GOOD HOUSEKEEPING

GOOD COOKING

GOOD HOUSEKEEPING

GOOD COOKING

Ebury Press
London

Published by Ebury Press
Division of The National Magazine Company Limited
Colquhoun House
27-37 Broadwick Street
London W1V 1FR

First Impression 1987

Good Cooking was first published in 36 parts as
Good For You by Orbis Publishing Limited in 1986.

ISBN 0 85223 670 0
Edited by *Veronica Sperling*
Art Direction by *Frank Phillips*
Designed by *Dave Brown*
Photography by *David Johnson* and *Simon Butcher*
Stylist *Kit Johnson*
Cover photograph by *Simon Butcher* of Tuna and Bean Salad with Orange Dressing
(recipe on page 148); Monkfish and Prawn Terrine (recipe on page 172);
Tomato and Pasta Soup (recipe on page 17); Lamb Chops with Rosemary (recipe
on page 87); Fruit Cheesecake (recipe on page 118); styled by *Cathy Sinker*

Filmset by Advanced Filmsetters (Glasgow) Ltd

Printed and bound in Italy by New Interlitho, S.p.a., Milan

CONTENTS

WHAT IS HEALTHY EATING?

Many people suspect healthy eating means forgoing many of their favourite foods and replacing them with boring or unfamiliar foods that have to be prepared in an unnecessarily complicated manner. How wrong they are!

In this book we show how favourite dishes—including cakes and puddings, roast meats and rich sauces—can be prepared in ways that are not only better for your health but make them taste better, too. We also introduce plenty of foods that may be new to you and explore exciting new ways of preparing more familiar ingredients and dishes.

We show you how you can improve your diet by cutting down on fats, sugar and salt, preserving vitamins and minerals, and increasing fibre—you may be surprised how easily you can do it. We provide a detailed but straightforward explanation of the principles behind the rules of sensible eating, to help you plan your own diet and explore even more ways of preparing food that is as attractive and tasty as any you have ever eaten—and good for you as well.

GROWTH, ENERGY AND HEALTH
Food supplies us with the materials for the growth and repair of body tissues, the energy we need for daily activities and the different elements necessary to enable the body to function properly. As the food we eat passes through our system, it is digested—that is, broken down into its constituents. These constituents are absorbed into the body, some entirely, some only in part, and what cannot be used is excreted.

In order to digest food the body secretes various chemical substances into the mouth, stomach and bowels. When the digested materials are absorbed into the body other chemicals carry them into the bloodstream. They are then used either for building the body tissues or providing energy stores.

The food we eat is intended to make up whatever has been lost from the tissues and energy stores in moving,

**AVOCADO AND CITRUS STARTER
SMOKED TROUT MOUSSE IN LEMON SHELLS**

breathing, thinking even—and to provide the small amounts of essential chemicals that the body needs to keep these chemical processes working, but is incapable of manufacturing itself.

This breaks down into two basic categories: proteins, fats and carbohydrates—what are often called the building blocks and fuel of the body machine; and vitamins and minerals. A properly-balanced intake of all these is essential to a healthy body.

GETTING THE BALANCE RIGHT
The proportions of the different kinds of food are very important. The healthy human body requires five parts of carbohydrate (starches and sugars) to one of protein and one of fat. An excess or deficiency of any of these could upset the delicate balance and lead to illness.

Carbohydrates are the principal source of energy. You could survive for quite a long time on a diet of white sugar and nothing else except water. But such a diet would provide nothing to keep the tissues healthy, nor would it replace any of the substances lost in keeping the body functioning. And because it has so little bulk, it would be easy to take in far more calories than needed, in order to feel full.

It is much better to obtain the necessary carbohydrate from the starch in potatoes and grains, and from the natural sugars of fruit and some vegetables—where the energy also comes packaged with essential nutrients.

Although carbohydrates are the principal source of energy in the human body, fats and proteins also provide a significant amount; fats, in fact, provide twice as many calories per gram as either protein or carbohydrate.

FATS AND CHOLESTEROL
All fats are made up of compounds of glycerol (common glycerine) with various acids, known generally as fatty acids. The molecules of these acids are made up of carbon, oxygen and hydrogen atoms; in some of them it is not possible, by any chemical process, to add any further hydrogen atoms to the molecule—these are called saturated acids; others do not have their full possible complement of hydrogen, and these are called unsaturated acids.

Animal fats are mostly saturated while most vegetable oils are unsaturated (but bear in mind that palm oil and coconut oil, for example, contain substantial amounts of saturated fat).

Polyunsaturated acids are those that are short of four or more hydrogen atoms. Corn, olive and sunflower oils are good sources of polyunsaturates. These help to keep down the level of cholesterol in the blood, while saturated fats tend to raise it.

All animal fats contain cholesterol, but it is absent from vegetable fats. It plays a very important part in the body, but the healthy liver produces sufficient cholesterol for all the body's needs after the first six months of life, and there is no need for any extra in the diet. In fact, it is known that high concentrations in the blood are associated with heart disease.

THE NEED FOR FIBRE
For a healthy diet and for the proper functioning of the intestines, you also need fibre or roughage. Fibre is what makes up the 'skeletons' of plants: the husks of grains, the shells of beans, the skins and flesh of fruit. It is composed of complex carbohydrates that the body cannot digest, so it passes through your intestines almost unchanged, trapping saturated fats, reducing the absorption of cholesterol, and swelling up in water to give you that comfortable full feeling, so that you don't get the need to nibble at snacks between meals.

And because refined and processed foods have not only the fibre removed but most of the minerals and vitamins as well, you can be sure that taking fibre in your diet will ensure that you also get enough of these essential substances.

So that is your guide for healthy eating. To help you follow it there are recipes for hundreds of mouth-watering dishes: snacks, main meals, teatime favourites and suppers. Remember that the secret of healthy eating is balance, and the occasional indulgence is easily corrected.

THE VITAL VITAMINS

Vitamins contribute to good health by enabling the body to function efficiently—for example, some are responsible for the growth and repair of body tissues, others for healthy skin, good vision and the development of strong teeth and bones. Unlike proteins, fats and carbohydrates, vitamins do not supply the body with energy, but some enable energy to be released in the body from the food we consume daily.

Each vitamin is made up of individual chemicals which give it its characteristic properties: for example, vitamin C is ascorbic acid, a name derived from antiscorbutic, meaning the ability to prevent and cure scurvy. The letters that denote each vitamin merely represent the order in which they were discovered. Thus vitamin A was the first; it was identified in 1911.

There are 13 major vitamins: A, C, D, E and K and eight B vitamins which work together and are known as the vitamin B complex. Vitamins are divided into two major groups: those which dissolve in water, and those which dissolve in fats.

The water soluble vitamins are all of the B vitamins and vitamin C. Because they dissolve in water they are easily lost in cooking and cannot be stored in the body. This means that foods which contain vitamins B and C must be eaten on a regular daily basis to keep the blood and cells saturated at all times with sufficient amounts for the body's needs. Those that are extra to requirements are excreted in the urine.

The fat soluble vitamins are A, D, E and K. They are stored in the liver, so that a daily intake is not essential; a good quantity of a rich source eaten once a week is usually sufficient.

MAJOR VITAMINS
The following is a brief guide to the major vitamins; it gives the main sources of each and the role they play in diet and nutrition.

Vitamin A is needed for normal growth, healthy skin and good vision and is responsible for renewing body tissues. It is manufactured by the body from carotene, which is found in green leafy vegetables and yellow and red vegetables such as spinach, cabbage, watercress, carrots and tomatoes. A pure form of vitamin A, called retinol, is found in some animal foods, including eggs, butter, liver, kidney and fish liver oils. In this case the vitamin has been manufactured from carotene in the body of the animal.

Light and air can cause some loss of vitamin A, as can cooking at high temperatures in fats.

Vitamin B_1 (*thiamine*) is needed to release the energy that is present in carbohydrates. It is found in pork, liver, wholewheat, yeasts, pulses and nuts. Of all the B vitamins, thiamine is most affected by cooking, especially by the addition of bicarbonate of soda.

Vitamin B_2 (*riboflavin*) releases energy from other foods and is essential for healthy skin and eyes. It is present in liver, red meat, milk and cheese. Exposure to light can result in loss of B_2; for this reason, bottled milk should not be left on the doorstep but should be stored in a dark place, preferably the refrigerator.

Vitamin B_6 (pyridoxin) maintains healthy body tissue, nerves and skin and helps in hormone production. It has been found to be helpful in treating premenstrual tension, although the reason for its effectiveness in this is not yet clear. It may also be prescribed during pregnancy to ease early signs of toxaemia—such as swelling feet and ankles. Vitamin B_6 is found in cereals, pulses, liver, avocados, fish, egg yolks, nuts and bananas.

Vitamin B_{12} is needed by rapidly dividing cells, such as those in the bone marrow and intestines. It is present in all foods of animal origin—liver and kidney, milk, eggs and cheese are rich sources. A deficiency of B_{12} can lead to anaemia; vegans—who eat no meat or dairy products—should take vitamin B_{12} supplements. Unlike other water-soluble vitamins, excess B_{12} can be stored in the liver. Adding bicarbonate of soda to cooking water destroys it.

Folic acid is part of the B complex. It is needed for the same reasons as B_{12} and is particularly important during preg-nancy. Folic acid is present in all living matter but leafy vegetables, liver, eggs, pulses, rice, bananas and oranges are the best sources. Lots is lost in cooking, because heating and reheating destroy it.

Vitamin C is important for maintaining healthy connective tissues and strong bones; it also aids the absorption of iron. It is found in citrus fruits, blackcurrants, green leafy vegetables, green peppers, potatoes—with new containing more than old—and liver.

A deficiency of vitamin C can—in extreme cases—lead to scurvy: when this occurs connective tissue breaks down, causing breakage of blood vessels and bleeding into the skin, joints and gums. Teeth are loosened, bruises appear and the body's resistance to infection is greatly lowered. Vitamin C is especially vulnerable to heat and air and can be lost in cooking. Smoking also impairs the absorption of vitamin C.

Vitamin D helps the body absorb calcium and is necessary for the growth and repair of body tissue, healthy gums and healthy bones. The most extreme form of vitamin D deficiency is rickets in babies and children and osteomalacia, or bone softening, in adults.

Cod liver oil is rich in vitamin D, as is fatty fish such as herrings, kippers and sardines; it is also added to some margarines. But the most important source of vitamin D is sunlight.

Vitamin E is claimed to help cure many ailments and even improve sexual performance, but as yet there is little evidence to support these claims. The most concentrated sources are wheat-germ oil, wholemeal bread, sunflower oil, eggs and breast milk. A deficiency is unlikely in adults eating a varied diet, but in a premature baby it could lead to anaemia. It is thought that the action of the contraceptive pill in the body impairs the absorption of vitamin E.

Vitamin K is used by the liver to produce substances in the bloodstream which initiate blood clotting. A deficiency is unlikely to occur because the vitamin is manufactured by bacteria in the intestines, which ensures a steady supply. It is present in leafy vegetables such as broccoli, lettuce, cabbage and spinach as well as cereals. Babies are given vitamin K at birth because they have no intestinal bacteria to produce their own, and the supply from the mother's bloodstream is quickly used up.

ALL ABOUT MINERALS

Compared with vitamins, minerals are often neglected—yet they are just as important, and, like vitamins, play an essential part in helping the body function. The best way to guard against a deficiency is to make sure you are eating a good, varied diet.

Minerals are substances that perform a wide range of functions in the body. Although not as fragile as vitamins, some minerals are water soluble and can be cooked out of foods; their action may also be inhibited by certain foods or substances that slow down or inhibit their absorption by the body.

There are about 25 minerals in the body which are present in differing quantities. A distinction is made between major minerals, which are needed by the body in relatively large—but not megadose—amounts, and trace minerals which are needed in tiny amounts. The distinction between the major minerals and the trace minerals does not mean that the first group is more important—a daily deficiency in one of the trace minerals can be just as serious as a deficiency in one of the major ones.

MAJOR MINERALS

Calcium, magnesium, sodium and potassium are important major minerals.

Calcium is the body's most vital mineral. It amounts to two per cent of the body's weight and is essential for the formation of healthy teeth and bones; it is also involved in nerve conduction and blood clotting. A network of hormones in the body maintains calcium levels in the blood and other body fluids; if you are deficient in calcium these hormones will draw on the calcium in the bones so that the functions of the mineral can continue. A deficiency in calcium thus causes the bones to deteriorate, leading to rickets in children and osteomalacia, in adults. Low calcium levels are also implicated in osteoporosis—easily-fractured brittle bones, particularly in post-menopausal women.

Magnesium is also important for healthy bones and it plays a part in the control of the body's chemical reactions. A magnesium deficiency may occur in young children who have suffered from diarrhoea over the course of two or three days; it is also common in alcoholics because of excretion of the mineral in the urine.

Sodium and its companion mineral *chloride* regulate the balance of water in the body as well as maintaining muscle and nerve activity. In the form of salt (sodium chloride) it is present in most processed foods; it is rare for our bodies to lack salt as the body conserves it.

Recent studies have shown that our daily sodium requirement is probably as low as 2 grams a day, but most of us eat much more than that because the Western diet is high in salt.

To avoid an excess of sodium do not add salt to foods at the table, but use alternate seasonings, such as lemon juice and herbs.

Potassium complements sodium in the body and may also counteract the effects of too much sodium. It is essential for healthy functioning of the nerves and muscles and it aids the release of energy from fats and carbohydrates. An excess or deficiency can have an effect on the heart and kidneys and cause muscle weakness.

TRACE MINERALS

Iron, zinc and iodine are the trace minerals which are essential for the healthy functioning of the body.

Iron is important for healthy blood; most of the iron absorbed by the body goes to the bone marrow to help in the production of healthy blood cells.

Because only a small percentage of iron consumed in food is absorbed, it is important to eat foods which contain significantly more than is actually needed. Although the body stores iron in the liver, spleen and other organs and bone marrow, if there is a deficiency these stores are eventually used up and anaemia may result.

Zinc aids the action of the enzymes responsible for mental and physical development; it also helps heal wounds. *Iodine* is involved in the production of the thyroid hormone, thyroxine; this promotes normal growth and maintains the body's metabolic rate.

Fluorine is the mineral from which fluoride is obtained. It is important for the health of teeth and bones and adding it to the water supply in many areas has helped fight dental decay. However, an excess of fluorine can be toxic and can also lead to mottling of the teeth; for this reason, fluoride supplements—other than those ingested through water—are not recommended.

MINERALS—YOUR DAILY REQUIREMENTS

Calcium, iron and zinc are the three minerals which many people are deficient in, so it is worth paying special attention to the stated daily requirements. The daily requirements of some minerals—such as potassium and fluorine—are not known; however, they are essential for a healthy functioning body.

SOURCE

Calcium	Magnesium	Potassium	Iron	Zinc	Iodine	Fluorine
Milk and dairy products; sardines; canned salmon eaten with bones; green leafy vegetables; citrus fruits; dried beans and peas	Many foods, especially green vegetables (eaten raw); nuts (especially almonds and cashews); soya beans; seeds; wholegrains	Many foods, including milk; fruit juice; bananas; dried fruits; meats; bran; peanut butter; dried beans and peas; potatoes	Liver; kidneys; red meat; egg yolk; green, leafy vegetables; dried fruits; dried beans and peas; potatoes; molasses; cereals	Meat; liver; eggs; poultry; seafood; milk and wholegrains	Seafood; iodized salt; sea salt	Fish; tea; drinking water in many areas

FUNCTION

Calcium	Magnesium	Potassium	Iron	Zinc	Iodine	Fluorine
Maintaining healthy bones and teeth; muscle contraction; blood clotting; absorption of vitamin B_{12}	Building bones and manufacturing proteins; constituent of many enzymes	Body water balance; muscle contraction; release of energy from carbohydrates, proteins and fats	Essential for healthy red blood cells needed for carrying oxygen around the body; also forms part of several enzymes	Aids the action of the enzymes responsible for healthy mental and physical development; it also helps wounds to heal	A constituent of the thyroid hormones which are essential for normal metabolism and reproduction	Formation of healthy teeth and bones; resistance to dental decay

AMOUNT

Calcium	Magnesium	Potassium	Iron	Zinc	Iodine	Fluorine
Adults: 500 mg per day. Pregnant and lactating women: 1200 mg per day. Adolescents: 700 mg per day. Children under 9: 600 mg per day	Adults and children: 300-400 mg per day		Women: 12 mg per day. Men: 10 mg per day	Adults and children: 10-15 mg per day; daily requirement increases in adolescence	Adults and children: 150 mg per day	

CALORIES

We have all heard of calories—the term usually comes up when dieting or weight loss is under discussion. But what exactly are they, and how are they measured? Outlined below are the facts about calories—information which is important to everyone, not just to slimmers.

The food we eat supplies us with the energy we need to function. Much of that energy is used up in simply staying alive: keeping the heart beating and the lungs breathing; and sustaining the other essential operations that keep the body running, from transmitting nerve signals to building new tissues. Energy is also required for daily activities—walking, working, eating, talking and so on. The energy that comes from food is measured in calories.

MEASURING ENERGY

A calorie is defined as the amount of energy in the form of heat required to raise the temperature of 1 gram of water by 1°C. In fact, in the body, about 75 per cent of the energy provided by food is used as heat, with only 25 per cent converted to work.

Calories provide a useful unit for measuring the potential energy content of any food, as well as the amount of energy consumed in a particular activity. The unit which is used by nutritionists is the larger Calorie, spelt with a capital C. This is equal to 1000 of the small calories. The term kilocalorie (kilo means 1000) therefore means the same as the term Calorie.

An alternative measurement which is increasingly being used is the Joule. The same rules apply: the unit is most commonly used in blocks of 1000, which are called kilojoules; 1 Joule is the same amount as 1 kilojoule. One Calorie is equal to 4.2 Joules.

CALORIE CONTENT

The food components that supply the body with calories are fat, carbohydrate and protein, with fat being more than twice as high in calories as either carbohydrate or protein.

Cooking oil is virtually 100 per cent fat, ordinary white sugar (sucrose) is virtually 100 per cent carbohydrate, but most foods contain proportions of the different components. The calorific value—the potential energy content—of a food is determined first by the proportions of one nutrient to another and second by their concentration.

Unrefined carbohydrates—which include wholemeal bread, pasta and grains —are not only a good source of calories but are also rich in fibre, vitamins and other nutrients and are therefore ideal foods from which to obtain energy. Four slices of wholemeal bread weighing approximately 100 g (4 oz) provide 216 calories, 9 g of protein and only 3 g of fat; similarly 100 g (4 oz) potato provides 87 calories, 2 g of protein and only 0.1 g of fat. Both bread and potatoes have a high water content which affects the 'energy density' of a food—the more water in food, the fewer calories.

HOW MANY DO YOU NEED?
The average adult takes in and uses up between 2000 and 2500 calories a day, although individuals vary. The amount of energy consumed depends upon age, sex and activity level, with one or two other factors, such as weight—the larger you are, the harder your body has to work, so you will burn up more calories. It also depends on how much of your body is fat; lean muscle tissue uses more calories than fat tissue.

About two thirds of your calorific intake is required for basic metabolic processes—heartbeat, respiration, digesting foods, eliminating wastes and so

on. Even spending 24 hours in bed will use up approximately 1500 calories for some individuals.

If you take in more calories than you use the excess is stored by the body as fat; if you take in less you will lose weight, mainly through a reduction in fat stores and, when they are exhausted, by burning up muscle protein.

Fat is our reserve source of energy. It is a highly concentrated fuel with more than twice the energy content of protein or carbohydrates. It is present in the body as an energy store and will continue to build up by reserving all the calories you take in and do not use.

Rather unfairly, some people seem to be particularly efficient at storing surplus energy. For others, the reverse is true; seemingly, no matter how much they eat they are able to burn off the calories in excess of their requirements.

CALORIE-CONTROLLED DIETS
Whatever your own metabolism it is clear that if you are putting on weight it is because you are taking in more calories in your food than you are able to use up. And the converse is also true; to lose weight you have to use up more energy than you take in.

There are many different types of diets—low-fat, high-fibre, high-protein, low-carbohydrate and fad diets such as the grapefruit diet. The success of any diet relies on the principle that less calories are eaten than used.

AVOIDING EMPTY CALORIES
Taking in energy is by no means the only reason for eating; your diet may provide you with more than enough calories to keep going but supply neither the right amount or balance of essential nutrients.

Refined sugar, alcohol and products with large quantities of sugar are sometimes called empty calories: although they provide energy, they have reduced amounts of vitamins and minerals; the sugar in these products provides energy and nothing else. Foods with a high fat content are also high in calories. It is all too easy, especially on a slimming diet which emphasises calorie-counting rather than recommending certain foods, to use up your calorie allowance on foods full of empty calories.

Instead, you should aim to take in as many calories as possible from unrefined foods high in carbohydrates—these include wholemeal bread, potatoes, pulses, pasta and grains such as rice.

CARBOHYDRATES

Carbohydrates form an important part of our everyday diet. There are, however, various sources of carbohydrate, some of which are nutritionally more valuable than others. Here we explain the role of carbohydrates and identify the best sources for a healthy diet.

A healthy body needs a balance of nutrients to function efficiently. The combination of proteins and fats with carbohydrates provides the building blocks and fuel for the body. As carbohydrates are digested they are turned into simple sugars which provide the body's main source of energy.

SUGAR
Refined, or processed, sugars are those that have been isolated from their natural state. They are absorbed into the bloodsteam very quickly and give a short, intensive burst of energy that is quickly exhausted. A period of low blood sugar follows as the balance of the blood is being restored. This may happen, for example, if you are hungry and eat something like a bar of choc-

olate rather than a balanced snack, because the instant energy is rapidly depleted. Unrefined carbohydrates, on the other hand, slow the absorption of sugar and thus prevent a sugar overload.

At present our carbohydrate intake is about 40 per cent of our total energy intake, including refined sugars. It is recommended that 50–55 per cent of our total energy should come from carbohydrates, mainly unrefined.

The most common forms of carbohydrates are starches and sugars. Starch is found in vegetables, grains and pulses; sugars are provided by fruit, vegetables, milk and milk products and by the refined sugar contained in confectionery, biscuits and cakes. Refined white sugar provides energy but no nutrients. Even the unrefined varieties, such as muscovado, could not be called nutritious, although they do contain traces of minerals.

For a healthy diet most carbohydrates should be taken in the form of unrefined starch from grains and cereals, pulses, vegetables and fruit. All of these sources offer a range of essential nutrients in addition to supplying carbohydrates, thereby making a major contribution to the total diet. They also provide various forms of non-digestible carbohydrate—

fibre—which is important for maintaining a healthy digestive system.

Milk is not a major source of carbohydrate, although it does provide some lactose, or milk sugar. Skimmed milk provides the same amount of lactose as whole milk.

THE CORRECT BALANCE
In poorer countries, approximately 80 per cent of the total calories are consumed mainly as carbohydrate, whereas in more affluent societies this may be only 50 per cent or less. During this century there has been a shift in the eating habits in many developed countries, resulting in increased consumption of animal products, such as meat, fish, poultry, eggs and dairy products. This has been accompanied by an emphasis on refining and purifying food and a rejection of many of those staple foodstuffs which used to make up the major part of the average diet. Research indicates that the increased intake of animal protein and fats has not meant a better general standard of health—quite the contrary. Conditions such as cancer, diabetes, high blood pressure, and heart and kidney diseases have increased in Western societies, whereas in poorer countries they are still fairly rare.

There is nothing wrong in eating

animal protein and fats in moderation, but when they are consumed in excess, and vegetables are neglected, the whole digestive system is thrown out of balance and disorders may result. In order to maintain health, therefore, the diet should include more whole grains and cereals, wholemeal pastas, wholemeal bread, vegetables and fruit. These provide natural energy-giving starches and sugars, some protein and plenty of fibre to make a satisfying meal which prevents hunger between meals. Pulses and grains eaten together supply complete protein—for example, lentils and rice, or bean and vegetable soup with wholemeal bread.

CALORIES

Carbohydrate, protein and fat are all needed to maintain a healthy body. The tendency has been, however, to consume more protein and fat but less carbohydrate. Fat has twice the calories of either carbohydrate or protein and because of excess consumption of fat in the Western diet this has generally meant that more calories than necessary are consumed. Overweight or obesity has usually been blamed on the dietary carbohydrates, and unfortunately, carbohydrates, such as bread, pasta and potatoes, have therefore been labelled fattening foods. This is largely unjustified; it is far more likely that the butter or margarine on bread and potatoes or the cheese and rich sauces accompanying pasta will cause an increase in weight, rather than the carbohydrates themselves. Combined with healthy low-fat toppings and sauces, carbohydrates are good nutritional value. Baked potatoes, for example, eaten with their skins, are an excellent staple food and can be eaten with savoury toppings or served with dishes such as salads or stews.

CHOLESTEROL

Cholesterol is a big buzz word since it has been identified as a factor which may cause heart disease. What exactly is cholesterol and how can we guard against its build-up? Here we explain its function and show how, by healthy eating, you can maintain it at a reasonable level in your body.

Cholesterol is a fatty substance which has a number of important roles in the body. It forms part of the cell membranes and the sheaths which protect the nerve fibres; it is involved in the manufacture of hormones, particularly the sex hormones and those which regulate the body's metabolism; and it plays an important part in the body's digestive system—bile salts are formed from cholesterol and these salts break down fats into small drops, aiding their digestion and absorption.

In addition, cholesterol is a constituent of vitamin D which is manufactured by the body from the action of sunlight on the skin.

Cholesterol is not an essential nutrient; our bodies make all the cholesterol we need from the fats, carbohydrates and proteins in food. It is manufactured in the liver and, to a lesser extent, in the wall of the small intestine. It is present in all animal tissues and is found in all foods of animal origin—meat, poultry, fish, eggs and dairy produce. It is virtually absent from plant foods.

INTAKE AND MANUFACTURE

Most people in the western world take in about 500–600 milligrams of cholesterol per day, half of which is absorbed into the blood from the intestinal tract, while the rest is excreted in the faeces. There is no risk of a cholesterol deficiency; if we eat little or no cholesterol, our bodies respond by making more. There is a fine balance between the amount of cholesterol we eat and the amount the body manufactures.

Cholesterol is carried through the blood linked to proteins called lipoproteins. Low density lipoproteins (LDLs) transport most of the cholesterol—about 50–75 per cent—and deliver it to the cells in the body. When the diet contains large amounts of saturated fats the liver correspondingly produces large amounts of LDLs, contributing to the build-up of cholesterol in the body.

High density lipoproteins (HDLs) carry a smaller amount of cholesterol. They transport it to the liver where it is excreted into the intestine in the form of bile. HDLs are considered to be the desirable lipoproteins to have; their ratio to LDLs is increased by brisk exercise and physical activity. Polyunsaturated fats are carried on HDLs and boost the HDL to LDL ratio. People who are overweight generally have low HDL levels; as they lose weight the percentage increases.

LINKS WITH HEART DISEASE

The causes of heart disease are complex and are thought to be due to a number of factors, including the amount and type of fat consumption; other factors include genetic make-up, lack of exercise, smoking, stress and a low-fibre diet.

A diet high in fat, particularly saturated fat, raises blood cholesterol levels. If blood cholesterol levels rise above the limits which are considered to be normal the risk of coronary heart disease increases.

REDUCING THE RISKS

To reduce the risk of heart disease it is important to control the amount of fat in your diet; try to reduce it to approximately one-third of all the food you eat. At the same time, limit your intake of foods which are rich in cholesterol.

To reduce the overall amount of fat in your diet, choose skimmed and semi-skimmed milk, low and medium-fat cheese and low-fat yogurt. Replace some of the red meat in your diet with poultry and fish as these foods are good sources of polyunsaturated fatty acids.

Foods which are high in cholesterol include liver, kidney, brain, fish roe and eggs; egg consumption should be limited to 4–5 per week, including those in complete dishes.

Certain foods tend to lower the levels of blood cholesterol; these include margarines which are high in polyunsaturates and corn, sunflower and safflower oils, which are also high in polyunsaturates and contain essential fatty acids.

CHOLESTEROL IN FOOD	
Meat	**mg per 100 g**
Beef, lean	82
Lamb, lean,	110
Brains	2,200
Chicken, light meat	74
Duck, breast meat	160
Liver	260–430
Pork, lean	110
Turkey, light meat	62
Dairy products	
Butter	230
Cheddar cheese	70
Edam cheese	72
Egg white	0
Egg, whole	450
Egg yolk	1,260
Milk, skimmed	2
Milk, whole	14
Parmesan cheese	90
Seafood	
Fish, oily	80
Fish, white	70
Prawns	200
Miscellaneous	
Lard	70+
Margarine (made of animal fat)	65
Margarine (made of vegetable fat only)	0
Vegetables and cereals	0

WHAT IS DIETARY FIBRE?

Despite the countless articles and the best-selling books championing its virtues, the role of fibre in the diet is not always clearly understood. Here we tell you exactly what fibre is, just why it is so important and where to get it.

Fibre, or roughage, is the name for a group of substances that are mainly types of carbohydrate (starches and sugar), found naturally in cereals, nuts, beans, fruit and vegetables. Unlike other carbohydrates, fibre is not fully broken down but instead passes completely through the digestive tract.

DIET AND DISEASE

Although the value of roughage in preventing constipation has long been recognised, in the past nutritionists have tended to dismiss fibre as an indigestible waste product with no dietary significance. Recent research, however, has linked insufficient fibre in the diet with a whole range of disorders, such as diverticulosis, haemorrhoids, gallstones and varicose veins and conditions as serious as heart disease, diabetes and cancer of the colon.

Sometimes called the diseases of affluence, all of these complaints are relatively common in western societies, where the typical diet is low in fibre. In contrast, their incidence is much lower in poorer, less developed countries, where the inhabitants eat far fewer refined foods and their intake of fibre is much greater, although this does not account for other lifestyle differences.

THE CASE FOR FIBRE

The most obvious, immediate effect of increasing fibre intake is that it is beneficial in treating constipation if you are a sufferer. Fibre stimulates the smooth efficient working of the bowels by acting like a sponge, absorbing many times its own weight in water, making the stools larger and softer and easier to pass. This may also help prevent such problems as haemorrhoids or inflammation of the bowel, thought to be brought about by the constant strain of passing hard faeces.

Fibre also tends to help the body pass food wastes through more quickly. It has been suggested that this plays a significant part in preventing cancer of the colon by reducing the length of time that cancer-causing substances stay within the system and by diluting their concentration.

One of the most important recent discoveries is that a high level of cholesterol in the blood, which has long been associated with coronary heart disease, can be reduced by certain types of fibre. One study has shown that eating 200 g (7 oz) of raw carrots every day for three weeks had the effect of reducing cholesterol levels by 11 per cent, as well as increasing the amount of fat excreted by 50 per cent.

A finding of particular significance to diabetics is the effect fibre appears to have on blood sugar levels. By increasing the level of fibre in their diet, under medical supervision, some diabetics have been able to reduce their insulin intake, and in some cases even discontinue its use.

BULK FOR STREAMLINING

Apart from any questions of health, a high-fibre diet has considerable attractions for slimmers; because it is filling, less food is eaten, particularly fatty foods which are high in calories. Many fibrous foods, especially fruits and vegetables, are low in calories anyway and, since the fibre absorbs a lot of water as it passes through the system, you are more likely to feel satisfied before you have exceeded your calorie limit.

What then is the best way to set about obtaining these considerable benefits? One particularly rich source of fibre—in fact, it has almost become synonymous with fibre—is bran. This consists of the outer layers of cereal grains such as wheat and is about 50 per cent fibre. In the 1970s, wheat bran was regarded as something of a cure-all. Books, newspapers and magazines championed bran by the spoonful as the key to being healthy and slim.

But merely sprinkling everything with bran is certainly not the best way to go about improving a low-fibre diet, for a number of reasons. There is no sense in expecting dramatic improvements in health by adding a little fibre to an otherwise unhealthy diet, when what is called for is an overall change in eating habits. Above all, it is important to realise that you cannot get all the possible benefits from fibre by eating only one type of fibrous food.

SOURCES AND VARIETIES

The term dietary fibre groups together many different kinds of fibre, each with different properties. Cereal fibre appears to be the most useful in dealing with intestinal problems, making waste material bulkier and softer and speeding the transit time through the body. The best sources of cereal fibre are unrefined cereals, such as wheat, and their products, including wholemeal bread, brown rice and wholemeal pasta.

The fibres in oats and pulses—dried beans, peas, lentils and so on—work quite differently: they form a sticky globular substance in the intestine which is thought to restrict the amount of fat the body absorbs from food, as well as affecting the absorption of sugar.

These gummy fibres can bring about a significant lowering in the blood cholesterol level and seem to be the most effective in lowering blood pressure and in dealing with blood sugar problems.

The richest sources are such pulses as red kidney beans, butter beans, chickpeas and lentils, and products containing oats, barley or rye such as porridge and rye bread.

Fruits and vegetables have many properties in common with oats and pulses. Pectin, found in many fruits and vegetables, particularly apples and carrots, has also reduced blood cholesterol levels in tests and been shown to have significant effects on blood sugar levels.

A high fibre content is not necessarily confined to chewy, nutty, typically fibrous foods. Sweetcorn, for example, is high in fibre, as are soft fruits such as raspberries and blackcurrants. Prunes, dried apricots and other dried fruits are particularly high in fibre: the fibre is concentrated by the removal of water.

GET IT NATURALLY

Despite the claims for fibre-added products, it is usually far better to get the fibre where it occurs naturally. For example, while high-fibre loaves of white bread combined with pulse fibre may have the same fibre content as wholemeal bread, wholemeal bread contains more B vitamins, as well as more minerals such as zinc and magnesium.

Eat more brown rice and wholemeal pasta and breakfast cereals made from whole grains or with oats. Eat more dried fruits such as apricots or prunes—try adding them to breakfast cereals or using them in cooking, to add fibre to meat dishes or to sweeten puddings in place of sugar. Eat plenty of fresh fruits and vegetables, including the skins wherever possible, and do not neglect pulses and nuts, which are also high in protein, vitamins and minerals.

ALTERNATIVE SEASONINGS

'Pass the salt' is one of the most frequently uttered phrases during meal times in many homes—and that is often after the food has been salted during cooking. Many of us add salt to food without even tasting it first. The experts say too much salt is bad for us. How can we cut down?

Salt (sodium chloride) is used in large quantities in many foods for extra flavour and for its preserving qualities. Most of us eat far more than is healthy.

Everyone needs some salt to maintain the fluid balance mechanism in the body, but in normal circumstances we obtain all the salt we need by eating cereals, bread, fruit, vegetables and dairy products. Medical evidence points to a link between high salt intake and high blood pressure, a condition which can lead to an increased risk of heart disease, kidney disease and stroke.

Since many people suffer from high blood pressure (hypertension) without being aware of it, it is wise for everyone to take less salt. It does no one any harm to eat less salt, and a low-salt diet can certainly do a lot of good. Besides the obvious health benefits, many people who have lowered their salt consumption report a heightened appreciation for the taste of food.

Many people add salt to food they cook and eat at home, and consume many processed and preserved foods to which salt has been added. It is estimated that most people eat an average of 8–12 grams (about $\frac{1}{2}$ oz), or about 15 ml (1 tbsp) of salt each day. Nutritional experts advise reducing this to 6 grams (about $\frac{1}{4}$ oz) a day or 5–10 ml (1–2 tsp). Remember, these quantities refer to total salt intake—not just what you deliberately add to food at the table.

SALT AWAY

You can lower your salt consumption in a number of ways. The simplest way is to stop adding salt to food at the table and to use as little as possible in cooking. Experiment instead with various herbs, spices and other flavourings so your food is flavourful enough and you do not miss the taste of salt.

Avoid or reduce your consumption of highly salted commercially prepared foods such as sausages, frankfurters, packaged and canned soups, stock cubes and high-salt yeast extracts. Start reading labels and lower your consumption of sodium, monosodium glutamate, sodium sulphate and other additives with the word 'sodium' in their names.

Use fresh or frozen vegetables. There is usually very little or no salt added to frozen vegetables, whereas large amounts are usually added to canned vegetables. Some canned food is now available to which no salt has been added, and their labels prominently advertise this fact. If you like snack foods such as crisps look for the unsalted varieties. Natural roasted nuts are now available from supermarkets without any added salt.

To remove excess salt from ham, bacon and salty fish, soak in cold water for at least 12 hours, then drain, place in a pan with cold water, bring to the boil and immediately drain again before cooking. Canned anchovies can be soaked in milk or water for 20 minutes, then drained.

LOW-SODIUM ALTERNATIVES

When you start to reduce your salt consumption, you may want to try one of the special low-sodium salt alternatives now on the market, but do not use these to excess. Many of them are made by replacing sodium with potassium, a mineral which in rare instances can upset an individual's sodium/potassium balance. However, you could well find that after several weeks of using a salt substitute you will be better able to wean yourself from salt.

Rock and sea salts, although they do contain tiny traces of minerals not found in pure salt, are not really preferable to other forms of salt.

Use fruit and vegetables as garnishes or flavourful accompaniments to main dishes. Apple sauce tastes good with pork, peaches with ham, and pineapple with chicken and pork. Use strong-flavoured vegetables in cooked dishes. Green peppers and mushrooms, for example, are versatile ingredients and can be added to many chicken, beef and fish dishes. Since salt is often used to cover up or give extra flavour to poorly cooked food, adding spices and herbs may eliminate the desire for added salt.

As you begin to use less salt, you may be surprised to find you do not miss it.

2 SOUPS AND STARTERS

Rich, well-flavoured stock is the basis of all good soups and sauces and essential for good cooking—and it is so simple to make.

A large stockpot, bubbling away at the back of the range and regularly replenished, was an almost ubiquitous feature years ago which has all but disappeared from the modern kitchen. In its place has come instant stock from powder, cubes and granules. Stock cubes are certainly useful but have a sameness of flavour and lack body. Nor do they have the nutritional value of a properly prepared stock and most tend to be highly seasoned, containing more salt than is desirable for good health.

THE MAKINGS OF THE STOCK
Stock is made by cooking the bones and trimmings of meat or fish with herbs, spices and vegetables such as carrots, onions, leeks and celery. They are gently simmered together to extract the flavours and the gelatine from the bones which helps give body to the stock. For convenience, vegetable bouillon cubes and granules, without added salt, flavouring or preservatives, are available from health food shops.

All meat, poultry and white fish bones can be used, along with the skin, leftover meat and other trimmings. If no bones are available they can be bought from the butcher, who will split them for you: breaking them up releases the gelatine which forms the stock into a delicious jelly when chilled.

Raw bones and chicken carcasses will make a stock with a fuller flavour than one made with bones from cooked meat. Always trim the fat from the bones or trimmings before adding to the pot.

In addition to the traditional flavourings, virtually any available vegetables can be used, although certain rather strong vegetables, such as turnips or cabbage, should be used sparingly. Potatoes can make the stock cloudy so they should be avoided.

A few black peppercorns are traditionally added and a bouquet garni greatly improves the flavour. This may be bought but it is far better to make your own if you can: tie together a sprig each of parsley, thyme, tarragon, rosemary and a bay leaf in a piece of muslin. Many cooks like the addition of an onion with two cloves stuck in it to the stock.

Since stock is always strained before use it does not matter if lots of small, loose herbs and spices are in it. A good pinch of salt can be added to the water to leach out the vitamins and minerals from the vegetables. Usually when cooking vegetables this should be avoided because of the goodness that is lost, but when making stock you are trying to extract the maximum value from the vegetables which are then discarded. However, avoid seasoning stocks that will be reduced after cooking.

PREPARATION
A good stock will take about 3 hours to cook, except for fish stocks which should only be cooked for 30 minutes, otherwise they will be bitter.

During the first part of cooking the stock should be skimmed of scum that rises to the surface. Never allow a stock to boil because it will turn cloudy. Follow the recipes given here to get good results every time.

Alternatively, a pressure cooker works very well. Place all the ingredients in the cooker, making sure that it is not more than half full and that there is sufficient liquid for your make of pressure cooker. Bring to the boil without the lid on, then skim off the fat and any scum. Fix the lid on, bring slowly to high pressure, reduce the heat and cook for 45 minutes. Reduce the pressure slowly before removing the lid.

Stock should be strained immediately it is cooked—vegetables left in stock may cause it to turn sour. Leave the stock to cool when the fat will rise to the surface. If it is to be used straightaway, degrease it with absorbent kitchen paper, or chill the stock and lift off the fat.

STORING THE STOCK
Stock will keep for up to 3 days stored in a covered container in the refrigerator. If the strained and degreased stock is boiled for about 2 minutes every other day, then it will keep for 1 week. Fish and vegetable stocks are best used on the day of making but can be kept in refrigerator up to 2 days.

Freeze stocks for up to 2 months. To take up less freezer space, stock can be reduced by boiling over high heat until reduced by one-half. Store in amounts calculated for future use or, conveniently, in ice-cube trays. Use the cubes of stock straight from the freezer and dilute with the same quantity of water as concentrated stock.

CHICKEN STOCK

MAKES 900 ml (1½ pints)
Minimal calories per serving
PREPARATION 15 minutes
COOKING 2–3 hours

**1 chicken carcass and trimmings
1 large onion, sliced
2 carrots, scrubbed and diced
2 celery sticks, trimmed and chopped
1 bouquet garni
a few black peppercorns
salt, to taste**

———1———

Break up the bones of the chicken carcass and put into a saucepan. Add any pieces of chicken meat and the cleaned giblets. Add the vegetables, bouquet garni, peppercorns, salt and water just to cover.

———2———

Bring to the boil, skimming off any scum from the surface, then cover with a tight-fitting lid. Lower the heat and simmer for 2–3 hours, skimming again if necessary.

———3———

Strain through a fine sieve and leave to cool. When cold, spoon the fat from the surface or degrease with absorbent kitchen paper. Alternatively, chill, then lift off the solid fat.
MICROWAVE Follow step 1, putting all ingredients into a large bowl. Cover. In step 2, cook 100% (High) 10 minutes, until boiling, then cook 20–30% (Defrost) 1 hour, skimming as necessary. Follow step 3.

FISH STOCK
Use 450–700 g (1–1½ lb) fish trimmings or white fish and make as for Chicken Stock, peeling the onion and simmering the stock only for 30 minutes. Do not use oily fish such as mackerel, herring or kipper fillets. Use on the same day or store, covered, in the refrigerator for up to 2 days.
MICROWAVE As Chicken Stock; cook 20–30% (Defrost) 15 minutes.

BEEF STOCK
Brown 450–900 g (1–2 lb) chopped marrow bones or knuckle of veal and 450 g (1 lb) stewing beef in a roasting pan at 220°C (425°F) mark 7 for 30 minutes. Place the bones, beef and vegetables in a large saucepan and make as for Chicken Stock.
MICROWAVE Preheat a browning dish 100% (High) 4–6 minutes or according to manufacturer's instructions. Add 15 ml (1 tbsp) oil, then add bones and beef. Cook 100% (High) 4 minutes, turning once. Place bones, beef and vegetables in a deep bowl, cover with water and cook 10 minutes, until boiling. Cover and cook 20–30% (Defrost) 1 hour.

VEGETABLE STOCK
Using stalks, peelings, outer leaves and any vegetables that are available, make as for Chicken Stock, simmering the stock for only 45 minutes.
MICROWAVE As Chicken Stock, cook 20–30% (Defrost) 30 minutes.

WHITE STOCK
Using 450–900 g (1–2 lb) blanched veal bones, make as Chicken Stock, adding 10 ml (2 tsp) lemon juice if desired. Bring to the boil, lower the heat and simmer for 4 hours to extract all the flavour.
MICROWAVE As Chicken Stock, cook 20–30% (Defrost) 1½ hours.

GOODNESS GUIDE
PROTEIN The chicken meat and bones are a good source of protein
MINERALS The bones are a rich source of calcium
VITAMINS The stocks retain vitamins A, B and C which are in the vegetables

Use these recipes as a guide for making delicious home-made stocks. They will add an excellent flavour to soups, sauces and gravies.

CHICKEN STOCK

15

CHUNKY VEGETABLE SOUP

LEEK AND POTATO SOUP

TOMATO AND RICE SOUP

CRAB BISQUE

CRAB BISQUE

A flavourful and nutritious soup, this version of Crab Bisque has a lower fat content than traditional bisques made with cream.

SERVES 4 200 calories per serving
PREPARATION 5 minutes
COOKING 10–15 minutes

40 g (1½ oz) polyunsaturated margarine
40 g (1½ oz) plain flour
600 ml (1 pint) fish stock
300 ml (½ pint) semi-skimmed milk
175 g (6 oz) white crab meat,
thawed if frozen
2 spring onions, finely chopped
salt and white pepper, to taste
lemon twists, to garnish

——1——
Melt the margarine, stir in the flour and cook for 1 minute. Gradually stir in the fish stock and the milk. Bring to the boil, lower the heat and simmer for 5 minutes.

——2——
Add the crab meat, spring onions and seasoning. Simmer for a further 5 minutes. Garnish each portion with a twist of lemon and serve.

MICROWAVE In step 1, put margarine in a bowl and cook 100% (High) 30–45 seconds to melt, add flour and cook 30 seconds, until bubbling. Whisk in hot stock (using only 450 ml [¾ pint]) and the milk. Cook 3½–4 minutes, until thickened and boiling. In step 2, add crab meat, onions and seasoning. Cook 1½–2 minutes, until heated through, stirring once.

16

CHUNKY VEGETABLE SOUP

This a very hearty soup. Served with some warm crusty wholemeal bread, it can make a complete meal.

SERVES 4 75 calories per serving
PREPARATION 10 minutes
COOKING 30 minutes

1 onion, skinned and thinly sliced
3 celery sticks, trimmed and chopped
3 carrots, scrubbed and chopped
1 parsnip, peeled and chopped
100 g (4 oz) swede, peeled and diced
1 potato, scrubbed and diced
1 garlic clove, skinned and crushed
900 ml (1½ pints) chicken stock
40 g (1½ oz) sweetcorn kernels
salt and pepper, to taste

———1———

Put the vegetables, except the sweetcorn, and garlic into a large saucepan with the stock. Bring to the boil, lower the heat and simmer very gently for 25–30 minutes or until the vegetables are just tender.

———2———

Using a slotted spoon, remove approximately half the vegetables. Place the remaining vegetables and stock in a blender or food processor and purée until smooth.

———3———

Return the purée to a clean pan and add the reserved vegetables, sweetcorn and seasoning. Heat through, then serve.

GOODNESS GUIDE
CHUNKY VEGETABLE SOUP
FIBRE Carrots, parsnips, swede, onion, celery, potato and sweetcorn all provide quantities of fibre
VITAMINS The substantial amount of vitamin C in all the vegetables is retained in the soup
FAT This very substantial soup has a minimal fat content

CRAB BISQUE
PROTEIN The crab, fish stock and milk make a high-protein soup
FAT Seafood generally is very low in fat; using semi-skimmed milk also keeps the fat to a minimum

MINERALS Rich in a number of essential minerals, seafood is the principal dietary source of iodine, needed for normal reproduction

LEEK AND POTATO SOUP

This soup can be served hot or cold.

SERVES 4 154 calories per serving
PREPARATION 5 minutes
COOKING 30 minutes

1 small onion, skinned and chopped
4 leeks, trimmed and coarsely chopped
2 large potatoes, peeled and coarsely chopped
300 ml (½ pint) vegetable or chicken stock
300 ml (½ pint) semi-skimmed milk
50 ml (2 fl oz) dry white wine
salt and pepper, to taste

———1———

Put the vegetables, stock and milk into a large saucepan. Bring to the boil, lower the heat and simmer for 20–25 minutes or until just tender. Place in a blender or food processor and purée until smooth.

———2———

Pour into a clean pan and add the wine and seasoning. Heat through, adding extra stock, if necessary. Serve at once or cool, then chill before serving.

MICROWAVE Follow step 1 using a deep bowl. Cover and cook 100% (High) 20 minutes, until tender, stirring 2 or 3 times. Continue as rest of step. In step 2, return soup to the cleaned bowl, add wine, seasoning and extra stock, if necessary. Cook 1½–2 minutes, until heated through. Serve at once or chill before serving.

GOODNESS GUIDE
FAT This is a low-fat version of classic Vichyssoise, using semi-skimmed milk in place of butter and cream
FIBRE There is a lot of fibre contained in the soup from the leeks, onion and potatoes
VITAMINS Like all home-made vegetable soups, this is rich in vitamin C

TOMATO AND RICE OR PASTA SOUP

Adding brown rice or pasta to this soup gives an interesting contrast in textures as well as increasing the fibre content.

SERVES 4 75 calories per serving
PREPARATION 10–15 minutes
COOKING 30 minutes

50 g (2 oz) brown rice or wholemeal pasta shapes
15 g (½ oz) polyunsaturated margarine
1 onion, skinned and chopped
1 garlic clove, skinned and crushed
2 celery sticks, trimmed and chopped
600 g (1¼ lb) canned peeled tomatoes
30 ml (2 tbsp) tomato purée
5 ml (1 tsp) whole grain mustard
salt and pepper, to taste
5 ml (1 tsp) chopped fresh thyme or 2.5 ml (½ tsp) dried thyme, plus extra, to garnish
croûtons, to serve (optional)

———1———

Put the rice or pasta into a small saucepan of boiling water. Simmer gently for 10–15 minutes or until the rice or pasta is tender.

———2———

Meanwhile, melt the margarine in a large saucepan and cook the onion for 3–5 minutes, until soft.

———3———

Add the garlic, celery, tomatoes with their juice, tomato purée and mustard. Season to taste with salt and pepper and simmer gently for 20 minutes. Put the soup in a blender or food processor and purée until smooth.

———4———

Return the soup to a clean pan and add the thyme, rice or pasta and 300 ml (½ pint) boiling water. Simmer for a further 4–5 minutes to heat through. Garnish with thyme and serve with croûtons, if wished.

GOODNESS GUIDE
FAT Very little fat is used in this soup; there is just a small amount of polyunsaturated margarine to soften the onion
FIBRE The brown rice or pasta, onion, celery and tomatoes help make this soup high in fibre
VITAMINS Tomatoes and tomato purée are high in vitamin A and all the vegetables supply vitamin C

CHILLIED CHICK-PEA SALAD

CRISPY BAKED MUSHROOMS WITH GARLIC DIP

CHINESE SWEETCORN AND CRAB SOUP

CHILLED TARRAGON AND VEGETABLE SOUP

CHILLED TARRAGON AND VEGETABLE SOUP

SERVES 4   145 calories per serving
PREPARATION 10 minutes
COOKING 25 minutes
CHILLING At least 1 hour

25 ml (1½ tbsp) corn oil
½ Spanish onion, skinned and finely chopped
1 garlic clove, skinned and crushed
2 celery sticks, trimmed and chopped
2 potatoes, peeled and chopped
20 ml (4 tsp) chopped fresh tarragon or
10 ml (2 tsp) dried
¾ Iceberg lettuce, shredded
600 ml (1 pint) vegetable stock
300 ml (½ pint) buttermilk
100 g (4 oz) natural Quark
salt, to taste
chopped fresh tarragon, to garnish

———1———
Heat the corn oil in a heavy-based saucepan, add the onion and cook, stirring, for 2 minutes. Add the garlic, celery and potatoes. Cook, stirring, until well coated with oil. Add half the tarragon and mix well.
———2———
Add the lettuce. Cover and cook over low heat for about 1 minute, until softened. Pour on the vegetable stock and bring to the boil. Lower the heat and cook, half covered, for 20 minutes.
———3———
Pour into a blender or food processor and blend until smooth. Transfer to a large bowl, cover and chill for at least 1 hour.
———4———
Whisk in the buttermilk, Quark and remaining tarragon. Season. Blend again, then cover and chill until ready to serve. Garnish with tarragon.

MICROWAVE Put oil and onion into bowl. Cover and cook 100% (High) 3 minutes. Stir in garlic, celery, potatoes and half the tarragon. Cover and cook 2 minutes. Add lettuce and boiling stock. Cover and cook 15 minutes. Complete recipe.

18

CHILLIED CHICK-PEA SALAD

SERVES 4 115 calories per serving
PREPARATION 10 minutes
COOKING None

1 garlic clove, skinned and crushed
10 ml (2 tsp) tahini
15 ml (1 tbsp) lemon juice
425 g (15 oz) can chick-peas, drained
and rinsed
1 small green chilli, cored, seeded and
thinly sliced
½ crisp lettuce, finely shredded
½ red pepper, cored, seeded and cut into thin
strips, to garnish
warm wholemeal pitta bread, to serve

——— 1 ———

Put the garlic, tahini and lemon juice
in a small bowl and stir to a smooth,
thick paste. Stir in 30 ml (2 tbsp)
cold water. Mix until smooth.

——— 2 ———

Place the chick-peas in a bowl, pour
over the tahini dressing and mix
well. Gently mix in the chilli.

——— 3 ———

Arrange the lettuce in a shallow
serving bowl and pile the chick-pea
mixture in the centre. Garnish with
strips of red pepper. Serve with
warm pitta bread.

GOODNESS GUIDE
CHILLIED CHICK-PEA SALAD

PROTEIN The chick-peas and tahini (made
from seasame seeds) are good sources of
plant protein. Serving the salad with pitta
bread provides good quality protein
FIBRE The chick-peas provide a type of
fibre which aids the control of sugar
absorption by the blood. Extra fibre is
present in the vegetables and bread.

*CHILLED TARRAGON AND
VEGETABLE SOUP*

MINERALS The cheese and buttermilk are
good sources of calcium
VITAMINS B-complex vitamins are provided
by the buttermilk and cheese. The
vegetables will retain some vitamin C after
cooking. Vitamin C aids the formation of
collagen and is also needed for a healthy
immune system

CRISPY BAKED MUSHROOMS WITH GARLIC DIP

*These baked mushrooms can be
made in advance and stored in the
refrigerator. Spearing the
mushrooms on wooden cocktail
sticks makes dipping easier.*

SERVES 4 120 calories per serving
PREPARATION 15 minutes
COOKING 15–20 minutes
CHILLING At least 30 minutes

100 g (4 oz) fine day-old wholemeal
breadcrumbs
30 ml (2 tbsp) grated Parmesan cheese
15 ml (1 tbsp) chopped fresh mixed herbs or
7.5 ml (½ tbsp) dried
225 g (8 oz) button mushrooms, trimmed
3 egg whites, lightly beaten

GARLIC DIP
100 g (4 oz) low-fat soft cheese
60 ml (4 tbsp) low-fat natural yogurt
1–2 garlic cloves, skinned and crushed
15 ml (1 tbsp) snipped fresh chives

——— 1 ———

Mix the breadcrumbs, Parmesan
cheese and herbs together on a large
flat plate.

——— 2 ———

Dip each mushroom in the egg
whites, then coat in the breadcrumb
mixture, pressing on firmly and
making sure that the mushroom is
completely covered. Repeat until all
the mushrooms are coated.

——— 3 ———

Place the mushrooms on a baking
sheet and chill for at least 30
minutes. Bake at 190°C (375°F)
mark 5 for 15–20 minutes, until
golden brown.

——— 4 ———

Meanwhile, put the cheese, yogurt,
garlic and chives in a bowl and mix
together. Spoon into a serving dish.
Serve the mushrooms hot, with the
garlic flavoured dip.

GOODNESS GUIDE

VITAMINS The breadcrumbs and cheeses
provide a range of B-complex vitamins,
necessary for energy production
FIBRE The mushrooms and breadcrumbs
provide fibre
PROTEIN Protein is present in the cheeses,
egg whites, breadcrumbs and mushrooms

CHINESE SWEETCORN AND CRAB SOUP

SERVES 4 155 calories per serving
PREPARATION 5 minutes
COOKING 15 minutes

900 ml (1½ pints) chicken stock
2.5 cm (1 inch) piece fresh
root ginger, peeled
1 garlic clove, skinned
225 g (8 oz) frozen sweetcorn kernels
10 ml (2 tsp) cornflour
175 g (6 oz) can crab meat
15 ml (1 tbsp) dry sherry
5 ml (1 tsp) sesame or corn oil
1 egg white
2 spring onions, trimmed and finely
chopped, to garnish

——— 1 ———

Put the stock in a saucepan with the
ginger and garlic. Bring to the boil,
then cover, lower the heat and
simmer for 5 minutes. Discard the
garlic and ginger.

——— 2 ———

Add the sweetcorn and cook for 5
minutes. In a small bowl, mix the
cornflour with 15 ml (1 tbsp) cold
water. Add to the soup and cook,
stirring, for 2 minutes, until thickened. Add the crab meat and cook
for a further 2 minutes, then add the
dry sherry.

——— 3 ———

Mix together the sesame oil and egg
white. Take the pan off the heat and
pour in this mixture, stirring gently.
Serve in individual bowls, garnished
with spring onions.

MICROWAVE Put boiling stock into a
bowl, add ginger and garlic. Cover
and cook 100% (High) 3 minutes.
Discard the ginger and garlic. Add
sweetcorn to stock, cover and cook
100% (High) 3 minutes. Blend
cornflour with 15 ml (1 tbsp) water.
Stir into the soup. Cook,
uncovered, 100% (High) 3 minutes,
stirring once, until thickened. Add
crab meat and sherry. Cook,
uncovered, 100% (High) 3 minutes.
Complete recipe.

GOODNESS GUIDE
FAT Crab meat is a low-fat
source of protein
MINERALS The crab meat and sweetcorn
both provide iron. The crab meat and all the
vegetables supply potassium

ITALIAN EGG SOUP

CREAM OF CELERY SOUP

MELON AND GRAPE COCKTAIL

MELON AND GRAPE COCKTAIL

This is an ideal starter to a large meal. If fresh mint is out of season, use grated citrus rind.

SERVES 4   75 calories per serving
PREPARATION   20 minutes
CHILLING   3–4 hours

1 large Galia or Charentais melon,
halved and seeded
175 g (6 oz) black grapes, halved and seeded
75 g (3 oz) seedless green grapes
juice of 2 oranges
juice of 2 limes
pinch of ground mixed spice
fresh mint sprigs, to decorate (optional)

————1————
Scoop the melon flesh into balls with a melon baller or peel and cut into fine dice.
————2————
Mix the melon in a bowl with the grapes, orange juice, lime juice and mixed spice. Cover and chill for 3–4 hours. Serve garnished with fresh sprigs of mint.

GOODNESS GUIDE
FIBRE   The grapes and melon are good sources of fibre
VITAMINS   The fruit is rich in vitamin C, one function of which is to maintain blood capillaries
MINERALS   The grapes and melon are good sources of potassium

20

SPRING PRAWN SOUP

CREAM OF CELERY SOUP

This delicately flavoured soup is ideal to serve before a chicken dish. For special occasions, swirl a little low-fat natural yogurt on the top.

SERVES 4   80 calories per serving
PREPARATION   15 minutes
COOKING   35 minutes

15 g ($\frac{1}{2}$ oz) polyunsaturated margarine
1 onion, skinned and finely chopped
1 garlic clove, skinned and crushed
6 celery sticks, trimmed
15 ml (1 tbsp) plain wholemeal flour
600 ml (1 pint) chicken stock
300 ml ($\frac{1}{2}$ pint) semi-skimmed milk
salt and pepper, to taste
celery leaves, to garnish

———1———
Melt the margarine and cook the onion for 4 minutes, until soft. Add the garlic and celery and cook gently for a further 5 minutes.
———2———
Stir in the flour and cook for 1 minute. Gradually stir in the stock, milk and seasoning. Bring to the boil, lower the heat, cover and simmer gently for 25–30 minutes or until the celery is very soft.
———3———
Purée in a blender or food processor until smooth. Reheat gently. Serve hot, topped with celery leaves.

GOODNESS GUIDE
FIBRE High amounts of fibre are provided by the onion, celery and flour
VITAMINS Some vitamin C is provided by the fresh vegetables
FAT The overall fat content is lower than in traditional cream of celery soup because semi-skimmed milk is used instead of whole milk

ITALIAN EGG SOUP

Based on a traditional Roman recipe, this is a filling and nutritious soup.

SERVES 4   90 calories per serving
PREPARATION   5 minutes
COOKING   5 minutes

2 eggs
25 ml (1$\frac{1}{2}$ tbsp) semolina
30 ml (2 tbsp) grated Parmesan cheese
grated nutmeg, to taste
salt and pepper, to taste
1 litre (1$\frac{3}{4}$ pints) chicken stock
chopped fresh parsley, to garnish

———1———
Whisk together the eggs, semolina, cheese, nutmeg and seasoning. Add 150 ml ($\frac{1}{4}$ pint) of the stock.
———2———
Bring the remaining stock to the boil, then whisk in the egg and semolina mixture. Lower the heat and simmer gently for about 3 minutes, until thickened. Serve at once, garnished with fresh parsley.

GOODNESS GUIDE
FIBRE The semolina contributes some fibre
VITAMINS The eggs contribute vitamins A, B complex and D. Vitamin D is vital for healthy teeth and bones and for assisting in calcium absorption. Cheese and semolina also contribute some B vitamins
MINERALS Cheese and semolina provide some calcium; iron is contributed by the eggs, semolina and chicken stock

SPRING PRAWN SOUP

SERVES 4   185 calories per serving
PREPARATION   5 minutes
COOKING   40 minutes
CHILLING   3–4 hours

275 g (10 oz) cooked prawns, peeled with shells reserved
2 spring onions, chopped
small bunch of parsley stalks
1 bay leaf
strip of thinly pared lemon rind
300 ml ($\frac{1}{2}$ pint) dry white wine
salt and pepper, to taste
20 g ($\frac{3}{4}$ oz) polyunsaturated margarine
20 g ($\frac{3}{4}$ oz) plain flour
150 ml (5 fl oz) low-fat natural yogurt
grated lemon rind and fresh dill sprigs, to garnish

———1———
Place the prawn shells in a saucepan with the spring onions, parsley stalks, bay leaf, the lemon rind and 600 ml (1 pint) water. Bring to the boil, lower the heat and simmer gently, covered, for 25 minutes.
———2———
Pour the prawn stock through a fine sieve and discard the shells and flavourings. Mix with the white wine and season. Reserve.
———3———
Melt the margarine. Stir in the flour and cook for 1 minute. Gradually stir in the stock and bring to the boil. Lower the heat, add two-thirds of the prawns and simmer gently for about 5 minutes. Purée in a blender or food processor until smooth. Set aside to cool, then stir in the yogurt. Chill for 3–4 hours.
———4———
Stir the remaining prawns into the soup. Serve garnished with lemon rind and sprigs of dill.

GOODNESS GUIDE
FAT Prawns are a low-fat source of protein, as is the yogurt
VITAMINS The prawns are a rich source of B complex vitamins, which are also present in the flour and yogurt
MINERALS Prawns are an excellent source of zinc. Calcium, potassium and iron are provided by the prawns and flour; the yogurt also provides calcium

HARICOT BEAN AND OLIVE SOUP

SERVES 4 145 calories per serving
PREPARATION 15 minutes
COOKING 1¾ hours
SOAKING Overnight

100 g (4 oz) dried haricot beans, soaked
overnight and drained
30 ml (2 tbsp) olive oil
1 onion, skinned and chopped
2 garlic cloves, skinned and crushed
900 ml (1½ pints) vegetable stock
2 celery sticks, trimmed and chopped
1 carrot, scrubbed and chopped
4 tomatoes, coarsely chopped
100 g (4 oz) French or dwarf beans, cut into
2.5 cm (1 inch) lengths
1 small red pepper, cored, seeded and diced
15 ml (1 tbsp) tomato purée
1 courgette, sliced
15 ml (1 tbsp) chopped fresh parsley
10 ml (2 tsp) chopped fresh basil or
5 ml (1 tsp) dried
10 ml (2 tsp) chopped fresh marjoram or
5 ml (1 tsp) dried
10 ml (2 tsp) chopped fresh thyme or
5 ml (1 tsp) dried
salt and pepper, to taste
25 g (1 oz) stoned black olives,
thinly sliced

1

Put the haricot beans in a saucepan with fresh water to cover and boil for 15 minutes.

2

Meanwhile, heat the oil in a large heavy-based saucepan, add the onion and cook, stirring, for 5 minutes. Add the garlic and cook for 2 minutes.

3

Drain the beans, rinse and add to the onion with the stock. Bring to the boil, then simmer, half covered, for about 1¼ hours.

4

Add the celery, carrot and tomatoes and cook, half covered, for a further 10 minutes, stirring occasionally. Add the French beans and red pepper and continue cooking for 2 minutes, then stir in the tomato purée, courgette, herbs and seasoning. Simmer, uncovered, for 5 minutes. Sprinkle the olives over the top and serve.

GOODNESS GUIDE

PROTEIN Serving bread with the soup will complement the protein in the beans
FIBRE The beans and vegetables provide an excellent amount of fibre which is important for good carbohydrate absorption and healthy intestines

HARICOT BEAN AND OLIVE SOUP

AVOCADO AND CITRUS STARTER

AVOCADO AND CITRUS STARTER

It is important to remove all the white pith from the grapefruit and the tangerine as it is very bitter.

SERVES 4 210 calories per serving
PREPARATION 15 minutes
COOKING None

finely grated rind and juice of 1 lime
5 ml (1 tsp) clear honey
2.5 ml ($\frac{1}{2}$ tsp) Dijon mustard
salt and pepper, to taste
45 ml (3 tbsp) olive oil
1 large grapefruit, peeled and segmented
2 large tangerines, peeled and segmented
1 large avocado, peeled, stoned
and thinly sliced
50 g (2 oz) strawberries, hulled
and thinly sliced
lime twists, to garnish

——— 1 ———

To make the dressing, put the lime rind and juice, honey, mustard and seasoning in a bowl and whisk together. Gradually whisk in the olive oil.

——— 2 ———

Arrange the grapefruit, tangerines, avocado and strawberries on 4 plates. Spoon over the dressing, garnish with lime twists and serve immediately.

GOODNESS GUIDE
VITAMINS Plenty of vitamin C is provided by the fruit. The avocado and tangerines supply a little carotene. The avocado is also a source of vitamin E which is a very important fat-soluble vitamin
FIBRE The avocado and the citrus fruit provide fibre

SMOKED TROUT MOUSSE IN LEMON SHELLS

Smoked mackerel may be used but it does not have such a delicate flavour.

SERVES 4 100 calories per serving
PREPARATION 40 minutes
COOKING None
CHILLING 2$\frac{3}{4}$ hours

175 g (6 oz) smoked trout, skinned
175 g (6 oz) natural Quark
10–15 ml (2–3 tsp) horseradish
pepper, to taste
4 large lemons
10 ml (2 tsp) powdered gelatine
2 egg whites
30 ml (2 tbsp) finely chopped fresh parsley,
to garnish
8 triangles of hot wholemeal toast, to serve

——— 1 ———

Flake the trout and discard all the bones, Put the flesh in a bowl with the Quark, horseradish and season-ing. Mix well, then set aside.

——— 2 ———

Cut the lemons in half lengthways. Scoop out all the flesh, pips and pith into a sieve and press to extract the juice. Reserve the lemon shells.

——— 3 ———

Sprinkle the gelatine over 60 ml (4 tbsp) lemon juice in a small bowl. Soak for 1 minute, then place over a saucepan of hot water and stir until the gelatine has dissolved.

——— 4 ———

Stir the gelatine liquid into the trout mixture. Whisk the egg whites until stiff, then fold into the mousse until evenly incorporated. Chill for about 45 minutes or until the mousse just holds its shape, then spoon into the reserved lemon shells. Chill for a further 2 hours, until firm. Sprinkle with chopped fresh parsley and serve with the hot toast.

GOODNESS GUIDE
VITAMINS The trout and cheese provide B vitamins. Vitamin C is found in lemon juice and parsley
FAT Trout is a medium fat fish. Using Quark makes this dish lower in fat than traditional mousses
PROTEIN The trout and cheese provide a good serving of protein

SMOKED TROUT MOUSSE IN LEMON SHELLS

PASTA SALAD WITH GREEN MAYONNAISE

PEPPERY CHEESE SOUFFLES

PEPPERY CHEESE SOUFFLES

These light soufflés are quick to prepare and are perfect before a simple beef or poultry meal, or on their own as a simple late-night supper.

SERVES 4   135 calories per serving
PREPARATION   10 minutes
COOKING   15 minutes

100 g (4 oz) low-fat soft cheese
50 g (2 oz) mature Cheddar cheese,
finely grated
15 ml (1 tbsp) grated Parmesan cheese
1.25 ml ($\frac{1}{4}$ tsp) mustard powder
5 ml (1 tsp) green peppercorns in brine,
drained and roughly chopped
50 ml (2 fl oz) dry sherry or white wine
2 eggs, separated

——————1——————
Lightly grease 4 ramekins and set aside. Mix the cheeses with the mustard and peppercorns. Mix in the sherry or wine and the egg yolks.

——————2——————
Whisk the egg whites until stiff, then carefully fold 15 ml (1 tbsp) into the cheese mixture, to soften. Fold in the remainder.

——————3——————
Spoon into the ramekins and bake at 200°C (400°F) mark 6 for about 15 minutes, until puffed and golden brown on top. Serve immediately.

GOODNESS GUIDE
PROTEIN Good protein is supplied by the cheese and eggs
VITAMINS The cheese and eggs provide B vitamins
MINERALS Calcium and potassium are provided by the cheese and eggs, with iron supplied by the eggs. Calcium is needed for strong bones, blood clotting and efficient nerve transmission

PASTA SALAD WITH GREEN MAYONNAISE

SERVES 4   225 calories per serving
PREPARATION   20 minutes
COOKING   About 15 minutes

100 g (4 oz) wholemeal pasta shells
4 spring onions, chopped
$\frac{1}{2}$ red pepper, cored, seeded and diced
75 g (3 oz) button mushrooms,
washed and trimmed
1 tomato, cut into small wedges, to garnish

GREEN MAYONNAISE
2 large garlic cloves, skinned and crushed
50 g (2 oz) frozen spinach
15 ml (1 tbsp) chopped fresh parsley
60 ml (4 tbsp) Greek strained yogurt
60 ml (4 tbsp) mayonnaise
15 ml (1 tbsp) lemon juice
grated nutmeg, to taste
salt and pepper, to taste

——————1——————
Cook the pasta in a large saucepan of boiling water for 2–3 minutes if fresh, 5–8 minutes if dried, or until tender but still firm. Drain, refresh the pasta in cold water and set aside.

MIXED PEPPER SOUP

COURGETTE AND TOMATO SOUP

COURGETTE AND TOMATO SOUP

This refreshing chilled summer soup is ideal as a seasonal starter. Serve with slices of wholemeal bread and a bowl of grated cheese.

SERVES 4 50 calories per serving
PREPARATION 10 minutes
COOKING 12 minutes
CHILLING 1½ hours

15 ml (1 tbsp) olive oil
2 garlic cloves, skinned and crushed
225 g (8 oz) courgettes, trimmed and sliced
15 ml (1 tbsp) chopped fresh basil
225 g (8 oz) tomatoes, chopped
salt and pepper, to taste
fresh basil leaves, to garnish

———1———

Heat the oil in a saucepan, add the garlic and courgettes and cook over a high heat for 2–3 minutes, stirring occasionally. Add the basil and 300 ml (½ pint) water. Cover and simmer gently for about 10 minutes or until the courgettes are tender.

———2———

Remove from the heat and allow to cool slightly, then purée in a blender or food processor until fine, but not smooth. Transfer to a bowl.

———3———

Add the tomatoes to the blender and process roughly. Add to the courgettes, mix well and season.

———4———

Chill for at least 1½ hours before serving. Pour into individual bowls and garnish with fresh basil leaves.

MICROWAVE Put the oil, garlic and courgettes into a bowl. Cover and cook 100% (High) 5 minutes. Add the basil and 300 ml (½ pint) boiling water. Cover and cook 100% (High) 8 minutes, until the courgettes are tender. Complete the recipe.

GOODNESS GUIDE

VITAMINS Vitamins A and C are provided by the tomatoes, courgettes and fresh basil. Vitamin A assists in the maintenance of healthy skin, hair and mucous membranes, and is also important for good dim-light vision

FIBRE All the vegetables supply fibre

MIXED PEPPER SOUP

This mixed pepper soup may be served hot or cold with wholemeal bread.

SERVES 4 80 calories per serving
PREPARATION 15 minutes
COOKING 35 minutes

30 ml (2 tbsp) corn oil
1 onion, skinned and chopped
30 ml (2 tbsp) chopped fresh root ginger
1 red pepper, cored, seeded
and roughly chopped
1 yellow pepper, cored, seeded
and roughly chopped
1 green pepper, cored, seeded
and roughly chopped
600 ml (1 pint) vegetable stock
60 ml (4 tbsp) low-fat natural yogurt
salt and pepper, to taste

———1———

Heat the oil in a large saucepan and cook the onion and ginger for 3–4 minutes or until softened. Add the peppers and cook for a further 1 minute. Pour in the stock, cover the pan and simmer for about 30 minutes or until the peppers are just tender.

———2———

Remove a few pieces of pepper from the pan and set aside. Purée the soup in a blender or food processor until smooth, then add the yogurt and seasoning. Return the soup to the pan and gently reheat without boiling. Add the reserved pieces of pepper to the soup before serving.

MICROWAVE Put the oil, onion and ginger into a bowl. Cover and cook 100% (High) 3 minutes, until softened. Add the peppers, cover and cook 100% (High) 3 minutes. Pour in 450 ml (¾ pint) boiling stock. Cover and cook 100% (High) 18–20 minutes, until tender. Follow step 2, reheating, uncovered, 100% (High) 2–3 minutes. Add the reserved pepper pieces to the soup.

GOODNESS GUIDE

VITAMINS Peppers are very high in carotene and vitamin C. Vitamin C, among its other functions, helps to maintain capillaries, bones and teeth

FIBRE The vegetables provide a good helping of fibre

———2———

To make the dressing, cook the garlic and spinach in a small non-stick pan, stirring, for about 10 minutes. Allow to cool. Purée the spinach with the parsley in a blender or food processor until smooth. Add the remaining dressing ingredients and season.

———3———

Combine the cooled pasta, spring onions, red pepper and mushrooms together in a bowl. Divide between 4 serving plates and spoon a little dressing over each. Garnish with tomato wedges.

GOODNESS GUIDE

FIBRE The wholemeal pasta and vegetables provide a good serving of fibre
VITAMINS Carotene is provided by the spinach, parsley and red pepper. All the vegetables provide plenty of vitamin C. The pasta and yogurt provide B-complex vitamins which, among other functions, help the body to utilise energy from carbohydrates, fats and protein

CARROT AND DATE SALAD

The mixture of sweet and tangy flavours in this salad is typical of Middle Eastern cookery.

SERVES 4   200 calories per serving
PREPARATION   15 minutes
COOKING   None

450 g (1 lb) carrots, scrubbed
and thinly sliced
150 ml ($\frac{1}{4}$ pint) unsweetened orange juice
100 g (4 oz) dried dates, rinsed,
stoned and chopped
50 g (2 oz) sunflower seeds
5 ml (1 tsp) chopped fresh parsley
15 ml (1 tbsp) olive oil
15 ml (1 tbsp) lemon juice
5 ml (1 tsp) Dijon mustard
lettuce leaves, to serve
peeled orange segments, to garnish

———1———

Place the carrots and orange juice in a saucepan. Bring to the boil, cover, lower the heat and simmer for 5 minutes, until the carrots are almost tender but still crunchy. Strain, reserving the orange juice.

———2———

In a small bowl mix the carrots with the dates, sunflower seeds and parsley. Mix the oil, lemon juice and mustard with the hot orange juice and pour over the carrots. Serve warm or cold on a lettuce leaf, garnished with orange segments.

GOODNESS GUIDE

VITAMINS This salad is rich in a range of vitamins which are crucial for keeping the body in good condition. The carrots and orange juice provide A, which is essential for healthy eyes and skin. With the lemon juice and parsley they also supply C, which is important for the health of cells, blood vessels, teeth and gums

CHICKEN NOODLE SOUP

SERVES 4   155 calories per serving
PREPARATION   15 minutes
COOKING   15 minutes

2 chicken breasts, 100–175 g (4–6 oz) each,
skinned, boned and cut into thin strips
900 ml (1$\frac{1}{2}$ pints) chicken stock
5 ml (1 tsp) mild curry powder
50 g (2 oz) Chinese egg noodles
30 ml (2 tbsp) chopped fresh parsley
salt and pepper, to taste

———1———

Place the chicken in a saucepan, add the stock and bring to the boil. Lower the heat, cover and simmer for 10 minutes or until chicken cooks through.

———2———

Strain the chicken, reserving the cooking liquid. Place the chicken back in the saucepan, add the curry powder and cook for 2–3 minutes over medium heat, stirring constantly so the curry powder coats all the chicken.

———3———

Gradually return the cooking liquid to the saucepan, then add the noodles, parsley and seasoning. Simmer for 10 minutes. Serve at once in individual bowls.

GOODNESS GUIDE

PROTEIN Proteins provide the building material for repair of worn body tissues and for growth. The chicken breasts and egg noodles make this a high-protein soup
FAT Chicken is one of the leanest of meats. With the skins removed from the breasts and no fat added during cooking, this soup is very low fat

AVOCADO PRAWNS WITH CHILLI DRESSING

CARROT AND DATE SALAD

CHICKEN NOODLE SOUP

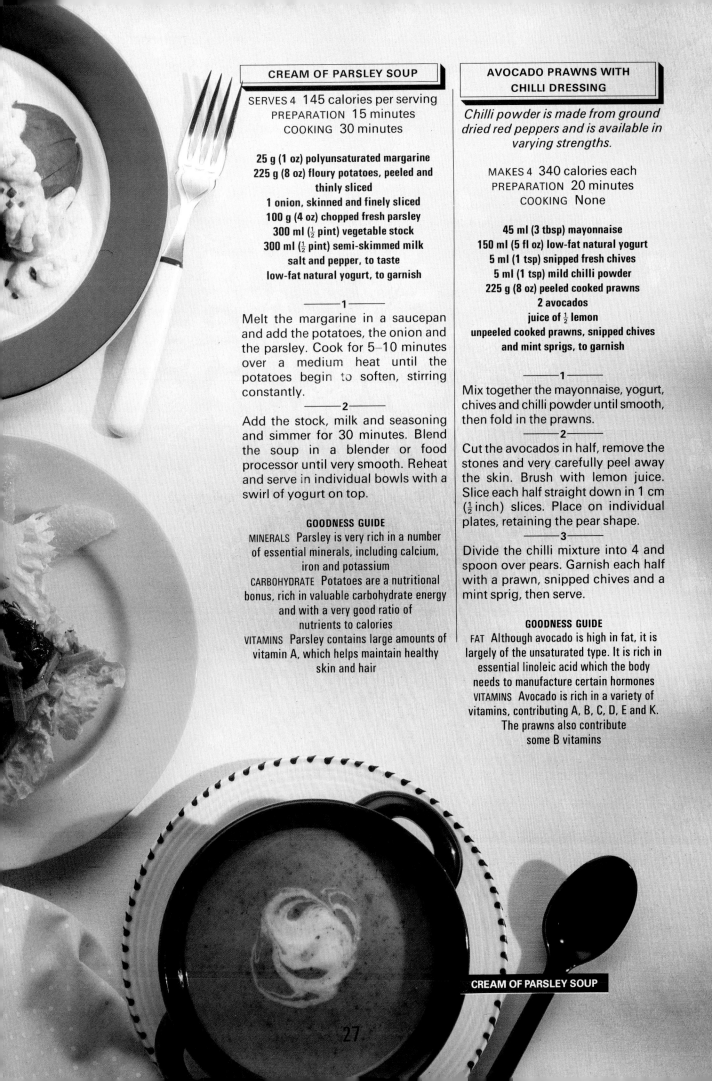

CREAM OF PARSLEY SOUP

SERVES 4   145 calories per serving
PREPARATION   15 minutes
COOKING   30 minutes

25 g (1 oz) polyunsaturated margarine
225 g (8 oz) floury potatoes, peeled and
thinly sliced
1 onion, skinned and finely sliced
100 g (4 oz) chopped fresh parsley
300 ml ($\frac{1}{2}$ pint) vegetable stock
300 ml ($\frac{1}{2}$ pint) semi-skimmed milk
salt and pepper, to taste
low-fat natural yogurt, to garnish

———1———

Melt the margarine in a saucepan
and add the potatoes, the onion and
the parsley. Cook for 5–10 minutes
over a medium heat until the
potatoes begin to soften, stirring
constantly.

———2———

Add the stock, milk and seasoning
and simmer for 30 minutes. Blend
the soup in a blender or food
processor until very smooth. Reheat
and serve in individual bowls with a
swirl of yogurt on top.

GOODNESS GUIDE

MINERALS Parsley is very rich in a number
of essential minerals, including calcium,
iron and potassium
CARBOHYDRATE Potatoes are a nutritional
bonus, rich in valuable carbohydrate energy
and with a very good ratio of
nutrients to calories
VITAMINS Parsley contains large amounts of
vitamin A, which helps maintain healthy
skin and hair

AVOCADO PRAWNS WITH CHILLI DRESSING

*Chilli powder is made from ground
dried red peppers and is available in
varying strengths.*

MAKES 4   340 calories each
PREPARATION   20 minutes
COOKING   None

45 ml (3 tbsp) mayonnaise
150 ml (5 fl oz) low-fat natural yogurt
5 ml (1 tsp) snipped fresh chives
5 ml (1 tsp) mild chilli powder
225 g (8 oz) peeled cooked prawns
2 avocados
juice of $\frac{1}{2}$ lemon
unpeeled cooked prawns, snipped chives
and mint sprigs, to garnish

———1———

Mix together the mayonnaise, yogurt,
chives and chilli powder until smooth,
then fold in the prawns.

———2———

Cut the avocados in half, remove the
stones and very carefully peel away
the skin. Brush with lemon juice.
Slice each half straight down in 1 cm
($\frac{1}{2}$ inch) slices. Place on individual
plates, retaining the pear shape.

———3———

Divide the chilli mixture into 4 and
spoon over pears. Garnish each half
with a prawn, snipped chives and a
mint sprig, then serve.

GOODNESS GUIDE

FAT Although avocado is high in fat, it is
largely of the unsaturated type. It is rich in
essential linoleic acid which the body
needs to manufacture certain hormones
VITAMINS Avocado is rich in a variety of
vitamins, contributing A, B, C, D, E and K.
The prawns also contribute
some B vitamins

CREAM OF PARSLEY SOUP

EGGS MIMOSA

SERVES 4 175 calories per serving
PREPARATION 20 minutes
COOKING None

4 eggs
45 ml (3 tbsp) low-fat natural yogurt
30 ml (2 tbsp) mayonnaise
15 ml (1 tbsp) capers, well drained
and chopped
1 bunch watercress, chopped
50 g (2 oz) seedless raisins, rinsed
salt and pepper, to taste
pinch of cayenne pepper
lettuce leaves
watercress sprigs, to garnish

———1———

To hard boil the eggs, place in a saucepan of boiling water, bring back to the boil and simmer for 10–12 minutes. Place under cold running water, tap the shells and leave until cold, then shell, cut in half lengthways and gently remove the yolks.

———2———

Mix together the yogurt, mayonnaise, capers, watercress, raisins and seasonings. Lay 1 or 2 lettuce leaves on each plate and place 2 egg white halves on top, cut side upwards. Divide the yogurt mixture between the eggs, and fill each of the cavities.

———3———

Sieve 2 of the egg yolks over the stuffed egg whites (use the remaining yolks in another dish). Garnish with sprigs of watercress.

GOODNESS GUIDE
EGGS MIMOSA
PROTEIN Eggs are a cheap source of excellent protein
VITAMINS Fresh vegetables such as watercress and lettuce contain essential folic acid, which helps form haemoglobin in red blood cells
FAT Egg yolk is high in saturated fat and cholesterol, so limit egg consumption to about 4 per week

SPICY MUNG BEAN SOUP
FIBRE Mung beans are exceptionally high in fibre
MINERALS The beans contribute large amounts of calcium, potassium, and, in particular, iron for healthy blood
VITAMINS Mung beans contribute large amounts of the B vitamins, particularly niacin, needed for energy production in cells, and folic acid

SPICY MUNG BEAN SOUP

Mung beans are small, round and green, with an 'eye'. They are available at health food shops, the larger supermarkets and specialist grocers.

7.5 ml (1½ tsp) olive oil
1 onion, skinned and sliced
1 fresh red chilli, seeded and finely chopped
1 garlic clove, skinned and sliced
1 cm (½ inch) piece fresh root ginger, peeled
finely pared rind of 1 orange
100 ml (4 fl oz) unsweetened orange juice
750 ml (1¼ pints) vegetable stock
225 g (8 oz) mung beans, soaked for 2–3 hours and drained
salt, to taste
15 ml (1 tbsp) chopped fresh coriander or parsley
1 orange, peeled and segmented
low-fat natural yogurt, to garnish

———1———

Heat the olive oil in a large saucepan, add the onion and cook, stirring, for 5 minutes or until the onion is softened but not browned. Add the chilli, garlic, ginger and half the orange rind and cook for 1 minute longer to blend the flavours.

———2———

Add the orange juice and bring to the boil. Boil until the liquid has reduced by half, then add the stock, mung beans and seasoning. Return to the boil, lower the heat and simmer, covered, for 30 minutes or until the beans are tender. Purée in a blender or food processor, then reheat. If the soup is thicker than preferred, adjust the consistency by adding additional orange juice.

———3———

Finely slice the remaining orange rind into matchstick-thin strips, called julienne strips. Pour the soup into bowls and stir the coriander. Arrange the orange segments on top, then place a spoonful of yogurt in the centre and a couple of shreds of orange rind on top. Serve at once.

MEDITERRANEAN PRAWN SALAD

SERVES 4 385 calories per serving
PREPARATION 20 minutes
COOKING None

5 ml (1 tsp) Dijon mustard
20 ml (4 tsp) lemon juice
30 ml (2 tbsp) olive oil
salt and pepper, to taste
2 avocados
1 small fennel bulb, finely sliced
5 ml (1 tsp) ground cumin
8 cooked Mediterranean prawns, thawed if frozen and peeled
5 ml (1 tsp) polyunsaturated margarine

———1———

To make the dressing, put the mustard into a bowl with the lemon juice and then slowly pour in the oil, whisking constantly. Season to taste.

———2———

Halve the avocados, peel, remove and discard the stone. Dice the avocado flesh and add to the dressing with the fennel slices. Gently mix so the avocado is well coated.

———3———

Sprinkle the cumin evenly over each prawn. Melt the margarine in a heavy-based frying pan, add the prawns and cook over low heat for 1 minute on each side.

———4———

Put the fennel and avocado mixture on to individual serving plates and top with the prawns. Serve at once.

GOODNESS GUIDE
MEDITERRANEAN PRAWN SALAD
FIBRE Avocados contain good amounts of fibre
FAT Although avocados are high in fat, it is polyunsaturated and contains fat-soluble vitamins, A, D and E
MINERALS Avocados provide iron. Prawns are a good source of calcium, potassium, iron, zinc and iodine

TARAMASALATA
VITAMINS Cod's roe is full of vitamins, including A, B-complex, C, D and E. Vitamin D is essential for calcium absorption. Vitamin E is found in all our cell membranes; it prevents the destruction of polyunsaturated fatty acids by oxygen which results in damage to the cells

TARAMASALATA

This classic Greek dip keeps well for 3–4 days if stored in the refrigerator in an airtight container.

SERVES 4   95 calories per serving
PREPARATION   10 minutes
COOKING   None

175 g (6 oz) smoked cod's roe, skinned
50 g (2 oz) fresh wholemeal breadcrubs
1 garlic clove, skinned and crushed
150 ml (5 fl oz) low-fat natural yogurt
juice of ½ lemon or 1 lime
pepper, to taste
15 ml (1 tbsp) snipped fresh chives
fresh chives and lemon and lime twists,
to garnish
toasted wholemeal bread fingers, to serve

Blend all the ingredients, except for the garnish and toast, in a blender or food processor until smooth and creamy, then adjust the seasoning. Garnish and serve with wholemeal toast fingers.

MEDITERRANEAN PRAWN SALAD

TARAMASALATA

SPICY MUNG BEAN SOUP

EGGS MIMOSA

29

GAZPACHO

A traditional chilled Spanish soup, Gazpacho is quick to make and acts as an excellent appetite stimulant.

SERVES 4 95 calories per serving
PREPARATION 10 minutes
COOKING None
CHILLING 30 minutes

225 g (8 oz) tomatoes, seeded and
finely diced
$\frac{1}{3}$ cucumber, peeled, seeded and finely diced
1 onion, skinned and chopped
1 small green pepper, cored, seeded
and diced
1 small red pepper, cored, seeded and diced
1 garlic clove, skinned and finely chopped
450 ml ($\frac{3}{4}$ pint) tomato juice, chilled
150 ml ($\frac{1}{4}$ pint) chicken or vegetable
stock, chilled
15 ml (1 tbsp) olive oil
45 ml (3 tbsp) red wine vinegar
few drops Tabasco sauce
salt and pepper, to taste
15 ml (1 tbsp) chopped fresh chives or mint
2 slices wholemeal bread, toasted and
cubed, and ice cubes, to serve

——— 1 ———
Reserve about a quarter of the tom-atoes, cucumber, onion and peppers for the garnish. Place the remaining vegetables in a blender or food processor with the garlic and tomato juice and blend until smooth.

——— 2 ———
Add the stock, oil, vinegar and Tabasco sauce and blend well. Season. Pour into a bowl, cover and chill for about 30 minutes.

——— 3 ———
Stir the soup and sprinkle with the fresh herbs. Serve with the reserved vegetables, wholemeal croûtons and ice cubes in separate bowls, to be added to the soup as desired.

GOODNESS GUIDE
VITAMINS This soup is rich in vitamin C, which is essential for defence against infection. The tomatoes and peppers also contribute vitamin A, which is important for dim-light vision
FIBRE The vegetables contribute good amounts of fibre

GOAT'S CHEESE TARTS

Goat's cheese is available from delicatessens and large supermarkets.

MAKES 4 275 calories each
PREPARATION 10 minutes
BAKING 30 minutes
CHILLING 30 minutes

50 g (2 oz) plain wholemeal flour
50 g (2 oz) plain flour
salt, to taste
50 g (2 oz) polyunsaturated margarine
fresh coriander sprigs, to garnish

CHEESE FILLING
50 g (2 oz) soft goat's cheese, any coarse
rind removed
1 egg, separated
100 ml (4 fl oz) semi-skimmed milk
salt and pepper, to taste
one of the following flavourings:
1 small red pepper, cored, seeded
and finely chopped;
30 ml (2 tbsp) snipped fresh chives;
8 green and 8 black olives, stoned and
chopped with 15 ml (1 tbsp) drained capers

——— 1 ———
Put flours and salt into a bowl. Rub in margarine until mixture resembles fine breadcrumbs. Add water to form a dough. Chill 30 minutes.

——— 2 ———
Divide the dough into 4. Roll out each piece to a round and use to line 4 individual Yorkshire pudding tins. Prick with a fork, bake blind at 200°C (400°F) mark 6 for 5 minutes. Lower oven temperature to 190°C (375°F) mark 5.

——— 3 ———
Meanwhile, cream the cheese with a fork. Beat in the egg yolk and gradually add milk. Season and add one of the flavourings. Whisk egg white until stiff. Fold into mixture.

——— 4 ———
Divide filling between pastry cases and bake for a further 25 minutes. Garnish and serve warm.

GOODNESS GUIDE
MINERALS The cheese, egg, milk and flour are excellent sources of calcium, which is important for bone strength and blood clotting
VITAMINS A range of B vitamins are provided by the pastry and the filling. B-complex vitamins aid the body in utilising food

ARTICHOKES VINAIGRETTE

To ring the changes, use lemon juice and finely grated rind and 15 ml (1 tbsp) Dijon mustard in place of the orange juice, rind and ginger.

SERVES 4 150 calories per serving
PREPARATION 10 minutes
COOKING 30 minutes

4 globe artichokes, each about 100 g (4 oz)
30 ml (2 tbsp) red wine vinegar
15 ml (1 tbsp) unsweetened orange juice
finely grated rind of $\frac{1}{2}$ orange
1.25–2.5 ml ($\frac{1}{4}$–$\frac{1}{2}$ tsp) very finely chopped
fresh root ginger
salt and pepper, to taste
90 ml (6 tbsp) olive oil
30 ml (2 tbsp) chopped fresh parsley,
tarragon, dill or chives (optional)
orange segments, to garnish

——— 1 ———
Cut the stem off each artichoke close to the base and discard any dry or discoloured leaves. Place on its side and, using a sharp knife, cut off the upper leaves about 2.5 cm (1 inch) from the top. Using scissors, cut off about 2.5 cm (1 inch) from the tops of the remaining leaves. Rinse well in cold water and drain.

——— 2 ———
Cook the artichokes, covered, in a large saucepan of simmering water for about 30 minutes or until a leaf pulled gently comes off easily. Drain, leave upside down until ready to serve.

——— 3 ———
To make the dressing, put vinegar, orange juice and rind, ginger and seasoning into a bowl and mix well. Gradually beat in the oil and add the herbs.

——— 4 ———
Serve the artichokes garnished with the orange segments and small bowls of vinaigrette dressing on the side. Remove the leaves one by one, dip the base in the dressing and pull through the teeth to eat the fleshy part. Eat the heart with a knife and fork, first discarding the hairy 'choke'.

MICROWAVE Place the prepared artichokes in a deep bowl with 60 ml (4 tbsp) water. Cover, cook 100% (High) 15–18 minutes, rearranging artichokes twice, until tender. Drain. Complete as recipe.

SPICY BEAN PATE

SERVES 4 190 calories per serving
PREPARATION 5 minutes
COOKING None
CHILLING At least 1 hour

400 g (14 oz) can cannellini beans, drained
and rinsed
1 garlic clove, skinned and crushed
15 ml (1 tbsp) lemon juice
30 ml (2 tbsp) low-fat natural yogurt
15 ml (1 tbsp) olive oil
15 ml (1 tbsp) chopped fresh parsley
salt and cayenne pepper, to taste
black olives, tomato wedges and small
lettuce leaves, to garnish
4 slices wholemeal bread, toasted and cut
into triangles, or Melba toast, to serve

—— 1 ——
Drain the beans well, patting away
any excess moisture with absorbent
kitchen paper. Place in a blender or
food processor and purée until well
blended and smooth.

—— 2 ——
Transfer to a bowl and add the
garlic, lemon juice, yogurt, oil and
parsley. Mix well and season to
taste. Cover the mixture and chill for
at least 1 hour.

—— 3 ——
Serve in a large bowl or on individual plates, garnished with olives,
tomato wedges and lettuce leaves.
Serve with the toast.

GOODNESS GUIDE
SPICY BEAN PATE
PROTEIN The cannellini beans and yogurt
are good, low-fat sources of protein
FIBRE The wholemeal bread and beans
provide excellent amounts of fibre of
different kinds. One is good for efficient
bowel movements, the other controls sugar
absorption into the blood
VITAMINS The beans, bread and yogurt
provide B vitamins, essential for energy
production in the body

ARTICHOKES VINAIGRETTE
VITAMINS The orange juice and fresh herbs
provide vitamin C, which is needed for
healthy blood capillaries
MINERALS Artichokes are a source of
potassium and calcium, both of which are
involved in the transmission
of nerve impulses

SPICY BEAN PATE

ARTICHOKES VINAIGRETTE

GAZPACHO

GOAT'S CHEESE TARTS

31

HEDGEROW SALAD

AVOCADO WITH BLUE CHEESE DRESSING

ORANGE AND GRAPEFRUIT CONSOMME

HEDGEROW SALAD

Health food shops and some large supermarkets sell dandelion leaves, primulas and nasturtiums.

SERVES 4   130 calories per serving
PREPARATION   10 minutes
COOKING   None

1 small bunch of dandelion leaves
a few leaves of chicory
1 small curly endive
50 g (2 oz) sorrel
8 primula or nasturtium flowers

DRESSING
50 g (2 oz) walnuts, halved
30 ml (2 tbsp) walnut oil
60 ml (4 tbsp) lemon juice
1 garlic clove, skinned and crushed
salt and pepper, to taste

————1————
Break the leaves into bite-size pieces and place in a large bowl. Sprinkle over the flowers.

————2————
Mix together the dressing ingredients and pour over the salad. Toss and serve immediately.

GOODNESS GUIDE
VITAMINS Endive is particularly rich in carotene, the form of vitamin A found in vegetables, which the body converts to retinol, the active vitamin A. The walnuts contribute B-complex vitamins, including thiamine, folic acid and B_6
MINERALS This salad is rich in minerals, including iron, calcium, potassium, magnesium and zinc

32

AVOCADO WITH BLUE CHEESE DRESSING

SERVES 4 290 calories per serving
PREPARATION 15 minutes
COOKING None
SOAKING 2 hours

30 ml (2 tbsp) raisins, rinsed
30 ml (2 tbsp) brandy
50 g (2 oz) blue cheese
60 ml (4 tbsp) low-fat natural yogurt
2 ripe avocados
4 lettuce leaves
watercress, to garnish

———1———
Soak the raisins in the brandy for 2 hours, then drain, reserving the brandy.

———2———
Blend the cheese and yogurt in a blender or food processor with the brandy until smooth and creamy.

———3———
Halve and peel the avocados and remove the stones. Lay each half on a lettuce leaf and place some raisins in each cavity. Spoon over the dressing, garnish with watercress and serve.

GOODNESS GUIDE
MINERALS Avocados are rich in potassium, which is important for fluid balance in the cells. They also contain calcium and iron
VITAMINS Avocados contribute a range of vitamins, including A, B-complex, C and E. Vitamin E is important for strong blood vessels and muscles and protects vitamin A from oxidation

CUCUMBER AND MINT WATER ICE

To save time, this savoury starter may be made in advance and stored in the freezer for 3–4 weeks.

SERVES 4 40 calories per serving
PREPARATION 10 minutes
COOKING None
FREEZING 3–4 hours

1 cucumber, about 225 g (8 oz), peeled and chopped
45 ml (3 tbsp) chopped fresh mint or 25 ml (1½ tbsp) dried
200 ml (7 fl oz) white wine
fresh mint sprigs, to garnish

———1———
Place the cucumber in a blender or food processor with the mint. Blend to a smooth purée, gradually adding the wine.

———2———
Transfer the mixture to a plastic freezerproof container and freeze for 3–4 hours. Whisk well twice during freezing to prevent ice crystals from forming. To serve, scoop the water ice into small bowls and garnish with fresh mint.

GOODNESS GUIDE
FIBRE The cucumber and the mint provide some fibre
VITAMINS Folic acid is provided by the cucumber and the mint. Folic acid helps in the formation of haemoglobin, the oxygen-carrying substance in red blood cells. The mint and cucumber also provide vitamin C, needed by the body for healthy bones and teeth

ORANGE AND GRAPEFRUIT CONSOMME

This chilled soup makes a refreshing start to a meal on a warm summer's evening. Pink or white grapefruit can be used.

SERVES 4 65 calories per serving
PREPARATION 15 minutes
COOKING None
CHILLING 2 hours

15 ml (1 tbsp) powdered gelatine
200 ml (7 fl oz) unsweetened orange juice
450 ml (¾ pint) unsweetened grapefruit juice
2 grapefruit, peeled and cut into segments
few drops of Angostura bitters (optional)
grapefruit segments and mint leaves, to garnish

———1———
Sprinkle the gelatine over 30 ml (2 tbsp) cold water in a heatproof bowl and leave to soak for 1 minute. Place over a pan of gently boiling water and stir until the gelatine is dissolved.

———2———
Mix the fruit juices together in a bowl. Add the gelatine and grapefruit with the Angostura bitters, if using, and stir.

———3———
Chill for 2 hours, until the consommé is very lightly gelled. Serve in soup plates, garnished with grapefruit segments and mint leaves.

GOODNESS GUIDE
FIBRE The grapefruit supplies a little fibre, necessary for healthy bowel movement
VITAMINS A good supply of vitamin C is provided by the fruit juices as well as by the grapefruit. Among its other qualities, vitamin C is needed for the manufacture and repair of connective tissues like collagen and cartilage in bones

SPRATS WITH GOOSEBERRY SAUCE

SPRATS WITH GOOSEBERRY SAUCE

SERVES 4 145 calories per serving
PREPARATION 30 minutes
COOKING About 5 minutes

350 g (12 oz) gooseberries, topped and tailed
30 ml (2 tbsp) light muscovado sugar
450 g (1 lb) sprats, cleaned
and heads removed
juice of 1 lemon
fresh dill, to garnish

———1———

Put the gooseberries, sugar and 150 ml ($\frac{1}{4}$ pint) water into a sauce-pan. Simmer for about 15–20 minutes, until thick, breaking up the gooseberries with a fork.

———2———

Meanwhile, brush the sprats with lemon juice and cook under a hot grill for $1\frac{1}{2}$–$2\frac{1}{2}$ minutes each side. Garnish with fresh dill and serve with the hot gooseberry sauce.

GOODNESS GUIDE
FAT Sprats are an oily fish but the fat is mostly polyunsaturated and a source of a fatty acid which prevents blood abnormally clotting
VITAMINS Vitamin D is present in the fish. The gooseberries are high in vitamin C
FIBRE One serving of the gooseberries provides one-tenth of the recommended daily amount of 30 g

CHINESE CABBAGE AND PRAWN SOUP

BAKED SMOKED SALMON MOUSSES

FRESH PEA SOUP

34

CHINESE CABBAGE AND PRAWN SOUP

This is a clear soup full of vegetable goodness. Serve with wholemeal bread for a satisfying meal on its own.

SERVES 4   145 calories per serving
PREPARATION   10 minutes
COOKING   About 25 minutes

30 ml (2 tbsp) corn oil
50 g (2 oz) French beans, trimmed and cut into 5 cm (2 inch) lengths
1 large carrot, scrubbed and cut into matchstick strips
1 small turnip, peeled and cut into matchstick strips
1.1 litres (2 pints) chicken stock
30 ml (2 tbsp) soy sauce, preferably naturally fermented shoyu
1.25 ml ($\frac{1}{4}$ tsp) sweet chilli sauce
30 ml (2 tbsp) medium dry sherry
15 ml (1 tbsp) light muscovado sugar
175 g (6 oz) Chinese leaves, finely shredded
75 g (3 oz) peeled cooked prawns

———1———
Heat the oil in a saucepan, add the beans, carrot and turnip and gently cook for 5 minutes. Add the stock, soy sauce, chilli sauce, sherry and sugar. Simmer for 15 minutes, until the vegetables are just tender.

———2———
Add the Chinese leaves and prawns and cook for 2–3 minutes, until the leaves are tender but still crisp. Serve immediately.

MICROWAVE   Put the oil into a bowl and cook, uncovered, 100% (High) 1 minute. Add beans, carrot and turnip. Cover the bowl. Cook 100% (High) 3 minutes. Add only 1 litre (1$\frac{3}{4}$ pints) boiling stock, the soy sauce, chilli sauce, sherry and sugar. Cook, covered, 100% (High) 10 minutes. Add Chinese leaves and prawns. Cook, covered, 100% (High) for 2 minutes.

FRESH PEA SOUP

If fresh peas are not readily available, use frozen; both require the same cooking time.

SERVES 4   120 calories per serving
PREPARATION   10–15 minutes
COOKING   30 minutes

30 ml (2 tbsp) corn oil
1 small onion, skinned and chopped
1 garlic clove, skinned and crushed
1.1 litres (2 pints) chicken stock
900 g (2 lb) fresh peas, shelled, or 450 g (1 lb) frozen
salt and pepper, to taste
low-fat natural yogurt, to garnish

———1———
Heat the oil in a saucepan. Add the onion and garlic and cook for 5 minutes, until softened. Add the stock and peas and bring to the boil, then simmer for 20–25 minutes, until the peas are very tender.

———2———
Cool slightly. Purée in a blender or food processor, until smooth. Return to the pan and add seasoning. Reheat and serve hot, garnished with a swirl of yogurt.

MICROWAVE   Put the oil, onion and garlic into a bowl. Cover and cook 100% (High) 2 minutes. Add only 900 ml (1$\frac{1}{2}$ pints) boiling stock and the peas. Cover, cook 100% (High) 10–12 minutes, or until peas are soft. Cool slightly and purée in a blender or food processor. Return to the bowl and season. Cook, uncovered, 100% (High) 2 minutes to heat. Complete the recipe.

GOODNESS GUIDE
FRESH PEA
FIBRE   The vegetables provide a good helping of fibre
VITAMINS   Peas contain vitamins A, C and folic acid

CHINESE CABBAGE AND PRAWN SOUP
VITAMINS   Chinese leaves provide large amounts of B vitamins, including niacin and folic acid, and vitamin C. All these are slightly reduced with the shredding and cooking
MINERALS   Calcium and iron are present in both the Chinese leaves and the prawns
FIBRE   The vegetables give fibre

BAKED SMOKED SALMON MOUSSES

SERVES 4   195 calories per serving
PREPARATION   20 minutes
COOKING   40 minutes

75 g (3 oz) smoked salmon, thinly sliced
1 egg, size 2
225 g (8 oz) cooked cod or haddock fillet, skinned and flaked
10 ml (2 tsp) cornflour
75 ml (5 tbsp) whipping cream
75 ml (5 tbsp) Greek strained yogurt
30 ml (2 tbsp) chopped fresh parsley
15 ml (1 tbsp) brandy
salt and pepper, to taste
parsley sprigs and lemon twists, to garnish

———1———
Lightly grease 4 ramekin dishes. Line each with a circle of grease-proof paper and a small piece of smoked salmon.

———2———
Roughly chop the remaining smoked salmon and place in a bowl. Add the egg, fish, cornflour, whipping cream, yogurt, parsley, brandy and seasoning. Mix together well.

———3———
Divide the mixture between the ramekins and cover each tightly with foil. Bake at 180°C (350°F) mark 4 for about 40 minutes, until firm when lightly touched.

———4———
Remove foil and run a sharp knife around the edge of each ramekin. Turn out and peel off the grease-proof paper. Serve hot or cold, garnished with parsley sprigs and lemon twists.

MICROWAVE   Follow steps 1 and 2. Divide mixture between the ramekins. Cover each ramekin with cling film. Cook 60% (Medium) 8–9 minutes, rearranging the dishes 3 or 4 times. Cook until only just set in the centres. Complete the recipe.

GOODNESS GUIDE
FAT   Salmon is a medium-fat fish and cod is a low-fat fish
PROTEIN   The salmon, cod, egg and yogurt provide a good helping of protein
MINERALS   The yogurt and salmon contribute calcium to the dish
VITAMINS   The salmon provides vitamin D

SPINACH AND YOGURT SOUP

STILTON PUFFS

AVOCADO AND FETA SALAD

BROCCOLI AND ORANGE SOUP

BROCCOLI AND ORANGE SOUP

SERVES 4 120 calories per serving
PREPARATION 20 minutes
COOKING 35–40 minutes

350 g (12 oz) broccoli, divided into stalks
and small florets
900 ml (1½ pints) chicken stock
25 g (1 oz) polyunsaturated margarine
1 onion, skinned and chopped
25 g (1 oz) plain flour
150 ml (¼ pint) semi-skimmed milk
rind and juice of 1 large orange, with rind
cut into fine strips
salt and pepper, to taste

———1———

Peel the broccoli stalks if thick and
roughly chop. Set aside with half the
broccoli florets.

———2———

Bring the stock to the boil in a
saucepan. Add the remaining florets
and simmer for 3 minutes. Remove
and reserve. Set the stock aside.

———3———

Heat the margarine in a saucepan,
add the onion and cook gently for 5
minutes. Add the flour and cook,
stirring, for 1 minute.

———4———

Gradually add the stock, stirring
until thickened and smooth. Add
the uncooked broccoli stalks and
florets. Simmer, covered, for 25
minutes.

———5———

Put the soup into a blender or food
processor and purée until smooth.
Return to the pan with the milk,
2.5 ml (½ tsp) of the orange rind, the
orange juice and seasoning. Reheat
the soup gently.

———6———

Before serving, add the broccoli
florets to the soup and reheat.
Sprinkle with remaining orange rind.

MICROWAVE Complete step 1. Put
half broccoli florets into a bowl
with 750 ml (1¼ pints) boiling
chicken stock. Cover, cook, 100%
(High) 4 minutes. Drain florets and
reserve. Set stock aside. Put
margarine and onion into a bowl.
Cover, cook 100% (High) 3
minutes, until softened. Stir in flour,
cook, uncovered, 100% (High)
½ minute. Gradually whisk in the
stock, add broccoli stalks, and
uncooked florets. Cover, cook
100% (High) 15 minutes, whisking
after 5 minutes. Purée soup, return

36

to bowl with milk, 2.5 ml ($\frac{1}{2}$ tsp) of the orange rind, orange juice and seasoning. Cook, uncovered, 100% (High) 1$\frac{1}{2}$ minutes. Add broccoli florets, cook, uncovered, 100% (High) $\frac{1}{2}$ minute to heat. Complete recipe.

AVOCADO AND FETA SALAD

Feta cheese is made from ewe's milk and has a sharp, salty taste. Buy white, moist and slightly crumbly cheese.

SERVES 4   245 calories per serving
PREPARATION   10 minutes
COOKING   None

2 small ripe avocados, peeled, stoned and cut into 16 slices
2 red eating apples, cored and cut into 16 slices
4 small tomatoes, quartered
100 g (4 oz) feta cheese, crumbled
MUSTARD DRESSING
15 ml (1 tbsp) cider cinegar
2.5 ml ($\frac{1}{2}$ tsp) Dijon mustard
30 ml (2 tbsp) sunflower oil
salt and pepper, to taste

———1———

Arrange overlapping slices of avocado and apple in a fan on 4 serving plates. Place 4 quarters of tomato at the base of each fan. Sprinkle the cheese over each salad.

———2———

Put the dressing ingredients in a screw-topped jar and shake to mix. Drizzle over each salad and serve.

GOODNESS GUIDE

AVOCADO AND FETA SALAD
FIBRE   The avocados, apples and tomatoes provide a good serving of fibre
VITAMINS   Vitamins A and C are supplied by the avocados and tomatoes and the cheese provides B vitamins. The avocados also supply the fat-soluble vitamins D and E. Vitamin E protects vitamin C from destruction

BROCCOLI AND ORANGE SOUP
VITAMINS   Vitamins A and C are supplied by the broccoli and orange. The milk provides B vitamins, especially riboflavin, which is essential for the utilisation of energy from food
MINERALS   Broccoli is a source of iron and calcium; extra calcium is found in the milk and flour
FIBRE   Fibre is provided by the broccoli, onion and orange

STILTON PUFFS

The unfilled puffs can be kept for one to two days in an airtight container.

MAKES 20   55 calories each
PREPARATION   20 minutes
BAKING   25 minutes

50 g (2 oz) polyunsaturated margarine
65 g (2$\frac{1}{2}$ oz) wholemeal flour
2 eggs
175 g (6 oz) low-fat soft cheese
50 g (2 oz) Stilton cheese, grated
2 celery sticks, finely chopped
15 ml (1 tbsp) milk
pepper, to taste
2.5 ml ($\frac{1}{2}$ tsp) yeast extract
finely chopped celery leaves, to garnish

———1———

Moisten two baking sheets, line with non-stick silicone paper and set aside. Put the margarine in a saucepan with 150 ml ($\frac{1}{4}$ pint) water. Heat gently to melt the margarine and then bring to the boil. Remove from the heat and quickly tip in all the flour, beating the mixture until it forms a soft dough in the centre of the pan. Cool for a few minutes.

———2———

Lightly beat the eggs and gradually add them to the flour mixture. Spoon about 20 heaped teaspoonfuls of the mixture, a little apart, over the baking sheets. Bake at 200°C (400°F) mark 6 for 20 minutes, until risen and golden brown.

———3———

Remove from the oven and slit the side of each puff with a sharp knife. Return them to the oven to bake for a further 5 minutes until they are crisp. Cool on a wire rack.

———4———

Mix together the cheeses, celery, milk and seasoning. Just before serving, fill each puff with some of the mixture. Smear a little yeast extract over the top of each puff and dip the top of each puff in the chopped celery leaves to garnish.

GOODNESS GUIDE

PROTEIN   The eggs, cheese, milk and flour make these puffs high in protein
VITAMINS   The flour, eggs and cheese provide good amounts of B vitamins. Fat-soluble vitamins A, D and E are found in the margarine and eggs

SPINACH AND YOGURT SOUP

Spinach combines well with yogurt and spring onions to give a refreshing chilled summer soup.

SERVES 4   90 calories per serving
PREPARATION   15 minutes
COOKING   5 minutes
CHILLING   1 hour

225 g (8 oz) young spinach leaves, washed and drained
4 spring onions, chopped
450 ml (15 fl oz) low-fat natural yogurt
5 ml (1 tsp) paprika
15 ml (1 tbsp) lemon juice
150 ml ($\frac{1}{4}$ pint) semi-skimmed milk
salt and pepper, to taste
4 ice cubes, to serve
paprika, spring onion and spinach, to garnish

———1———

Put the spinach leaves in a saucepan with only the water that clings to the leaves. Cover and cook for 5 minutes, until wilted. Drain well, pressing out any excess water.

———2———

Chop the spinach roughly, then place in a blender or food processor with the spring onions and 225 ml (8 fl oz) yogurt. Purée until smooth. Add the remaining yogurt, the paprika, lemon juice, milk and seasoning. Blend until mixed. Chill for 1 hour.

———3———

Divide the soup between 4 serving bowls and drop an ice cube into each. Sprinkle with a little paprika and garnish with spring onion and spinach before serving.

MICROWAVE   Put washed spinach leaves into a bowl. Cover, cook 100% (High) 3 minutes until leaves are wilted. Drain well, pressing out excess water. Complete recipe.

GOODNESS GUIDE

VITAMINS   Spinach is a rich source of vitamins A and C. Vitamin A maintains the mucous membranes that line the mouth, respiratory and urinary tracts, which are the first line of defence against infection
FIBRE   The spinach and spring onions supply fibre

QUICK CHICKEN LIVER PATE

CHILLED SPRING ONION SOUP

CHINESE-STYLE HOT AND SOUR SOUP

PASTA WITH TOMATO SAUCE

PASTA WITH TOMATO SAUCE

In this unusual pasta starter, the pasta twirls are served hot with a cold frothy tomato sauce.

SERVES 4   315 calories per serving
PREPARATION   5 minutes
COOKING   3–10 minutes

5 ml (1 tsp) corn oil
100 g (4 oz) dried or fresh wholemeal
pasta twirls
225 g (8 oz) dried or fresh spinach
pasta twirls
30 ml (2 tbsp) chopped fresh parsley,
to garnish

FRESH TOMATO SAUCE
450 g (1 lb) tomatoes, chopped
20 ml (4 tsp) chopped fresh tarragon or
10 ml (2 tsp) dried
5 ml (1 tsp) dried thyme
1 garlic clove, skinned and crushed
salt and pepper, to taste

———1———
Bring a large pan of water to the boil and add the corn oil. Add the pasta, stir and cook for 3 minutes for fresh pasta, 10 minutes for dried.
———2———
Meanwhile, make the sauce. Purée the tomatoes in a blender or food processor. Add the tarragon, thyme, garlic and seasoning. Blend again, until the sauce is pink and frothy.
———3———
Drain the pasta and divide between 4 plates. Spoon the sauce on top and sprinkle with chopped parsley.

GOODNESS GUIDE

PASTA WITH TOMATO SAUCE
CARBOHYDRATE AND VITAMINS   Pasta is an excellent source of carbohydrate energy and also provides B vitamins, especially thiamine. Vitamins A and C are provided by tomatoes and herbs

QUICK CHICKEN LIVER PATE
VITAMINS   Liver is full of vitamins, including vitamins A and C as well as some D and E. It also provides B-complex vitamins and is the richest source of B_{12} and folic acid

QUICK CHICKEN LIVER PATE

This pâté is high in iron, as chicken livers are a rich source. Serve with wholemeal bread.

SERVES 4 225 calories per serving
PREPARATION 5 minutes
COOKING 7 minutes
COOLING AND CHILLING 3 hours

450 g (1 lb) chicken livers, trimmed
40 g (1½ oz) polyunsaturated margarine
1 small onion, skinned and chopped
2 cloves
8 allspice berries
10 black peppercorns
5 ml (1 tsp) dried thyme
10 ml (2 tsp) dry sherry
salt and pepper, to taste
1 egg, hard-boiled, and 15 ml (1 tbsp) toasted sunflower seeds, to garnish
1 stick wholemeal French bread, warmed, to serve

———1———

Rinse the livers and place in a saucepan. Cover with cold water, bring to the boil and simmer gently for 5–7 minutes, until no longer pink.

———2———

Meanwhile, melt the margarine in a small saucepan. Add the onion and cook for about 5 minutes, until soft. Add the cloves, allspice, peppercorns and thyme and stir over low heat for 2 minutes.

———3———

Drain the livers and put them into a blender or food processor. Remove the spices from the onion and discard. Add the onion to the livers and blend briefly. Add the sherry and seasoning and coarsely blend.

———4———

Scoop the mixture into a dish and smooth the surface. Leave to cool for 1–2 hours, then chill for 1 hour.

———5———

Finely chop the egg white into a bowl. Sieve in the yolk. Use to garnish the pâté with the sunflower seeds. Serve with warmed bread.

MICROWAVE Rinse livers. Put into a bowl with 60 ml (4 tbsp) water. Part cover. Cook 100% (High) 6–7 minutes, stirring twice, until no longer pink. Put margarine, onion, cloves, allspice, peppercorns and thyme into a bowl. Cover, cook 100% (High) 5 minutes. Complete recipe.

CHINESE-STYLE HOT AND SOUR SOUP

Adjust the seasonings to suit your own taste, in this delicious Oriental soup.

SERVES 4 90 calories per serving
SOAKING 20 minutes
PREPARATION 5 minutes
COOKING 30 minutes

25 g (1 oz) dried Chinese mushrooms
1 cm (½ inch) piece fresh root ginger, peeled
1 carrot, scrubbed and halved
1 spring onion, white part only, chopped
45 ml (3 tbsp) soy sauce, preferably naturally fermented shoyu
225 g (8 oz) can bamboo shoots
100 g (4 oz) tofu, cubed
120–150 ml (8–10 tbsp) malt vinegar
7.5–10 ml (1½–2 tsp) pepper
10–15 ml (2–3 tsp) dry sherry
1 egg, beaten (optional)

———1———

Wash the mushrooms and then soak them in 300 ml (½ pint) warm water for 20 minutes.

———2———

Put the mushrooms and their soaking liquid in a saucepan and add 300 ml (½ pint) cold water, the ginger, carrot and spring onion. Bring to the boil and simmer, half-covered, for 15–20 minutes. Add 15 ml (1 tbsp) soy sauce and strain into a clean saucepan. Reserve mushrooms; discard ginger, carrot and onion.

———3———

Slice the mushrooms and return to the stock. Add the bamboo shoots and tofu and simmer gently. Stir in the remaining soy sauce and gradually add the vinegar and seasoning, tasting to get the desired blend of hot and sour. Add the sherry.

———4———

Remove from the heat and stir in the beaten egg, if using. It will cook in the heat of the soup. Serve at once.

GOODNESS GUIDE

FAT As only one egg yolk is used and the remaining ingredients are low in fat, the overall fat content of this soup is very low
PROTEIN The tofu and egg are excellent sources of protein

CHILLED SPRING ONION SOUP

Make double the quantity of this nutritious soup and freeze the leftovers for up to 3–4 months.

SERVES 4 115 calories per serving
PREPARATION 10 minutes
COOKING 15–20 minutes
COOLING AND CHILLING 5 hours

15 spring onions
25 ml (1½ tbsp) corn oil
2 potatoes, peeled and sliced
3 celery sticks, chopped
salt and pepper, to taste
150 ml (5 fl oz) low-fat natural yogurt
extra yogurt, to garnish

———1———

Trim the green tops from the spring onions and reserve. Roughly chop the onion bulbs. Heat the oil in a saucepan and add the potatoes, celery and chopped spring onion bulbs. Cook, stirring, for about 1 minute, then add 600 ml (1 pint) of cold water. Bring to the boil, stir and simmer, covered, for 15–20 minutes, until vegetables are soft.

———2———

Pour the soup into a blender or food processor and purée until smooth. Season and leave to cool for about 4 hours.

———3———

Whisk the yogurt into the cooled soup and add a little water to thin the soup, if necessary. Chill for 1 hour. Serve chilled, garnished with the spring onion tops and yogurt.

MICROWAVE Put oil, potatoes, celery and chopped spring onion bulbs into a bowl. Cover, cook 100% (High) 3 minutes. Add 600 ml (1 pint) boiling water. Cover, cook 100% (High) 12 minutes, until vegetables are soft. Complete recipe.

GOODNESS GUIDE

VITAMINS The fresh vegetables provide vitamin C and the yogurt supplies B-complex vitamins
MINERALS Yogurt provides large amounts of calcium and together with the vegetables provides potassium
FIBRE The vegetables are a good source of fibre

POACHED ASPARAGUS WITH ORANGE SAUCE

Although asparagus is more expensive than most other vegetables, it is nice to use it when in season for a starter or side dish.

SERVES 4   125 calories per serving
PREPARATION   10 minutes
COOKING   20 minutes

450 g (1 lb) fresh asparagus, trimmed and scraped
150 ml ($\frac{1}{4}$ pint) dry white wine
juice of 1 orange
150 ml ($\frac{1}{4}$ pint) Greek strained yogurt
1 egg, size 2
salt, to taste
finely pared rind of 1 orange, finely shredded, and orange slices, to garnish

—— 1 ——

Tie the asparagus in a bundle and cover tips with a cap of foil. Stand, tips uppermost, in a deep saucepan of boiling water, lower the heat and simmer for 15 minutes, until tender. Drain well.

—— 2 ——

Meanwhile, place the wine and orange juice in a small saucepan and boil for 7–8 minutes, until reduced by two-thirds.

—— 3 ——

Beat together the yogurt and egg in a small heatproof bowl over a pan of simmering water. Cook for about 10 minutes, whisking continuously until thickened, then gradually stir in the reduced liquid and season. Spoon the sauce over the asparagus tips and garnish.

MICROWAVE Put prepared asparagus spears in one layer with tips toward centre in a microwave oven dish. Add 75 ml (3 fl oz) water. Part cover, cook 100% (High) 7–8 minutes, turning dish twice. For sauce, use only juice of $\frac{1}{2}$ orange and 45 ml (3 tbsp) wine. Put into a bowl and cook, uncovered, 100% (High) 1$\frac{1}{2}$ minutes. Whisk into yogurt and egg in a bowl. Cook, uncovered, 100% (High) 2–2$\frac{1}{2}$ minutes, whisking 2 or 3 times. Garnish and serve.

GOODNESS GUIDE
VITAMINS Asparagus is a source of vitamins A and C. Vitamin A is needed for healthy skin, hair and mucous membranes. It is also essential for vision in dim light. The egg and yogurt supply B complex vitamins
PROTEIN The egg and yogurt provide good amounts of easily digested protein

POACHED ASPARAGUS WITH ORANGE SAUCE

HOT MUSHROOM MOUSSE

SERVES 4 270 calories per serving
PREPARATION 15 minutes
COOKING 50–60 minutes

20 g (¾ oz) polyunsaturated margarine
20 g (¾ oz) plain wholemeal flour
300 ml (½ pint) semi-skimmed milk
salt and pepper, to taste
75 g (3 oz) button mushrooms,
finely chopped
75 g (3 oz) fresh wholemeal breadcrumbs
2 eggs, separated
30 ml (2 tbsp) chopped fresh parsley
30 ml (2 tbsp) grated Parmesan cheese
12 small button mushrooms

CHIVE SAUCE
45 ml (3 tbsp) low-fat natural yogurt
45 ml (3 tbsp) mayonnaise
1.25 ml (¼ tsp) lemon juice
15 ml (1 tbsp) snipped fresh chives

1
Lightly grease and line a 450 g (1 lb) loaf tin or 15 cm (6 inch) soufflé dish with greaseproof paper.

2
Melt the margarine in a saucepan. Stir in the flour and cook for 1 minute. Stir in the milk and bring to the boil. Add the seasoning and chopped mushrooms. Simmer for 5 minutes.

3
Beat the breadcrumbs, egg yolks, parsley and cheese into the sauce. Whisk the egg whites until stiff, then fold into the mixture.

4
Spoon the mixture into the prepared loaf tin, adding the whole mushrooms at random. Level the surface and cover with a piece of lightly greased aluminium foil.

5
Stand in a roasting pan and add hot water to come halfway up the sides of the loaf tin. Bake at 170°C (325°F) mark 3 for 45 minutes, until the mousse is set.

6
Meanwhile, make the sauce. Mix together the yogurt, mayonnaise, lemon juice and chives. Cover and chill until ready to serve.

7
Turn the loaf out on to a warm serving dish. Serve, cut into slices, accompanied by the sauce.

MICROWAVE Follow step 1, using a soufflé or loaf dish. In step 2, put margarine in a bowl and cook 100% (High) 20 seconds to melt. Stir in flour and cook 30 seconds. Gradually whisk in milk, then cook 4 minutes, whisking 2 or 3 times. Add seasoning and chopped mushrooms. Cook 1½–2 minutes. Follow steps 3 and 4, but do not cover. In step 5, put container in a large dish and add hot water. Cook 60% (Medium) 13–15 minutes, until mousse is just set in the centre, turning dish 2 or 3 times. Make sauce and serve.

GOODNESS GUIDE
VITAMINS B-complex vitamins are supplied by the milk, mushrooms, breadcrumbs, cheese and yogurt
MINERALS Potassium and magnesium are contributed by the dairy products and flour, which also supply calcium. Calcium and magnesium are important for healthy bones. Potassium helps to regulate the body's water balance

HOT MUSHROOM MOUSSE

41

STRIPY AVOCADO AND CHEESE MOUSSES

An easy-to-prepare and impressive starter which can be made the evening before and stored, covered, in the refrigerator.

SERVES 4 115 calories per serving
PREPARATION 10 minutes
COOKING None
CHILLING 2 hours or overnight

1 large ripe avocado
1 garlic clove, skinned and crushed
1.25 ml ($\frac{1}{4}$ tsp) cayenne pepper
15 ml (1 tbsp) lemon juice
1–2 drops Tabasco sauce (optional)
salt and pepper, to taste
30 ml (2 tbsp) natural Quark
2.5 ml ($\frac{1}{2}$ tsp) paprika
1 celery stick, trimmed and finely chopped
7.5 ml (1$\frac{1}{2}$ tsp) powdered gelatine
strips of red pepper, to garnish

——— 1 ———

Scoop the flesh out of the avocado and place in a blender or food processor. Add the garlic, cayenne pepper, lemon juice and Tabasco sauce, if using, and purée until smooth. Season.

——— 2 ———

Put the Quark into a bowl, sprinkle in the paprika and mix in the celery and seasoning.

——— 3 ———

Sprinkle the gelatine on to 30 ml (2 tbsp) cold water in a heatproof bowl and leave to soak for 1 minute. Place over a pan of gently boiling hot water and stir until the gelatine is dissolved. Stir 5 ml (1 tsp) into the cheese mixture. Pour the remainder into the avocado mixture and blend briefly until mixed.

——— 4 ———

Pour half of the avocado mixture into 4 wine glasses. Top with the cheese mixture, dividing it evenly. Finish with the avocado mixture.

——— 5 ———

Cover and chill for at least 2 hours or overnight. Just before serving, garnish with strips of red pepper.

GOODNESS GUIDE

VITAMINS AND FAT Avocados provide vitamins C and E, as well as carotene. B-complex vitamins are also present, especially folic acid which is needed by rapidly dividing cells such as those in bone marrow. The fat-soluble vitamins A and E rely on the valuable unsaturated fat to be absorbed by the body

STRIPY AVOCADO AND CHEESE MOUSSES

WARM VEGETABLE SALAD

This summer salad can be cooked on a barbecue or under a grill. The vegetables are cooked whole, then thinly sliced and served with an oil and vinegar dressing.

SERVES 4 · 160 calories per serving
PREPARATION 15 minutes
COOKING 20 minutes

4 onions, skinned
2 red peppers
2 yellow peppers
6 courgettes
1 aubergine
45 ml (3 tbsp) olive oil
30 ml (2 tbsp) red wine vinegar
2 garlic cloves, skinned and crushed
15 ml (1 tbsp) chopped fresh thyme salt and pepper, to taste

——— 1 ———

Parboil the onions whole for 5 minutes, then drain thoroughly. Rub the onions, peppers, courgettes and aubergine with 15 ml (1 tbsp) of the olive oil.

——— 2 ———

Place the vegetables on the rack over a preheated barbecue, or under a medium grill, keeping the peppers 10 cm (4 inches) away from the source of heat. Cook for 15–20 minutes, turning the vegetables once or twice, until they are tender.

——— 3 ———

Meanwhile, prepare the dressing. Mix the remaining olive oil with the red wine vinegar, garlic, thyme and seasoning.

——— 4 ———

Remove the cooked vegetables from the barbecue or grill with tongs. Leave to cool slightly. Slice the vegetables quite thinly, including any charred pieces of vegetable skin for flavour. Discard the core and seeds from the peppers.

——— 5 ———

Place the warm vegetables in a shallow serving dish. Spoon the prepared dressing over the top and serve immediately.

GOODNESS GUIDE

VITAMINS All of the vegetables provide vitamin C and the peppers also provide vitamin A. Vitamin A is essential for low-light vision and for the maintenance of healthy skin and surface tissues, especially those which excrete mucus

FIBRE All the vegetables provide fibre

WARM VEGETABLE SALAD

43

3 MAIN DISHES

SIMMERING GOODNESS

Casseroles can add variety to every-day meals and, because they can be made in advance—their flavour improves when cooked ahead of time—they are excellent for entertaining. Casseroling is a particularly healthy cooking method because the nutrients from the ingredients pass into the cooking liquid. The casserole liquid therefore becomes enriched during the long, slow cooking.

Both casseroling and stewing describe a long, slow method of cooking in a simmering liquid. The main difference between the two is that casseroling refers to the dish in which the ingredients cook. While stews are often cooked on top of the stove in a saucepan, casseroles are made in a dish with a tight-fitting lid to prevent evaporation, and with a heavy base so that the food does not burn or stick. Flameproof casserole dishes can be used either on top of the stove or in the oven; ovenproof or heatproof dishes are only suitable for use in the oven.

MEAT AND VEGETABLES CASSEROLES

Casseroling is particularly suitable for foods which will benefit from long, slow cooking in moist heat. Tough cuts of meat—especially chuck, shin and leg of beef—all require slow cooking to become tender and succulent. For these cuts, oven cooking is preferable—cooking in the oven is gentler than stewing on top of the stove and is therefore the best way to cook many meat casseroles.

Casseroles containing meat are usually flavoured with herbs and spices and are cooked in stock or a combination of stock and alcohol such as wine or beer; water may also be added to the cooking liquid. Root vegetables such as carrots and leeks are often cooked with the meat, while delicate vegetables—mushrooms and courgettes, for example—may be added at the end of cooking time. Some classic meat casseroles, such as chilli con carne, have beans added to them; this reduces the amount of meat eaten, an important factor in a healthy diet.

Vegetable casseroles such as ratatouille make delicious and healthy alternatives to dishes based on meat. Slow cooking allows the various flavours to mingle and most of the nutrients are retained in the liquid which forms part of the dish. The addition of cooked beans or other pulses to a vegetable casserole makes a nutritious and substantial main course and, when served with rice or another grain such as burghul, a well-balanced meal. Nuts can also be added to vegetable stews. They are high in fibre and protein and also make a very healthy and interesting alternative to meat.

BRAISING

Braised dishes are similar to casseroles and stews, and consist of large pieces of meat or poultry placed on a bed of vegetables with little added liquid. The meat cooks in the steam created by the vegetables and absorbs their flavours. Some vegetables can also be braised. Red cabbage is delicious cooked with apples and a little added liquid, while celery, which is traditionally braised in butter, can be braised in chicken stock for a low-fat dish.

QUICK CASSEROLES

Quick casseroles are made by combining ingredients which require a short cooking time or just heating through. They are often combined in a roux-based sauce and are an excellent way to use up leftovers as well as an imaginative way to combine meat, vegetables, pasta or grains to make healthy one-pot meals. Fish, which requires a short cooking time, is often used as an ingredient in a quick casserole. A breadcrumb or grated cheese topping adds flavour and texture, with the breadcrumbs contributing fibre and both toppings adding protein.

MAKING HEALTHY CASSEROLES

For maximum nutrition and flavour only fresh ingredients should be used; ideally, vegetables should be prepared just before cooking. Excess fat should be trimmed from meat, and chicken dishes will be less fatty if the skin is removed.

Traditionally, casseroles are made by first browning the ingredients to seal in the juices and add colour to the dish. If you are following this method, use an oil which is high in polyunsaturated fat such as corn or soya and brown the meat

in a non-stick pan, or cast iron pan which needs only a light coating of oil.

As an alternative to browning the ingredients, casseroles can be made by simply layering the ingredients in the dish and covering them with cold liquid. In this method the finished casserole is paler in colour, but the juices will help to make a richly-flavoured and nutritious liquid. It is better not to use this method when cooking fatty meat, which will benefit from an initial browning in order that some fat can be drained off. This will improve flavour and reduce fat intake.

Seasoning casseroles at the start of cooking encourages the juices to run out and these flavour the cooking liquid. However, if the cooking liquid is to be reduced at the end of cooking, season when the liquid has been reduced to avoid over-salting the dish. For healthy cooking, get into the habit of seasoning with herbs and spices instead of salt.

To thicken casseroles, flour can be stirred into the ingredients during cooking. Some recipes suggest coating chunks of meat with seasoned flour before browning and this, too, will thicken the liquid. Cornflour or wholemeal flour can also be used for thickening—blend a little with cooking liquid before stirring into the ingredients. As a tasty and healthy alternative, casseroles can be thickened with grated or puréed vegetables such as potatoes or root vegetables such as carrots, parsnips, turnips and swede.

If a creamy sauce is desired, use low-fat natural yogurt rather than cream or soured cream. Stir it in at the end of cooking, making sure that the cooking liquid has stopped bubbling, otherwise the yogurt may curdle.

REHEATING AND FREEZING

Casseroles usually improve in flavour when reheated, which is why it is a good idea to make them a day in advance. It is not advisable to make them for more than one day in advance for fear of encouraging bacteria. When a casserole is subsequently reheated, it is important that it reach boiling point: it should then be boiled for at least 10–15 minutes. Once the casserole has cooled any fat will rise to the surface and it will be easy to spoon it from the top of the dish, or de-grease with a piece of crumpled absorbent kitchen paper. If the dish is refrigerated the fat will harden and can easily be spooned off the casserole.

Most casseroles can be frozen but when cooking for the freezer do not add any dairy ingredients until the dish is reheated. Before placing in the freezer allow the casserole to cool, remove all fat—it becomes rancid during storage—and place in a rigid container with 1 cm ($\frac{1}{2}$ inch) head space to allow for expansion during freezing. Chunks of food should be submerged in the liquid to help prevent freezer 'burn'. Most casseroles can be frozen for up to two months, but those with spicy ingredients and those rich in garlic tend to take on a musty taste after two weeks.

BETTER WAYS TO ROAST

For flavour and enjoyment, roasting is one of the very best ways of preparing meat. And from a health point of view, the fat loss that can be achieved during cooking makes it highly recommended. Here we look at the choosing and preparing of meat, and different ways of cooking it to achieve the tastiest—and healthiest—results.

All the recent guidelines for a healthier diet recommend a considerable reduction in the amount of fat we consume. The 1983 NACNE report on food and health in Britain specifically recommended that the average intake of saturated fats, which are found in large quantities in red meat, should be halved.

The main advantage of roasting is that it can considerably reduce the amount of fat in the cooked dish, which makes it particularly suitable for fatty meats such as pork and lamb. And it is a first-rate means of bringing out the full flavour of the meat.

THE CHOICE OF MEAT
Roasting is generally best suited for tender cuts of meat; the cheaper cuts, which are perfectly good for stewing, braising and so on, tend to get tough and stringy when subjected to the intense dry heat of roasting.

A large joint always roasts better than a small one because its size allows the outside to be properly crisped while the inside is cooked but not dried out. However, it is far better to buy a small lean cut of expensive meat such as sirloin of beef or leg of lamb, than a larger, less expensive joint that would be much fattier.

Of course, one widely available and very economical source of lean meat is chicken, and, better still, turkey. They have a lower overall fat content than red meat, with a higher proportion of unsaturated fats. All game is also very lean, including pheasant, rabbit and venison, with a healthy ratio of unsaturated to saturated fats.

All frozen meat should be thawed thoroughly before cooking. For poultry this is absolutely essential—if the centre of the chicken is not sufficiently thawed it may not get hot enough to kill off bacteria during cooking. Frozen meat should be put into the refrigerator to thaw slowly; thawing meat too fast can damage both the texture and flavour. Chilled meat should be removed from the refrigerator about an hour before cooking, to bring it to room temperature.

METHODS OF ROASTING
Roasting can be be done in a number of ways. Oven-roasting is the most common method, for which there are two basic approaches: quick-roasting at a high temperature, which is only really suitable for top-quality meats; and slow-roasting at a low temperature, which produces juicy, more tender meat with less shrinkage. The drawback with the slower method is that to prevent the meat drying out during the longer cooking time it may need frequent basting, with fats and juices that would otherwise have drained off. This results in succulent meat but meat with a higher fat content.

Whichever method is chosen, the meat must be weighed first to calculate the cooking time for the manner in which it will be cooked; for example, on or off the bone, stuffed or rolled.

INTO THE OVEN
To roast the meat, put it on a rack in a roasting pan so that the fat can drain off into the pan. For slow-roasting, place the pan in the middle of the oven, preheated to 200°C (400°F) mark 6, and cook for 10 minutes to seal the surface and trap the juices. Reduce the heat to 180°C (350°F) mark 4 and cook for the times indicated below.

For medium beef, allow 20 minutes per 450 g (1 lb) and 20 minutes extra. For rare beef, cook for 15 minutes per 450 g (1 lb) and 15 minutes extra, and for well done, 25 minutes per 450 g (1 lb) plus 25 minutes extra. Lamb requires 20–25 minutes per 450 g (1 lb); this will still be slightly pink on the inside—add an extra 20 minutes if you prefer it well done. Pork and veal must both be well-cooked right through but must not be dry: allow 30–35 minutes per 450 g (1 lb) plus 30–35 minutes extra. The quick-cooking method, at 220°C (425°F) mark 7, generally takes 5–10 minutes less per 450 g (1 lb).

For roasting poultry, times will vary according to weight, with heavier birds taking proportionally less time to cook. Turkey will take about 20 minutes per 450 g (1 lb) for birds up to 5.5 kg (12 lb) and about 15 minutes per 450 g (1 lb) for birds over that weight. Cooking times for chicken are similar.

Duck and goose are both very fatty and can be cooked at a high temperature without basting; the meat will not dry out. The skin of these birds should be pricked all over to allow the fat to drain off. Cook for about 20 minutes per 450 g (1 lb) at 200°C (400°F) mark 6, pouring off surplus fat from the pan during cooking. Use the same method with goose, which requires a slightly shorter cooking time.

COVERED COOKING
The joint or bird can be cooked in foil, which prevents fat spattering all over the oven and cooks the meat well. The foil can be used to wrap up the meat completely like a parcel, or placed over the pan in which the meat is placed on the rack. The parcel method is less desirable as the meat sits in fatty juices and air cannot circulate around it.

Covering the pan with a sheet of foil is probably the healthiest approach to roasting. The meat cooks in the steam produced under the foil and therefore retains its moisture. This is a particularly useful method for slightly tougher meat which is tenderised by the moist heat. Since the meat is kept moist there is no need to baste it.

Covering the meat with foil is more like pot roasting, and cooking times or oven temperatures need to be increased accordingly. If the meat is to be browned, remove the foil for the last 20–30 minutes cooking time.

Clear plastic roasting bags can also be used—the meat bastes and browns during roasting, so they are not removed until cooking is finished. But, as with wrapping in foil, the meat sits in its own fats and juices rather than being raised above them on a rack, so its not such a healthy cooking method.

Covered roasting pans work in much the same way. Here again, the meat should be placed on a rack to raise it above the base of the pan. If you do not have a rack, however, a tight fitting covered roasting pan or casserole has the advantage of keeping the meat moist without requiring additional fat. Use only the sediment for making gravy.

One other method to consider is spit-roasting. Strictly speaking, the method called roasting—cooking the meat in fats and juices in the oven—is really baking. With the introduction of the rotisserie the traditional method of spit-roasting has been revived. It can produce even better results than cooking in an oven; the meat revolves as it cooks, basted by its own juices, and cooks through evenly.

BETTER BRAISING AND POT ROASTING

Braising and pot roasting are both gentle ways of cooking which preserve the flavour of the food, prevent it from drying out and shrinking and, most important, retain most of the nutrients during cooking.

These two long, slow cooking methods are quite similar. In the past, the term braising usually referred to cooking either on the hob or in the oven; pot roasting meant cooking on the hob only. The main difference in the current usage of the terms, however, is that while braised meat is cooked on a bed of vegetables with just enough stock, wine or other liquid to keep it moist, pot roasted meat cooks in its own juices or with a very small amount of liquid.

Both methods are suitable for beef topside, flank, silverside or braising steak. Leg or shoulder of lamb joints—boned and stuffed if wished—can also be cooked by either method. Whole chicken and any pork joints from the leg, loin or hand and spring can be braised or pot roasted, and both techniques are perfect for veal joints, which have a tendency to dry out when roasted.

For either method, meat can be marinated in olive oil, wine and herbs and chilled overnight. The marinade can then be used for the cooking liquid. Bring the meat to room temperature before cooking.

BRAISING MEAT
For braising meat, use a flameproof casserole or heavy-based saucepan into which the meat will fit snugly. If you use a dish or pan that is too large, the liquid will boil away. The dish or pan must have a tight-fitting lid so that steam cannot escape during cooking. The meat should rest on a bed of vegetables such as diced onion, carrots and celery—known as a mirepoix—which should all be cut to roughly the same size so they cook in the same amount of time.

Lightly brush the base of the casserole or pan with oil and heat, then add the meat and cook until all the surfaces are browned and sealed. Remove the meat, add the vegetables and quickly cook them in the same way. Drain off any excess fat, then add the seasonings and herbs. Place the meat on top of the vegetables and add enough liquid to come about two-thirds of the way up the vegetables. Cover and simmer very gently on top of the stove or in the oven until tender, checking occasionally to see if extra liquid is needed.

During cooking the vegetables will disintegrate and thicken the liquid. If there is too much liquid left at the end of the cooking time, the meat and vegetables can be removed and the liquid boiled until it is reduced. Alternatively, it can be thickened with cornflour. Any excess fat in the liquid should be skimmed off before thickening.

POT ROASTING MEAT
For pot roasting, follow the same method as for braising but use less liquid or none at all. The liquid should not boil during cooking or it will toughen the meat. Because there is less liquid, pot roasted joints may need turning over and basting several times.

BRAISING VEGETABLES
Braising is also a delicious method of cooking vegetables and, as with braising meat, the results are very nutritious because none of the vitamins and minerals are thrown away with the cooking water. A variety of vegetables, from slightly tough root vegetables to leafy green vegetables and tender asparagus, can be cooked this way.

Prepare the vegetables as usual just before cooking. Unless absolutely necessary, vegetables should not be peeled as most of the vitamins are just below the skin. Cut the vegetables into even-sized pieces and quickly brown them in hot oil, following the method used for meat. Browning, however, is unnecessary for leafy green vegetables and asparagus because they are quite delicate and do not have the same type of exposed edges as other vegetables when cut.

Add just enough liquid to the pan to keep the vegetables moist during cooking, checking occasionally to see that they do not dry out. Vegetables such as spinach and cabbage need only the water that clings to the leaves after rinsing as they will produce their own liquid while cooking. Serve the braised vegetables with the cooking juices so none of the nutrients are wasted.

BRAISING CHART

Simmer the meat and vegetables over a low heat on top of the cooker, or cook at 180°C (350°F) mark 4

Beef

Blade bone	45 mins per 450 g (1 lb)
Brisket	45 mins per 450 g (1 lb)
Chuck	45 mins per 450 g (1 lb)
Silverside	45 mins per 450 g (1 lb)
Top rib	45 mins per 450 g (1 lb)
Top rump/thick flank	45 mins per 450 g (1 lb)

Lamb

Stuffed shoulder of lamb	45 mins per 450 g (1 lb)
Stuffed and rolled breast of lamb	45 mins per 450 g (1 lb)

Pork

All cuts	30 mins per 450 g (1 lb)

Veal

Stuffed rolled breast of veal	25 mins per 450 g (1 lb)

Poultry

Whole chicken	30 mins per 450 g (1 lb)
Whole turkey	20 mins per 450 g (1 lb)

Offal

Whole hearts	
Calf's	1–1½ hours
Lamb's	1¼ hours
Pig's	1½ hours
Oxtail pieces	45 mins per 450 g (1 lb)
Tongue	
Whole calf's tongue	1½ hours
Whole ox's tongue	2 hours

Fish

Whole fish	20 mins per 450 g (1 lb)

Cooking times: A minimum cooking time of 2 hours should be allowed for joints weighing less than 1.5 kg (3 lb).

SIMPLE WAYS TO STEAM

Steaming is a versatile and healthier way to cook food. Flavour, colour and texture are less altered than with most other methods of cooking. Less water-soluble vitamins and minerals are lost because the food is not immersed in water and steaming is an excellent way of cooking without adding any fat.

There are two methods of steaming; direct and indirect. In the first, the food is placed in a container with a perforated base. The container is then placed over a pan of boiling water. Steam from the boiling water rises through the perforations to cook the food.

If wine or stock are used instead of water, then the steamed food will absorb some of the flavour. Salt, if used, should be added after cooking, otherwise moisture will be drawn from the food causing it to dry or toughen.

In indirect steaming, the food is placed in a basin which is then set in the boiling water. This method is generally used for puddings.

Topping up with boiling water is important in steaming; as the water evaporates, add more boiling water from the kettle. If the food is being steamed in a basin, the water should only come halfway up the sides and you should work quickly so that there is no interruption in cooking. An upturned saucer placed under the basin will rattle as the water level sinks—a sign to top up.

VEGETABLES

When vegetables are steamed they lose fewer nutrients than when boiled. They can be steamed in the top pan of a double steamer, or in a colander which is placed over a pan of boiling water and covered with foil so that steam cannot escape. A particularly useful item for steaming vegetables is a metal trivet—the collapsible type fits most saucepans. The trivet containing the vegetables stands over a quantity of boiling water and the vegetables cook in the steam. Another type of trivet, designed to fit into a wok, is suitable for cooking Chinese-style shredded vegetables. A tiered bamboo steamer can either be placed in a large wok or deep saucepan. Vegetables and other foods can be steamed simultaneously, with the item that takes the longest to cook at the base. The top basket must be tightly covered so none of the steam escapes.

Vegetables can be steamed by wrapping them in pieces of aluminium foil and placing them in boiling water. The parcels should be loosely wrapped but watertight, with space for steam to circulate. This method works well with young, fresh beans or peas, and with young root vegetables if they are cut into even pieces.

A combination of boiling and steaming is used to cook asparagus. They are placed upright in a deep pan, propped up with crumpled foil. The stems cook in boiling water while the delicate tips are cooked by steaming.

FISH AND MEAT

Steaming is an excellent way to cook fish: all the flavour and nutrients are retained and the fish keeps its bright appearance. Whole fish—such as small trout—can also be stuffed and steamed in a double steamer, as can fillets of white fish which can be steamed between heatproof plates over a pan of rapidly boiling water.

Fish, especially salmon steaks, are also excellent steamed in watertight aluminium foil parcels in the same way as vegetables.

Braising is a form of steaming that is good for cooking tough cuts of meat. Meat, which is usually first lightly sautéed, is placed on a bed of vegetables with little or no added liquid. During cooking, in a tightly covered casserole, the meat becomes tender and absorbs the flavours of the vegetables.

GRAINS

Rice can be steamed in a tiered bamboo steamer, or in a rice steaming ball—suspended from the saucepan's handle, it floats in boiling water and the rice comes out moulded in to a round shape.

Burghul, a processed cracked wheat, is used in Middle Eastern dishes. It can be first soaked, then gently steamed until it is tender.

Couscous, a type of semolina used in North African cuisine, cooks in the steam of the stew with which it is to be eaten. Traditionally it is made in a couscousier, a double pan with a large base which cooks the couscous in the smaller pan above. A couscousier can be made using a covered and lined metal sieve or colander set inside a saucepan. Make sure no steam can escape.

PUDDINGS

Savoury suet puddings, such as steak and kidney, and sweet puddings, such as sponge and Christmas puddings, are usually cooked by steaming. In one method, the mixture is placed in a covered heatproof basin which stands in a covered pan of boiling water; the water should come about halfway up sides of the basin. It is important to use a basin which fits easily into the saucepan so that you can get it in and out, and which gives space for the steam to circulate.

A second method of steaming puddings is really a type of steam boiling: the mixture is wrapped in a cloth, the ends of which are secured by the pan lid; the pudding base sits in the boiling water.

BETTER WAYS TO BOIL

Boiling vegetables to death is something of a national habit—drowned in hot, salty water they not only have a mushy consistency but also lose most of their vitamins and minerals. But fortunately there is good boiling as well as bad boiling, and if you learn to boil in a healthy way you will conserve the nutrients in the food. Fruit and vegetables will taste better too, because minerals give them much of their flavour. We tell you how to prepare and boil your food the healthiest way.

Vegetables are an excellent source of vitamins and minerals, but often by the time they reach our plates most of their goodness has been boiled away. Prolonged boiling in large amounts of water with added bicarbonate of soda can cause as much as 80–100 per cent vitamin C loss, as well as a drop in other vitamins and water soluble minerals.

LESS WATER, LESS TIME

The first step towards better boiling is to cut the length of time that vegetables are exposed to heat. Heat reduces the amounts of vitamins B and C and, when combined with exposing the vegetables to air, further destruction of vitamin C occurs. Vitamin A is also destroyed by exposure to air.

All vegetables—including the root varieties—should be placed in water that is already boiling. The traditional idea of starting to cook potatoes in cold water means that more vitamins are lost because they are soaking in cold water before the water comes to the boil. In addition, instead of drowning the vegetables in water, use only a few spoonsful. Even for potatoes, 1 cm ($\frac{1}{2}$ inch) of water is enough, if the potatoes are cut into 5 cm (2 inch) cubes. Of course, as soon as cold vegetables are added to

BOILING TIMES FOR VEGETABLES

For healthy boiling, bring the water to the boil, add the vegetables in small amounts and keep on a high heat until the water comes back to the boil. Turn down the heat; if the pan lid rattles, reduce the heat further.

Cook the vegetables in 1 cm ($\frac{1}{2}$ inch) boiling water, preferably in a 1.7 litre (3 pint) saucepan. Times given are for 225 g (8 oz) of vegetables.

VEGETABLES	*SIZE*	*BOILING TIME*
Turnips	4 cm (1$\frac{1}{2}$ inch) chunks	7–8 minutes
French Beans	4 cm (1$\frac{1}{2}$ inch) lengths	4–5 minutes
Carrots	1 cm ($\frac{1}{2}$ inch) slices	6–7 minutes
Cabbage	1.5 cm ($\frac{3}{4}$ inch)	3–4 minutes
Brussels sprouts	Boil whole	7–8 minutes
Swedes	2.5–4 cm (1–1$\frac{1}{2}$ inch) chunks	14–15 minutes
Courgettes	1 cm ($\frac{1}{2}$ inch) slices	3–4 minutes
Parsnips	Peeled and cut into 4 lengthways (if old and tough, remove core first)	3–4 minutes
Potatoes	5 cm (2 inch) chunks	19–20 minutes
Broad beans	Boil whole	4–5 minutes
Peas	Boil whole	2–3 minutes
Broccoli florets	1 cm ($\frac{1}{2}$ inch) stems	4–6 minutes

boiling water, the temperature of the water falls; it must therefore be brought back to boiling point quickly by keeping the pan on maximum heat. Because less water is used, the boiling temperature will be regained quickly.

Cutting vegetables into small pieces helps them to heat up more quickly and ensures that the temperature of the water does not drop too sharply when the vegetables are placed in it. However, when a plant is cut, and its surfaces exposed—whether by peeling, chopping or shredding—a chemical reaction takes place which rapidly destroys vitamin C. To minimise this effect, the shorter the time between chopping and heating, the better. A good practice to follow is to cut the vegetables while the water is heating. The size of the vegetable pieces will vary according to what is required for the recipe, the size of the saucepan and the type of vegetable being cooked.

Light is also destructive to vitamins, especially to vitamins C and B_2 (riboflavin). This is another reason for chopping vegetables just before you cook them. If you have to prepare them early, put in a bowl and cover tightly with a lid or aluminium foil and place in the refrigerator.

Vegetables should be stored in a cool dark place; so should nuts and pulses, good sources of the B vitamins that are adversely affected by exposure to light.

Another factor that reduces the vitamin content of vegetables is the process called leaching: the vegetables' vitamins dissolve into the cooking water, and their nutritional value is lost. Adding salt to boiling vegetables, especially at the beginning of cooking time, accelerates the leaching process. Because salt attracts moisture, the juices in the vegetables that carry the vitamins and minerals will be drawn out more quickly; therefore boil without adding salt. However, if you make a habit of saving the cooking water and storing it in the refrigerator, you can counteract the effects of leaching by using it as vitamin-and-mineral-rich stock for soups and sauces.

BOILING WITHOUT BURNING

You can still boil your vegetables, and lose very few of their nutrients by following the above guidelines and using the right sort of pans.

To boil without burning, use a heavy pan with a thick base and a tight-fitting lid. Stainless steel pans conduct heat less efficiently than aluminium or cast iron, but some have a sandwich of copper or aluminium in their base to hasten heating, so weight is the best guide to their worth. Enamelled cast iron pans are good for cooking fruit and vegetables; if they are not enamelled, the iron may react with food, darkening the colour. A heavy pan with a lid will conserve vitamins because the pan cannot boil dry when it is tightly covered. The food is then quickly cooked through by a combination of boiling and steaming.

Finally, the fresher the fruit and vegetables, the less the *risk* of them boiling dry. Fruit and vegetables which are picked from the garden and cooked immediately need less water than those that are purchased; this is because the plants' natural moisture has not dried out and toughened the fibres.

Frying is a quick method of cooking in hot oil or fat. It is not usually recommended for healthy eating because it adds extra fat to the diet; however, it makes food tastier, and can add colour and texture to a dish. If you want to fry—and everyone does from time to time—it's well worth following a few simple guidelines which will keep fat and oil to a minimum and at the same time retain all the food's nutrients.

The great advantage of frying is that the food comes into immediate contact with the hot fat, sealing in all the flavour and nutrients. What happens is that the surface is sealed and the inside of the food cooks quickly in the heat of its own steam. But to get the full advantages from frying, use pure vegetable oils and good quality ingredients.

TYPES OF FAT AND OIL

For healthy cooking, and for the best possible results, choose your fat with care. Pure vegetable oils, such as sunflower, safflower, soya and corn, are all high in polyunsaturated fats and should generally be used. Olive oil, which contains monounsaturated fats, is also a healthy oil for cooking, although very expensive. But blended vegetable oils should be avoided because they often contain coconut or palm oil which are high in saturated fat.

Lard, hard margarines and butter are also high in saturated fat and are not recommended for healthy cooking.

SMOKING TEMPERATURES

The oil you use should have a high smoking temperature so that it can be heated without burning. Different oils vary widely in the smoking temperatures—the point just before the oil begins to burn—from 150°C (300°F) to 230°C (450°F). For successful frying, choose an oil that has a smoking temperature of at least 200°C (400°F). Sunflower and corn oil both have high smoking temperatures, whereas butter, margarine and olive oil have low smoking temperatures.

Make sure the oil does not reach smoking temperature before you start to cook. The warning sign is a slight blue haze rising from the surface of the hot oil. At this stage, the fat begins to break down. As the temperature rises the rate of decomposition increases rapidly, and

acrolein is formed which has an unpleasant acrid smell and is indigestible. Beyond this point the oil will reach flashpoint temperature and will catch fire; never leave the pan unattended.

RE-USING OIL

Oil can be re-used once, so long as it has not been over-heated. Oil which has an unpleasant smell, looks thick or is dark should be discarded as it may contain impurities such as salt or water which will spatter on heating. If you are going to re-use oil strain it through a metal sieve into a clean saucepan and leave to cool before re-bottling.

DEEP-FRYING

In deep-frying the food is immersed in hot oil to give even cooking. It is very important to make sure that the food is fried at the correct temperature—this is vital for healthy cooking. If the oil is too hot, the food will burn on the outside and may be raw inside—especially if cooked from frozen. If the oil is not hot enough, the food will not be sealed; it will absorb oil and become soggy.

To make sure that the oil has reached the correct temperature, it is best to use a thermometer. Failing this, the temperature of the oil can be tested by dropping a 2.5 cm (1 inch) cube of bread into the oil to see how long it takes to become crisp and brown. At 180°C (350°F) it will take 60 seconds; at 190°C (375°F) it takes 40 seconds and at 200°C (400°F) it takes 20 seconds. The temperature required will vary according to the food, but in most cases the oil should reach at least 200°C (400°F).

The ideal equipment for deep frying is an electric, thermostatically-controlled deep fryer. However, you can deep fry successfully and safely using a heavy-based deep saucepan with a frying basket. If you do not have a frying basket, remove the food with a slotted metal spoon. The pan should be less than half full of oil, so that it does not overflow when food is added.

To get the best results from deep frying, make sure that the food is in even-sized pieces so it cooks in the same time. It is advisable to coat the food with batter, egg and wholemeal breadcrumbs or flour to prevent it from burning on the outside or breaking up.

Cook the food in small batches: if you add it all at once you will lower the temperature of the oil and the food will absorb it. Allow the oil to re-heat between batches and turn the food occasionally with a slotted spoon to ensure even cooking. Once the food has browned, drain it well in the basket or

slotted spoon over the pan, then place it on sheets of absorbent kitchen paper and turn once or twice to remove excess oil. Serve at once to retain crispness.

SHALLOW FRYING

Shallow frying seals the surface and, with some items, little further cooking is necessary. But with thick cuts of meat, reduce the temperature once the surface has browned.

For healthy shallow frying use a non-stick pan; to minimise the amount of oil, smear a little all over the pan with a brush or a piece of absorbent paper.

DRY-FRYING

This is a healthy method of shallow frying; the food cooks in its own fat and oil is not added to the pan. It is ideal for foods such as bacon, sausages and minced meat which will cook in their own fat. But to dry-fry you must use a good non-stick or cast iron pan.

STIR-FRYING

In stir-frying the accent is on vegetables—they retain all their nutrients, colour and bite when cooked correctly by this method. It is a good method of cooking for cutting down on the amount of meat in the diet—as the meat is shredded very finely it goes a long way and is usually served with vegetables.

The food should be chopped or shredded just before cooking. The ingredients are then placed in the pan and turned continuously for even cooking.

SAUTÉING

Sautéing is similar to, but slightly different from, shallow frying. It is often used for whole pieces of meat—such as chicken breasts—as the first stage in a recipe, and for vegetables which have been first partially cooked in water. The food is placed in a little oil and is moved continuously to seal and brown it. A well-seasoned, straight-side, heavy-based pan is ideal for sautéing.

CASSEROLES

Meat and some vegetables are often fried before casseroling or stewing. To reduce the amount of fat in the dish, fry the meat well in advance and leave in the pan to cool. The excess fat will then rise to the surface and can be lifted off with a spoon or skimmed off with absorbent kitchen paper before re-heating. As an alternative to this first stage of frying, all the ingredients can be added raw to the casserole and cooked from cold.

To reduce the amount of fat in the dish, all the fat should be trimmed from the meat; this includes the skin of poultry, as the layer of fat lies just beneath it.

ALL ABOUT FISH

For a country completely surrounded by the sea, we do not make adequate use of the valuable food resource it provides. As a nation we eat only about 6.8 kg (15 lb) of fish per head per year, yet fish provide excellent low-fat protein, and freshly-caught fish are one of the most delicious foods you can cook.

Fishermen in Britain land a great variety of fish. Yet only about a dozen types, out of 160 species of fish in the Mediterranean and Atlantic, are regularly in demand. The bulk of the European catch consists mainly of cod, hake, herring, mackerel, pilchard and anchovies.

The value of fish in the diet is frequently underestimated. Fish is a good source of high-grade protein. It is much more readily digestible than meat.

The amount of fat in different fish varies widely, but most is polyunsaturated and considered very valuable. It contains eicosapentaenoic acid (EPA), considered to help prevent abnormal blood clotting, and is therefore beneficial in the prevention of heart attacks. The flesh of white fish such as cod and plaice contains very little fat, while oily fish such as herring and trout contain from 10–12 per cent, distributed throughout the flesh.

Oily fish also contain valuable amounts of vitamins A and D. White fish livers are rich in these vitamins, and oils from cod and halibut are recognised as very concentrated dietary supplements.

Fish muscle contains a well-balanced supply of minerals, including iodine. If the bones are eaten as well, as for example in sardines and canned salmon, these are good sources of calcium and phosphorus. Potassium and sodium are found in most fish, and iodine and fluorine in sea fish. Iron content is highest in oily fish.

CLASSIFICATION OF FISH

Fish can be classified into four groups: white, oily, freshwater fish and shellfish.

There are two types of white fish: round and flat. Each can be recognised by its shape, distinctive markings and colour. Flat fish, as the name suggests, are flat in shape. They include Dover sole, halibut, plaice and skate. Round fish include cod, mullet and hake. Oily fish are so named because oil is evenly distributed throughout the flesh, giving these fish their characteristic darker colour. Herring, mackerel and sprats are examples of oily fish.

Freshwater fish include trout and salmon. Much of the freshwater fish now available come from fish farms. The fish produced are of a consistent quality and size and are less expensive than other fish.

All shellfish are sea fish; they include molluscs, such as whelks, winkles and mussels, and crustaceans, such as lobsters and crabs.

PRESERVING FISH

Fish are sometimes preserved by salting, curing, smoking or canning. Many of these processes incorporate additives such as artificial dyes and flavourings, but traditional methods of smoking without the addition of chemicals are fortunately now becoming more popular.

It is often difficult to buy fresh fish, especially in inland rural areas. However, modern methods of quick freezing aboard ship, as soon as the fish has been caught and filleted, ensure that the quality of frozen fish is high. As well as frozen whole fish, fish can be bought frozen in the form of prepared fillets, steaks, fingers and cakes. As a rule, try to avoid the brightly coloured breaded variety which contains artificial colouring.

BUYING AND STORING

Many fish are available all year round. However, there are some months when their colour, texture and flavour are at their best. Buy fish from a reputable retailer who has a quick turnover and obtains fresh supplies daily—the fresh fish counters in larger supermarkets are generally very good, as are many specialist fishmongers.

Fish from the sea should smell of sea water, not of fish, and the scales should be firmly attached. The eyes should be bright and prominent, the gills red, and any natural markings, such as the orange dots on plaice, should be bright and clear. The flesh of steaks and cutlets should be plump and firm. Avoid fish which show signs of staleness: grey, dull skin, opaque eyes, a dried appearance or a strong fishy smell.

When buying frozen fish, look for tightly sealed packages which show no signs of damage or frost formation. Store frozen white fish for up to six months and oily fish for up to four months. Thaw frozen fish overnight in the refrigerator, covered. When storing fish at home, remove from the shop wrapping and place in a polythene bag or a rigid container to prevent strong flavours tainting other foods. Keep in the coolest part of the refrigerator for no more than two days before eating.

COOKING

Allowing for wastage, quantities per person are as follows: approximately 350 g (12 oz) whole white fish; 225 g (8 oz) dressed fish; and 175 g (6 oz) fillets or cutlets. As oily fish is richer than white fish, slightly smaller quantities can be served.

With over 50 varieties of fish available in Britain and the countless way of preparing them, fish are an asset to any cook's menu. They can be cooked in a variety of ways, including sautéing, baking, grilling, steaming and poaching. Fish are also suitable for microwaving, barbecuing and stir-frying.

ALL ABOUT SHELLFISH

The coast around Britain provides some of the finest shellfish in the world. The varieties of shellfish range from the undeniably extravagant lobsters and oysters to the humbler and cheaper but equally excellent cockles, mussels and winkles. With more common delicacies such as prawns and scallops, too, there is shellfish for every occasion.

Now that more people are turning to fish as an alternative form of protein to meat, there is a growing interest in the part shellfish can play in our diets. Shellfish contains valuable amounts of most B-complex vitamins and is an excellent source of a well balanced supply of many minerals, particularly potassium, calcium, iron, zinc and iodine. It is high in the type of protein which provides all the essential amino acids and is extremely low in fat. Apart from cockles, oysters and scallops, which are low in cholesterol, most shellfish contains high levels.

Shellfish has low levels of thiamine and the vitamins A, C and D; to produce a balanced meal, serve shellfish with its traditional accompaniments of brown bread, lemon and watercress or with a salad and mayonnaise.

BUYING SHELLFISH

When selecting shellfish, freshness is of paramount importance. Ideally you should buy live specimens, but unless you are lucky enough to live by the sea this may not be possible. However, modern fishing, transportation and packaging methods ensure shellfish reach the shops in the freshest condition.

Always buy shellfish from a reputable shop or market stall which has a fast turnover. Traditional fish shops are becoming something of a rarity, but an increasing number of supermarkets are introducing fresh fish counters with a supply of shellfish in season.

If you are buying live crabs, lobsters or crawfish, they should appear to be reasonably lively and should have both their main claws. When cooked, they should have shells intact with no signs of damage and should feel heavy.

Dublin Bay prawns are most commonly sold already cooked. Like shrimps and prawns they should have prominent eyes and feel firm, dry and crisp.

Fresh mussels, clams and oysters should always be sold live. Their shells should be undamaged and tightly closed. This also applies to cockles, although they are usually sold cooked and removed from their shells.

Scallops are often alive inside their tightly-closed shells, but they are sometimes opened by the fishmonger and displayed attached to their bottom shell. They should have firm white flesh and orange roe or coral.

Live whelks should recoil into their shells when touched. However, like winkles, they are usually sold cooked.

Frozen shellfish is widely available, especially prawns, either peeled or in their shells. Patronise a shop that stores its frozen food correctly and has a fast turnover of stock. The packaging should be undamaged, and the contents should feel frozen solid.

Canned prawns, crab meat, oysters, clams and mussels are found in many grocers and supermarkets. Canned smoked oysters and mussels are particularly delicious. Cockles and mussels are often packed in jars in brine or vinegar.

STORING SHELLFISH

Fresh shellfish should be eaten on the day of purchase. Frozen shellfish must be stored at −18°C (0°F) or colder, for up to 2 months. Once thawed, it should be consumed immediately and never refrozen. It is not practical to freeze shellfish at home unless you have access to a supply of absolutely fresh shellfish, and your freezer has a fast-freeze control. Prepared dishes containing shellfish may be frozen for up to 2 months.

TYPES OF SHELLFISH

Shellfish are divided into two groups. Crustaceans have jointed shells; molluscs have hinged or single shells.

Crustaceans

Crabs found around the coast of Britain include velvet crabs, spider crabs and brown crabs, the most common, which are grey-brown when alive and red when cooked. The females often contain red coral or roe.

Lobsters are dark blue when alive, changing to scarlet when cooked. Males have larger claws than the females which have wider tails containing the coral.

Crawfish are similar to lobster, but have no claws, so all the meat is in the tail. They are prepared in the same way as lobster, but are in scant supply and usually sold frozen.

Crayfish are miniature freshwater lobsters, rarely seen in the shops.

Dublin Bay prawns are also known as Norway lobster, scampi and langoustine. They look like tiny lobsters with elongated claws and are pale pink when alive and become a darker pink when they are cooked.

Prawns are grey when alive and turn to pink when they are cooked. They vary in size and most small prawns are boiled and frozen, peeled or in the shell.

Shrimps sold in this country include brown shrimps which are actually grey-brown in colour, turning pale pink when cooked, and the larger pink shrimps.

Molluscs

Oysters have rough, knobbly shells. The slow-growing Natives are superior to the faster growing Pacific variety.

Scallops have fan-shaped shells which are pinky brown in colour, and flat on one side. Queen scallops are smaller and have pink shells.

Clams have strong brown shells and vary in size according to the variety. They are not widely available.

Cockles are usually sold cooked, removed from their tiny fan-shaped shells.

Mussels have shells of varying sizes, and a range of colours from blue-black to golden brown.

Whelks have an attractive spiralling shell. They are usually sold cooked.

Winkles are much smaller than whelks and have a black shell.

SHELLFISH AVAILABILITY

Crustaceans	
Crab	April to December
Crawfish	April to October
Crayfish	all year
Dublin Bay prawn	all year
Lobster	April to November
Prawn	all year
Shrimp	February to October
Molluscs	
Clam	all year
Cockle	May to December
Mussel	September to March
Oyster	September to April
Scallop	September to March
Whelk	February to August
Winkle	April to October

SPINACH AND RICOTTA CANNELLONI

CHICKEN KEBABS

CHICKEN KEBABS

Herbs and grated orange rind flavour these nutritional kebabs. Serve with boiled brown rice and a salad.

MAKES 4 295 Calories each
PREPARATION 10 minutes
COOKING 15 minutes

MARINATING At least 4 hours

100 ml (4 fl oz) dry white wine
60 ml (4 tbsp) lemon juice
30 ml (2 tbsp) olive oil
1 garlic clove, skinned and crushed
15 ml (1 tbsp) chopped fresh tarragon or
10 ml (2 tsp) dried
grated rind of 1 orange
pepper, to taste
450 g (1 lb) boned chicken breasts, skinned
and cubed
225 g (8 oz) chicken livers, thawed if
frozen, halved
2 oranges, peeled and segmented, and
watercress sprigs, to garnish

—— 1 ——
Mix together the wine, lemon juice, olive oil, garlic, tarragon, orange rind and pepper.

—— 2 ——
Pour the marinade over the chicken and livers, reserving about 75 ml (5 tbsp) for basting, and set aside for at least 4 hours, turning the pieces several times.

—— 3 ——
Thread the chicken pieces and the livers evenly on to 4 long skewers and place under the grill.

—— 4 ——
Grill the kebabs for about 15 minutes, basting occasionally with the reserved marinade, and turning once during cooking. Serve hot, garnished with the orange segments and the sprigs of watercress.

GOODNESS GUIDE
FAT With lean white chicken, this high-protein dish is very low fat
VITAMINS Chicken livers are a rich source of vitamins A and B, expecially B_{12}. Watercress is high in A and C
FIBRE Fibre is contributed by the watercress and orange segments

SPINACH AND RICCOTTA CANNELLONI

This is a perfect dish to cook in advance and freeze. Reheat just before serving, for a quick meal.

SERVES 4 600 calories per serving
PREPARATION 45 minutes
COOKING 45 minutes

450 g (1 lb) fresh spinach, stems removed
and rinsed, or 225 g (8 oz) frozen, thawed,
chopped and drained
275 g (10 oz) ricotta cheese
1 egg, size 2, beaten
5 ml (1 tsp) grated nutmeg
salt and pepper, to taste
16 cannelloni tubes
two 400 g (14 oz) cans tomatoes
1 garlic clove, skinned and crushed
1 small onion, skinned and finely chopped
5 ml (1 tsp) dried mixed herbs
100 g (4 oz) mozzarella cheese, thinly sliced
fresh basil sprigs, to garnish

—— 1 ——
Lightly oil an ovenproof dish and set aside. If using fresh spinach, cook only in the water that clings to the leaves after rinsing, for 5 minutes. Drain well and coarsely chop.

FISH AND VEGETABLE PIE

Put the spinach, ricotta cheese, egg and nutmeg in a bowl, mix well and season. Fill the cannelloni tubes with the mixture. Arrange in a single layer in the prepared dish.

———3———

Roughly chop the tomatoes and add them with their juice, garlic, onion and herbs into a saucepan. Season, bring to the boil, lower the heat and simmer for 15–20 minutes, until slightly thickened.

———4———

Purée in a blender or food processor and pour over the cannelloni. Cover with aluminium foil and cook at 200°C (400°F) mark 6 for 35 minutes, until cannelloni is tender.

———5———

Remove the foil and arrange the cheese slices over the top. Return to the oven, cook for a further 10 minutes, until bubbling and golden, and serve.

MICROWAVE In step 1, place spinach in a large bowl, cover and cook 100% (High) 5 minutes, stirring twice. Drain well and chop coarsely. Follow step 2. Make tomato sauce as in step 3 and pour over the cannelloni. Cover and cook 15 minutes, giving dish a half turn once. In step 5, uncover and arrange cheese slices on top. Cook 4 minutes, until cheese is bubbling and melted.

FISH AND VEGETABLE PIE

Serve this protein-rich dish with a green vegetable or salad for a delicious family meal.

SERVES 4 700 calories per serving
PREPARATION 45 minutes
COOKING 45 minutes

1.1 kg (2½ lb) mixed white fish fillets, such as cod, coley or fresh or smoked haddock
100 g (4 oz) sweetcorn kernels, thawed if frozen
100 g (4 oz) button mushrooms, sliced
3 tomatoes, chopped
3 celery sticks, trimmed and sliced
900 ml (1½ pints) semi-skimmed milk
45 ml (3 tbsp) cornflour
salt and pepper, to taste

POTATO TOPPING
1.4 kg (3 lb) floury potatoes, peeled and cut into 5 cm (2 inch) pieces
150 ml (¼ pint) semi-skimmed milk
salt and pepper, to taste

———1———

To make the topping, cook the potatoes in boiling water for 20 minutes, until tender. Drain, mash with the milk and season.

———2———

Meanwhile, put the fish in a pan and cover with cold water. Bring to the boil, then lower the heat and simmer for 15 minutes, until cooked. Drain and flake fish, discarding any bones and the skin.

———3———

Put the fish, sweetcorn, mushrooms, tomatoes and celery in an ovenproof dish. Blend 150 ml (¼ pint) milk with the cornflour. Bring remaining milk to the boil, then lower the heat and add the cornflower mixture, stirring until thickened. Season. Pour the sauce over fish mixture and stir gently to mix.

———4———

Spoon the potatoes over the fish. Cook at 180°C (350°F) mark 4 for 45 minutes, until lightly browned.

GOODNESS GUIDE

SPINACH AND RICOTTA CANNELLONI
FIBRE Spinach, tomatoes and onion provide a high fibre content
PROTEIN This cooked dish is very high in protein

FISH AND VEGETABLE PIE
FIBRE Fibre is supplied by the potatoes, celery and sweetcorn
VITAMINS The potatoes, tomatoes and celery all provide vitamin C; the fish provides B vitamins, needed for the body to release energy from food

53

MEATLESS SHEPHERD'S PIE

SERVES 4 370 Calories per serving
PREPARATION 40 minutes
COOKING 1½ hours

75 g (3 oz) green lentils
75 g (3 oz) red lentils
1 large onion, skinned and chopped
1 bay leaf
5 ml (1 tsp) ground cumin
salt and pepper, to taste
550 g (1¼ lb) potatoes, scrubbed
40 g (1½ oz) polyunsaturated margarine
150 ml (¼ pint) semi-skimmed milk, plus
60 ml (4 tbsp)
2.5 ml (½ tsp) grated nutmeg
100 g (4 oz) parsnips, scrubbed and cut into
1 cm (½ inch) cubes
100 g (4 oz) cauliflower florets
100 g (4 oz) leeks, thickly sliced
50 g (2 oz) canned or frozen
sweetcorn kernels
30 ml (2 tbsp) plain wholemeal flour
15 ml (1 tbsp) chopped fresh parsley
chopped fresh parsley, to garnish

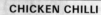

MEATLESS SHEPHERD'S PIE

—————1—————
Pick over the lentils, removing any stones, and wash thoroughly. Put into a saucepan with the onion, bay leaf, cumin and pepper. Cover with 900 ml (1½ pints) water, bring to the boil, cover and simmer for about 40 minutes or until the lentils are tender.

—————2—————
Meanwhile, cook the potatoes in boiling water for about 15 minutes, until soft. Drain and peel, then mash with 15 g (½ oz) margarine, 30 ml (2 tbsp) milk, the nutmeg and seasoning. Set aside.

—————3—————
Cook the parsnips in boiling water for 8 minutes; add the cauliflower and leeks for the last 4 minutes. Drain well.

—————4—————
Drain off all but 30 ml (2 tbsp) cooking liquid from the lentils, and discard the bay leaf. Mash the lentils and add the cauliflower, parsnips, leeks and sweetcorn kernels.

—————5—————
Melt 15 g (½ oz) margarine in a small saucepan, stir in the flour and cook for 1 minute. Remove the pan from the heat and gradually stir in remaining milk. Return the pan to the heat and cook, stirring, for 2 minutes or until the sauce thickens. Remove from the heat, season with pepper and stir in the parsley. Add the sauce to the lentil mixture, stir well, then put into a 1.1 litre (2 pint) ovenproof pie dish.

—————6—————
Pile the mashed potato on top of the lentil mixture, mark the top with a fork and dot with the remaining 15 g (½ oz) margarine. Cook at 190°C (375°F) mark 5 for 30–40 minutes.

MICROWAVE Place lentils in a microwave oven dish with 600 ml (1 pint) boiling water. Cover, cook 100% (High) 8–10 minutes, stirring once. Add all the vegetables (except potatoes) and seasoning. Cover and cook 5 minutes. Stand covered. Put potatoes into a bowl with 75 ml (3 fl oz) water. Cover, cook 8–10 minutes, stirring twice. Mash and set aside. Put margarine into a bowl and cook, uncovered, 45 seconds. Stir in flour and cook 30 seconds. Whisk in milk and cook, 2½–3 minutes, whisking twice. Add with seasoning and parsley to mashed lentil mixture and place in microwave oven dish. Follow step 6 and cook, uncovered, 8–9 minutes.

GOODNESS GUIDE
PROTEIN Lentils are a low-fat source of protein. There is also protein in the milk
FAT This dish is low in saturated fats and contains very little cholesterol

CHICKEN CHILLI

Give your chicken a Mexican flair with this complete meal-in-a-casserole. Serve with brown rice or wholemeal noodles.

SERVES 4 290 calories per serving
PREPARATION 5 minutes
COOKING 1½ hours
SOAKING Overnight

100 g (4 oz) dried red kidney beans,
soaked overnight
2 chicken breasts, each about
175 g (6 oz), skinned
2 chicken legs, each about
100 g (4 oz), skinned
15–30 ml (1–2 tbsp) plain wholemeal flour
15 ml (1 tbsp) corn oil
1 onion, skinned and finely sliced
1 garlic clove, skinned and crushed
2 fresh green chillies, seeded
and finely chopped
5 ml (1 tsp) chilli powder
pepper, to taste
225 g (8 oz) tomatoes, chopped
150 ml (¼ pint) chicken or vegetable stock

CHICKEN CHILLI

STUFFED VINE LEAVES

STUFFED VINE LEAVES

————1————
Drain the beans and boil for 10–15 minutes in a saucepan of fresh water. Drain, cover again with fresh water, bring to the boil and cook for 30 minutes or until the beans are tender. Drain. Put the beans in the base of a 2.3 litre (4 pint) ovenproof casserole.

————2————
Coat the chicken joints in the flour. Heat the oil in a frying pan and cook the chicken for 5–8 minutes or until browned all over. Place on top of the kidney beans.

————3————
Lightly cook the onion and garlic in the remaining oil in the frying pan for 3 minutes, then add the green chillies, chilli powder and pepper and cook for a further 2 minutes. Add the tomatoes and continue cooking for 5 minutes, stirring occasionally. Add the stock, stir and pour over the chicken joints and beans. Stir to mix.

————4————
Cover and cook the casserole at 190°C (375°F) mark 5 for 40–45 minutes or until chicken is cooked. Serve Chicken Chilli hot straight from the casserole.

GOODNESS GUIDE
FIBRE Pulses and vegetables contribute fibre
PROTEIN Pulses such as kidney beans are cheap, low-fat sources of protein. Chicken is another source of excellent low-fat protein
FAT As only a small amount of oil has been used, this dish is low in fat

---

SERVES 4 210 calories per serving
PREPARATION 12–15 minutes
COOKING 40–45 minutes

225 g (8 oz) packet vine leaves, drained and rinsed
15 ml (1 tbsp) corn or olive oil
1 onion, skinned and grated
225 g (8 oz) minced lean lamb
50 g (2 oz) fresh wholemeal breadcrumbs
50 g (2 oz) canned or bottled chestnuts, drained and finely chopped
grated rind and juice of 1 orange
10 ml (2 tsp) chopped fresh mint or 5 ml (1 tsp) dried
pepper, to taste
200 ml (7 fl oz) vegetable stock
orange slices, to garnish

————1————
Separate the vine leaves, put into a mixing bowl and pour boiling water over. Set aside until ready to use.

————2————
Heat the oil in a saucepan and cook the onion for 2 minutes or until transparent, then add the lamb and cook quickly, stirring, for a further 3 minutes or until browned. Remove from the heat, drain off any fat and mix in the breadcrumbs, chestnuts, orange rind and juice, mint and pepper. Mix together.

————3————
Drain the vine leaves and remove the stems. Put each leaf shiny side down on a flat board and spoon about 1 dessertspoon of the lamb mixture into the centre. Fold the leaf over to encase the filling completely, forming a neat parcel. With the smaller leaves, overlap 2 or 3 of the leaves together before adding the stuffing and folding.

————4————
Put the stuffed leaves close together in a shallow 1.1 litre (2 pint) oven-proof dish, pour the stock over, cover and cook at 190°C (375°F) mark 5 for 35–40 minutes or until the filling is cooked through. Serve hot, garnished with orange slices.

MICROWAVE Follow step 1, then put oil and onion into a bowl. Cook, uncovered, 100% (High) 2 minutes, stirring once. Add lamb, cook, uncovered, 100% (High) 2 minutes, stirring well after 1 minute. Add remaining ingredients and follow step 3, then put stuffed leaves into a shallow microwave oven dish. Pour stock over, cover, cook 100% (High) 15 minutes.

GOODNESS GUIDE
FIBRE Vine leaves are packed with fibre. The wholemeal breadcrumbs and chestnuts also contribute fibre
FAT Using lean minced lamb and only a little oil keeps fat relatively low
MINERALS Lamb, vine leaves and wholemeal breadcrumbs are sources of potassium, iron and zinc. The vine leaves and breadcrumbs also provide calcium

CHICK-PEA STROGANOFF

Low-fat yogurt is a healthy substitute for soured cream in this Stroganoff sauce. The use of chick-peas as an alternative to the traditional beef makes an interesting and nutritious vegetable dish.

SERVES 4 270 calories per serving
PREPARATION 10 minutes
COOKING 10 minutes

30 ml (2 tbsp) corn oil
2 onions, skinned and sliced
1 garlic clove, skinned and crushed
225 g (8 oz) mushrooms, sliced
400 g (14 oz) can chick-peas, drained
350 g (12 oz) tomatoes, cut into wedges
300 ml (10 fl oz) low-fat natural yogurt
15 ml (1 tbsp) chopped gherkin
salt and pepper, to taste
15 ml (1 tbsp) chopped fresh parsley
1 gherkin, to garnish

──── 1 ────

Heat the oil in a large frying pan or saucepan, then add the onions and cook for 3 minutes. Add the garlic and mushrooms and cook for 2 minutes. Add the chick-peas and tomato wedges and cook, stirring, for 3 minutes, until the chick-peas are lightly browned and the tomatoes are softened.

──── 2 ────

Stir in the yogurt and chopped gherkin and season. Heat gently, stirring, but do not boil or the yogurt may curdle.

──── 3 ────

Turn into a serving dish, sprinkle with the chopped parsley and garnish with a gherkin 'fan': slice the gherkin lengthways from the wide end three or four times, leaving the stalk end intact, then spread them open. Serve at once.

GOODNESS GUIDE

CHICK-PEA STROGANOFF
PROTEIN The combination of chick-peas and yogurt provides protein which can be fully utilised

SPINACH PIE
VITAMINS This is a vitamin-rich dish, with vitamins A and C from the spinach, C from the onion, and B vitamins from the milk, cheese, flour and spinach
MINERALS The iron provided by the spinach, egg and flour is more easily absorbed into the body because of the presence of the vitamin C

OXTAIL AND CRANBERRY CASSEROLE
VITAMINS Cranberries are high in vitamin C, and essential B vitamins are provided by the oxtail
MINERALS Oxtail is a source of potassium, iron and zinc. Zinc is essential for healthy skin

CHICK-PEA STROGANOFF

56

SPINACH PIE

OXTAIL AND CRANBERRY CASSEROLE

OXTAIL AND CRANBERRY
CASSEROLE

SERVES 4 335 calories per serving
PREPARATION 20 minutes
CHILLING 3 hours
COOKING 3–4 hours

SPINACH PIE

*This tasty spinach and cheese pie
makes a substantial meal and is
good served with a tomato salad.*

SERVES 4 435 calories per serving
PREPARATION 30 minutes
BAKING 30 minutes
CHILLING 30 minutes

700 g (1½ lb) fresh spinach or 350 g (12 oz)
frozen spinach
25 g (1 oz) polyunsaturated margarine
2 onions, skinned and chopped
1 garlic clove, skinned and crushed
40 g (1½ oz) plain wholemeal flour
300 ml (½ pint) semi-skimmed milk
2.5 ml (½ tsp) dried oregano
2.5 ml (½ tsp) dried marjoram
salt and pepper, to taste
225 g (8 oz) ricotta or low-fat soft cheese

PASTRY
175 g (6 oz) plain wholemeal flour
1.25 ml (¼ tsp) salt
65 g (2½ oz) polyunsaturated margarine
15 ml (1 tbsp) milk or beaten egg, to glaze

———1———
Cook the fresh spinach with just the
water that clings to the leaves for
about 5 minutes, until wilted. Drain
well; set aside. If using frozen spinach, cook, stirring, for 10 minutes.

———2———
To make the pastry, put the flour
and salt in a bowl and rub in the
margarine. Stir in 30 ml (2 tbsp)
cold water and mix to a dough.
Cover and chill 30 minutes.

———3———
Heat the margarine, add the onion
and garlic and cook for 5 minutes.
Stir in the flour, then gradually add
the milk, herbs and seasoning. Bring
to the boil, stirring, until thickened,
then simmer for 1 minute.

———4———
Pour about one third of the onion
sauce into the base of a 900 ml
(1½ pint) pie dish. Arrange a third of
the cooked spinach on top and
crumble over half the cheese.
Repeat, then top with the remaining
sauce and a layer of spinach,
doming up slightly in the centre.

———5———
Turn dough out on to a lightly
floured surface, knead gently and
roll out to 5 cm (2 inches) wider
than the top of the pie dish. Dampen
the rim of the pie dish, then cut a
2.5 cm (1 inch) wide strip from the
outer edge of the dough and place it
on the dish rim.

———6———
Brush the pastry rim lightly with
water and put on the pastry lid,
pressing it down. Flute the edges
and decorate with pastry trimmings,
if liked. Brush the top of the pie with
the milk or beaten egg. Bake at
200°C (400°F) mark 6 for 30
minutes, until the pastry is crisp and
golden brown. Serve hot.

about 1 kg (2¼ lb) oxtail, well trimmed and
cut into joints
3 onions, 1 skinned and quartered, 2 skinned
and chopped
1 carrot, scrubbed and cut into large
pieces
1 bay leaf
salt and pepper, to taste
30 ml (2 tbsp) corn oil
2 celery sticks, sliced
30 ml (2 tbsp) plain flour
175 g (6 oz) fresh or frozen cranberries

———1———
Place the oxtail joints, quartered
onion, carrot and bay leaf in a large
saucepan with 1 litre (1¾ pints)
water. Season and bring to the boil.
Cover and simmer for 2–3 hours.

———2———
Remove the oxtail joints with a
slotted spoon and set aside. Chill the
stock for about 3 hours or until the
fat solidifies on the surface. Remove
the fat.

———3———
Heat the oil in a saucepan, add the
chopped onion and celery and cook
for 5 minutes. Stir in the flour, then
add 600 ml (1 pint) of the skimmed
oxtail stock and bring to the boil,
stirring, until thickened.

———4———
Place the oxtail joints in a casserole
dish and scatter over the cranberries.
Pour over the sauce and cover. Cook
at 180°C (350°F) mark 4 for about 1
hour, until heated through.

BEEF TERIYAKI

Try sake, the Japanese rice wine, in this dish, instead of sherry. Sake is available from larger off-licences.

SERVES 4 205 calories per serving
PREPARATION 10 minutes
COOKING 5–15 minutes
MARINATING 30 minutes

4 beef steaks, such as sirloin, rump or fillet, each about 100 g (4 oz), trimmed of fat
30 ml (2 tbsp) soy sauce, preferably naturally fermented shoyu
30 ml (2 tbsp) dry sherry or sake
2.5 ml ($\frac{1}{2}$ tsp) finely grated fresh root ginger
1 garlic clove, skinned and crushed
2 spring onions, to garnish

———1———
Place the steaks in a dish in a single layer. Mix together the soy sauce, dry sherry or sake, ginger and garlic and pour over the steaks. Marinate for at least 30 minutes, turning the steaks occasionally.

———2———
Meanwhile, trim the spring onions top and bottom and slice the bulbs lengthways. Remove a small portion of each bulb and cut into long thin shreds. Place the spring onions in chilled water for 5 minutes, to form 'tassels'.

———3———
Cook the steaks under a hot grill for 5–15 minutes, until rare, medium or well done, turning once and basting with the remaining marinade.

———4———
Place the steaks on a warm serving platter or individual plates and spoon over any remaining marinade juices. Scatter the spring onion shreds over the top, garnish with the spring onion tassels, and serve at once.

GOODNESS GUIDE
PROTEIN The beef provides a good supply of protein, which is needed for tissue replacement
MINERALS Beef provides an easily absorbed source of iron
VITAMINS Beef is a source of B-complex vitamins, one of which is B$_{12}$. This is as necessary as iron for healthy red blood cells

CHICKEN A LA KING

SERVES 4 320 calories per serving
PREPARATION 15 minutes
COOKING 15 minutes

40 g (1$\frac{1}{2}$ oz) polyunsaturated margarine
1 onion, skinned and chopped
100 g (4 oz) mushrooms, sliced
1 green or red pepper, cored, seeded and sliced
40 g (1$\frac{1}{2}$ oz) plain wholemeal flour
150 ml ($\frac{1}{4}$ pint) chicken stock
150 ml ($\frac{1}{4}$ pint) semi-skimmed milk
30–45 ml (2–3 tbsp) dry sherry (optional)
10 ml (2 tsp) tomato purée
salt and pepper, to taste
350–450 g (12 oz–1 lb) cold cooked chicken meat, skinned and cut into bite-sized pieces
15 ml (1 tbsp) chopped fresh parsley

———1———
Melt the margarine in a saucepan, add the onion and cook for 3 minutes. Add the mushrooms and cook 2 minutes, then stir in the green or red pepper and cook for 1 minute, stirring.

———2———
Stir in the flour, add the stock and milk and bring to the boil, stirring, until the sauce is thickened. Add sherry, if using, purée and seasoning.

———3———
Add the chicken and simmer gently to reheat. Stir in a little more warmed milk to make a thinner sauce if necessary. Sprinkle with the parsley and serve at once.

MICROWAVE Put margarine and onion into a dish. Cover and cook 100% (High) 3 minutes. Add mushrooms and green or red pepper and cook, uncovered, 100% (High) 2 minutes. Blend in flour, stock and milk and cook, uncovered, 100% (High) 4 minutes, stirring 2 or 3 times. Add sherry, tomato purée, seasoning and chicken. Cook, uncovered, 100% (High) 3–4 minutes.

GOODNESS GUIDE
VITAMINS The chicken, milk and flour are sources of B vitamins; the vegetables provide vitamin C; vitamin A comes from the sweet pepper and tomato purée
MINERALS The meat, flour and vegetables contribute potassium, needed for fluid balance in the cells

VEGETABLE KORMA

SERVES 4 325 calories per serving
PREPARATION 30 minutes
COOKING 30 minutes

450 g (1 lb) potatoes, scrubbed
30 ml (2 tbsp) corn oil
1 onion, skinned and sliced
225 g (8 oz) aubergine, diced
1 garlic clove, skinned and crushed
10 ml (2 tsp) grated fresh root ginger
10–15 ml (2–3 tsp) curry powder
225 g (8 oz) carrots, scrubbed and thinly sliced
225 g (8 oz) leeks, trimmed and sliced
100 g (4 oz) peas or green beans
50 g (2 oz) sultanas (optional)
300 ml (10 fl oz) low-fat natural yogurt
25 g (1 oz) flaked almonds, toasted

———1———
If the potatoes are large, cut into 5 cm (2 inch) chunks. Otherwise, leave whole. Cook in boiling water for 10 minutes, then drain and leave to cool.

———2———
Heat the oil in a large saucepan, add the onion and aubergine and cook for 5 minutes. Add the garlic, ginger and curry powder and cook for 1 minute. Add the potatoes, carrots, leeks, peas and sultanas, if using. Stir to coat well.

———3———
Stir the yogurt. Cover the pan and simmer gently for about 30 minutes, stirring occasionally, until the vegetables are tender but still slightly crisp. To serve, sprinkle with nuts.

MICROWAVE Place potatoes in a bowl with carrots and 75 ml (3 fl oz) water. Cover and cook 100% (High) 5 minutes. Drain. Put oil, onion and aubergine into a bowl, cover and cook 100% (High) 5 minutes. Add garlic, ginger and curry powder, cook, uncovered, 100% (High) 1 minute. Mix in potatoes, carrots, leeks, peas and sultanas. Stir in yogurt and cook, covered, 100% (High) 15–20 minutes.

GOODNESS GUIDE
FIBRE The vegetables, sultanas and nuts contribute a good deal of fibre
PROTEIN The low-fat yogurt and almonds provide most of the protein in this dish
MINERALS Potassium is supplied by the vegetables, nuts, sultanas and yogurt

VEGETABLE KORMA

BEEF TERIYAKI

CHICKEN A LA KING

CHEESY CAULIFLOWER

This is a colourful alternative to the usual cauliflower cheese and the nuts add a pleasant crunchy taste. It is important not to overcook the cauliflower so, if preferred, steam whole or divided into florets.

SERVES 4 150 calories per serving
PREPARATION 5 minutes
COOKING 30 minutes

1 cauliflower, about 900 g (2 lb), trimmed
2 tomatoes, finely chopped
50 g (2 oz) Brazil nuts, chopped
50 g (2 oz) button mushrooms, chopped
50 g (2 oz) Edam cheese, finely grated
salt and pepper, to taste
parsley sprigs, to garnish

———1———

Trim the base of the cauliflower and remove the outer leaves. Place the cauliflower in a large saucepan of boiling water and cook for 10–15 minutes, until tender, then drain.

———2———

Place the cauliflower in an oven-proof dish. Sprinkle the remaining ingredients over and cook at 190°C (375°F) mark 5 for 15 minutes or until the cheese is golden brown. Serve immediately, garnished with the parsley sprigs.

MICROWAVE Put the cauliflower, stalk end up, into a deep bowl with 150 ml ($\frac{1}{4}$ pint) water. Cover and cook 100% (High) 5 minutes. Turn the cauliflower over, cover, and cook for a further 7–8 minutes. Put the drained cauliflower in the microwave dish, add remaining ingredients and cook, uncovered, 100% (High) for 3 minutes, turning twice.

GOODNESS GUIDE

PROTEIN The nuts, cheese and mushrooms provide protein
FIBRE The cauliflower, tomatoes, nuts and mushrooms contribute fibre
VITAMINS Cauliflower provides vitamin C, as do the tomatoes and mushrooms. The nuts and cheese are sources of B-complex vitamins

SPARE RIBS IN BARBECUE SAUCE

SERVES 4 505 calories per serving
PREPARATION 25 minutes
COOKING 1 hour

1.4 kg (3 lb) pork spare ribs
50 g (2 oz) tomato chutney
350 g (12 oz) canned pineapple in natural juice, drained and finely chopped
15 ml (1 tbsp) Worcestershire sauce
45 ml (3 tbsp) clear honey
5 ml (1 tsp) Dijon mustard
2.5 cm (1 inch) piece fresh root ginger, peeled and finely chopped
spring onion tassel, to garnish

———1———

Place the spare ribs in a large saucepan and cover with water. Bring to the boil, then simmer for 10 minutes. Drain and transfer to an ovenproof dish. Cook at 200°C (400°F) mark 6 for 15 minutes.

———2———

Place the remaining ingredients in a saucepan, bring to the boil and cook over a high heat for 10 minutes.

———3———

Remove the ribs from the oven and drain off the fat. Pour the sauce over the drained ribs and continue cooking for 1 hour, turning occasionally. Transfer the ribs to a large serving dish and pour the sauce over.

GOODNESS GUIDE

SPARE RIBS IN BARBECUE SAUCE
FIBRE Pineapple contributes fibre
VITAMINS Lean pork meat is a rich source of thiamine, one of the B vitamins. Although some is lost during preparation, this dish still provides a good amount. The pineapple contributes some vitamin C

VEGETABLE SAMOSAS
FAT The fact that these samosas are cooked in the oven and not deep-fried makes them far lower in fat than the traditional variety. Also, the ingredients themselves are low in fat
FIBRE The wholemeal flour and the vegetables provide good amounts of fibre
VITAMINS All the vegetables provide vitamin C. Because vitamin C is water-soluble, it is necessary for us to get a supply every day

VEGETABLE SAMOSAS

Easy blend dried yeast—which doesn't need to be activated in warm liquid to reconstitute—is now available. Simply mix it together with the flour before adding remaining ingredients.

MAKES 12 105 calories each
PREPARATION 20 minutes
BAKING 25 minutes
RISING 40 minutes

5 ml (1 tsp) easy blend dried yeast or 10 ml (2 tsp) fresh yeast
225 g (8 oz) plain wholemeal flour
100 ml (4 fl oz) semi-skimmed milk
1 egg
30 ml (2 tbsp) corn oil
salt, to taste

VEGETABLE FILLING
15 ml (1 tbsp) corn oil
1 onion, skinned and finely chopped
1 garlic clove, skinned and finely chopped
5 ml (1 tsp) curry powder
2.5 ml ($\frac{1}{2}$ tsp) ground cumin
2.5 ml ($\frac{1}{2}$ tsp) ground coriander
2.5 ml ($\frac{1}{2}$ tsp) ground ginger
2.5 ml ($\frac{1}{2}$ tsp) ground turmeric
juice of 1 lemon
1 carrot, scrubbed and finely chopped
1 small green pepper, cored, seeded and finely chopped
1 celery stick, trimmed and finely sliced
60 g (2$\frac{1}{2}$ oz) frozen peas
coriander sprigs, to garnish

———1———

In a bowl mix together the easy blend dried yeast and 100 g (4 oz) flour. Warm the milk until tepid and add to the flour and yeast mixture, stirring well. If using fresh yeast, mix

it to a paste with a little of the warm milk and then add the remaining milk and half the flour. Cover and leave in a warm place for 40 minutes.

———2———

Meanwhile, begin to make the filling. Put the corn oil into a saucepan and heat gently. Add the onion and garlic and cook for 5 minutes, then add the curry powder, cumin, coriander, ginger and turmeric and cook for 2 minutes. Mix in the lemon juice and remove from the heat.

———3———

When the flour mixture has risen, add the egg, reserving a little for glazing, corn oil, remaining flour and salt. Knead the dough on a lightly floured surface for 10 minutes. Roll the dough out very thinly to a 40.5 × 30.5 cm (16 × 12 inch) rectangle and cut into twelve 10 cm (4 inch) squares.

———4———

Spoon the onion mixture into a bowl and add all the vegetables. Place 15 ml (1 tbsp) of the filling slightly off-centre on each of the dough squares. Moisten two adjacent edges of each square with water and fold the unmoistened corner over to form a triangle. Press the edges down firmly to seal them.

———5———

Prick the top of each patty with a fork, brush with remaining egg and bake at 200°C (400°F) mark 6 for 25 minutes. Garnish with coriander.

SPARE RIBS IN BARBECUE SAUCE

CHEESY CAULIFLOWER

VEGETABLE SAMOSAS

61

POUSSINS FLORENTINE-STYLE

SERVES 4 600 calories per serving
PREPARATION 12–15 minutes
COOKING 30–40 minutes

4 poussins, each about 450 g (1 lb)
juice of 2 small lemons
25 ml (1½ tbsp) corn oil
pepper, to taste
10 ml (2 tsp) chopped fresh thyme or
5 ml (1 tsp) dried
225 g (8 oz) frozen spinach
300 ml (½ pint) semi-skimmed milk
1 onion, skinned and studded with 3 cloves
7.5 cm (3 inch) piece carrot, scrubbed
7.5 cm (3 inch) piece celery
1 bay leaf
2 blades mace
25 g (1 oz) polyunsaturated margarine
25 g (1 oz) plain flour
25 g (1 oz) Emmenthal cheese, grated

———1———

Lay each bird on its breast and cut along centre of backbone with a sharp knife. Turn bird over and lay it flat on a board. Bang centre of bird to break breastbone. Thread 2 skewers through body, leg and wing to wing. Blend lemon juice, oil, pepper and thyme and brush over the birds, reserving remaining mixture. Put under a medium grill and cook, turning occasionally and brushing with remaining lemon mixture, 25–30 minutes, until cooked. Keep warm.

———2———

Meanwhile, cook the spinach according to package instructions, then purée in a blender or a food processor. Keep hot. Put the milk into a saucepan with the onion, carrot, celery, bay leaf and mace and heat. Remove from the heat, cover and infuse for 5–10 minutes. Strain.

———3———

Melt margarine in a clean pan, stir in flour and cook for 1 minute. Stir in the milk off the heat. Bring to boil, stirring, and cook for 2 minutes, until thickened.

———4———

Put the poussins on top of the spinach purée in a shallow oven-proof dish. Pour the sauce over, sprinkle with the grated cheese and brown under a hot grill for 5 minutes.

GREEK-STYLE KEBABS

SERVES 4 235 calories per serving
PREPARATION 10 minutes
COOKING 8–10 minutes
CHILLING 30 minutes

14 stoned black olives
175 g (6 oz) lean minced leg of lamb
1 garlic clove, skinned and crushed
1 onion, skinned and finely chopped
75 g (3 oz) fresh brown breadcrumbs
25 ml (1½ tbsp) tomato purée
15 ml (1 tbsp) sesame seeds
pepper, to taste
8 shallots or small onions, skinned
1 red pepper, cored, seeded and cubed
30 ml (2 tbsp) olive oil
45 ml (3 tbsp) lemon juice
10 ml (2 tsp) chopped fresh coriander

———1———

Finely chop 6 of the olives and put in a mixing bowl with the lamb, garlic, onion, breadcrumbs, tomato purée and sesame seeds. Season and mix together well. Form into 12 small sausage-shapes, cover and chill for 30 minutes.

———2———

Thread 4 kebab skewers with the lamb rolls, shallots, pepper and reserved olives. Blend the olive oil, lemon juice and coriander together and brush over the kebabs.

———3———

Cook under a moderatlely hot grill for 8–10 minutes or until cooked, turning and brushing occasionally with the oil mixture.

GOODNESS GUIDE

POUSSINS FLORENTINE-STYLE
PROTEIN Poussin, like all chicken, is a good source of protein. Further protein is contributed by the milk and cheese
VITAMINS Spinach is an excellent source of vitamins A and C and folic acid

GREEK-STYLE KEBABS
FIBRE The vegetables and breadcrumbs provide a fair amount of fibre
MINERALS Lamb is a good source of potassium, iron and zinc. Zinc is essential for the action of the enzymes needed to release carbon dioxide from the blood into the lungs

CURRIED BEANS

SERVES 4 260 calories per serving
PREPARATION 12 minutes
COOKING 1½–1¾ hours
SOAKING At least 8 hours

100 g (4 oz) dried chick-peas, rinsed and soaked at least 8 hours
100 g (4 oz) dried red kidney beans, rinsed and soaked at least 8 hours
30 ml (2 tbsp) corn oil
1 onion, skinned and chopped
1 garlic clove, skinned and crushed
175 g (6 oz) aubergine, diced
1 green pepper, cored, seeded and sliced
10 ml (2 tsp) grated fresh root ginger
10 ml (2 tsp) ground coriander
10 ml (2 tsp) ground cumin
2.5–5 ml (½–1 tsp) ground turmeric
pepper, to taste
225 g (8 oz) can pineapple chunks in natural juice, drained, with juice reserved
300 ml (½ pint) vegetable stock
1 banana, peeled and sliced

———1———

Put the chick-peas and beans with their soaking water in a large saucepan. Boil for 10 minutes, drain, then cover again with fresh water. Bring to the boil again, lower the heat, cover and simmer for 35–45 minutes, until tender. Drain and reserve.

———2———

Heat the oil in the rinsed-out pan and cook the onion, garlic, aubergine and green pepper for 5 minutes. Add the spices and pepper and cook for a further 2 minutes. Add the pineapple juice to the pan with the stock and the reserved chick-peas and red kidney beans.

———3———

Stir well, cover and simmer gently for 30 minutes, stirring occasionally. Add the pineapple and banana and cook for 15–10 minutes longer, until the fruit has been thoroughly heated. Transfer to a serving bowl and serve hot.

GOODNESS GUIDE

FIBRE The beans, vegetables and fruit make this a high-fibre dish
VITAMINS The beans are a good source of thiamine and niacin, which help the release of energy from the carbohydrates in the beans, vegetables and fruit
PROTEIN Pulses are a good source of vegetable protein, which is enhanced if eaten with a cereal

CURRIED BEANS

POUSSINS FLORENTINE-STYLE

GREEK-STYLE KEBABS

LAMB TAGINE

TARRAGON CHICKEN

TARRAGON CHICKEN

SERVES 4 370 calories per serving
PREPARATION 10 minutes
COOKING 1¼ hours

1.6 kg (3½ lb) oven-ready chicken
1 onion, skinned
1 large lemon, sliced
1 bunch fresh tarragon, trimmed
225 ml (8 fl oz) dry white wine
salt and pepper, to taste
15 g (½ oz) polyunsaturated margarine
15 ml (1 tbsp) plain flour
150 ml (5 fl oz) low-fat natural yogurt
tarragon sprig, to garnish

———1———

Line a roasting pan with a piece of aluminium foil large enough to enclose the chicken. Place the chicken in the lined pan and put the onion and half the lemon slices inside the chicken cavity.

———2———

Arrange the remaining lemon slices and the tarragon leaves over the chicken, pour the wine over and season. Bring the foil edges together to enclose the chicken.

———3———

Cook at 200°C (400°F) mark 6 for 1 hour. Open the foil and cook for a further 15–20 minutes, until the skin is golden brown.

———4———

Remove the chicken from the foil and keep warm. Pour the juices into a saucepan and skim off the fat, then bring to the boil.

———5———

Mix together the margarine and flour to make a paste, and stir gradually into the cooking juices. Cook for 3–4 minutes, stirring continuously until thick and smooth. Remove from the heat. Add the yogurt and seasoning. Gently reheat and serve the sauce separately with the chicken.

MICROWAVE Prepare the chicken, then place breast side down in a deep bowl. Add wine and seasoning. Cover and cook 100% (High) 10 minutes. Turn chicken over and add lemon slices and tarragon. Cover and cook 100% (High) 15 minutes, until tender. Remove chicken and skin off fat, reserving cooking liquid. Blend margarine and flour in a bowl. Whisk in cooking liquid. Cook, uncovered, 100% (High) 2 minutes, whisking once. Add yogurt and cook, uncovered, 100% (High) 1 minute. Season to taste.

GOODNESS GUIDE
PROTEIN The chicken meat and yogurt are good, low-fat sources of protein
VITAMINS The B-complex vitamins in the chicken and yogurt are involved in many processes in the body, including the utilisation of energy from carbohydrates, fats and proteins

LAMB TAGINE

SERVES 4 720 calories per serving
PREPARATION 12–15 minutes
COOKING 2½ hours
SOAKING Overnight

900 g (2 lb) boned lean lamb, trimmed of fat
and cut into large cubes
45 ml (3 tbsp) olive oil
1.25 ml (¼ tsp) salt
1 onion, skinned and sliced
10 ml (2 tsp) ground coriander
2.5 ml (½ tsp) saffron threads
1 cinnamon stick
5 ml (1 tsp) ground ginger
2.5 ml (½ tsp) ground cumin
juice of 1 lemon
450 g (1 lb) mixed dried fruit, such as
prunes, apples, pears and apricots, rinsed,
soaked overnight and drained
45 ml (3 tbsp) clear honey
25 g (1 oz) toasted sesame seeds

———1———

Put the lamb, oil, salt, onion, coriander, saffron, cinnamon stick, ginger, cumin and lemon juice in a heavy-based saucepan. Pour over about 450 ml (¾ pint) water, or just enough to cover the lamb. Cover tightly with a well-fitting lid and simmer over a very low heat for 2 hours.

HADDOCK-STUFFED COURGETTES

2

Add the fruit and honey. Cook, uncovered, for 20 minutes. Remove the lamb and fruit with a slotted spoon. Skim off any fat, then boil the liquid until reduced to about 150 ml (¼ pint). Discard the cinnamon stick.

3

Return the lamb and fruit to the pan and heat through. Serve hot, sprinkled with the sesame seeds.

MICROWAVE Put lamb, oil, salt, onion, coriander, saffron, cinnamon stick, ginger, cumin, lemon juice and 150 ml (¼ pint) water in a bowl. Cover, and cook 100% (High) 15 minutes, then 60% (Medium) 35 minutes. Add the fruit and honey, cover, and cook 60% (Medium) 15 minutes, until lamb is tender. Remove lamb and fruit. Skim off fat and cook 100% (High) 4–5 minutes to reduce. Return lamb and fruit to liquid and cook, uncovered, 100% (High) 2–3 minutes. Complete the recipe.

GOODNESS GUIDE

FIBRE The dried fruit supplies a good amount of fibre

VITAMINS The lamb contains the B-complex vitamins riboflavin, thiamine and niacin

MINERALS Lamb provides iron, which is needed for the formation of haemoglobin, a constituent of red blood cells that carries oxygen to the body cells

---

HADDOCK-STUFFED COURGETTES

SERVES 4 135 calories per serving
PREPARATION 20 minutes
COOKING 25–30 minutes

4 large courgettes, about 100 g (4 oz) each
450 g (1 lb) haddock fillets, skinned
5 ml (1 tsp) ground cumin
5 ml (1 tsp) ground coriander
1.25 ml (¼ tsp) turmeric
45 ml (3 tbsp) low-fat natural yogurt
1 egg, size 2, separated
fresh coriander sprigs, to garnish

1

Trim the ends from the courgettes, then cut them in half and scoop out and discard the seeds. Place the courgette shells in a saucepan of boiling water and cook for about 5 minutes, until just tender. Drain well and set aside

2

Place the haddock in a saucepan of just enough simmering water to cover. Poach for 8–10 minutes, until cooked through and the fish flakes easily. Drain well, then flake, discarding any bones.

3

Put the fish, cumin, coriander, turmeric, yogurt and egg yolk in a bowl and mix well.

4

Whisk the egg white and using a metal spoon, carefully fold into the fish mixture. Spoon into the prepared courgette shells and place in an ovenproof dish in a single layer.

5

Cook at 200°C (400°F) mark 6 for 25–30 minutes, until the stuffing is pale golden brown and the courgettes are tender. Garnish with coriander sprigs and serve hot.

MICROWAVE Prepare the courgettes, then place in a bowl with 60 ml (4 tbsp) water. Cover and cook 100% (High) 7 minutes, until tender. Drain. Put haddock into a dish with 30 ml (2 tbsp) water. Cover and cook 100% (High) 5 minutes. Drain well, flake and discard any bones. Follow steps 3 and 4, putting filled courgettes into dish. Cook, uncovered, 100% (High) 6–7 minutes, turning dish once. Garnish with coriander sprigs and serve hot.

GOODNESS GUIDE

MINERALS The egg, spices and courgettes provide iron and calcium, with more calcium being provided by the yogurt. All the ingredients provide potassium

VITAMINS The haddock, egg and yogurt are sources of B complex vitamins. The courgettes provide vitamin C, which aids the absorption of the iron

LEMON SOLE IN LETTUCE

SERVES 4 220 calories per serving
PREPARATION 15 minutes
COOKING 22 minutes

**16 large lettuce leaves, thick
stalks removed
8 lemon sole fillets, about 100 g (4 oz)
each, skinned
15 ml (1 tbsp) lemon juice
salt and pepper, to taste
100 g (4 oz) peeled cooked prawns
15 ml (1 tbsp) chopped fresh dill
150 ml ($\frac{1}{4}$ pint) fish stock or dry white wine
lemon slices, to garnish**

———1———

Drop the lettuce leaves into a large
saucepan of boiling water and simmer
for 2 minutes. Drain and rinse in cold
water until the leaves are chilled.
Dry on absorbent kitchen paper,
then spread out on a flat surface.

———2———

Sprinkle the fillets with a little of the
lemon juice and season. Arrange a
few prawns in the centre of each
fillet and sprinkle over half the dill.
Fold the fish into thirds to enclose
the prawns.

———3———

Place each folded fillet on a lettuce
leaf and roll up again, folding the
edges to form a neat parcel.

———4———

Place the fish parcels in a non-stick
frying pan and sprinkle over the
remaining lemon juice, stock or
wine and pepper to taste. Cover and
cook gently for 15 minutes, until
tender.

———5———

Remove the fish to a warmed serving
dish. Boil the cooking juices until
reduced to about 90 ml (6 tbsp). Stir
in the remaining dill and pour over
the fish. Serve with lemon slices.

MICROWAVE Put lettuce leaves into
a bowl with 60 ml (4 tbsp) water.
Cover and cook 100% (High)
2 minutes. Complete steps 1, 2
and 3. Arrange fillets in a shallow
dish. Add remaining lemon juice
and only 75 ml (5 tbsp) stock or
wine and seasoning. Cover and
cook 100% (High) 8 minutes.
Remove fillets and cook juices,
uncovered, 3 minutes. Complete
the recipe.

GOODNESS GUIDE
MINERALS Prawns are rich in minerals,
particularly calcium, magnesium, iron and
zinc. Magnesium helps build bones and
manufacture proteins. Zinc aids the action
of the enzymes responsible for mental and
physical development, and helps
wounds to heal
FAT Sole and prawns are low-fat
sources of protein

RASPBERRY CHICKEN WITH PEACHES

SERVES 4 255 calories per serving
PREPARATION 10 minutes
COOKING 20–25 minutes
MARINATING 2 hours

**4 boneless chicken breasts, about
150 g (5 oz) each, skinned
250 g (9 oz) raspberries
30 ml (2 tbsp) lemon juice
30 ml (2 tbsp) clear honey
15 ml (1 tbsp) olive oil
30 ml (2 tbsp) red wine vinegar
15 ml (1 tbsp) soy sauce, preferably
naturally fermented shoyu
1 garlic clove, skinned and crushed
2.5 ml ($\frac{1}{2}$ tsp) mustard powder
salt and pepper, to taste
2 peaches, skinned, halved and stoned
sprigs of coriander, to garnish**

———1———

Make 3 slashes across the back and
front of each chicken breast, but do
not cut right through. Arrange in a
shallow dish.

———2———

Reserve 25 g (1 oz) raspberries for
serving and place the remainder in a
blender or food processor with the
lemon juice. Purée until smooth.
Rub the purée through a sieve and
discard the seeds.

———3———

Add the honey, oil, vinegar, soy
sauce, garlic, mustard powder and

LEMON SOLE IN LETTUCE

RASPBERRY CHICKEN WITH PEACHES

seasoning to the raspberry sauce. Mix well and pour over the chicken breasts. Cover and marinate for about 2 hours.

4

Drain the chicken, reserving the marinade, and place in the grill pan. Cook under a moderate grill for 20–25 minutes, turning frequently and basting with the marinade.

5

Brush the peach halves with marinade and arrange around the chicken breasts for the last 5 minutes of cooking to warm through.

6

To serve, spoon any sauce remaining in the grill pan over the chicken and garnish with coriander sprigs. Fill the peach halves with the reserved raspberries and serve with the chicken.

MICROWAVE Follow steps 1, 2 and 3. Arrange chicken on a rack. Cook, uncovered, 100% (High) 7 minutes, turning once and basting. Brush peaches with marinade. Add to rack at outside edge. Cook, uncovered, 100% (High) 3 minutes.
Complete recipe.

GOODNESS GUIDE
PROTEIN Chicken is a low-fat source of protein
VITAMINS Chicken is a source of B-complex vitamins, which are important for energy production in the body

APRICOT AND REDCURRANT STUFFED PORK

SERVES 4 265 calories per serving
PREPARATION 45 minutes
COOKING 55 minutes

25 g (1 oz) brown rice
550–700 g (1¼–1½ lb) pork fillet
½ small onion, skinned and chopped
50 g (2 oz) redcurrants
100 g (4 oz) apricots, chopped
100 g (4 oz) cooking apple, peeled, cored and chopped
finely grated rind of 1 small orange
30 ml (2 tbsp) chopped fresh parsley
salt and pepper, to taste
30 ml (2 tbsp) unsweetened orange juice
5 ml (1 tsp) no-added-sugar apricot jam

1

Put the rice in 150 ml (¼ pint) of boiling water. Reduce the heat. Cover and simmer for 30 minutes, or until just tender and all the liquid is absorbed.

2

Meanwhile, split open the pork fillet lengthways, without cutting it in half. Spread the meat out flat, cut side down, cover with greaseproof paper and pound with a flat mallet to form a 30 × 20.5 cm (12 × 8 inch) rectangle.

3

Put the onion in a bowl with the redcurrants, apricots, apple, orange rind, 15 ml (1 tbsp) chopped parsley, seasoning and cooked rice. Mix together well.

4

Spoon the stuffing over the pork fillet and spread to within 4 cm (1½ inches) of the edge. Fold over the 2 short ends of the port fillet, then roll up, Swiss-roll fashion, from a long side. Tie the roll with string at 4 cm (1½ inch) intervals.

5

Place the meat on a piece of aluminium foil and spoon 15 ml (1 tbsp) orange juice over. Wrap the foil loosely around the meat and seal the top. Place on a baking sheet. Cook at 190°C (375°F) mark 5 for 45 minutes. Fold back the foil, baste the meat with the cooking juices and cook for further 10 minutes.

6

Remove the meat from the oven and keep warm on a serving plate. Pour the juices from the foil into a saucepan and add the remaining orange juice and jam. Bring to the boil and cook until reduced by half. Strain, then stir in the remaining chopped parsley.

7

Remove the string and serve the meat, cut into slices, with a little sauce poured over. Serve the remaining sauce separately.

MICROWAVE Put rice into bowl with 120 ml (8 tbsp) boiling water. Cover, cook 100% (High) 2 minutes, then 60% (Medium) 9 minutes, stirring twice. Stand or drain, if necessary. Complete steps 2, 3 and 4. Put pork into a dish, spoon 15 ml (1 tbsp) orange juice over. Cover, cook 100% (High) 15 minutes, turning dish twice. Remove, keep warm. Add remaining orange juice and jam to the juices in the dish. Cook, uncovered (High) for about 5 minutes or until reduced.
Complete recipe.

GOODNESS GUIDE
MINERALS The rice and pork provide iron, and the apricots and rice, calcium. All the ingredients provide potassium, which is needed for the body's water balance. In hot weather it is important to eat many potassium-rich foods to replace that lost in perspiration
VITAMINS The pork and brown rice provide thiamine, important for energy production in the body

APRICOT AND REDCURRANT STUFFED PORK

VEAL ESCALOPES WITH MUSHROOMS

BAKED HALIBUT TANDOORI-STYLE

BAKED HALIBUT TANDOORI-STYLE

SERVES 4   190 calories per serving
PREPARATION   9–10 minutes
COOKING   20–25 minutes
MARINATING   24 hours

4 halibut steaks, about 175 g (6 oz) each
75 ml (5 tbsp) low-fat natural yogurt
30 ml (2 tbsp) white wine vinegar
2 garlic cloves, skinned and crushed
1 onion, skinned and finely chopped
15 ml (1 tbsp) paprika
5 ml (1 tsp) garam masala
2.5 ml ($\frac{1}{2}$ tsp) turmeric
1 red chilli, seeded and finely chopped
5 ml (1 tsp) grated fresh root ginger
juice of 1 lemon
lemon wedges, chopped fresh coriander and
green chilli flower, to garnish

————1————
Wash the halibut steaks under cold
running water, drain and then place
the steaks in a large shallow dish.
————2————
Put all the remaining ingredients,
except those for the garnish, into a
blender or food processor and purée
until smooth. Pour over the fish.
Cover with aluminium foil and leave
to marinate in a cool place for 24
hours, turning occasionally.

————3————
Cook the fish, still covered with foil,
at 180°C (350°F) mark 4 for 20–25
minutes, until cooked through.
————4————
Serve the fish, garnished with lemon
wedges, coriander and chilli flower.
Serve the sauce, separately.

MICROWAVE   Place fish in a shallow
dish. Follow step 2.
Cover with pierced cling film and
cook 100% (High) 7–8 minutes,
turning dish twice. Remove the fish.
If necessary, reduce fish juices in
uncovered dish 100% (High)
3 minutes. Complete recipe.

GOODNESS GUIDE
MINERALS Yogurt is rich in calcium, needed
for healthy bones. The dried spices are rich
in iron and calcium. All the ingredients
supply potassium, which is involved with
sodium in maintaining the body's
fluid balance
FAT This is a very low-fat dish, using low-
fat white fish, low-fat yogurt and no oil in
the cooking

VEAL ESCALOPES WITH MUSHROOMS

*As this dish tastes quite rich, it is
best accompanied by a mixed
green salad.*

SERVES 4   250 calories per serving
PREPARATION   10 minutes
COOKING   about 15 minutes

30 ml (2 tbsp) corn or olive oil
450 g (1 lb) veal escalopes, cut into
narrow strips
1 onion, skinned and finely chopped
100 g (4 oz) button mushrooms
2 courgettes, cut into narrow strips
finely pared rind of 1 lemon, cut into
matchstick strips
juice of 1 lemon
150 ml ($\frac{1}{4}$ pint) chicken stock
150 ml ($\frac{1}{4}$ pint) dry white vermouth
pepper, to taste
45 ml (3 tbsp) low-fat natural yogurt
parsley sprig, to garnish

————1————
Heat the oil in a frying pan and cook
the veal strips for 2 minutes, until
browned. Remove from the pan.
————2————
Add the onion, mushrooms and
courgettes to the pan and cook for 3
minutes, until the onions are just
beginning to soften.

LAMB AND BEAN CASSEROLE

3

Add the lemon rind to the pan with the lemon juice, stock, vermouth and seasoning. Cook, stirring occasionally, for 5–8 minutes, until the liquid is reduced by half.

4

Return the veal to the pan. Cover and cook for 3 minutes or until the veal is thoroughly reheated. Remove from the heat, swirl in the yogurt, garnish with parsley sprig and serve.

MICROWAVE Put oil into a browning dish and heat, uncovered, 100% (High) 1–2 minutes. Add veal and cook, uncovered, 100% (High) 4–5 minutes, turning twice. Remove veal. Add onion, mushrooms and courgettes and cook, uncovered, 100% (High) 3 minutes. Add 75 ml (3 fl oz) each stock and vermouth. Add lemon strips, juice and seasoning. Cook, uncovered, 100% (High) 5–8 minutes, until reduced. Add veal. Cook, uncovered, 100% (High) 1–2 minutes to heat through. Complete recipe.

GOODNESS GUIDE
MINERALS Veal contains a good amount of easily assimilated animal iron
VITAMINS Veal is a rich source of the B vitamins thiamine, niacin and riboflavin, all of which are involved in energy production in the body from carbohydrates
FAT Veal escalopes are the leanest cuts of meat on the calf

LAMB AND BEAN CASSEROLE

This casserole is based on a cassoulet, a recipe for beans and meat that originated in the Languedoc region of southern France.

SERVES 4   360 calories per serving
PREPARATION 5 minutes
COOKING 5 hours
SOAKING Overnight

100 g (4 oz) dried black-eye beans, soaked overnight
1.1 litres (2 pints) vegetable stock
3 garlic cloves, skinned and chopped
2 bay leaves
15 ml (1 tbsp) corn oil
50 g (2 oz) unsmoked lean bacon, chopped
4 slices lean, boneless lamb, about 100 g (4 oz) each
1 bouquet garni
pepper, to taste
75 g (3 oz) fresh brown breadcrumbs
25 g (1 oz) rolled oats

1

Drain the beans, rinse well and drain again. Put into a large saucepan with the stock, garlic and bay leaves. Bring to the boil for 10–15 minutes, then cover.

2

Lower the heat and simmer for 45 minutes. Drain, reserving the cooking liquid, and set aside the beans. Discard the bay leaves.

3

Heat the oil in the rinsed pan and cook the bacon and lamb for 5 minutes, until the lamb is browned. Add the beans and cook for a further 2 minutes. Pour in half the reserved stock and add the bouquet garni and seasoning. Cover the gently simmer for 3 hours, gradually adding the remaining stock during this time.

4

Discard the bouquet garni, then turn the mixture into a 1.1 litre (2 pint) ovenproof dish. Mix the breadcrumbs with the rolled oats and sprinkle over the top.

5

Cook at 180°C (350°F) mark 4 for about 1 hour, until the topping is crisp and light golden brown. Serve the casserole piping hot.

GOODNESS GUIDE
MINERALS This dish is high in potassium. High-potassium, low-sodium diets are believed to help reduce high blood pressure
PROTEIN The lean lamb and pulses are low-fat sources of protein
VITAMINS The meat, pulses, breadcrumbs and oats provide a wide range of B-complex vitamins, which are involved in the synthesis of red blood cells

STUFFED SEA TROUT

SERVES 4 535 calories per serving
PREPARATION 15 minutes
COOKING 40 minutes

1.4 kg (3 lb) sea trout, cleaned and boned,
with head removed
75 ml (3 fl oz) dry white wine

FENNEL AND ALMOND STUFFING
25 g (1 oz) polyunsaturated margarine
½ small onion, skinned and finely chopped
1 small fennel bulb, trimmed and
finely chopped
1 garlic clove, skinned and crushed
50 g (2 oz) fresh wholemeal breadcrumbs
50 g (2 oz) flaked almonds, toasted and
finely chopped
grated rind and juice of ½ lemon
pepper, to taste

———1———

Make the stuffing. Melt the margarine in a non-stick frying pan. Cook the onion, fennel and garlic for about 5 minutes, until soft. Stir in the breadcrumbs, almonds, lemon rind and juice and season.

———2———

Open out the fish and spread the stuffing evenly along one side. Fold over and put on a lightly greased piece of aluminium foil large enough to enclose the fish. Pour the wine over and seal the foil edges together. Carefully transfer to a roasting pan.

———3———

Cook at 190°C (375°F) mark 5 for 35–40 minutes, until the fish is cooked through and the skin flakes easily when tested with a fork. Open out the foil and carefully transfer the fish to a serving dish, then pour over any cooking juices and serve.

GOODNESS GUIDE
PROTEIN Sea trout, in common with most fish, is an excellent source of protein
SALT Fennel, garlic and lemon help bring out the full flavour of the fish so there is no need to add any salt
VITAMINS The fish, bread and almonds are high in B vitamins
FIBRE The wholemeal breadcrumbs and almonds in the stuffing are high in fibre

TURKEY TUSCANY

SERVES 4 640 calories per serving
PREPARATION 10 minutes
COOKING 40 minutes

40 g (1½ oz) polyunsaturated margarine
700 g (1½ lb) turkey escalopes, skinned and
cut into strips
1 garlic clove, skinned and crushed
1 onion, skinned and thinly sliced
1 green pepper, cored, seeded and cut into
thin strips
1 yellow or red pepper, cored, seeded and
cut into thin strips
2 courgettes, thinly sliced
75 g (3 oz) button mushrooms, sliced
4 tomatoes, roughly chopped
10 ml (2 tsp) dried oregano
15 ml (1 tbsp) chopped fresh basil or 7.5 ml
(½ tbsp) dried
150 ml (¼ pint) chicken stock
salt and pepper, to taste
30 ml (2 tbsp) tomato purée
350 g (12 oz) spinach noodles
basil sprigs, to garnish (optional)

———1———

Melt 15 g (½ oz) of the margarine in a large non-stick frying pan, add the turkey strips and cook for 5 minutes. Remove from the pan and set aside.

———2———

Melt the remaining margarine in the pan. Add the garlic, onion, peppers and courgettes and cook gently for about 5 minutes, until soft.

———3———

Add the mushrooms, tomatoes, herbs, chicken stock, turkey strips, and seasoning. Cover and cook for 20 minutes. Remove the lid, add tomato purée and cook for a further 10 minutes.

———4———

Meanwhile, cook the noodles in boiling water for 8–10 minutes or until tender.

———5———

Drain well and place on a warmed serving dish. Top with the turkey mixture and garnish with basil sprigs. Serve at once.

GOODNESS GUIDE
PROTEIN Like chicken, turkey is a good low-fat source of animal protein
FAT Turkey has an even lower fat content than chicken—the skinned meat is only about 3 per cent fat, and of this a high proportion is polyunsaturated
FIBRE The vegetables provide this dish with plenty of fibre

SPINACH AND EGG CRUMBLE

SERVES 4 410 calories per serving
PREPARATION 20 minutes
COOKING 15–20 minutes

1 onion, skinned and chopped
15 g (½ oz) polyunsaturated margarine
2 garlic cloves, skinned and crushed
450 g (1 lb) chopped frozen spinach, thawed
5 ml (1 tsp) grated nutmeg
pepper, to taste
4 eggs

CRUMBLE
100 g (4 oz) plain wholemeal flour
50 g (2 oz) plain flour
5 ml (1 tsp) mustard powder
pinch of cayenne pepper
50 g (2 oz) polyunsaturated margarine
50 g (2 oz) mature Cheddar cheese, grated

———1———

Put the onion and margarine in a saucepan over a gentle heat. Cover and cook until the onion is translucent, shaking the pan occasionally to prevent sticking.

———2———

Add the garlic, spinach, nutmeg and seasoning and cook gently for 2–3 minutes, stirring occasionally.

———3———

Meanwhile, prepare the crumble. Mix the flours with the mustard powder and cayenne pepper and rub in the margarine and cheese.

———4———

Divide the spinach mixture between 4 small heatproof dishes, making a well in the centre of each. Break an egg into each and cover with the crumble mixture.

———5———

Bake at 200°C (400°F) mark 6 for 15–20 minutes, until the crumble begins to brown and the eggs are set but not too hard.

GOODNESS GUIDE
FIBRE The spinach and the wholemeal flour in the crumble combine to give the dish a high-fibre content
MINERALS Spinach is very high in both iron and calcium, as are eggs
VITAMINS Eggs are rich in A, D, E and B vitamins. The vitamin C in the spinach helps the body absorb the iron more easily

70

TURKEY TUSCANY

SPINACH AND EGG CRUMBLE

STUFFED SEA TROUT

71

CARROT, ONION AND EGG LOAF

MAKES 12 SLICES 95 calories each
PREPARATION 15–20 minutes
COOKING 1¼ hours
COOLING 1 hour

**1 parsnip, peeled and halved
2 carrots, scrubbed and grated
2 courgettes, trimmed and grated
2 onions, skinned and chopped
100 g (4 oz) fresh wholemeal breadcrumbs
salt and pepper, to taste
1 egg, beaten
100 g (4 oz) Double Gloucester or mature
Cheddar cheese, grated
3 eggs, hard-boiled and shelled**

———1———
Lightly grease a 900 g (2 lb) loaf tin
and line with lightly greased greaseproof paper. Cook the parsnip in
boiling water for 5 minutes. Drain
and leave to cool slightly, then grate.

———2———
Put the parsnip, carrots and courgettes into a bowl. Mix in the onions,
breadcrumbs and seasoning. Add
the beaten egg and 50 g (2 oz) of
the grated cheese. Combine the
ingredients thoroughly.

———3———
Place one-third of the vegetable
mixture in the tin and spread out
evenly. Arrange the hard-boiled eggs
down the centre.

———4———
Cover with the remaining vegetable
mixture and press firmly to level the
surface. Sprinkle over the remaining
cheese and press lightly.

———5———
Bake, on a baking sheet, at 180°C
(350°F) mark 4 for 1 hour. If
necessary, cover loaf with foil during
cooking to prevent overbrowning.

———6———
Leave the loaf to cool in the tin for 1
hour. To serve, turn out on to a
serving plate and remove lining
paper, then slice.

MICROWAVE Lightly grease a 900 g
(2 lb) loaf tin. Put parsnip into a
bowl with 45 ml (3 tbsp) water.
Cover, cook 100% (High)
2 minutes. Drain, cool, grate.
Complete steps 2, 3, and 4 omitting
cheese on top. Cover, cook 100%
(High) 13 minutes, turning tin 3
times. Add cheese on top, cover,
cook further 2–3 minutes. Cool,
turn out, remove paper. Serve.

GOODNESS GUIDE
PROTEIN The eggs and cheese provide a
good serving of protein
VITAMINS The eggs, cheese and
breadcrumbs provide B vitamins
MINERALS Eggs and wholemeal breadcrumbs
provide iron, calcium and also zinc which is
necessary for healthy skin and
reproduction. Zinc deficiency leads to loss
of taste

SPICY SCALLOPS

*Serve these delicious scallops on a
bed of steamed, shredded
Chinese leaves.*

SERVES 4 160 calories per serving
PREPARATION 10 minutes
COOKING 6–8 minutes

**350 g (12 oz) queen scallops, fresh or frozen,
thawed
10 ml (2 tsp) Chinese sweet chilli sauce
100 g (4 oz) carrots, scrubbed
3 celery sticks
15 ml (1 tbsp) dry sherry
15 ml (1 tbsp) soy sauce
5 ml (1 tsp) tomato purée
30 ml (2 tbsp) corn oil
5 ml (1 tsp) grated fresh root ginger
15 ml (1 tbsp) chopped spring onion**

———1———
Mix the scallops with the chilli
sauce and set aside. Cut the carrots
and celery into thin matchsticks. Mix
the sherry, soy sauce and tomato
purée with 30 ml (2 tbsp) water.

SPICY SCALLOPS

CARROT, ONION AND EGG LOAF

2

Heat half the oil in a large frying pan or wok. Add the carrot and celery and stir-fry over a high heat for 1 minute. Remove vegetables from pan with a slotted spoon and set aside.

3

Heat the remaining oil in the pan, then add the ginger and spring onion and stir-fry briefly over high heat. Add the scallops and turn them in the oil to seal them on all sides.

4

Lower the heat to medium, add the soy sauce mixture to the pan and stir well. Return the vegetables to the pan and stir well. Stir-fry for 3–4 minutes, until the scallops feel firm. Serve the dish hot.

GOODNESS GUIDE

MINERALS Rich in minerals, scallops provide calcium, magnesium and potassium—all necessary for nerve impulse and muscle contraction and relaxation. They are also an excellent source of iron, one serving supplying a quarter of the daily recommended amount for adults of 10 milligrams

CHINESE CHICKEN WITH RICE

SERVES 4   360 calories per serving
PREPARATION 10 minutes
COOKING 45 minutes

75 g (3 oz) brown rice
30 ml (2 tbsp) corn or olive oil
1 garlic clove, skinned and crushed
1 onion, skinned and thinly sliced
1 large red or green pepper, cored, seeded and cut into thin strips
75 g (3 oz) button mushrooms, sliced
450 g (1 lb) cooked chicken meat, skinned and cut into strips
3–4 canned water chestnuts or bamboo shoots, sliced
225 g (8 oz) fresh beansprouts (optional)
10 ml (2 tsp) cornflour
15 ml (1 tbsp) soy sauce
150 ml ($\frac{1}{4}$ pint) chicken stock
15 ml (1 tbsp) dry sherry
lime slices and fresh coriander, to garnish

1

Put the brown rice in 450 ml ($\frac{3}{4}$ pint) boiling water. Cover and simmer for about 30 minutes, until tender and liquid has been absorbed.

2

Heat the oil in a large frying pan or wok. Add the garlic, onion, red or green pepper and mushrooms. Cook for 3 minutes, stirring.

3

Add the rice and cook for 2 minutes. Stir in the chicken, water chestnuts or bamboo shoots and beansprouts if using. Cook for 2–3 minutes, stirring frequently.

4

Dissolve the cornflour in the soy sauce and mix with the chicken stock and sherry. Add to the pan and bring to the boil, stirring. Cook for 2–3 minutes, stirring all the time, until the liquid has thickened. Garnish and serve.

GOODNESS GUIDE

FAT Only a little oil has been used in this dish to keep it low in fat
FIBRE The brown rice and vegetables provide a good serving
VITAMINS Vitamin C is provided by all the fresh vegetables. B vitamins are present in the chicken, brown rice and beansprouts

CHINESE CHICKEN WITH RICE

73

CURRIED WHITE FISH

SERVES 4 245 calories per serving
PREPARATION 10 minutes
COOKING About 20 minutes

30 ml (2 tbsp) corn oil
1 onion, skinned and finely chopped
1 garlic clove, skinned and crushed
10–15 ml (2–3 tsp) mild curry paste
5 ml (1 tsp) coriander seeds, crushed
200 ml (7 fl oz) fish or chicken stock
5 ml (1 tsp) cornflour
200 ml (7 fl oz) low-fat natural yogurt
finely grated rind of $\frac{1}{2}$ lime
450 g (1 lb) thick haddock fillet, skinned and
cut into 2.5 cm (1 inch) cubes
100 g (4 oz) button mushrooms, sliced
pepper, to taste
30 ml (2 tbsp) olive oil
$\frac{1}{2}$ head Chinese leaves, finely shredded
juice of 1 lime
10 ml (2 tsp) chopped fresh coriander
15 ml (1 tbsp) toasted pumpkin seeds,
sprigs of fresh coriander and thin wedges of
lime, to garnish

——— 1 ———
Heat the corn oil in a saucepan and cook the onion for 3 minutes. Add the garlic, curry paste and coriander seeds and cook for a further 1 minute. Stir in the stock and bring to simmering point.

——— 2 ———
Mix the cornflour with 15 ml (1 tbsp) water to make a smooth paste and stir into the yogurt. Blend into the hot stock mixture. Add the lime rind, haddock, mushrooms and seasoning. Cover and simmer gently for 15 minutes.

——— 3 ———
Meanwhile, heat the olive oil in a large deep frying pan or wok. Add the Chinese leaves, lime juice and chopped coriander and stir-fry for 3–4 minutes.

——— 4 ———
Spoon the hot fish curry on to a serving dish. Sprinkle with the pumpkin seeds and garnish with coriander sprigs and lime wedges. Serve with the stir-fried Chinese leaves.

GOODNESS GUIDE
MINERALS Fish, vegetables, seeds and yogurt are high in potassium which is vital for nerve transmission, digestion, growth and body fluid balance
VITAMINS The fish, yogurt and pumpkin seeds provide B vitamins and the vegetables and herbs are rich in vitamin C

RATATOUILLE CHEESE PIE

SERVES 4 490 calories per serving
PREPARATION 15 minutes
COOKING 1 hour
RISING 40 minutes

30 ml (2 tbsp) corn oil
1 onion, skinned and chopped
2 garlic cloves, skinned and crushed
1 aubergine, sliced
2 courgettes, trimmed and sliced
$\frac{1}{2}$ red pepper, cored, seeded and chopped
$\frac{1}{2}$ green pepper, cored, seeded and chopped
450 g (1 lb) tomatoes, chopped
2.5 ml ($\frac{1}{2}$ tsp) dried thyme
1.25 ml ($\frac{1}{4}$ tsp) ground coriander
15 ml (1 tbsp) chopped fresh parsley
150 g (5 oz) Mozzarella cheese, diced
salt and pepper, to taste

PASTRY
225 g (8 oz) plain wholemeal flour
1.25 ml ($\frac{1}{4}$ tsp) salt
2.5 ml ($\frac{1}{2}$ tsp) easy blend yeast
1 egg, size 3, beaten
30 ml (2 tbsp) corn oil
sesame seeds, for sprinkling

——— 1 ———
Lightly grease a rectangular 20 × 25 cm (8 × 10 inch) ovenproof dish and set aside. To make the pastry, place the flour, salt and yeast in a bowl. Add a third of the beaten egg and the oil and mix well, adding about 100 ml (4 fl oz) tepid water to form a fairly stiff dough. Knead lightly. Cover the bowl with a clean cloth and leave to rise in a warm place for 40 minutes.

——— 2 ———
Meanwhile, make the filling. Heat the oil in a large saucepan or frying pan. Add the onion and cook for about 5 minutes, until soft. Add the garlic and cook for 1–2 minutes, then mix in the sliced aubergine, sliced courgettes, chopped red and green peppers and chopped tomatoes. Add the thyme and coriander. Cover, and cook over moderate heat for 30 minutes, stirring occasionally.

——— 3 ———
Remove the lid, stir, then boil the mixture vigorously for 1–2 minutes to thicken. Pour into the ovenproof dish and mix in the parsley, cheese and seasoning.

——— 4 ———
Knock back the dough and roll out thinly on a lightly floured surface. Use to cover the vegetable mixture and brush with half the remaining beaten egg. Bake at 200°C (400°F) mark 6 for 15 minutes.

——— 5 ———
Brush with the remaining egg and sprinkle over sesame seeds. Bake for a further 5 minutes. Serve hot.

GOODNESS GUIDE
FAT The yeast pastry has a relatively low fat content
FIBRE Wholemeal pastry and the vegetables provide a large amount of fibre
MINERALS Wholemeal flour and cheese are excellent sources of calcium

RATATOUILLE CHEESE PIE

STUFFED SPRING GREEN PARCELS

Brown rice and almonds give a good texture to the high-fibre stuffing in the cabbage parcels.

SERVES 4   245 calories per serving
PREPARATION   25 minutes
COOKING   1 hour 20 minutes

50 g (2 oz) brown rice
350 g (12 oz) large spring green leaves,
washed and stalks removed
2.5 ml (½ tsp) olive oil
1 onion, skinned and chopped
75 g (3 oz) blanched almonds,
chopped and toasted
15 ml (1 tbsp) chopped fresh parsley
5 ml (1 tsp) grated lemon rind
25 g (1 oz) raisins, rinsed
2.5 ml (½ tsp) paprika
salt and pepper, to taste
225 g (8 oz) button mushrooms, sliced
225 ml (8 fl oz) vegetable stock
15 g (½ oz) polyunsaturated margarine
15 g (½ oz) plain flour
75 ml (3 fl oz) low-fat natural yogurt

— 1 —

Put the rice in a saucepan of 300 ml (½ pint) boiling water, cover and simmer for 30 minutes, until tender and all the water has been absorbed.

— 2 —

Meanwhile, blanch the spring green leaves in boiling water for 2 minutes. Drain and rinse under cold water. Leave to drain well.

— 3 —

Heat the oil in a non-stick frying pan and cook the onion over gentle heat for 5 minutes. Drain on absorbent kitchen paper to remove excess oil. Place in a bowl and add the rice, nuts, parsley, lemon rind, raisins, paprika and seasoning. Mix well.

— 4 —

Lay out 8 large spring green leaves on a work surface and arrange the remaining leaves on top, to provide a casing for the stuffing. Divide the stuffing between the leaves, placing it in mounds in the centre. Fold the sides of the leaves over and roll up to form small neat parcels.

— 5 —

Put the mushrooms in the base of a shallow ovenproof dish just large enough to hold the parcels. Arrange the parcels on top and pour in the stock. Cover and cook at 190°C (375°F) mark 5 for 40 minutes.

— 6 —

Remove the vegetable parcels to a serving plate and keep warm. Strain the stock into a pan, reserving the mushrooms. Blend together the margarine and flour and add to the stock in small pieces. Simmer, stirring, for 1 minute or until thickened. Add the mushrooms and reheat for 1 minute.

— 7 —

Remove from the heat and stir in the yogurt. Pour over the spring green parcels and serve.

GOODNESS GUIDE

FIBRE Plenty of fibre is provided by the brown rice, nuts and vegetables
PROTEIN The combination of rice, nuts and yogurt gives a good source of protein
VITAMINS B-complex vitamins are present in the rice, nuts and yogurt. The spring greens and almonds are particularly rich in the B vitamin, folic acid

CURRIED WHITE FISH

STUFFED SPRING GREEN PARCELS

SALMON AND PRAWN LASAGNE

COLD SPICED PORK WITH NECTARINE

GADO GADO

GADO GADO

This traditional Indonesian salad is made of a mixture of cooked and raw vegetables which may be varied according to seasonal availability. It is served with a spicy sauce.

SERVES 4 260 calories per serving
PREPARATION 40 minutes
COOKING 15 minutes

100 g (4 oz) French beans, topped and tailed
225 g (8 oz) white cabbage, finely shredded
100 g (4 oz) carrots, scrubbed and cut into
matchsticks
100 g (4 oz) fresh beansprouts
5 cm (2 inch) piece cucumber, sliced
4 eggs, hard-boiled and sliced

PEANUT SAUCE
50 g (2 oz) desiccated coconut
15 ml (1 tbsp) corn or groundnut oil
1 small onion, skinned and finely chopped
75 g (3 oz) natural crunchy peanut butter
5 ml (1 tsp) hot chilli powder
5 ml (1 tsp) light muscovado sugar
15 ml (1 tbsp) lime juice

76

——— 1 ———

Bring a saucepan of water to the boil, add the beans and cook for 2 minutes. Add the cabbage and cook for a further 1 minute. Drain, then run under cold water until completely cold. Drain well.

——— 2 ———

Put the blanched vegetables in a large shallow bowl with the carrots and beansprouts and mix well. Arrange the cucumber and eggs slices alternately over the vegetables. Chill while preparing the sauce.

——— 3 ———

To make the peanut sauce, place the coconut in a bowl and pour over 300 ml (½ pint) boiling water. Leave to infuse for 20 minutes, then strain through a sieve over a bowl, using a wooden spoon to press out as much liquid as possible. Reserve the liquid and discard the coconut.

——— 4 ———

Heat the oil in a saucepan, add the onion and cook for about 5 minutes until softened. Add the peanut butter, chilli powder and sugar and mix well. Stir in the strained coconut liquid and bring to the boil. Simmer for 5 minutes until the sauce has thickened. Remove from the heat, stir in the lime juice and leave to cool. Serve the salad with some of the sauce poured over the remainder served separately.

MICROWAVE Put beans into a bowl with 300 ml (½ pint) boiling water. Cover, cook 100% (High) 2 minutes. Add cabbage, cook 100% (High) 2 minutes. Complete steps 1, 2 and 3. Put oil and onion into a bowl. Cover, cook 100% (High) 4 minutes until softened. Mix in peanut butter, chilli powder and sugar. Add coconut liquid. Cook, uncovered, 100% (High) 5–6 minutes until thickened. Complete recipe.

GOODNESS GUIDE

VITAMINS There is vitamin C in the fresh vegetables, and B-complex and E vitamins in the eggs and peanuts. Vitamin E is frequently destroyed by commercial cooking and processing, deep frying and deep freezing
PROTEIN The eggs and peanut butter provide a good supply of protein

---

SALMON AND PRAWN LASAGNE

SERVES 4 495 calories per serving
PREPARATION 20 minutes
COOKING 50 minutes

10 ml (2 tsp) corn oil
450 ml (¾ pint) semi-skimmed milk
1 small onion, skinned and studded with
4 cloves
2 blades mace
4 black peppercorns
7.5 cm (3 inch) piece carrot, scrubbed
7.5 cm (3 inch) piece celery
1 bay leaf
150 g (5 oz) wholemeal lasagne
50 g (2 oz) polyunsaturated margarine
25 g (1 oz) plain wholemeal flour
25 g (1 oz) plain flour
15 ml (1 tbsp) chopped fresh dill or
10 ml (2 tsp) dried
220 g (7½ oz) can red or pink salmon, drained
and roughly flaked
100 g (4 oz) white crab meat, flaked
100 g (4 oz) peeled cooked prawns
30 ml (2 tbsp) grated Parmesan cheese
unpeeled prawns and dill, to garnish

——— 1 ———

Grease a 1.7 litre (3 pint) square or rectangular ovenproof dish with 5 ml (1 tsp) of the oil. Put the milk into a saucepan with the onion, mace, peppercorns, carrot, celery and bay leaf. Bring to simmering, then remove from the heat, cover and set aside while cooking pasta.

——— 2 ———

Add the remaining oil to a large saucepan of boiling water. Add the lasagne strips and cook for 8–10 minutes or until just tender. Drain.

——— 3 ———

Strain the milk. Melt the margarine in a saucepan, stir in the flours and cook for 2 minutes. Remove from the heat and gradually stir in the milk. Return the pan to the heat, bring to the boil, stirring constantly, and cook until the sauce is thick and smooth. Remove from the heat and mix in the dill, salmon, crab meat and prawns.

——— 4 ———

Put one-third of the fish sauce in the base of the greased dish and cover with half the lasagne. Top with a further third of the sauce, cover with the remaining lasagne, then finish with sauce. Sprinkle with the Parmesan cheese. Cook at 180°C (350°F) mark 4 for 35–40 minutes or until golden brown. Serve hot, garnished with prawns and dill.

COLD SPICED PORK WITH NECTARINE

SERVES 4 245 calories per serving
PREPARATION 15 minutes
COOKING 40 minutes
MARINATING 1 hour

30 ml (2 tbsp) clear honey
45 ml (3 tbsp) soy sauce, preferably
naturally-fermented shoyu
pinch of Chinese five-spice powder
(optional)
450 g (1 lb) pork fillet, trimmed of excess fat
1 ripe nectarine
watercress, to garnish

——— 1 ———

For the marinade, mix together the honey, soy sauce and five-spice powder, if using. Place the pork in a dish. Pour over the marinade and rub it well into the meat. Leave to marinate for 1 hour, turning occasionally.

——— 2 ———

Place the pork on a wire rack over a roasting tin half filled with hot water. Roast at 180°C (350°F) mark 4 for 20 minutes. Turn the meat over, brush with more marinade, then return to the oven for 20 minutes, until the meat is cooked through and tender. Set aside to cool.

——— 3 ———

Thinly slice the pork and halve, stone and cut the nectarine into thin slices. Arrange the pork and nectarine slices alternately, radiating from the centre of a serving dish. Garnish with watercress.

GOODNESS GUIDE

COLD SPICED PORK WITH NECTARINE
FAT Using lean pork and no oil for cooking makes this dish low in fat
VITAMINS Pork provides B-complex vitamins, especially thiamine. Vitamins A and C are supplied by the nectarine

SALMON AND PRAWN LASAGNE
FIBRE Wholemeal pasta and flour give this dish a high fibre content
MINERALS Large amounts of calcium are provided by the prawns, milk, cheese and flour

MAIN DISHES

BEEF OLIVES WITH MUSHROOM STUFFING

SERVES 4 300 calories per serving
PREPARATION About 15 minutes
COOKING 45 minutes

8 thin slices topside, 75 g (3 oz) each
15 g ($\frac{1}{2}$ oz) polyunsaturated margarine
150 ml ($\frac{1}{4}$ pint) dry red wine
salt and pepper, to taste
15 ml (1 tbsp) tomato purée
finely chopped fresh parsley, to garnish

MUSHROOM STUFFING
75 g (3 oz) button mushrooms, finely
chopped
5 ml (1 tsp) Dijon mustard
1 small carrot, scrubbed and grated
1 courgette, grated
15 ml (1 tbsp) bran
10 ml (2 tsp) tomato purée

――――1――――
Beat the beef slices between sheets of damp greaseproof paper until almost double in size.

――――2――――
To make the stuffing, mix together mushrooms, mustard, carrot, courgette, bran and 10 ml (2 tsp) tomato purée. Divide mixture between the beef slices and spread evenly over. Roll up and secure at both ends with fine string.

――――3――――
Melt the margarine in a flameproof casserole and brown the prepared beef olives over a medium heat. Pour over the red wine and seasoning. Cover and cook for 45 minutes, until tender. Transfer beef olives to a serving dish, discard the string and keep hot.

――――4――――
Skim the fat from the cooking liquid, then add the remaining tomato purée and adjust seasoning. Heat through and pour over beef olives. Garnish and serve at once.

MICROWAVE Follow the recipe to step 3. Use a browning dish to brown the prepared beef olives with the margarine. Continue cooking in the browning dish if large enough or arrange them in a single layer in a dish. Pour over the wine and season. Cover and cook at 60% (Medium) 15 minutes, until tender. Stand 5 minutes, then finish as the recipe but after pouring over the sauce, cover and cook at 100% (High) 2 minutes.

GOODNESS GUIDE
MINERALS Red meat is an excellent source of iron. The beef in its dish contains over half an adult's daily recommended requirement
FAT Beef can be fatty, but topside is one of the leaner cuts. Be sure to trim any visible fat from the meat before it is cooked

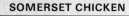

SOMERSET CHICKEN

SERVES 4 520 calories per serving
PREPARATION About 15 minutes
COOKING 1$\frac{1}{4}$ hours

4 chicken breasts, about 175 g (6 oz) each,
skinned, boned and cut into bite-sized
pieces
30 ml (2 tbsp) plain wholemeal flour
2 onions, skinned and chopped
175 g (6 oz) button mushrooms, thinly sliced
10 ml (2 tsp) dried mixed herbs
30 ml (2 tbsp) finely chopped fresh parsley
salt and pepper, to taste
900 g (2 lb) floury potatoes, scrubbed and
thinly sliced
300 ml ($\frac{1}{2}$ pint) dry cider
300 ml ($\frac{1}{2}$ pint) chicken or vegetable stock
parsley sprig, to garnish

――――1――――
Toss the chicken in the flour and place in a casserole. Cover with the onions, mushrooms, herbs, chopped parsley and seasoning.

78

RATATOUILLE PASTIES

SOMERSET CHICKEN

—— 2 ——

Arrange the potato slices neatly over the top, then pour over the cider and stock. The potatoes should be just covered with the liquid. Add extra stock if necessary

—— 3 ——

Cover and cook at 190°C (375°F) mark 5 for 1 hour. Remove cover and cook for a further 15 minutes, until browned on top. Serve hot, garnished with a parsley sprig.

GOODNESS GUIDE

SOMERSET CHICKEN

FAT Using lean skinned chicken breasts cooked this way, with no fats added, gives the dish a very low fat content

SALT With plenty of herbs for flavouring, salt can be kept to a minimum

FIBRE The onions, potatoes and wholemeal flour supply good amounts of fibre

RATATOUILLE PASTIES

VITAMINS The flour, cheese and egg provide plenty of B vitamins, while the egg and margarine supply vitamins A, D and E

FIBRE The aubergines, courgettes and wholemeal flour make these a good source of fibre.

RATATOUILLE PASTIES

Good hot or cold, these pasties add nourishment to a packed lunch or picnic.

MAKES 4 495 calories each
PREPARATION About 25 minutes
COOKING 20–30 minutes

175 g (6 oz) plain flour
175 g (6 oz) plain wholemeal flour
pinch of salt
50 g (2 oz) polyunsaturated margarine
50 g (2 oz) mature Cheddar cheese, finely grated
1 egg, beaten, to glaze
25 g (1 oz) Parmesan cheese, finely grated

RATATOUILLE FILLING
1 small aubergine, diced
1 courgette, thinly sliced
1 onion, skinned and chopped
1 small green pepper, cored, seeded and cut into strips
225 g (8 oz) can tomatoes
5 ml (1 tsp) ground coriander
5 ml (1 tsp) dried oregano
15 ml (1 tbsp) tomato purée

—— 1 ——

Place the filling ingredients, except tomato purée, in a saucepan. Cover, bring to the boil, lower heat and simmer for 20 minutes, stirring.

—— 2 ——

Uncover, add tomato purée and cook for a further 5 minutes, until the mixture has thickened. Set aside the filling to cool.

—— 3 ——

Meanwhile, make the pastry. Place the flours and salt in a bowl and rub in the margarine until the mixture resembles fine breadcrumbs. Stir in the Cheddar cheese and 150 ml ($\frac{1}{4}$ pint) chilled water. Mix lightly to form a soft dough.

—— 4 ——

Knead the dough on a lightly floured surface and divide into 4 equal-sized pieces. Roll out each into a 20 cm (8 inch) round.

—— 5 ——

Place one quarter of the filling in the centre of each pastry round. Dampen the edges and fold over to form a pasty. Seal edges well, flute and make a small hole in the top of each so the pasties do not burst open during baking.

—— 6 ——

Lightly grease a baking sheet. Transfer the pasties to the baking sheet, then brush with beaten egg and dredge with Parmesan cheese. Cook at 190°C (375°F) mark 5 for 20–30 minutes, until golden brown and cooked through. Serve the pasties hot or cold.

APRICOT-STUFFED LAMB

BUTTER BEANS AND PARSLEY

PRAWN PILAFF

PRAWN PILAFF

The pleasantly nutty flavour of brown rice complements the prawns.

SERVES 4 560 calories per serving
PREPARATION About 10 minutes
COOKING About 45 minutes

25 g (1 oz) polyunsaturated margarine
2 onions, skinned and chopped
2 garlic cloves, skinned and crushed
350 g (12 oz) brown rice
900 ml (1½ pints) hot chicken stock
1 red pepper, cored, seeded and diced
1 green pepper, cored, seeded and diced
225 g (8 oz) frozen sweetcorn kernels
salt and pepper, to taste
450 g (1 lb) peeled cooked prawns, thawed if frozen
30 ml (2 tbsp) lemon juice

———1———

Melt the margarine, then add the onions and garlic and cook 3–5 minutes, until soft.

———2———

Add the rice and cook, stirring, for 1 minute. Pour in the stock, stir well, cover and cook over a low heat for 30 minutes, until the rice is almost cooked and tender.

———3———

Uncover, add peppers and sweetcorn and season. Cook for a further 10 minutes, until all the liquid has been absorbed and the rice is tender. Stir in the prawns and lemon juice and heat through for 2–3 minutes.

MICROWAVE Place the margarine, onion and garlic in a dish, cover and cook at 100% (High) 4 minutes. Stir in the rice and stock. Cover and cook at 100% (High) 14 minutes, then at 60% (Medium) 8 minutes. Add the peppers, sweetcorn and seasoning. Cover and cook at 100% (High) 4 minutes. Stir in prawns and juice and cook 2 minutes.

GOODNESS GUIDE

FAT The overall fat content of this satisfying dish is very low. Prawns make a useful low-fat source of protein
FIBRE The brown rice and sweetcorn provide large amounts of fibre
MINERALS Prawns are rich in iodine, zinc and other essential minerals

APRICOT-STUFFED LAMB

Leg of lamb is the leanest lamb cut. Because there is so little waste it is better value than less expensive cuts.

SERVES 4–6 515–345 calories per serving
PREPARATION 20 minutes
COOKING 1½ hours

1.6–1.8 kg (3½–4 lb) leg of lamb, well trimmed and boned
apricot halves and watercress sprigs, to garnish

APRICOT AND WALNUT STUFFING
50 g (2 oz) ready-to-eat dried apricots, rinsed
40 g (1½ oz) walnut halves, chopped
50 g (2 oz) fresh wholemeal breadcrumbs
1 egg, size 6
5 ml (1 tsp) dried mixed herbs
salt and pepper, to taste

———1———

To make the stuffing, chop the apricots and put in a bowl with the walnuts, breadcrumbs, egg and herbs. Mix well and season.

———2———

Spoon the stuffing into the boned cavity in the lamb, packing down. Using fine string and a trussing needle, sew up the cavity. Place the joint on a meat rack in a roasting pan and cover with foil.

———3———

Cook at 200°C (400°F) mark 6 for 1½ hours, until cooked through. Remove the foil 30 minutes before the end of cooking time to brown the meat. Stand in a warm place for 10 minutes before carving, garnish and serve.

MICROWAVE Follow the recipe to step 3. Weigh the stuffed joint, place on a roasting rack in a dish and cover with greaseproof paper. Cook at 60% (Medium) about 10 minutes per 450 g (1 lb). Cover in foil and stand 15–20 minutes before carving.

GOODNESS GUIDE

FAT Although lamb is quite a fatty meat, trimming before cooking and roasting on a rack helps reduce the fat content
FIBRE The stuffing adds a good amount of fibre to the dish. Breadcrumbs, dried apricots and walnuts are all excellent sources

BUTTER BEANS AND PARSLEY

SERVES 4 400 calories per serving
PREPARATION 20 minutes
COOKING 30 minutes

3 leeks, trimmed and thickly sliced
3 courgettes, thickly sliced
25 g (1 oz) polyunsaturated margarine
25 g (1 oz) plain flour
450 ml (¾ pint) semi-skimmed milk
salt and pepper, to taste
two 400 g (14 oz) cans butter beans, drained and rinsed
90 ml (6 tbsp) chopped fresh parsley
25 g (1 oz) fresh wholemeal breadcrumbs
50 g (2 oz) mature Cheddar cheese, grated

———1———

Cook the leeks and courgettes in 2.5 cm (½ inch) boiling water until just tender, then drain.

———2———

Melt the margarine in a saucepan, then add the flour and cook for 1 minute. Add the milk, stirring until thick. Bring to the boil, lower the heat and season.

———3———

Add the leeks, courgettes, butter beans and 60 ml (4 tbsp) of the parsley to the sauce and mix well. Turn the mixture into an ovenproof serving dish.

———4———

Mix together breadcrumbs, cheese and remaining parsley and sprinkle over evenly. Bake at 200°C (400°F) mark 6 for 30 minutes.

MICROWAVE Place the leeks in a dish with 60 ml (4 tbsp) water, cover and cook at 100% (High) 5 minutes. Add the courgettes, cover and cook 6 minutes. Leave covered while making the sauce. Melt the margarine in a bowl at 100% (High) 30 seconds. Stir in the flour, then the milk. Cook for 5 minutes, whisking after 2 minutes, then every minute. Follow step 3, using a 1.1 litre (2 pint) dish. In step 4 cook at 100% (High) 3 minutes.

GOODNESS GUIDE

PROTEIN This vegetable dish is high protein and makes a good alternative to a meat main course
FAT Semi-skimmed milk and a small amount of cheese is used to help keep the overall fat content low
FIBRE The vegetables, beans and breadcrumbs provide fibre

LAYERED FISH TERRINE

STUFFED CABBAGE ROLLS

STUFFED CABBAGE ROLLS

Lentils are a good source of protein; unlike many other pulses, they do not have to be soaked before cooking.

MAKES 8   100 calories each
PREPARATION   30 minutes
COOKING   40 minutes

175 g (6 oz) green lentils
8 large green cabbage leaves
1 large onion, skinned and finely chopped
15 ml (1 tbsp) sunflower oil
30 ml (2 tbsp) tomato purée
1 red pepper, cored, seeded and
finely chopped
5 ml (1 tsp) ground mixed spice
400 g (14 oz) can chopped tomatoes
150 ml ($\frac{1}{4}$ pint) vegetable stock
few drops of Tabasco sauce or to taste

———1———
Place the lentils in a small saucepan, add cold water to cover and bring to the boil. Lower the heat and simmer for about 20 minutes, until tender, then drain.

———2———
Meanwhile, in another saucepan, blanch the cabbage. Place in boiling water and cook for 4–5 minutes. Drain and set aside to cool.

———3———
In a clean saucepan cook the onion in the oil for about 3 minutes until soft. Add the tomato purée, red pepper and mixed spice and cook for 2–3 minutes, stirring occasionally.

Add the lentils and remove from the heat.

———4———
Place a little of the mixture into the centre of each cabbage leaf and fold to form a parcel. Place in a shallow ovenproof dish in a single layer.

———5———
Mix the tomatoes and their juice with the vegetable stock, season with a little Tabasco and pour over the parcels.

———6———
Cover with a piece of aluminium foil and bake at 180°C (350°F) mark 4 for 40 minutes, until tender. Serve immediately.

GOODNESS GUIDE
FIBRE All of the vegetables contribute a substantial amount of fibre

FAT Very little fat is used and that present is polyunsaturated

PROTEIN The lentils supply protein; serving this with yogurt or rice would make the protein more efficiently used by the body

LAYERED FISH TERRINE

The quantity of fish in this colourful terrine makes it rich in protein—and it is filling, too.

SERVES 4   245 calories per serving
PREPARATION   40–45 minutes
COOKING   1 hour 10 minutes

200 g (7 oz) can tuna in oil, drained and with
oil reserved
1 small onion, skinned and
roughly chopped
10 ml (2 tsp) tomato purée
2 eggs
anchovy essence, to taste
salt and pepper, to taste
225 g (8 oz) fresh haddock fillet
15 ml (1 tbsp) white wine vinegar
6 black peppercorns
1 bay leaf
40 g (1$\frac{1}{2}$ oz) plain flour
45 ml (3 tbsp) lemon juice
50 g (2 oz) French beans, thawed if frozen,
cut into 1 cm ($\frac{1}{2}$ inch) lengths
15 g ($\frac{1}{2}$ oz) polyunsaturated margarine
30 ml (2 tbsp) chopped fresh parsley

PIQUANT TURKEY DRUMSTICKS

remaining lemon juice. Bring to the boil, stirring, add the chopped parsley and cook for a further 2 minutes.

———11———

Turn the terrine out on to a serving dish; serve with the parsley sauce and garnish.

GOODNESS GUIDE

FAT Oily fish contain more fat than white fish but most of it is the preferred polyunsaturated type. The terrine's overall fat content is low

VITAMINS Both the haddock and the tuna provide some B vitamins; tuna is also rich in vitamin D

FIBRE The French beans add some fibre

PIQUANT TURKEY DRUMSTICKS

The spicy basting sauce in the recipe not only adds flavour, but also helps to keep the turkey meat moist.

MAKES 4 190 calories each
PREPARATION 10 minutes
COOKING 1 hour

30 ml (2 tbsp) tomato purée
30 ml (2 tbsp) Worcestershire sauce
15 ml (1 tbsp) red wine vinegar
30 ml (2 tbsp) sunflower oil
1 garlic clove, skinned and crushed
few drops Tabasco sauce (optional)
4 turkey drumsticks, weighing about
1½ kg (3 lb), skinned and scored
watercress, to garnish

———1———

Mix together the tomato purée, Worcestershire sauce, vinegar, oil, garlic and Tabasco. Rub well into the drumsticks, particularly where the flesh is scored.

———2———

Place on a wire rack set in a small roasting pan and cook with any remaining liquid at 190°C (375°F) mark 5 for about 1 hour. Baste with the liquid and turn occasionally, until the drumsticks begin to brown and the flesh shrinks away from the bones. Garnish with watercress and serve at once.

GOODNESS GUIDE

FAT Like chicken, turkey is a rich source of animal protein that is very low in fat. Only a little polyunsaturated oil is added here

VITAMINS Turkey supplies a range of B vitamins. There is also some A and C provided by the tomato purée

———1———

Line a 900 g (2 lb) loaf tin with lightly greased greaseproof paper. Put the reserved oil from the can of tuna in a frying pan with the onion. Cover and fry gently for 2–3 minutes or until the onion is soft.

———2———

Put the onion in a blender or food processor with the tuna, tomato purée, 1 egg and the anchovy essence. Add seasoning. Purée until smooth, then scrape into a bowl and set aside.

———3———

Put the haddock in a saucepan with 600 ml (1 pint) water, the vinegar, black peppercorns and bay leaf. Simmer for 15 minutes until the fish flakes when toasted with a fork.

———4———

Remove from the saucepan, reserving the cooking liquid, and cool slightly. Strain the cooking liquid and set aside.

———5———

Skin the haddock and put the flesh in the blender or food processor. Measure 100 ml (4 fl oz) cooking liquid from the haddock and set the rest aside for the sauce. Mix a little of this measured stock with 25 g (1 oz) of the flour to form a smooth paste, heating the rest of stock in a saucepan. Gradually pour the hot stock on to the flour paste, stirring

all the time. Return to the pan and bring to the boil, stirring constantly. Cook for 2–3 minutes to form a thick paste.

———6———

Add the mixture to the blender or food processor with the remaining egg, 30 ml (2 tbsp) lemon juice and seasoning and blend until smooth.

———7———

Place the beans in a little boiling water and cook for 2–3 minutes or until just tender, then drain.

———8———

Spread the haddock mixture into the prepared tin in an even layer. Sprinkle the beans over the haddock, then gently spread the tuna mixture over the top. Cover tightly with foil, place in a roasting tin and pour in enough hot water to come halfway up the sides of the loaf tin.

———9———

Cook at 200°C (400°F) mark 6 for 1 hour or until mixture is set. Leave to stand in the roasting tin for a further 5 minutes.

———10———

Meanwhile, make the sauce. Melt the margarine in a saucepan. Add the remaining flour and cook for 1 minute, stirring continuously. Remove from the heat and gradually stir in 300 ml (½ pint) of the reserved haddock cooking liquid and the

SPINACH BAKE

SERVES 4 425 calories per serving
PREPARATION 20 minutes
BAKING 30–35 minutes

225 g (8 oz) broccoli, in florets
450 g (1 lb) spinach, trimmed and rinsed
225 g (8 oz) fresh tagliatelle
20 g ($\frac{3}{4}$ oz) polyunsaturated margarine
20 g ($\frac{3}{4}$ oz) plain flour
400 ml (14 fl oz) semi-skimmed milk
75 g (3 oz) button mushrooms, sliced
salt and pepper, to taste
75 g (3 oz) Edam cheese, grated
30 ml (2 tbsp) fresh wholemeal breadcrumbs
15 ml (1 tbsp) chopped fresh basil or
oregano or 7.5 ml (1$\frac{1}{2}$ tsp) dried

———1———
Lightly grease an ovenproof dish and set aside. Blanch the broccoli in boiling water for 5 minutes. Drain, refresh in cold running water and drain again.

———2———
Cook the spinach in a covered saucepan with just the water clinging to the leaves for about 5 minutes, until just tender. Drain and press out excess moisture.

———3———
Meanwhile, put the tagliatelle in a saucepan of boiling water, cook for 4 minutes or until just tender. Drain.

———4———
Melt the margarine in a saucepan and stir in the flour. Cook over a gentle heat for 1 minute. Stir in the milk off the heat, then bring to the boil. Lower the heat and add the mushrooms and seasoning and simmer for 3 minutes.

———5———
Spread the spinach in the base of the ovenproof dish. Stir the broccoli and tagliatelle into the sauce with half the cheese, then spoon over the spinach. Sprinkle with the breadcrumbs, herbs and remaining cheese. Bake at 190°C (375°F) mark 5 for 30–35 minutes, until bubbling and golden. Serve immediately.

GOODNESS GUIDE
FIBRE A great deal of fibre is provided by the broccoli, spinach and wholemeal breadcrumbs
VITAMINS Vitamins A and C are contributed by the broccoli and spinach. The cheese, vegetables and flour contribute B complex vitamins
MINERALS Calcium is provided by the broccoli, spinach, milk and cheese, and iron by the broccoli and spinach

VEGETARIAN TOFU KEBABS

SERVES 4 205 calories per serving
PREPARATION 15 minutes
COOKING 8 minutes
CHILLING 3–4 hours

450 g (1 lb) tofu, cut into 2.5 cm
(1 inch) cubes
1 large red pepper, cored, seeded and cubed
1 large green pepper, cored, seeded
and cubed
grated rind and juice of 2 limes or 1 lemon
45 ml (3 tbsp) olive oil
salt and pepper, to taste
30 ml (2 tbsp) low-fat natural yogurt
30 ml (2 tbsp) soy sauce, preferably
naturally fermented shoyu
1 garlic clove, skinned and finely chopped
1.25 ml ($\frac{1}{4}$ tsp) ground cumin
1.25 ml ($\frac{1}{4}$ tsp) curry powder
8 cherry tomatoes or 4 tomatoes,
cut into wedges
shredded lettuce, to serve

———1———
Put the tofu and pepper cubes into a shallow dish. Mix together the lime rind and juice, olive oil, seasoning, yogurt, soy sauce, garlic and spices. Spoon evenly over the tofu and peppers. Cover and chill for 3–4 hours, turning the tofu and peppers occasionally.

———2———
Remove the tofu and pepper cubes from the marinade and thread on to skewers, alternating with the tomatoes. Grill for 3–4 minutes, turn, brush with the marinade and cook for a further 3–4 minutes. Serve on a bed of shredded lettuce.

GOODNESS GUIDE
FAT Tofu is a very low-fat source of protein and the olive oil is monounsaturated, so the overall saturated fat content is low
VITAMINS The fresh vegetables contribute vitamin C for maintaining bones and capillaries; the peppers are a particularly rich source
MINERALS Tofu contributes both calcium and iron

CHINESE-STYLE FISH

SERVES 4 415 calories per serving
PREPARATION 20 minutes
COOKING 40 minutes

2 whiting, each about 700 g (1$\frac{1}{2}$ lb), gutted
and cleaned
salt and pepper, to taste
30 ml (2 tbsp) chopped fresh coriander
1 cm ($\frac{1}{2}$ inch) piece fresh root ginger, peeled
and finely chopped or 1.25 ml ($\frac{1}{4}$ tsp)
ground ginger
grated rind and juice of 1 lemon
1 garlic clove, skinned and finely chopped
1 small yellow pepper, cored, seeded and
cut into thin strips
1 small red pepper, cored, seeded and cut
into thin strips
1 onion, skinned and thinly sliced
2 sticks celery, trimmed and finely chopped
45 ml (3 tbsp) olive oil
fresh coriander sprigs, to garnish

———1———
Season the fish inside and out. Mix together the coriander, ginger, lemon rind and garlic and press into the cavities of both fish.

———2———
Put a large piece of lightly greased foil on top of a baking sheet. Spread the vegetables evenly along the centre of the foil and put the fish on top. Sprinkle with the olive oil and lemon juice.

———3———
Pull the edges of the foil up over the fish, pinch together and seal. Cook at 190°C (375°F) mark 5 for 35 minutes. Fold back the foil and cook for a further 5 minutes. Garnish and serve at once.

MICROWAVE Follow step 1. In step 2 put fish in a baking dish or roasting bag with vegetables. In step 3 cover and cook 100% (High) 10 minutes, turning dish 2 or 3 times. Stand 4–5 minutes before serving.

GOODNESS GUIDE
FIBRE The vegetables provide a good amount of fibre
FAT The dish is low in saturated fat because whiting is a low-fat fish and olive oil is monounsaturated
VITAMINS All the fresh vegetables contribute vitamin C, and B complex vitamins are provided by the fish and vegetables

SPINACH BAKE

VEGETARIAN TOFU KEBABS

CHINESE-STYLE FISH

PAELLA

SERVES 4   835 calories per serving
PREPARATION 20 minutes
COOKING 1 hour 40 minutes

60 ml (4 tbsp) olive oil
4–6 chicken drumsticks, skinned
1 garlic clove, skinned and crushed
1 onion, skinned and chopped
225 g (8 oz) tomatoes, cut into wedges
1 red pepper, cored, seeded and diced
1 green pepper, cored, seeded and diced
100 g (4 oz) frozen peas
10 ml (2 tsp) ground turmeric
450 g (1 lb) brown rice
1.2 litres (2 pints) chicken stock
600 ml (1 pint) fresh mussels
100 g (4 oz) peeled cooked prawns
50 g (2 oz) flaked almonds, toasted
salt and pepper, to taste
lemon wedge, parsley sprig and unpeeled
prawns, to garnish

1
Heat the oil in a paella pan or large saucepan, add the drumsticks and cook for 15–20 minutes, until brown. Remove from the pan with a slotted spoon and keep warm. Add the garlic and onion to the pan and cook for 3–5 minutes, until softened. Pour off any excess fat.

2
Add the tomatoes, peppers, peas and turmeric and cook, stirring, for 5 minutes. Return the chicken to the pan and stir in the rice and stock. Bring to the boil, stirring constantly, reduce the heat and simmer for 40–45 minutes or until most of the stock has been absorbed and the rice is tender.

3
Meanwhile, prepare the mussels (see Mediterranean Fish Stew, right). Cook the prepared mussels in 1 cm ($\frac{1}{2}$ inch) boiling water until they all open. Drain. Stir the mussels, prawns and almonds into the chicken and rice mixture and heat through for 5 minutes. Season.

4
Serve the Paella in the cooking pan, garnished with the lemon wedge, the parsley sprig and a few prawns.

GOODNESS GUIDE
FIBRE The brown rice and vegetables provide a great deal of fibre
FAT With monounsaturated olive oil and skinless chicken this dish is low in saturated fat. Prawns are also low in fat
MINERALS Calcium, for blood clotting and strong bones, is provided by the prawns and mussels. The mussels are also a good source of iron, important for the production of red blood cells

MEDITERRANEAN FISH STEW

Serve sprinkled with parsley and with lots of crusty wholemeal bread to soak up the delicious juices.

SERVES 4   395 calories per serving
PREPARATION 15 minutes
COOKING 30 minutes

12 fresh mussels
1 onion, skinned and thinly sliced
30 ml (2 tbsp) olive oil
1 garlic clove, skinned and crushed
450 g (1 lb) tomatoes, skinned, seeded
and chopped
300 ml ($\frac{1}{2}$ pint) dry white wine
450 ml ($\frac{3}{4}$ pint) fish stock
15 ml (1 tbsp) chopped fresh dill or
5 ml (1 tsp) dill weed
10 ml (2 tsp) chopped fresh rosemary or
5 ml (1 tsp) dried
15 ml (1 tbsp) tomato purée
salt and pepper, to taste
450 g (1 lb) monkfish fillet, skinned and cut
into large chunks
4 jumbo prawns, peeled
225 g (8 oz) squid, cleaned and cut into rings

1
To clean the mussels, put in a large bowl and scrape well under cold running water. Discard any that are open. Rinse until there is no trace of sand in the bowl.

PAELLA

MEDITERRANEAN FISH STEW

―――2―――

In a large saucepan or flameproof casserole, gently cook the onion in the olive oil for 3–4 minutes. Add the garlic and tomatoes and cook for a further 3–4 minutes.

―――3―――

Add the white wine, stock, herbs, tomato purée and seasoning and bring to the boil. Lower the heat and simmer for a further 5 minutes.

―――4―――

Add the monkfish and simmer for 5 minutes. Add the prawns and squid and simmer for a further 5 minutes. Add the prepared mussels, cover the pan and cook for 3–4 minutes, until the shells open. Discard any of the mussels that do not open. Ladle the stew into individual bowls and serve at once.

GOODNESS GUIDE

FIBRE Some fibre is contributed by the onion and tomatoes

VITAMINS The monkfish and shellfish contribute B complex vitamins, and the tomatoes provide vitamin C

MINERALS The shellfish is a good source of iodine, which is stored in the thyroid gland and very important for normal growth

LAMB CHOPS WITH ROSEMARY

Redcurrants and apple complement the flavour of lamb.

SERVES 4 260 calories per serving
PREPARATION 10 minutes
COOKING 20 minutes
MARINATING 3–4 hours

4 lean lamb chops, well trimmed
150 ml ($\frac{1}{4}$ pint) unsweetened apple juice
15 ml (1 tbsp) chopped fresh rosemary or
7.5 ml ($\frac{1}{2}$ tbsp) dried
salt and pepper, to taste
1 garlic clove, skinned and chopped
2 large eating apples
juice of 1 lemon
60 ml (4 tbsp) redcurrants, thawed if frozen
fresh rosemary sprigs, to garnish

―――1―――

Put the lamb chops into a shallow dish with the apple juice, rosemary, seasoning and garlic. Cover and marinate in the refrigerator for 3–4 hours.

―――2―――

Halve the apples crossways, then core and brush with the lemon juice. Stand the apple halves in an oven-proof dish and cover with foil. Bake at 190°C (375°F) mark 5 for 12–15 minutes, until just tender.

―――3―――

Meanwhile, remove the lamb chops from the marinade and grill for 5–6 minutes. Turn the chops over, brush with a little marinade and grill for a further 5–6 minutes.

―――4―――

Fold back the foil from the apples, fill each half with redcurrants and return to the oven for 3 minutes.

―――5―――

Arrange the cooked chops on a serving dish, with the apple halves placed around them, and garnish with rosemary sprigs.

GOODNESS GUIDE

FIBRE The apples and redcurrants provide some fibre

FAT Fat is kept to a minimum by trimming the fat off the chops and grilling without added fat

VITAMINS Many B complex vitamins are contributed by the lamb, particularly B_{12} which assists the functioning of the nervous system

LAMB CHOPS WITH ROSEMARY

TROUT WITH HOLLANDAISE SAUCE

SERVES 4 480 calories per serving
PREPARATION 20 minutes
COOKING 20 minutes

4 trout, each 175–200 g (6–7 oz), gutted and
heads removed
150 ml (¼ pint) dry white wine
5 ml (1 tsp) coriander seeds
1 onion, skinned and sliced
lemon slices and watercress sprigs,
to garnish

HOLLANDAISE SAUCE
100 g (4 oz) polyunsaturated margarine
2 egg yolks
15 ml (1 tbsp) lemon juice
salt and pepper, to taste

1
Lay the trout in a shallow ovenproof
dish large enough to hold them in a
single layer. Add the wine and
150 ml (¼ pint) water, sprinkle with
the coriander seeds and lay the
onion over the top of the trout.
Cover with foil and cook at 190°C
(375°F) mark 5 for 20 minutes.

2
Carefully remove the trout from the
cooking liquid, reserving the liquid.
Skin each trout, leaving the tail
intact. Place on a serving dish and
keep warm.

3
Make the Hollandaise Sauce. Melt
the margarine in a saucepan. Strain
and reheat cooking liquid to boiling,
then put 25 ml (1½ tbsp) into the
warmed goblet of a food processor
or blender. Discard the remaining
liquid. Add the egg yolks and turn
the blender to low speed, then
gradually add the margarine to the
egg yolk mixture drop by drop, with
the motor still running. Add the
lemon juice and seasoning.

4
Spoon the sauce over the fish,
garnish with lemon slices and watercress sprigs and serve immediately.

GOODNESS GUIDE
MINERALS Besides protein, the main value
of trout and other fish is their high mineral
content. Trout is a source of potassium,
calcium, magnesium and iron, all of which
are important minerals
FAT Trout contain a low amount of fat and
the sauce is far lower in fat than the usual
Hollandaise Sauce

BUTTER BEAN CASSEROLE

SERVES 4 370 calories per serving
PREPARATION 10 minutes
COOKING 1½ hours
SOAKING 8–12 hours

350 g (12 oz) dried butter beans, soaked
8–12 hours
225 g (8 oz) swede, peeled and chopped
225 g (8 oz) parsnips, peeled and
roughly chopped
150 ml (¼ pint) dry cider
5 ml (1 tsp) dried oregano
400 g (14 oz) can tomatoes
30 ml (2 tbsp) tomato purée
100 g (4 oz) courgettes, sliced
100 g (4 oz) French beans, cut into 2.5 cm
(1 inch) lengths
salt and pepper, to taste
100 g (4 oz) fresh wholemeal breadcrumbs
30 ml (2 tbsp) chopped fresh rosemary or
15 ml (1 tbsp) dried
rosemary sprig, to garnish

1
Drain the butter beans, place in a
saucepan of boiling water and cook
for 10–15 minutes. Drain again and
rinse under cold running water.

TROUT WITH HOLLANDAISE SAUCE

BUTTER BEAN CASSEROLE

2

Place in a large casserole, with 450 ml (¾ pint) water, the swede, parsnips, cider, oregano, tomatoes with their juice and tomato purée. Cover and cook at 190°C (375°F) mark 5 for 45 minutes. Stir in the courgettes, French beans and seasoning and cook for a further 15 minutes.

3

Sprinkle with the breadcrumbs and rosemary and continue cooking un-covered for a further 30 minutes. Serve immediately, garnished with rosemary sprig.

GOODNESS GUIDE

PROTEIN The beans and breadcrumbs supply proteins that together are as beneficial as the protein in meat, but without the fat
FIBRE Each serving supplies much of the recommended daily intake of 30 g (1¼ oz) of fibre; most of this comes from the beans but the bread and vegetables also supply lots

MANGO CHICKEN PARCELS

Cooking the chicken in foil parcels seals in the flavour. Use ripe mangoes, recognised by their sweet aroma.

SERVES 4 205 calories per serving
PREPARATION 15 minutes
COOKING 25–30 minutes

4 boneless chicken breasts, each about 100–175 g (4–6 oz), skinned
2 fresh mangoes
2.5 cm (1 inch) fresh root ginger, peeled and finely chopped
pepper, to taste
lime slices and wedges and fresh coriander sprigs, to garnish

1

Slash the chicken breasts vertically, but do not cut all the way through. Place on individual pieces of foil large enough to make a secure parcel around the chicken.

2

Peel and remove all the flesh from the mangoes and discard the stones. Place the flesh in a bowl with the ginger and mash with a fork.

3

Spread evenly over the chicken and season. Seal the foil around the chicken and place on a baking sheet. Cook at 190°C (375°F) mark 5 for 25–30 minutes, until the chicken is cooked through. Open the parcels and garnish with the lime and coriander sprigs. Serve immediately, leaving the chicken in the foil.

MICROWAVE Follow steps 1 and 2 putting chicken into lightly greased greaseproof paper. In step 3 seal the paper well and place in a microwave oven dish as near the edges as possible. Cook 100% (High) 11–12 minutes, rearranging the parcels twice. Follow recipe and serve in paper.

GOODNESS GUIDE

SALT The strong flavour of the mangoes and ginger makes the addition of salt unnecessary
MINERALS Mangoes are a good source of potassium, which is needed to maintain the water balance in the body
VITAMINS Mangoes are rich in vitamins A and C

MANGO CHICKEN PARCELS

MUSTARD RABBIT

Rabbit is a tasty and very lean meat; its flavours are complemented well by the sharpness of the mustard.

SERVES 4   365 calories per serving
PREPARATION   20 minutes
COOKING   1¼ hours

15 g (½ oz) polyunsaturated margarine
15 ml (1 tbsp) corn oil
2 carrots, scrubbed and sliced
2 leeks, trimmed and sliced
1 large onion, skinned and chopped
900 g (2 lb) rabbit pieces, thawed if frozen
25 ml (1½ tbsp) plain wholemeal flour
600 ml (1 pint) chicken stock
30 ml (2 tbsp) Meaux mustard
150 ml (5 fl oz) Greek strained yogurt

———1———

Melt the margarine and oil in a flameproof casserole. Add carrots, leeks and onion and cook for 5 minutes.

———2———

Toss rabbit joints in the flour, shaking off the excess and reserving. Add rabbit to pan and cook for 5 minutes, turning, until sealed. Add reserved flour, stock and mustard to pan and stir well. Bring to the boil, lower the heat, cover and simmer about 1 hour, stirring occasionally.

———3———

Using a slotted spoon, transfer rabbit and vegetables on to a plate. Simmer the liquid until reduced by half, stirring occasionally. Remove from heat, stir in the yogurt and return the rabbit and vegetables to the pan. Reheat gently and serve.

MICROWAVE   Put half the margarine and oil in a dish with carrots, leeks and onion. Cover and cook 100% (High) 4 minutes, stirring once. Remove vegetables. Coat the rabbit pieces. Add rest of margarine and oil to dish and cook for 30 seconds. Add the rabbit joints and cook, uncovered, 100% (High) 7 minutes, turning twice. Stir in 300 ml (½ pint) boiling stock and mustard. Cook, covered, 100% (High) 20–25 minutes, stirring twice. Follow step 3, do not simmer liquid. Add the yogurt, rabbit and vegetables. Cook, uncovered, 100% (High) 3–4 minutes, until hot. Serve.

MONKFISH THERMIDOR

Monkfish has a similar taste to lobster, star of the classic French dish, and is very much cheaper.

SERVES 4   335 calories per serving
PREPARATION   10 minutes
COOKING   35 minutes

700–900 g (1½–2 lb) boned and skinned monkfish, cubed
3 shallots, skinned and chopped
15 ml (1 tbsp) chopped fresh tarragon or 5 ml (1 tsp) dried
150 ml (¼ pint) dry white wine
300 ml (½ pint) semi-skimmed milk
45 ml (3 tbsp) cornflour
5 ml (1 tsp) made English mustard
25 g (1 oz) Parmesan cheese, grated
50 g (2 oz) Gruyère cheese, grated

———1———

Put the monkfish into a saucepan with the shallots, tarragon and wine, cover and simmer for 18–20 minutes or until the flesh flakes easily. Using a slotted spoon, remove fish and reserve the cooking liquid.

———2———

Blend together the milk and cornflour and add to the cooking liquid with mustard and Parmesan cheese. Bring to the boil and stir until smooth and thick. Add the fish and transfer to a 1.1 litre (2 pint) shallow ovenproof serving dish.

———3———

Sprinkle over the Gruyère cheese and put under a hot grill for 5–10 minutes, until golden brown.

GOODNESS GUIDE

MONKFISH THERMIDOR

PROTEIN   Monkfish is an excellent source of low-fat protein, which is also supplied in this recipe by the milk and cheese. Parmesan is a particularly high-protein cheese

FAT   The sauce is made by the blended method, which eliminates the inclusion of fat. Using strong flavoured cheeses such as Gruyère and Parmesan means only a little cheese is required

MUSTARD RABBIT

FAT   Rabbit is a very low-fat source of protein and, like all game, contains a very healthy proportion of unsaturated to saturated fats

LAMB WITH ASPARAGUS SAUCE

If you grow your own asparagus, or have a friend who does, this is a good way of using up any awkwardly-sized spears.

SERVES 4   300 calories per serving
PREPARATION   15 minutes
COOKING   30–35 minutes

12–14 fresh asparagus spears, scraped and with ends trimmed
25 g (1 oz) polyunsaturated margarine
1 onion, skinned and chopped
300 ml (½ pint) chicken or vegetable stock
salt and pepper, to taste
4 lean lamb chops, each 175–225 g (6–8 oz), well trimmed of fat

———1———

Cut off asparagus tips and reserve, then slice the stalks. Melt margarine in a saucepan, add the onion and asparagus stalks and cook gently for 5 minutes. Add the stock and seasoning, bring to the boil, lower the heat, cover and simmer for 20 minutes, until tender. Purée the mixture in a blender or food processor until smooth. Return to pan to reheat, and adjust the seasoning.

———2———

Grill lamb chops for 10–15 minutes, turning once, until cooked as desired. Meanwhile, cook reserved asparagus tips in boiling water for 5 minutes, until just tender. Drain and keep warm.

———3———

Serve the chops with asparagus tips on a bed of sauce. Hand remaining sauce separately.

GOODNESS GUIDE

VITAMINS   Lamb is a good source of B group vitamins. These are involved in a number of complex reactions, including the release of energy from carbohydrates, proteins and fats. As B vitamins are not stored by the body for very long, a regular supply is essential

FIBRE   The asparagus and onion contribute a good amount of fibre to this dish

MUSTARD RABBIT

MONKFISH THERMIDOR

LAMB WITH ASPARAGUS SAUCE

PANCAKE PIZZA

Tomatoes, basil and mozzarella cheese give this dish a very Italian flavour.

SERVES 4   365 calories per serving
PREPARATION   45 minutes
BAKING   20–25 minutes

100 g (4 oz) plain wholemeal flour
1 egg, beaten
300 ml ($\frac{1}{2}$ pint) semi-skimmed milk
30 ml (2 tbsp) corn oil

FILLING
75 ml (3 fl oz) dry white wine
800 g (1 lb 12 oz) can tomatoes
1 onion, skinned and chopped
30 ml (2 tbsp) chopped fresh basil or
15 ml (1 tbsp) dried
75 g (3 oz) stuffed olives, chopped
30 ml (2 tbsp) tomato purée
salt and pepper, to taste
175 g (6 oz) mozzarella cheese

———1———

To make the filling, put the wine, tomatoes with their juices, onion and basil in a saucepan. Bring to the boil and simmer for 10 minutes, until the onion is soft. Add the olives and tomato purée and cook for a further 5–10 minutes, until thick. Season.

———2———

To make pancakes, put the flour into a bowl. Make a well in the centre and add the egg, whisking continuously. Gradually add the milk, drawing in the flour from the outside of the bowl, to form a smooth batter.

———3———

Heat the oil in a 20.5 cm (8 inch) frying pan until very hot. Pour off oil into a heatproof container. Add just enough batter to coat the base of pan and swirl lightly. Cook for 3–4 minutes, turn over and cook for a further 3–4 minutes. Make 7 pancakes with remaining batter.

———4———

Put one pancake in a heatproof dish and spread a little filling over. Grate half of the mozzarella and sprinkle a little over the filling. Top with another pancake and repeat process, finishing with a tomato layer. Slice the remaining mozzarella and arrange on top. Bake at 180°C (350°F) mark 4 for 20–25 minutes, until golden brown.

MICROWAVE   In step 1 put wine, drained tomatoes, onion and basil in a bowl. Cook, uncovered, 100% (High) 5 minutes. Add the olives, tomato purée and cook, uncovered, 100% (High) 5 minutes. Follow steps 2 and 3. In step 4, use a microwave oven dish. Cook, uncovered, 100% (High) 5–6 minutes, until heated through.

GOODNESS GUIDE
FIBRE   Made with wholemeal flour, these pancakes are an excellent source of the fibre necessary for the proper functioning of the intestines. The onion, tomato and olives also supply a useful amount of fibre
PROTEIN   A high-protein content is provided by the combination of milk, egg, cheese and flour

VEGETABLES WITH CHEESE DUMPLINGS

SERVES 4   365 calories per serving
PREPARATION   25 minutes
COOKING   30 minutes

15 g ($\frac{1}{2}$ oz) polyunsaturated margarine
15 ml (1 tbsp) corn oil
450 g (1 lb) swede, peeled and cubed
225 g (8 oz) parsnips, peeled and sliced
4 carrots, scrubbed and sliced
3 celery sticks, trimmed and sliced
1 large onion, skinned and chopped
1 red or green pepper, cored, seeded and chopped
1.1 litres (2 pints) vegetable stock
2.5 ml ($\frac{1}{2}$ tsp) dried rosemary
5 ml (1 tsp) dried mixed herbs
225 g (8 oz) cauliflower, cut into florets
225 g (8 oz) broccoli, cut into florets

CHEESE DUMPLINGS
175 g (6 oz) self-raising wholemeal flour
1.25 ml ($\frac{1}{4}$ tsp) baking powder
2.5 ml ($\frac{1}{2}$ tsp) salt
30 ml (2 tbsp) chopped fresh parsley
25 g (1 oz) Parmesan cheese, grated
50 g (2 oz) mature Cheddar cheese, grated

VEGETABLES WITH CHEESE DUMPLINGS

PANCAKE PIZZA

1

Melt margarine and oil in large flameproof casserole, add the swede, parsnips, carrots, celery, onion and pepper and cook for 5 minutes, until soft. Add the stock and dried herbs, and bring to the boil. Lower the heat and simmer, covered, for 15–20 minutes, until vegetables soften.

2

To make the dumplings, put the flour, baking powder, salt, parsley and cheeses in a bowl and mix well together. Add 100 ml (4 fl oz) water and, using a round bladed knife, mix lightly to form a soft dough. Divide into 12 pieces and form into balls.

3

Add the cauliflower and broccoli to casserole and place dumplings evenly around top. Cover and simmer for 15–20 minutes, until dumplings have doubled in size. Serve hot.

GOODNESS GUIDE

FIBRE The vegetables and wholemeal dumplings contribute a very substantial amount of fibre. One helping supplies at least one-third of the recommended daily intake for adults

VITAMINS Particularly rich in vitamin C, this dish also contains useful amounts of B vitamins from the flour and cheese

---

HADDOCK AND PRAWN STIR-FRY

SERVES 4 320 calories per serving
PREPARATION 20 minutes
COOKING 10 minutes

225 g (8 oz) can pineapple slices in natural juice, drained, with juice reserved
15 ml (1 tbsp) soy sauce, preferably naturally fermented shoyu
60 ml (4 tbsp) malt vinegar
30 ml (2 tbsp) light muscovado sugar
15 ml (1 tbsp) tomato purée
30 ml (2 tbsp) dry sherry
30 ml (2 tbsp) cornflour
45 ml (3 tbsp) corn oil
450 g (1 lb) haddock fillet, skinned and cut in bite-size pieces
1 small onion, skinned and sliced
1 red pepper, cored, seeded and thinly sliced
2 carrots, scrubbed and sliced
2.5 cm (1 inch) piece of fresh root ginger, peeled and chopped
225 g (8 oz) can water chestnuts, drained and sliced
100 g (4 oz) button mushrooms, sliced
225 g (8 oz) fresh beansprouts
175 g (6 oz) peeled cooked prawns, thawed

1

Cut each pineapple slice into chunks. Make up reserved juice to 300 ml ($\frac{1}{2}$ pint) with water. Add the soy sauce, vinegar, sugar, tomato purée, sherry and cornflour. Mix together until smooth.

2

Heat 15 ml (1 tbsp) oil in a large non-stick frying pan or wok. Add the haddock and stir-fry for about 5 minutes, until just cooked. Transfer to a plate and keep hot.

3

Rinse the pan, add remaining oil and cook the onion, pepper, carrots and ginger over a high heat for 3 minutes, stirring constantly. Add the pineapple, water chestnuts and mushrooms and stir-fry for a further 2 minutes. Stir the pineapple juice mixture and add to the pan. Bring to the boil, stirring. Add bean-sprouts, prawns and haddock and heat through. Serve at once.

GOODNESS GUIDE

FAT Haddock and prawns are very low-fat seafood. Not much fat has been used in the recipe and the quick stir-frying method reduces fat absorption

VITAMINS Lots of vitamin C is present in the fresh vegetables and the method of cooking means that a large amount is retained

HADDOCK AND PRAWN STIR-FRY

WEST COUNTRY COD

SERVES 4   155 calories per serving
PREPARATION   8–10 minutes
COOKING   25–30 minutes

4 cod fillets, each about
175 g (6 oz), skinned
1 onion, skinned and thinly sliced
pepper, to taste
thinly pared rind of 1 orange, cut into 7.5 cm
(3 inch) strips
juice of 1 orange
150 ml ($\frac{1}{4}$ pint) medium-dry cider
100 ml (4 fl oz) fish stock
10 ml (2 tsp) chopped fresh coriander
coriander sprigs, to garnish

———1———

Wipe the fish with absorbent kitchen paper and put in a shallow 1.1 litre (2 pint) ovenproof dish. Cover the fish with the onion, seasoning and orange rind.

———2———

Mix the orange juice with the cider and fish stock to make 300 ml ($\frac{1}{2}$ pint) liquid. Pour over the fish, cover and cook at 190°C (375°F). mark 5 for 20–25 minutes or until the fish is cooked through and flakes easily when tested with a fork. Place the fish, onion and orange strips on a serving dish and keep warm.

———3———

Strain the cooking liquid into a small saucepan and boil rapidly for 5 minutes or until the liquid is reduced by half. Pour over the fish and sprinkle with the coriander. Garnish and serve hot.

MICROWAVE Put prepared fish into a microwave oven dish and add remaining ingredients, but use only the juice of $\frac{1}{2}$ orange, 75 ml (3 fl oz) cider and no stock. Cover, cook 100% (High) 8 minutes, turning dish twice. Complete recipe.

GOODNESS GUIDE

PROTEIN Fish is an important source of protein and should be eaten at least twice a week for the other nutrients it contains
VITAMINS Cod contains niacin, which is important for energy production in the cells. The onion contains some vitamin C, as does the orange

FARMHOUSE CHICKEN BREASTS

SERVES 4   260 calories per serving
PREPARATION   15 minutes
COOKING   25 minutes

15 ml (1 tbsp) polyunsaturated margarine
$\frac{1}{2}$ small carrot, scrubbed and finely chopped
$\frac{1}{2}$ small onion, skinned and finely chopped
$\frac{1}{2}$ celery stick, trimmed and finely chopped
$\frac{1}{2}$ leek, finely chopped
1 garlic clove, skinned
4 boneless chicken breasts, each about
200 g (7 oz), skinned
200 ml (7 fl oz) chicken stock
50 ml (2 fl oz) low-fat natural yogurt
salt and pepper, to taste
cooked carrot slices and celery sticks,
to garnish

———1———

Melt the margarine in a heavy-based casserole. Add the carrot, onion, celery, leek and whole garlic clove. Cook for 5 minutes or until softened but not browned.

———2———

Place the chicken breasts on top of the vegetables and add the stock. Cover and simmer for 15 minutes or until the breasts are cooked through. Transfer the chicken breasts to a warm plate with a slotted spoon and keep warm.

———3———

Discard the garlic clove, then pour the mixture into a blender or food processor and purée until smooth. Return to the pan and reheat. Just before serving, mix in the yogurt and seasoning. Serve the chicken breasts with a little sauce spooned over them and garnished with cooked carrot slices and celery.

GOODNESS GUIDE

FAT The fat in this dish is kept low by using low-fat yogurt, skinned chicken breasts and only a little oil
PROTEIN Chicken and yogurt are two sources of easily digested protein
VITAMINS Chicken is a good source of niacin and riboflavin, which help promote energy production in the cells

STIR-FRIED LIVER

This flavourful dish will not only appeal to people who enjoy eating liver, but may also tempt those who do not usually care for it.

SERVES 4   160 calories per serving
PREPARATION   8–10 minutes
COOKING   15–18 minutes

15 ml (1 tbsp) corn oil
8 button onions, skinned
15 ml (1 tbsp) plain wholemeal flour
pepper, to taste
225 g (8 oz) lamb's liver, cut into thin strips
1 red pepper, cored, seeded and cut into
thin strips
1 green pepper, cored, seeded and cut into
thin strips
100 g (4 oz) button mushrooms
2 fresh rosemary sprigs
25 ml (1$\frac{1}{2}$ tbsp) soy sauce, preferably
naturally fermented shoyu
150 ml ($\frac{1}{4}$ pint) vegetable stock
100 g (4 oz) beansprouts

———1———

Heat the oil in a large frying pan or wok and cook the onions for 5–7 minutes or until browned. Remove from the pan and keep hot.

———2———

Season the flour with pepper and coat the liver strips. Quickly cook in the oil left in the pan for about 3 minutes, until browned. Return the onions to the pan with the red and green peppers and mushrooms. Add the rosemary sprigs, the soy sauce and the seasoning.

———3———

Pour the stock over and cook quickly for 5 minutes, stirring occasionally. Add the beansprouts and continue to cook for a further 2–3 minutes or until the beansprouts are heated through. Discard the rosemary and check the seasoning. Place on a warmed serving dish and serve hot.

GOODNESS GUIDE

MINERALS Liver is a good source of easily-absorbed iron. Iron is used to make red blood cells which transport oxygen around the body. Liver also contains high amounts of zinc
VITAMINS Liver is rich in B_{12} and folic acid, which are necessary for the formation of healthy red blood cells

FARMHOUSE CHICKEN BREASTS

WEST COUNTRY COD

STIR-FRIED LIVER

LAMB AND APRICOT PILAFF

FENNEL AND CHEESE MOUSSE

TURKEY TONNATO

LAMB AND APRICOT PILAFF

Substitute cubes of chicken for the lamb, if liked, and cook for only 5–10 minutes before adding rice.

SERVES 4 605 calories per serving
PREPARATION 15 minutes
COOKING 1 hour 20 minutes

100 g (4 oz) burghul wheat
15 ml (1 tbsp) olive oil
450 g (1 lb) lean boneless lamb, such as leg or fillet, well trimmed and cut into bite-sized cubes
1 onion, skinned and finely chopped
1 garlic clove, skinned and crushed
10 ml (2 tsp) tomato purée
5 ml (1 tsp) ground cinnamon
2.5 ml ($\frac{1}{2}$ tsp) powdered saffron or turmeric
salt and pepper, to taste
175 g (6 oz) brown rice
75 g (3 oz) ready-to-eat dried apricots, rinsed and roughly chopped
50 g (2 oz) seedless raisins, rinsed
25 g (1 oz) pine nuts or blanched almonds, toasted, and fresh coriander leaves, to garnish

————1————

Put the burghul in a large bowl, pour over enough warm water to cover, then leave to soak.

————2————

Meanwhile, heat the oil in a heavy flameproof casserole or saucepan, add the cubes of lamb and cook over high heat until browned on all sides. Remove with a slotted spoon and drain on absorbent kitchen paper.

————3————

Lower the heat, add the onion to the pan and cook gently, stirring frequently, until soft and lightly coloured. Add the garlic, tomato purée, cinnamon, saffron or turmeric and seasoning. Cook for a further 2–3 minutes, stirring, until the mixture gives off a spicy aroma.

————4————

Pour in 600 ml (1 pint) water and bring to the boil, stirring. Lower the heat, return the lamb to the pan, cover and simmer for 30 minutes.

————5————

Add the rice to the pan, stir once, then cover again and simmer for a further 20 minutes.

————6————

Stir in the apricots, raisins and 300 ml ($\frac{1}{2}$ pint) boiling water. Cover, and simmer for a further 20 minutes or until the rice is tender and has absorbed most of the liquid.

96

7

Drain the burghul, and wring out in a clean cloth to extract as much moisture as possible. Fold gently into the pilaff and heat through.

8

Turn the pilaff into a warmed serving dish. Garnish with the pine nuts or almonds and coriander leaves and serve hot.

GOODNESS GUIDE

MINERALS Iron is present in the lamb, apricots and grains. The absorption of iron by the body is aided by the vitamin C in the vegetables

VITAMINS B-complex vitamins are contributed by the lamb, grains and nuts

---

FENNEL AND CHEESE MOUSSE

SERVES 4 330 calories per serving
PREPARATION About 1 hour
COOKING 1¾ hours
COOLING 1 hour
CHILLING At least 1 hour

450 g (1 lb) fennel bulbs, trimmed and roughly chopped, with feathery tops reserved
50 g (2 oz) Roquefort or Blue Stilton cheese, any rind removed
450 g (1 lb) curd cheese
2 eggs
5 ml (1 tsp) chopped fresh herb fennel or 2.5 ml (½ tsp) dried
pepper, to taste
10 carrots, scrubbed
juice of 2–3 oranges, to taste
orange segments, to garnish (optional)

1

Grease and line the base of a 900 g (2 lb) loaf tin and set aside. Bring 1.7 litres (3 pints) water to the boil in a large saucepan, add the fennel and cook for about 10 minutes or until tender.

2

Remove the fennel with a slotted spoon, reserving the water in the pan. Drain the fennel well, then pat dry with absorbent kitchen paper.

3

Purée the fennel in a blender or food processor. Crumble in the blue cheese, then add the curd cheese, eggs, half of the herb fennel and seasoning. Purée until smooth.

4

Cut 4 of the carrots into thin strips. Return the fennel water to the boil, add the carrot strips and blanch for 2 minutes. Remove the strips with a slotted spoon, reserving the water, drain and pat dry.

5

Pour half of the puréed mixture into the loaf tin. Arrange the blanched carrot strips on top, then cover with the remaining mixture.

6

Cover with greased foil, place in a roasting tin and add enough boiling water to the roasting tin to come halfway up the sides of the loaf tin. Bake at 180°C (350°F) mark 4 for 1¾ hours, or until the mousse feels firm when pierced with a skewer.

7

Meanwhile, make the carrot sauce. Roughly chop the remaining carrots and add to the reserved vegetable water. Bring to the boil and simmer for 30–40 minutes, until the carrots are soft and most of the liquid has evaporated. Purée the carrots and liquid in a blender or food processor with the remaining herb fennel, the orange juice and seasoning. Cover and chill.

8

Drain off any surface liquid from the mousse. Leave to cool, then chill for at least 1 hour. To serve, run a knife carefully around the edge of the mousse to loosen it, then turn out and peel off the paper. Garnish. Serve with the sauce.

GOODNESS GUIDE

VITAMINS The vegetables provide vitamin C, necessary for a healthy immune system. The cheese provides B vitamins

PROTEIN The cheese and eggs provide plenty of protein

TURKEY TONNATO

Turkey fillets are a low-fat substitute for the veal traditionally used in the Italian dish Vitello Tonnato. The chilling time ensures that the turkey will absorb the flavour of the tuna.

SERVES 4 285 calories per serving
PREPARATION 30 minutes
COOKING 10–15 minutes
CHILLING 24–48 hours

450 g (1 lb) turkey fillets, thawed if frozen
60–90 ml (4–6 tbsp) dry white wine or cider (optional)
1 carrot, scrubbed and roughly chopped
2 celery sticks, trimmed
1 small onion, skinned and quartered
2 bay leaves
6 black peppercorns
100 g (3½ oz) can tuna in vegetable oil, drained
45 ml (3 tbsp) mayonnaise
45 ml (3 tbsp) lemon juice
pepper, to taste (optional)
50 g (2 oz) can anchovy fillets, drained and soaked in milk for 20 minutes
about 20 capers

1

Put the turkey fillets in a heavy flameproof casserole or saucepan. Pour over 750 ml (1¼ pints) cold water and the wine or cider, if using. Add the carrot, celery, onion, bay leaves and peppercorns. Bring slowly to the boil.

2

Lower the heat, cover and simmer gently for 10–15 minutes, or until the turkey is just tender when pierced with a skewer.

3

Remove from the heat and leave the turkey to cool in the poaching liquid. Transfer the turkey to a board, reserving the poaching liquid, and cut into neat, thin slices. Arrange on a serving platter, cover and set aside.

4

Boil the poaching liquid rapidly until reduced to about 60 ml (4 tbsp). Strain and leave to cool.

5

Sieve the tuna into a bowl, pressing the fish through the sieve with the back of a spoon. Stir in the poaching liquid, mayonnaise, lemon juice and seasoning and mix well until smooth. Spoon the dressing over the turkey, ensuring the meat is covered.

6

Drain and rinse the anchovies, pat dry with absorbent kitchen paper, then cut each one in half length-ways. Arrange the anchovies over the turkey in a lattice pattern, then place the capers in the 'windows' of the lattice.

7

Cover and chill for 24–48 hours. Remove from the refrigerator at least 1 hour before serving.

GOODNESS GUIDE

FAT The oils present in the tuna and anchovies are believed to aid in the prevention of heart disease

VITAMINS This dish provides plenty of B-complex vitamins including those involved in red blood cell formation

CHILLI CON CARNE

This recipe for chilli con carne uses cubes of beef. This is more traditional than minced beef which is often used instead. Add chillies and chilli powder according to taste. Serve with brown rice or wholemeal rolls.

SERVES 4   425 calories per serving
PREPARATION 15 minutes
COOKING 3–3½ hours
SOAKING Overnight

175 g (6 oz) dried red kidney beans, soaked overnight and drained
30 ml (2 tbsp) olive oil
2 large onions, skinned and chopped
2 garlic cloves, skinned and crushed
1 fresh green chilli, seeded and chopped
5 ml (1 tsp) dried oregano
2.5–5 ml (½–1 tsp) mild chilli powder
10 ml (2 tsp) ground cumin
7.5 cm (3 inch) cinnamon stick
1 bay leaf
700 g (1½ lb) lean chuck steak, trimmed of all fat and cut into 2.5 cm (1 inch) cubes
400 g (14 oz) can tomatoes
15 ml (1 tbsp) tomato purée
2.5 ml (½ tsp) dark muscovado sugar
2.5 ml (½ tsp) malt vinegar
30 ml (2 tbsp) chopped fresh coriander
salt and pepper, to taste
coriander sprig, to garnish

———1———

Place the beans in a large saucepan and cover with cold water. Bring to the boil and boil rapidly for 10 minutes. Drain, cover with fresh water and simmer for 50 minutes or until tender.

———2———

Meanwhile, heat the oil in a flame-proof casserole and cook the onions for 5 minutes, until softened. Add the garlic, green chilli, oregano, chilli powder, cumin, cinnamon and bay leaf and cook for 1–2 minutes, stirring constantly.

———3———

Add the meat to the casserole and cook for 5–6 minutes, until browned on all sides.

———4———

Stir in the remaining ingredients with 150 ml (¼ pint) water. Bring to the boil. Drain the beans and add to the casserole, then cover tightly and cook at 170°C (325°F) mark 3 for 2–2½ hours, until the meat is tender. Garnish with a coriander sprig.

NASI GORENG

SERVES 4 420 calories per serving
PREPARATION 10 minutes
COOKING 40 minutes

225 g (8 oz) brown rice
30 ml (2 tbsp) groundnut or corn oil
1 large onion, skinned and chopped
1 garlic clove, skinned and crushed
1 green chilli, seeded and chopped
½ green pepper, cored, seeded and cut into strips
50 g (2 oz) button mushrooms, sliced
100 g (4 oz) cooked chicken meat, skinned and diced
100 g (4 oz) peeled cooked prawns
50 g (2 oz) shelled unsalted peanuts
50 g (2 oz) frozen peas
2 spring onions, trimmed and finely chopped
15 ml (1 tbsp) soy sauce, preferably naturally fermented shoyu
2.5 ml (½ tsp) dark muscovado sugar
salt and pepper, to taste
3 tomatoes, cut into wedges, shredded lettuce and a green chilli flower, to garnish

———1———

Put the rice in 600 ml (1 pint) boiling water in a saucepan. Cover and simmer for 30 minutes or until the rice is just tender and the liquid has been absorbed.

———2———

Heat the oil in a large frying pan or wok and cook the onion, garlic, chilli and green pepper, until the onion is soft. Add the mushrooms and cook for a further 2–3 minutes, stirring occasionally.

———3———

Stir in the chicken, prawns, peanuts and cooked rice and cook for 3–4 minutes, stirring, until hot.

———4———

Add the remaining ingredients and continue cooking, stirring, for 1–2 minutes until heated through. Spoon on to a heated serving dish. Garnish.

MICROWAVE Put rice and 600 ml (1 pint) boiling water into a bowl. Part cover and cook 100% (High) 5 minutes, then cook 60% (Medium) 20–25 minutes or until rice is tender and the liquid absorbed. Put oil, onion, garlic, chilli and green pepper into a dish. Cover and cook 100% (High) 4 minutes, stirring once. Add mushrooms, cook ½ minute. Stir in remaining ingredients and cook 4–5 minutes, stirring twice. Complete recipe.

CASSEROLED GROUSE

Grouse is available from 12 August to early December. It makes an impressive meal for a special occasion.

SERVES 4 260 calories per serving
PREPARATION 15 minutes
COOKING About 1½ hours
MARINATING 24 hours

2 dressed grouse, about 450 g (1 lb) each
8 shallots, skinned
2 garlic cloves, skinned and crushed
3 carrots, scrubbed and sliced
4 celery sticks, trimmed and sliced
thinly pared rind and juice of 1 orange
10 juniper berries, crushed
3 bay leaves
15 ml (1 tbsp) corn oil
30 ml (2 tbsp) red wine vinegar
pepper, to taste
60 ml (4 tbsp) port
600 ml (1 pint) chicken stock
15 g (½ oz) cornflower
2 oranges, peeled and sliced, and chopped parsley, to garnish

———1———

Cut the grouse in half lengthways, discard the skin and remove the feet. Wipe with a clean damp cloth.

———2———

Slice 2 of the shallots and put in a large ovenproof casserole with the garlic, 1 carrot and 1 celery stick. Place the grouse on top.

———3———

Put the orange rind and juice in a small bowl with the juniper berries, bay leaves, corn oil, red wine vinegar, seasoning and 45 ml (3 tbsp) of the port. Pour over the grouse. Cover and leave to marinate in a cool place for 24 hours, turning occasionally.

———4———

Remove the bay leaves. Add the remaining shallots, carrots and celery and pour the stock over, mixing the stock with the marinade. Cover and cook at 180°C (350°F) mark 4 for 1½ hours or until the grouse are tender.

———5———

Place the grouse and vegetables on a serving dish and keep warm. Strain the stock and reserve 300 ml (½ pint). Blend the cornflour with 15 ml (1 tbsp) cold water to make a smooth paste. Heat the reserved stock and when gently boiling stir in the cornflour. Cook, stirring, until thickened. Continue cooking for a further 2 minutes.

—6—

Add the remaining port and pour over the grouse. Garnish with the orange slices and chopped parsley and serve immediately.

GOODNESS GUIDE

CASSEROLED GROUSE
FAT Grouse, like other game, is low in fat
FIBRE The vegetables provide some fibre

CHILLI CON CARNE
PROTEIN The red kidney beans and beef provide protein
MINERALS The beef and beans supply iron, zinc and potassium. The vegetables provide extra potassium
VITAMINS B vitamins are provided by the beef and beans. Vitamin C is provided by the vegetables
FIBRE The red kidney beans and vegetables provide fibre

NASI GORENG
FIBRE Fibre is supplied by the rice, peanuts and vegetables
VITAMINS A range of B vitamins are provided by the rice, chicken, prawns and peanuts. The green pepper and tomatoes supply carotene. All the vegetables supply vitamin C

CHILLI CON CARNE

NASI GORENG

CASSEROLED GROUSE

99

FAMILY BEEF CASSEROLE

This delicious casserole is filling, yet light enough for a summer meal. Complete the dish with wholemeal noodles and a crisp green salad.

SERVES 4 435 calories per serving
PREPARATION 15 minutes
COOKING 2 hours

700 g (1½ lb) chuck steak, trimmed of excess
fat and cubed
15 ml (1 tbsp) plain flour
175 g (6 oz) button mushrooms
16 button onions, skinned
150 ml (¼ pint) red wine
400 g (14 oz) can whole tomatoes
3 celery sticks, trimmed and sliced
1 sprig fresh thyme or 5 ml (1 tsp) dried
15 ml (1 tbsp) whole grain mustard
salt and pepper, to taste
10 black olives, stoned

———1———

Toss the meat in the flour and shake off any excess. Put the meat, mushrooms, onions, wine, tomatoes, celery, thyme, mustard and seasoning in a flameproof casserole and mix well. Bring gently to the boil and remove from the heat.

———2———

Cover the casserole and cook at 180°C (350°F) mark 4 for 2 hours, until the meat is tender. Add the olives and heat through. Serve at once.

GOODNESS GUIDE

MINERALS Beef is a source of iron, zinc and potassium
VITAMINS B-complex vitamins, including B_{12}, are supplied by the beef. B_{12} and iron are two important components for the blood cell formation, B_{12} also aids nervous system functioning. The fresh vegetables contribute vitamin C
FIBRE The vegetables supply fibre

RED TROUT EN PAPILLOTE

SERVES 4 290 calories per serving
PREPARATION 15 minutes
COOKING 25 minutes
MARINATING 1–4 hours

4 red trout, about 350 g (12 oz) each,
cleaned and boned, with heads removed
finely grated rind and juice of 2 limes
60 ml (4 tbsp) olive oil
30 ml (2 tbsp) anise-flavoured liqueur
(optional)
6 spring onions, trimmed and finely chopped
salt and pepper, to taste

———1———

Cut 4 pieces of foil large enough to enclose each trout and place a fish in the centre of each piece.

———2———

In a small bowl, mix together the lime rind and juice, olive oil, liqueur (if using), spring onions and seasoning. Spoon into the trout.

———3———

Fold over the edges of the foil to seal in the juices and make neat parcels. Place the parcels side by side in an ovenproof dish or baking tin and leave to marinate for 1–4 hours.

———4———

Cook at 190°C (375°F) mark 5 for 20 minutes. Open the foil and cook for a further 5 minutes or until the trout flesh flakes easily when tested with a fork. Place the parcels on a serving platter or individual plates. If liked, remove the fish from the parcels and pour the cooking juices over to serve.

MICROWAVE Put each trout into a plastic cooking bag and arrange in a baking dish. Follow step 2, using 30 ml (2 tbsp) olive oil. Lightly seal and snip bags for steam release. Cook 100% (High) 10–12 minutes, rearranging twice and turning over once. Remove from bags and serve.

GOODNESS GUIDE

PROTEIN Trout is an excellent source of protein
VITAMINS Fish contains niacin and B_6, crucial for protein metabolism
FAT Trout is a medium-fat fish. The oils present in fish are thought to help prevent heart disease

WHOLEWHEAT SALAD

SERVES 4 305 calories per serving
PREPARATION 5 minutes
COOKING 20–25 minutes
COOLING 30 minutes
CHILLING 2–3 hours
SOAKING Overnight

225 g (8 oz) wholewheat grain, soaked
overnight and drained
45 ml (3 tbsp) olive oil
30 ml (2 tbsp) lemon juice
salt and pepper, to taste
100 g (4 oz) ready-to-eat dried apricots,
rinsed and cut into small pieces
½ cucumber, diced

———1———

Put the wholewheat in a large saucepan of cold water. Bring to the boil, then simmer for 20–25 minutes, until the wheat is tender but still firm to the bite.

———2———

Meanwhile, in a large bowl, whisk together the oil, lemon juice and salt and pepper.

———3———

Drain the wholewheat and add to the dressing in the bowl. Toss well, then leave to cool for about 30 minutes.

———4———

Stir in the apricots and cucumber then cover and chill for 2–3 hours. Stir again before serving.

MICROWAVE Put wholewheat into a bowl with 450 ml (¾ pint) boiling water. Part cover, cook 100% (High) 10 minutes, until tender but still firm to the bite. Complete recipe.

GOODNESS GUIDE

FIBRE The wholewheat grain and apricots supply fibre
MINERALS Iron and calcium are contributed by the wholewheat grain and apricots. The fruit and grain also supply potassium
VITAMINS The vitamin C in the lemon juice and cucumber aids the body's absorption of the iron. The wheat is a good source of B vitamins, especially thiamine

RED TROUT EN PAPILLOTE

WHOLEWHEAT SALAD

FAMILY BEEF CASSEROLE

LIVER WITH APPLE AND SAGE

Instead of liver with bacon or liver with onion, try this more unusual combination—liver with apple and sage. Serve with brown rice

SERVES 4 215 calories per serving
PREPARATION 10 minutes
COOKING About 10 minutes

450 g (1 lb) lamb's liver, cut into thin strips
15 ml (1 tbsp) plain wholemeal flour
30 ml (2 tbsp) corn oil
1 onion, skinned and thinly sliced
1 garlic clove, skinned and crushed
15 ml (1 tbsp) chopped fresh sage
200 ml (7 fl oz) apple juice
4 cloves or 1.25–2.5 ml ($\frac{1}{4}$–$\frac{1}{2}$ tsp) ground cloves
salt and pepper, to taste
2 green eating apples, cored and thinly sliced
fresh sage sprigs, to garnish

———1———

Lightly dust the liver with the flour. Heat the oil in a large frying pan, add the onion and garlic and cook over a medium heat for 2 minutes. Add the chopped sage and cook for a further 1 minute.

———2———

Add the liver and cook briskly for about 3 minutes, turning the strips once. Stir in the apple juice, cloves or ground cloves and seasoning and bring to the boil, stirring. Add the apples and simmer gently for 2 minutes. Serve immediately garnished with fresh sage sprigs.

GOODNESS GUIDE

VITAMINS AND MINERALS Liver is particularly rich in iron and the B vitamins folic acid and B_{12}, which are all essential for the formation of healthy red blood cells
FIBRE The apples, onion and flour provide fibre necessary for healthy intestinal movements

MEATBALLS IN ORANGE SAUCE

SERVES 4 275 calories per serving
PREPARATION About 10 minutes
COOKING About 35 minutes
CHILLING 1 hour

350 g (12 oz) finely minced lean beef
1 small onion, skinned and finely chopped
75 g (3 oz) fresh wholemeal breadcrumbs
15 ml (1 tbsp) chopped fresh parsley
15 ml (1 tbsp) chopped fresh tarragon
1 large garlic clove, skinned and crushed
15 ml (1 tbsp) chopped unblanched almonds
salt and pepper, to taste
1 egg, beaten
15 ml (1 tbsp) low-fat natural yogurt
30 ml (2 tbsp) corn oil
1 large leek, cut into thin strips
300 ml ($\frac{1}{2}$ pint) chicken stock
rind of $\frac{1}{2}$ orange, cut into thin strips
150 ml ($\frac{1}{4}$ pint) unsweetened orange juice
10 ml (2 tsp) cornflour
1 orange, peeled and sliced, to garnish

———1———

Combine the minced beef, onion, breadcrumbs, herbs, garlic, almonds, seasoning, egg and yogurt. Mix well. Form into walnut sized balls, and chill for 1 hour.

———2———

Heat the oil in a saucepan or deep frying pan. Add the meatballs and cook until evenly coloured all over. Add the leek and cook for a further 1 minute.

———3———

Stir in the stock, orange rind and juice and bring to the boil. Blend the cornflour with 30 ml (2 tbsp) water and stir into the sauce. Simmer gently for 25 minutes until the meatballs are cooked through, stirring occasionally. Garnish with orange slices and serve.

GOODNESS GUIDE

FAT The use of lean meat, low-fat yogurt and only a little oil reduces the fat content of the dish
FIBRE The flour, leeks and almonds provide fibre
MINERALS The meat, breadcrumbs and almonds are rich in iron, which is needed for healthy blood cells

GREEK-STYLE MACKEREL

SERVES 4 430 calories per serving
PREPARATION 15 minutes
COOKING 12–15 minutes

4 small mackerel, about 250 g (9 oz) each, heads removed, gutted and cleaned
pepper, to taste
2 lemons, thinly sliced
2 garlic cloves, skinned and finely chopped
15 ml (1 tbsp) chopped fresh oregano or 5 ml (1 tsp) dried
15 ml (1 tbsp) olive oil
fresh oregano, to garnish

YOGURT SAUCE

1 egg yolk
150 ml (5 fl oz) Greek strained yogurt
finely grated rind of 1 lemon
15 ml (1 tbsp) capers, roughly chopped

———1———

Season the mackerel with pepper inside and out. Place the lemon slices, garlic and oregano in the cavity of each fish. Make three shallow cuts on both sides of each of the fish.

———2———

Brush the fish with oil and cook under a medium grill for 12–15 minutes, until the flesh flakes easily when tested with a fork, gently turning the fish carefully halfway through cooking.

———3———

Meanwhile, make the sauce. Beat together the egg yolk and yogurt, then add the lemon rind and capers. Arrange the fish on a dish. Garnish with oregano. Serve with the sauce.

MICROWAVE Complete step 1. Brush fish with oil, arrange in a browning dish. Part cover, cook 100% (High) 7–8 minutes, turning fish over after first 4 minutes. Complete step 3.

GOODNESS GUIDE

VITAMINS AND MINERALS Mackerel and egg yolk are rich in vitamin D which is essential for calcium absorption and metabolism. The egg and yogurt contain calcium, necessary to maintain strong bones and develop healthy teeth in children. Mackerel provides essential fatty acids.

102

LIVER WITH APPLE AND SAGE

GREEK-STYLE MACKEREL

MEATBALLS IN ORANGE SAUCE

4 DESSERTS

MAKING PASTRY
HEALTHIER

Pastry forms the basis of many dishes we enjoy. Traditionally it is made from plain flour and saturated fats such as butter or hard margarine. Made from wholemeal flour — or half wholemeal, half plain — and poly-unsaturated fats, it is much healthier. It can be as light and appetising as that made with white flour and, with practice, can even be used in recipes which call for a delicate choux or rough puff pastry.

Recipes which specify white flour can be made successfully by substituting wholemeal flour, or half wholemeal, half plain, usually in the quantity two thirds flour to one third fat. Always roll out wholemeal dough thinly, as the pastry is a little heavier than that made with white flour. Pastry is measured according to the amount of flour in the recipe. Therefore, 225 g (8 oz) pastry means it has been made with 225 g (8 oz) flour and probably 100 g (4 oz) fat.

It is a good idea to get to know what pastry ingredients do; this will help in handling them and adapting recipes.

FLOURS

Wholemeal flour is the healthiest of all flours because it contains 100 per cent of the wheat — the whole grain is milled. It produces a pastry which is rich in fibre and nutrients.

Wheatmeal flour contains 80–90 per cent of the grain, but some of the bran has been removed. Like white flour, it has added 'improvers' which bleach the flour. It is therefore better to use unbleached white flour and wholemeal, which have no additives.

Stoneground flour takes its name from a grinding process. Both wholemeal and wheatmeal are available in a stoneground version.

Soft (plain) white flour is traditionally used in pastry and is also used for making fine-textured white bread. Although it contains approximately 70 per cent of the wheat grain the bran and wheatgerm are removed, leaving the starch and protein.

Strong (plain) white flour is used in bread-making; the word 'strong' in the title refers to the fact that it is high in the protein called gluten, which enables it to stretch and coagulate during baking. Its elasticity makes it suitable for flaky rough puff and choux pastry, where a pliable dough is essential to achieve a successful result.

FATS

Fats are used in pastry to provide the 'shortening' agent — they ensure that the pastry is dry, crisp and crumbly. When using half wholemeal or half plain (white) flour, or when using all wholemeal, the proportions of fat to flour are 1:2: 50 g (2 oz) fat; 100 g (4 oz) flour.

Butter or hard margarines are most often used in pastry-making, but because these are high in saturated fats it is healthier to substitute white vegetable margarine or yellow soft tub margarine — both of which are high in polyunsaturated fat. Low-fat spreads are not suitable for pastry because they have a high water content and produce a hard, unappetising result.

To get the best results make sure that the margarine is well chilled; if possible, use it straight from the refrigerator and rub it in with light, cool fingers. Polyunsaturated margarine produces crumbs when rubbed in to the flour — in the same way that butter does. It is a good idea to grate this margarine into the flour as this makes it easy to rub in evenly.

OILS

Using oils in pastry-making produces a very short pastry. Sunflower oil, which is high in polyunsaturates, is ideal; do not use blended vegetable oils as these may contain cheap oils which will not only give a poor texture and flavour but may also be high in saturated fats.

Pastry made with oils is slightly greasy, so it is suitable for savoury rather than sweet dishes. If using wholemeal flour, let the pastry rest for 10 minutes before rolling out; if using white flour, roll it out immediately, as the dough dries quickly and is difficult to handle if left for even a short time or if it is chilled.

LIQUIDS

Chilled water is usually used to bind pastry together. Both wholemeal and wheatmeal flour absorb more water than plain (white) flour; when making the wholemeal pastry add just enough water for the dough to bind — if you add too much, and knead too vigorously, the pastry will be tough, but if you add too little, the cooked pastry will fall apart.

Enriched pastries may be bound together with egg yolk and water or, for a creamier result, egg yolk and natural Quark. When a recipe calls for milk, semi-skimmed or skimmed milk may be substituted for a pastry that is lower in fat. Lemon juice is added to flaky, rough puff and puff pastry because it makes the dough more elastic.

BASIC PASTRY

MAKES 225 g (8 oz) pastry
PREPARATION 5–10 minutes
BAKING None
CHILLING 30 minutes

100 g (4 oz) plain wholemeal flour
100 g (4 oz) plain flour
pinch of salt (optional)
100 g (4 oz) polyunsaturated margarine

Mix the flours and salt together in a bowl and rub in the margarine until the mixture resembles fine breadcrumbs. Gradually add 120 ml (8 tbsp) cold water, mixing to a smooth, soft dough. Wrap in cling film and chill 30 minutes.

NUTTY PASTRY
Add 15 ml (1 tbsp) poppy seeds and 30 ml (2 tbsp) finely chopped toasted nuts to the above recipe with the water.

ENRICHED PASTRY
Add 1 beaten egg yolk and 30 ml (2 tbsp) natural Quark in place of 45 ml (3 tbsp) of the water.

GOODNESS GUIDE

FIBRE Higher in protein, vitamins and certain minerals than plain flour, wholemeal flour also supplies three times as much fibre.
FAT The saturated fats traditionally used in baking have been linked with increased blood cholesterol levels, whereas the polyunsaturated fats used here tend to lower the levels

ALTERNATIVE SWEETENERS

From being highly regarded as a cheap pure energy source, sugar has become a dietary pariah, with experts recommending substantial reductions in the amount we consume. Is sugar so bad for us? If it is harmful, what are the alternatives for those of us with a sweet tooth?

High in calories and low in nourishment, sugar accounts on average for one fifth of our total food intake, amounting to about 45 kg (100 lb) per year for every man, woman and child in the United Kingdom. (These figures represent the sugar that the individual adds to food and that added by manufacturers to their products.) Excessive sugar consumption is the primary source of tooth decay and is also a major contributing factor to obesity and even hardening of the arteries and coronary heart disease.

The advice from health authorities is to cut sugar consumption by at least half. That means *all* sugar consumption; even unrefined raw cane sugars have the same detrimental effects.

WHAT IS SUGAR?
Sugar comes in many different forms, but what we are usually referring to when we talk about sugar is sucrose. Sucrose is extracted from sugar cane or sugar beet, and is refined in varying degrees, starting with a black treacly liquid and ending up, in the case of white sugar, as pure crystals.

Refined sugar provides no vitamins or minerals or any other nutrients; its only significant contribution is calories which provide energy. The less refined the sugar, the more vitamins and minerals there are (see panel). To make use of the energy present in sugar, the body requires certain vitamins, particularly vitamin B_1 (thiamine), and this is present in molasses. Therefore, when using sugar as a sweetener, it is preferable to use raw cane sugar, such as dark or light muscovado, which contains molasses.

OTHER COMMON SUGARS
Sucrose is a compound of fructose and glucose. Fructose—fruit sugar—is the sweetest known sugar and is found in fruit and some vegetables. Glucose, also known as dextrose, occurs naturally in a few foods, as well as being made in our bodies. Maltose—malt sugar—comes from barley and is one of the by-products of beer making. Lactose is a milk sugar found in mammal's milk.

As they naturally occur, all these sugars come with a wide variety of essential nutrients; for example, when you eat a piece of fruit you are taking in the sugar but you are also ingesting minerals, vitamins and fibre as well. When these sugars are refined, they have no real nutritional benefits. Fructose may have some advantage over other naturally-occurring sugars since it provides more sweetness from fewer calories; a number of food manufacturers are substituting fructose for sucrose in their products because less is required.

CANE SUGAR VARIETIES
RAW CANE SUGARS
Molasses, or black Barbados, sugar contains about 20 per cent molasses and is almost black in colour. It is the least refined of all cane sugars and therefore contains the highest amount of minerals, such as calcium and B vitamins, particularly thiamine.

Dark muscovado sugar is sometimes called Barbados sugar. It contains about 13 per cent molasses and has a strong rich taste.

Light muscovado sugar has a finer grain than dark muscovado; it contains about 6 per cent molasses. Both light and dark muscovado are less refined than demerara sugar.

Demerara sugar contains about 2 per cent molasses.

Golden granulated contains about 0.5 per cent molasses and is the most refined of all raw cane sugars.

REFINED CANE SUGARS
Soft brown and *London Demerara sugars* are manufactured white sugars coated with syrup and caramel colouring. Refined molasses may be added. They contain minute amounts of vitamins and minerals, and add no goodness to the diet.

White sugar is the most refined of all cane sugars. It contains no molasses; the resultant sugar is virtually pure sucrose, containing no minerals or vitamins. White sugar is sold in many forms: lumps, granules (the standard packet sugar); caster and icing sugar; and preserving sugar.

HEALTHY ALTERNATIVES
The outstanding alternative to refined sugar in cooking is dried fruit. Full of concentrated goodness, since most of the water content has been removed, it is extremely high in fibre, with minerals such as potassium, phosphorus and calcium in most varieties and large amounts of B-complex vitamins. Vitamin A is found in apricots and peaches.

Dried apricots are one of the most useful ingredients for sweet cooking without added sugar. Dried peaches have similar nutritional value. Both go very well in fruit salads, purées, pies and stuffings for poultry.

Dates have the highest natural sugar content of all dried fruits and can add a great deal of sweetness to puddings, breads and cakes. Prunes and figs are also good in puddings, cakes and biscuits. Apples are one of the few fruits that retain most of their vitamin C when they are dried. They are a useful addition to crumbles and pies for sweetening fresh, less sweet fruits such as gooseberries or rhubarb, as are most dried fruit. Like dried apricots, they are also a tasty sweetener to add to muesli or to other breakfast cereals.

Also extremely useful are the vine fruit—currants, raisins and sultanas—all of which are types of dried grapes. They are particularly good for baking; use sultanas to sweeten stuffed baked apples, for example.

Most dried fruit will need washing and soaking before use. Even ready-to-eat dried fruit should be well rinsed to remove any preservatives, such as sulphur dioxide, that may have been added.

Carob is a rich dark sweetener that is a very useful substitute for cocoa or chocolate. Produced from the Mediterranean carob, or locust, bean, it is available in bar or powder form from health food shops and larger supermarkets. It is naturally sweeter than cocoa so carob products need far less added sugar than chocolate and it is lower in fat so carob products contains less calories. Carob contains E and some B vitamins, as well as calcium, magnesium and iron.

There are also a number of spices and herbs which can be combined with foods to create sweet flavours without adding sugar. These include cinnamon, cardamom, allspice, nutmeg, ginger and coriander.

Fruit juices, such as apple and orange, are another useful alternative to refined sugar. They can be combined with fresh and dry fruits to make spreads and jams; if these are kept in the refrigerator, there is no need to add sugar as a preservative but eat within 3 weeks.

Coconut in moderation is a worthwhile alternative sweetener. It has a high protein content and is rich in potassium and iron. A little desiccated coconut sprinkled on fresh fruit makes the fruit taste much sweeter; it also goes well in cakes and biscuits. However, coconut is very high in fats, almost all of them saturated, so it should only be used in small amounts. Fortunately it has a strong flavour so less of it is needed.

Honey is the first known sweetener used by humans, and until the 1600s it was the only one used in Europe. But, apart from being sweet, smooth and sticky, what is it? Is it better for us than refined sugars?

Honey has a high carbohydrate content in the form of simple sugars. Its real value lies in helping us to cut down on the amount of sugar we eat—an average of 100 g (4 oz) a day. As honey is sweeter than sugar, less of it can be used to get the same sweet taste in food.

Using honey can also save some calories—as honey contains approximately 23 per cent water, this dilutes the calorific value. Weight for weight, honey has fewer calories than refined sugar— 290 calories per 100 g (4 oz) compared to sugar's 390 calories per 100 g (4 oz).

FUEL FOR ENERGY

The main sugars in honey are glucose and fructose. Glucose is quickly absorbed into the bloodstream, providing fuel for energy, whereas fructose is more slowly absorbed and thus is more slowly released for energy. The combination of sugars gives both an immediate source of energy and a longer lasting source, without causing a sharp rise in blood sugar levels.

In general we do not need sugar or honey for energy—we get energy from other types of food. It is important that honey should not be given to children under one year of age as it may contain an organism responsible for botulism in infants. Honey is, however, an easily digestible source of carbohydrates and is therefore useful for old people and invalids—especially where intake of carbohydrates from other foods is restricted.

NUTRIENTS

Refined sugar does not provide vitamins, minerals or any other nutrients, but honey has traces of a wide range of minerals including potassium, calcium and phosphorus, and a few vitamins— B-complex, C, D and E—and amino acids. However, experts dismiss the nutritional value of these non-sugar components as being too small to be of significance, compared with those obtained from other foods in a normal diet.

Most honey contains a tiny amount of pollen which collects in the bottom of the jar or inside the lid. Pollen contains every known nutrient and is believed by many, though it has not been proven scientifically, to have beneficial effects when taken regularly.

A WHOLE FOOD

The honeycomb is the natural form of all honeys, and there are many different flavours of honeycomb, depending on which flowers the bees visited to suck up the nectar to make the honey. A blend of honeys gathered from a variety of English blossoms is used to make English honey. Greek herbal blossoms give the world-famous, dark, clear and slightly thick Hymettus honey. Other delicious varieties include pure orange blossom, heather, acacia, clover, rosemary and sunflower.

All honey sold in Britain is pure, as no additives are allowed. It is also generally immune from pesticide traces, as any chemicals kill the bees before they can take polluted nectar back to the hive. Honey is, therefore, eaten in a form as near to a natural food as possible. Set honey is just as natural as clear honey and is achieved by a mixing process at the packers. Creamed honey has been whisked to make it softer.

In wholefood baking, honey, molasses and unrefined sugar are preferred to refined sugar. For cooking, clear honey is best. It is easier to use than set honey and mixes well with other ingredients. It can be used to flavour natural yogurt, fruit salad, biscuits, cakes, sauces and milk drinks. Honey is hygroscopic, which means it attracts water; therefore, cakes and breads made with honey tend to stay fresh and moist longer than those made with other sweeteners.

Over the years honey has had a reputation for improving general health: it has been used as a treatment for complaints ranging from sore throats to digestive infections. Honey is certainly effective in killing bacteria and is useful in treating wounds, sores and burns. Unlike sugar, honey does not irritate the lining of the stomach and is therefore easier on the digestive system.

Although the use of honey should be limited for really healthy eating—a little honey goes a long way—it is a delicious way of satisfying the sweetest tooth.

SOME TIPS FOR USING HONEY

● Use a mild flavoured honey such as clover or acacia to sweeten drinks unless you want the honey flavour to come through.

● If honey goes solid you can soften it by sitting the jar in a saucepan of warm water.

● Use slightly lower cooking temperatures when using honey. Honey burns more easily than sugar and the natural enzymes contained in raw or unheated honey will be destroyed at 46°C (114°F) and over.

● The easiest way to measure honey accurately is to put the jar on the scales, weigh it and remove spoonfuls until the scales drop by the required amount.

● Lightly grease the spoon before measuring and the honey will roll off smoothly, eliminating a sticky mess.

● For weighing larger amounts, put the mixing bowl on the scales, register its weight, then pour in the honey to obtain the required weight.

● If properly stored in a screw-topped jar in a cool place pure honey does not go bad. Recently a pot of edible honey over 5,000 years old was discovered in Egypt.

● Honey on the comb should be kept in an airtight container in a cool place. It should be eaten within three months.

APRICOT AND KIWI FRUIT CUPS

Non-stick silicone paper is useful when baking biscuits that are fragile. The fine film of oil on the paper makes it easy to lift off the cooked biscuits. Greased greaseproof paper is a good alternative.

SERVES 4 200 calories per serving
PREPARATION 15 minutes
BAKING 10 minutes

1 egg white
25 g (1 oz) light muscovado sugar
25 g (1 oz) plain wholemeal flour
25 g (1 oz) flaked almonds, chopped
25 g (1 oz) polyunsaturated margarine, melted
60 ml (4 tbsp) whipping cream
60 ml (4 tbsp) Greek strained yogurt
1 kiwi fruit, peeled and finely chopped
2 kiwi fruit, sliced, to decorate
3 apricots, stoned and finely chopped

——1——
Line 2 baking sheets with non-stick silicone paper. Whisk the egg white until stiff, then lightly fold in the sugar, flour and almonds with a metal spoon. Fold in the margarine.

——2——
Place 8 spoonfuls of the mixture, spaced well apart, on the baking sheets. With the back of the spoon smooth out each spoonful thinly to a 7.5 cm (3 inch) round. Bake at 190°C (375°F) mark 5 for 8–10 minutes, until golden.

——3——
Using a palette knife, quickly lift the biscuits, one at a time, from the baking sheets and place over a small orange or the base of a small glass so that they will set in a cup shape. Allow a moment or two for each biscuit to harden, then remove to a wire rack to cool. If the remaining biscuits begin to harden before being shaped, return them to the oven for a few minutes.

——4——
Whip the cream until quite thick, then lightly whisk in the yogurt. Fold in the chopped kiwi fruit and apricots.

——5——
Fill each biscuit cup with the fruit cream and serve decorated with kiwi fruit slices.

GOODNESS GUIDE
FIBRE Fibre is provided by the fruit, wholemeal flour and almonds
VITAMINS The kiwi fruit and apricots provide vitamin C and the almonds and flour supply vitamins B and E
MINERALS Iron, calcium and zinc are supplied by the flour and almonds. Zinc aids the action of the enzymes responsible for mental and physical development

APRICOT AND KIWI FRUIT CUPS

GOLDEN FRUIT JELLY

The jelly can be made with any fresh fruit in season; no other sweetening is necessary

SERVES 4   150 calories per serving
PREPARATION 20 minutes
COOKING None
CHILLING At least 3 hours

20 g ($\frac{3}{4}$ oz) powdered gelatine
750 ml (1$\frac{1}{4}$ pints) unsweetened apple juice
1 banana
1 dessert apple
1 ripe pear
low-fat natural yogurt, to serve

———1———
Mix the gelatine and 75 ml (5 tbsp) water in a heatproof bowl and leave for about 5 minutes, until softened. Put the bowl over a saucepan of gently simmering water until the gelatine dissolves. Remove from the heat and leave to cool slightly. Stir in the apple juice and mix well.

———2———
Meanwhile, prepare the fruit. Peel and slice the banana, core and dice the apple and core and dice the pear. Place the fruit in a 1.1 litre (2 pint) decorative jelly mould. Pour the liquid into the jelly mould and chill until set.

———3———
To unmould, lightly draw a knife that has been dipped in hot water around the rim of the mould, then place the mould in hot water for 2–3 seconds. Put a damp serving plate over the mould and invert quickly, holding with both hands and shaking sharply. Remove mould.

GOODNESS GUIDE
SUGAR No processed sugar is added; the natural sweetness of the fresh fruit and juice is sufficient
FAT This dessert is fat-free
PROTEIN Serving with yogurt makes this into a protein-rich dessert
FIBRE The fruit and leaving it unpeeled provides lots

UPSIDE-DOWN FRUITY PUDDING

Serve with mixed whipping cream and yogurt instead of double cream.

SERVES 4   505 calories per serving
PREPARATION 15 minutes
BAKING 35 minutes

150 g (5 oz) polyunsaturated margarine
75 g (3 oz) light muscovado sugar
2 eggs
50 g (2 oz) self-raising flour
50 g (2 oz) self-raising wholemeal flour
225 g (8 oz) can unsweetened pineapple with 30 ml (2 tbsp) juice reserved
3 ready-to-eat dried apricots, rinsed and halved

———1———
Cream 100 g (4 oz) of the margarine with 50 g (2 oz) of the sugar and eggs until pale and light. Stir the flours together and fold into the mixture with pineapple juice.

———2———
Grease a 20.5 cm (8 inch) sandwich tin with the remaining margarine and sprinkle with the remaining muscovado sugar.

———3———
Arrange the fruit over the base and cover with the cake mixture. Bake at 180°C (350°F) mark 4 for 35 minutes or until springy to the touch. Turn out and serve in slices hot or cold.

GOODNESS GUIDE
FIBRE This dessert is very high in fibre, which is provided by fruit—especially the dried apricots—and the wholemeal flour
PROTEIN The eggs provide protein, supplemented by the wholemeal flour

CAROB MOUSSES

A healthier version of chocolate mousse, everyone's favourite dessert.

SERVES 4   330 calories per serving
PREPARATION 10 minutes
COOKING None
CHILLING 1$\frac{1}{2}$ hours

two 42 g (1$\frac{1}{2}$ oz) plain carob bars
25 g (1 oz) light muscovado sugar
15 ml (1 tbsp) brandy
150 ml (5 fl oz) Greek strained yogurt
150 ml (5 fl oz) whipping cream, whipped
4 pecan nuts or walnuts, to decorate

———1———
Break the carob into a heatproof bowl, add sugar and brandy. Place the bowl over a pan of simmering water and melt the carob, stirring occasionally. Cool for 1–2 minutes.

———2———
Mix the yogurt with the carob mixture and fold in the cream. Spoon into glasses and chill 1$\frac{1}{2}$ hours. Decorate and serve.

GOODNESS GUIDE
FAT Carob is a low-fat alternative to chocolate or cocoa powder. Mixing the cream with yogurt keeps the fat content down
SUGAR Carob is naturally sweet, so only a little sugar has been added

CAROB MOUSSES

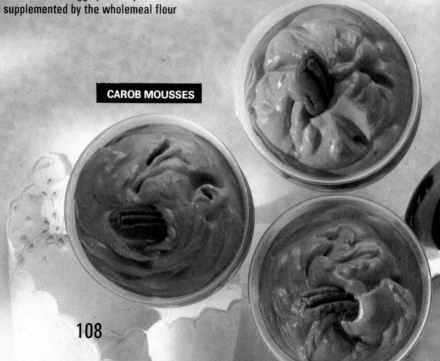

108

BANANA AND GRAPE BRÛLÉE

SERVES 4   230 calories per serving
PREPARATION   10 minutes
GRILLING   3 minutes
CHILLING   1 hour

2 bananas
225 g (8 oz) black grapes, seeded and halved
150 ml (5 fl oz) soured cream
150 ml (5 fl oz) Greek strained yogurt
25 g (1 oz) light muscovado sugar

———1———

Peel and slice the bananas, then mix with grapes; spoon into 4 ramekins. Mix the soured cream and yogurt and spoon over each. Cover and chill 1 hour. Sprinkle each with a little sugar and grill.

GOODNESS GUIDE
VITAMINS   Bananas and grapes are good sources of vitamin C, and the yogurt provides B vitamins
MINERALS   Both fruits are high in potassium; yogurt and soured cream provide calcium
FAT   Mixing soured cream with yogurt reduces the fat level

UPSIDE-DOWN FRUITY PUDDING

BANANA AND GRAPE BRULEE

GOLDEN FRUIT JELLY

109

BAKED STUFFED APPLES

Try these accompanied by Greek strained yogurt, and experiment with different nuts for the topping.

MAKES 4 170 calories each
PREPARATION 15 minutes
BAKING 40–50 minutes

4 cooking apples, each about 225 g (8 oz)
50 g (2 oz) ready-to-eat dried apricots,
rinsed and coarsely chopped
75 g (3 oz) fresh dates, stoned, or dried
dates, rinsed and chopped
juice of $\frac{1}{2}$ lemon
20 ml (4 tsp) clear honey
a little extra honey and a few toasted flaked
almonds, to serve

——— 1 ———

Core the apples. Scoop out the centre of each to leave a hollow about 2.5 cm (1 inch) in diameter. Using a sharp knife, cut a ring around the middle of the outside of each apple just into the skin. Place in a shallow, ovenproof dish and add 1 cm ($\frac{1}{2}$ inch) water.

——— 2 ———

Mix together the apricots, dates and lemon juice and use to fill the apples. Spoon 5 ml (1 tsp) of the honey into each apple centre.

——— 3 ———

Bake at 180°C (350°F) mark 4 for 40–50 minutes, until the apples are cooked through and tender when tested with a cocktail stick or skewer. Drizzle with the extra honey and sprinkle with toasted almonds. Serve at once.

MICROWAVE Follow step 1. Arrange apples in a circle in a round dish, add 30 ml (2 tbsp) water. Follow step 2. In step 3, cook 100% (High) 8–9 minutes until just tender, turning apples 3 times. Stand 2–3 minutes and complete step.

GOODNESS GUIDE

FIBRE High amounts of dietary fibre are provided by the dates, apricots and apples
SUGAR Only a small amount of added sugar, in the form of honey, is needed because most of the sweetness is provided by the fruit
FAT This is a very low-fat dessert

OLD-FASHIONED FRUIT PIE

MAKES 6 SLICES 160 calories each
PREPARATION 20 minutes
BAKING 35–40 minutes
CHILLING 30 minutes

1 eating apple
1 pear
175 g (6 oz) blackcurrants, trimmed from
stalks, thawed if frozen
25 ml (1$\frac{1}{2}$ tbsp) cornflour
15 ml (1 tbsp) light muscovado sugar
a little semi-skimmed milk and 30 ml
(2 tbsp) light muscovado sugar, to glaze

PASTRY
50 g (2 oz) self-raising wholemeal flour
50 g (2 oz) plain flour
50 g (2 oz) polyunsaturated margarine

——— 1 ———

To make the pastry, place the flours in a bowl. Add the margarine and rub in until the mixture resembles fine breadcrumbs. Stir in 25 ml (1$\frac{1}{2}$ tbsp) chilled water and mix lightly to a soft dough. Chill for 30 minutes.

BAKED STUFFED APPLES

OLD-FASHIONED FRUIT PIE

2

Turn out on to a lightly floured work surface and knead lightly. Divide the dough into two parts, one slightly larger than the other. Roll out the larger one and line a 19 cm (7½ inch) loose-bottomed flan tin.

3

Peel, core and slice the apple and pear. Mix with the blackcurrants, cornflour and sugar and place in the pastry case.

4

Roll out the reserved dough into a circle just large enough to cover the filling. Place over the fruit, seal the edges and trim away the excess dough. Cut 2 or 3 small slits in the centre of the pastry lid. Use the extra dough to make decorations. Brush with a little milk and sprinkle over the sugar.

5

Bake at 190°C (375°F) mark 5 for 35–40 minutes, until golden brown and the filling is cooked through. Cool for 5 minutes, then remove flan ring. Serve hot or cold.

GOODNESS GUIDE

FIBRE The fruit and wholemeal flour contribute good amounts of fibre
VITAMINS Blackcurrants are one of the richest sources of vitamin C
MINERALS Blackcurrants are also a good source of iron, calcium, magnesium and potassium

MARBLED PUDDING

If you do not have a steamer, put the basin in a pan of boiling water so it is half covered and reduce the cooking time by 15 minutes. Serve with Custard Sauce (page 122).

SERVES 4–6 450–300 calories per serving
PREPARATION 15 minutes
COOKING 1½ hours

75 g (3 oz) plain flour
5 ml (1 tsp) baking powder
100 g (4 oz) polyunsaturated margarine
100 g (4 oz) light muscovado sugar
2 eggs
60 ml (4 tbsp) semi-skimmed milk
65 g (2½ oz) plain wholemeal flour
10 ml (2 tsp) carob powder

1

Line the base and lightly grease a 900 ml (1½ pint) heatproof pudding basin and set aside. Sift together the plain flour and half the baking powder, then beat in half the amounts of all the remaining ingredients except the wholemeal flour and carob powder.

2

In another bowl, sift together the wholemeal flour, carob powder and remaining baking powder, adding any bran left in the sieve, then beat in the remaining ingredients. Spoon alternate heaped spoonfuls of the plain and carob mixtures into the pudding basin and lightly smooth the top.

3

Cover with a double thickness of lightly greased greaseproof paper or aluminium foil pleated in the centre, to allow for expansion, and secure with string.

4

Cook in a steamer over a large saucepan of boiling water for 1½ hours, topping up with extra boiling water when necessary, until a wooden cocktail stick or fine skewer pierced into the centre comes out clean. Turn out carefully on to a serving plate. Serve hot.

GOODNESS GUIDE

FAT This dish is lower in fat than traditional steamed puddings because semi-skimmed milk is used. Polyunsaturated margarine replaces saturated shredded beef suet
FIBRE Carob provides some fibre

MARBLED PUDDING

ORANGE MOUSSES

MAKES 4 120 calories each
PREPARATION 30 minutes
BAKING None
CHILLING 2–3 hours

4 sweet oranges
15 ml (1 tbsp) gelatine
15 ml (1 tbsp) light muscovado sugar
75 ml (3 fl oz) Greek strained yogurt
50 ml (2 fl oz) whipping cream
a few orange segments and mint sprigs,
to decorate

———1———

Over a large bowl, cut the top third off the oranges to make a zigzag edge. Remove all the flesh from the oranges and press through a sieve, then make the juice up to 300 ml ($\frac{1}{2}$ pint) with a little water if necessary. Reserve the orange shells.

———2———

Put half the juice into a saucepan, add the gelatine and leave for 5 minutes. Over a low heat, dissolve the gelatine by stirring, then add the sugar, stirring until dissolved. Pour into a bowl. Stir in the remaining juice and leave until the mixture sets around the edges of the bowl.

———3———

Fold the yogurt into the orange mixture. Whip the cream until it forms soft peaks and fold in to the mixture. Leave for 10–15 minutes, until it holds its shape. Pile into the reserved orange shells. Chill for 2–3 hours or until set. Serve chilled, decorated with orange segments and mint sprigs.

MICROWAVE Follow step 1. In step 2, put half the juice in a bowl, add gelatine, soak 5 minutes. Cook 100% (High) 1 minute or until gelatine is dissolved. Stir in sugar. Add remaining juice, leave until setting around the edges. Follow step 3.

GOODNESS GUIDE
FAT A small amount of whipping cream mixed with yogurt has been used instead of double cream for a lower fat content
VITAMINS Oranges contribute a good amount of vitamin C
FIBRE The oranges also provide some dietary fibre

LEMON MERINGUE PIE

MAKES 6 SLICES
210 calories per slice
PREPARATION 30 minutes
BAKING 40 minutes
CHILLING 30 minutes

finely grated rind and juice of 1 lemon
25 g (1 oz) light muscovado sugar
25 g (1 oz) cornflour
2 egg yolks

PASTRY
50 g (2 oz) plain flour
50 g (2 oz) plain wholemeal flour
50 g (2 oz) polyunsaturated margarine

MERINGUE
2 egg whites
50 g (2 oz) caster sugar

———1———

To make pastry, place flours in a bowl, add margarine and rub in until it resembles fine breadcrumbs. Add 25 ml (1$\frac{1}{2}$ tbsp) chilled water; mix to a dough. Chill 30 minutes.

———2———

Knead on a lightly floured surface, then roll out into a circle and line a 20.5 cm (8 inch) fluted flan dish.

———3———

Line the pastry with a sheet of greaseproof paper and baking beans and bake at 200°C (400°C) mark 6 for 10 minutes, until set. Remove paper and beans and return to the oven for 5 minutes.

———4———

To make the filling, put 300 ml ($\frac{1}{2}$ pint) water, the lemon rind and juice and sugar in a saucepan and bring to the boil, stirring to dissolve the sugar. In a bowl, blend the cornflour with a little water to make a smooth paste, then pour the boiling lemon and sugar mixture into the bowl, stirring constantly. Return to the saucepan and heat, stirring, until boiling, thickened. Remove from the heat and cool for 5 minutes.

———5———

Mix in the egg yolks, one at a time. Spoon into the pastry case, cover with foil and bake at 200°C (400°F) mark 6 for 20 minutes.

———6———

Whisk the egg whites until frothy. Gradually add the sugar, whisking constantly until the meringue is stiff. Spoon over the filling. Increase oven temperature to 220°C (425°F) mark 7 and bake for 5–10 minutes, until lightly tinged golden brown. Cool.

CREME CARAMEL

SERVES 4 205 calories per serving
PREPARATION 15 minutes
BAKING 1–1$\frac{1}{4}$ hours
CHILLING At least 3 hours

100 g (4 oz) light muscovado sugar
3 eggs
568 ml (1 pint) semi-skimmed milk
1 vanilla pod or 1.25 ml ($\frac{1}{4}$ tsp) vanilla essence
25 g (1 oz) dried skimmed milk powder
sliced strawberries, to decorate (optional)

———1———

Put half the sugar and 90 ml (6 tbsp) water into a saucepan. Stir over a low heat until the sugar dissolves, then boil rapidly without stirring until a deep golden brown. Pour into a 15 cm (6 inch) soufflé dish and cool.

———2———

Place the semi-skimmed milk and vanilla pod in a saucepan and slowly bring to the boil from the heat. Whisk together the eggs, remaining sugar and vanilla essence if used, and stir in the dried skimmed milk.

———3———

Remove the vanilla pod from the saucepan. (Rinse the pod and store for future use.) Pour the milk on to the egg mixture, whisking until the sugar and milk powder dissolve. Strain into the soufflé dish and cover. Place in a roasting pan half-filled with boiling water and bake at 170°C (325°F) mark 3 for 1–1$\frac{1}{4}$ hours, until set. Cool and chill for at least 3 hours or overnight.

———4———

To turn out, place a serving dish over the top of the soufflé dish. Hold the two dishes firmly together and turn over. Give a sharp shake to release the suction, then set aside for a few minutes so the caramel drains over the custard. Decorate with strawberries, if liked.

GOODNESS GUIDE

CREME CARAMEL
MINERALS A good amount of calcium is provided by the milk
PROTEIN This is high in protein

LEMON MERINGUE PIE
VITAMINS Lemon juice contains vitamin C
FAT The polyunsaturated margarine means less saturated fat

LEMON MERINGUE PIE

CRÈME CARAMEL

ORANGE MOUSSES

RASPBERRY BOMBE

This delicious and stunning looking dessert requires only 25 ml (1½ tbsp) added sugar—use less if you wish.

SERVES 4   75 calories per serving
PREPARATION 20 minutes
FREEZING 7 hours

225 g (8 oz) raspberries, fresh or thawed if frozen
25 ml (1½ tbsp) light muscovado sugar
10 ml (2 tsp) Crème de Cassis (blackcurrant liqueur)
225 g (8 oz) low-fat natural set yogurt
1 egg white, size 2

———1———
Put 175 g (6 oz) raspberries in a blender or food processor with half the sugar and the liqueur, and blend to make a purée. Reserve remaining raspberries for decoration. Pour into a freezerproof bowl; gently fold in the yogurt.

———2———
Put the bowl in the freezer for 1 hour or until ice crystals begin to form around the edge.

———3———
Whisk the egg white until stiff, then whisk in the remaining sugar and fold through the purée. Pour into a 900 ml (1½ pint) decorative freezer-proof mould.

———4———
Return to the freezer and leave at least 6 hours, until set. Stir at least once during this time.

———5———
Turn out of the bowl and decorate with reserved raspberries. Cut into slices to serve.

GOODNESS GUIDE

RASPBERRY BOMBE
FIBRE Raspberries are high in fibre
VITAMINS Raspberries are rich in vitamin C

PLUM CLAFOUTIS
PROTEIN Eggs, milk, cheese and almonds provide rich protein
VITAMINS Plums contain A and C

PEACH SOUFFLE
VITAMINS The peaches provide vitamin A and some C

CHESTNUT WHIPS
MINERALS The yogurt and chestnuts provide some calcium

PLUM CLAFOUTIS

Serve the clafoutis hot, straight from the oven, or chilled

MAKES 6 SLICES   170 calories each
PREPARATION 15 minutes
BAKING 25–30 minutes

450 g (1 lb) plums, halved and stoned

BATTER
50 g (2 oz) low-fat cheese
50 g (2 oz) ground almonds
25 g (1 oz) light muscovado sugar
2 eggs, lightly beaten
60 ml (4 tbsp) semi-skimmed milk
50 g (2 oz) polyunsaturated margarine, melted

———1———
Lightly grease a 20.5 cm (8 inch) round flan dish and arrange the plums in it in a circular pattern.

———2———
To make the batter, beat the cheese, ground almonds and sugar together, then gradually whisk in the eggs and milk. Fold in the margarine and pour the batter over the plums.

———3———
Bake at 200°C (400°F) mark 6 for 25–30 minutes, until set.

CHESTNUT WHIPS

Chestnuts are high in fibre. Whipped with egg whites and yogurt, chestnut purée makes a creamy dessert.

MAKES 4–6   305–200 calories each
PREPARATION 15 minutes
CHILLING 2 hours

425 g (15 oz) can unsweetened chestnut purée
300 ml (10 fl oz) Greek strained yogurt
finely grated rind and juice of ½ orange
10 ml (2 tsp) clear honey
2 egg whites
grated plain carob bar, to decorate

———1———
Beat the chestnut purée and yogurt together until smooth. Add the orange rind, juice and honey and beat again.

———2———
Whisk the egg whites until stiff. Stir 2 large spoonfuls into the chestnut mixture to soften it, then gently fold in the remaining egg white and spoon into 4–6 individual glasses. Chill for at least 2 hours until ready to serve, then grate a little carob on top of each.

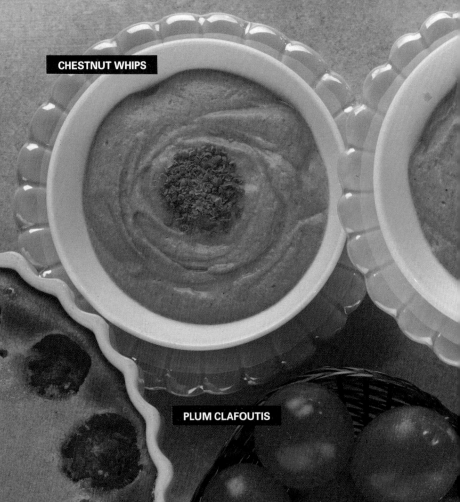

CHESTNUT WHIPS

PLUM CLAFOUTIS

GOLDEN PEACH SOUFFLE

GOLDEN PEACH SOUFFLE

This fruit soufflé is perfect after a large meal because it is made without a flour base. Serve it as soon as it is cooked, as it will collapse quickly.

SERVES 4 80 calories per serving
PREPARATION 15 minutes
BAKING 40–50 minutes

425 g (15 oz) can unsweetened peaches, drained
15 ml (1 tbsp) clear honey
2 egg yolks, beaten
3 egg whites

———1———
Lightly grease a 1.1 litre (2 pint) soufflé dish. Place the peaches and honey in a blender or food processor and purée until smooth.

———2———
Mix into the egg yolks. Whisk the egg whites until stiff, then carefully fold them into the peach mixture until well incorporated.

———3———
Pour into the prepared dish and bake at 190°C (375°F) mark 5 for 40–50 minutes, until golden and well risen.

RASPBERRY BOMBE

RHUBARB AND ORANGE CHIFFON PIE

MAKES 6 SLICES   245 calories each
PREPARATION   30 minutes
COOKING   10 minutes
CHILLING   1–2 hours

450 g (1 lb) rhubarb, trimmed, washed and
finely chopped
grated rind and juice of 1 small orange
2 eggs, separated
50 g (2 oz) light muscovado sugar
10 ml (2 tsp) powdered gelatine
thinly pared orange rind and whipped
cream, to decorate

BISCUIT CRUST
50 g (2 oz) polyunsaturated margarine
150 g (5 oz) wholemeal digestive biscuits,
crushed

——— 1 ———

To make the crust, melt the margarine and stir in the biscuit crumbs until well mixed. Turn into a 20.5 cm (8 inch) flan or pie dish and press evenly over the base and sides. Cover with cling film and chill.

——— 2 ———

Put the rhubarb and orange rind and juice in a saucepan and simmer gently, stirring occasionally, for about 10 minutes, until reduced to a pulp. Beat with a wooden spoon until smooth. Whisk the egg yolks and sugar together, then whisk into the rhubarb.

——— 3 ———

Dissolve the gelatine in 30 ml (2 tbsp) water in a heatproof bowl over a pan of gently steaming hot water. Cool slightly, then stir into the rhubarb mixture. Leave in a cold place until it begins to thicken and just set.

——— 4 ———

Whisk the egg whites until stiff, then fold into the rhubarb mixture. Pour into the biscuit crust, swirling the top for decoration. Chill for 1–2 hours, until set. Decorate with orange rind strips and swirls of cream.

GOODNESS GUIDE

FIBRE The rhubarb and wholemeal digestive biscuits make this a high-fibre dessert
VITAMINS The orange and rhubarb supply plenty of vitamin C
FAT Polyunsaturated margarine has replaced the hard fats traditionally used in biscuit crusts

MAGIC LEMON PUDDING

This pudding separates out during cooking to give a creamy sauce under a layer of sponge.

SERVES 4   280 calories per serving
PREPARATION   15 minutes
BAKING   40–45 minutes

finely grated rind and juice of 1 lemon
50 g (2 oz) polyunsaturated margarine
75 g (3 oz) light muscovado sugar
2 eggs, separated
300 ml ($\frac{1}{2}$ pint) semi-skimmed milk
50 g (2 oz) self-raising wholemeal flour
lemon slices, to decorate

——— 1 ———

Lightly grease a 1.1 litre (2 pint) ovenproof dish. Mix together the lemon rind, margarine and sugar and beat until pale and fluffy, then beat in the egg yolks.

——— 2 ———

Add the lemon juice with the milk and flour and stir. Whisk the egg whites until stiff, then fold in.

——— 3 ———

Pour the mixture into the prepared dish and stand in a roasting pan with enough water to come half way up the side of the dish.

——— 4 ———

Bake at 190°C (375°F) mark 5 for 40–45 minutes or until lightly browned and the top is set. Serve hot, decorated with lemon slices.

MICROWAVE Follow steps 1, 2 and 3 using a microwave oven dish. In step 4, cook 100% (High) for 20 minutes, turning the dish 3 or 4 times, until just set in the centre. Serve hot.

GOODNESS GUIDE
VITAMINS The pudding is rich in vitamins, with C from the lemon juice and B group vitamins from the milk, flour and eggs. Eggs also contribute vitamins A, D and E
MINERALS The eggs and flour supply iron, which is better absorbed in the presence of vitamin C; they and the milk also supply calcium

MAGIC LEMON PUDDING

RHUBARB AND ORANGE CHIFFON PIE

BROWN BREAD ICE CREAM

This is an old-fashioned favourite that has a delicious praline-like flavour.

SERVES 4   290 calories per serving
PREPARATION 20 minutes
COOKING None
FREEZING 4 hours

**100 g (4 oz) fresh wholemeal
breadcrumbs, including crusts
75 g (3 oz) light muscovado sugar
150 ml (5 fl oz) whipping cream
300 ml (10 fl oz) low-fat natural yogurt
1 or 2 egg whites (optional)
chopped walnuts, to decorate**

———1———

Mix the breadcrumbs with 50 g (2 oz) of the sugar and spread on a baking sheet. Bake at 200°C (400°F) mark 6 for 10–15 minutes, turning occasionally, until crisp and lightly browned. Alternatively, toast under the grill, turning frequently to prevent burning. Set aside to cool, then break up with a spoon.

———2———

Whip the cream until thick, then stir in the yogurt and remaining sugar. Stir in the toasted breadcrumbs, reserving 25 g (1 oz) for the topping. Whisk the egg whites, if using, and fold into the mixture.

———3———

Pour into a freezerproof container and freeze for 4 hours, until firm. Transfer to the refrigerator to soften 30 minutes before serving. To serve, scoop into serving dishes and sprinkle with reserved crumbs and walnuts.

GOODNESS GUIDE

FIBRE The wholemeal breadcrumbs in this recipe provide a substantial fibre content
FAT This ice cream is much lower in fat than most; the fat has been reduced by substituting low-fat yogurt for two-thirds of the cream; whipping cream itself is lower in fat than double cream
MINERALS The wholemeal breadcrumbs supply iron, calcium and zinc. The yogurt is rich in calcium

BROWN BREAD ICE CREAM

EXOTIC FRUIT SALAD

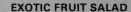
EXOTIC FRUIT SALAD

All these tropical fruits should be available at large supermarkets. You can add or substitute others, either fresh or canned in natural juices.

SERVES 4–6   165–110 calories
per serving
PREPARATION 30 minutes
COOKING None
CHILLING At least 30 minutes

**900 g (2 lb) ripe pineapple
1 mango or small papaya
1 guava or banana, sliced
1 passion fruit or pomegranate
4 lychees or rambutans
1 kiwi fruit**

———1———

Cut the pineapple in half lengthways, with the leaves attached. Remove the core in a wedge from each half and discard. Cut out the flesh, cut into small chunks and place in a bowl. Scrape out the remaining flesh and juice with a spoon and add to the bowl.

———2———

Peel the mango or papaya and discard the stone or seeds. Cut the flesh into cubes and add to the pineapple with the guava or banana.

———3———

Cut the passion fruit or pomegranate in half, and scoop out the seeds with a teaspoon. Add the seeds to the pineapple.

———4———

Peel the lychees or rambutans and cut in half. Remove the stones and add to the bowl of fruit.

———5———

Peel the kiwi fruit and cut the flesh into round slices. Add to the bowl of fruit and stir.

———6———

Spoon the fruit salad into the pineapple halves. Cover and refrigerate until required.

GOODNESS GUIDE

VITAMINS Mango and papaya are rich in vitamin A, while all the fruit contribute plenty of vitamin C
FIBRE All the fruit supply fibre; fibre is believed to have a significant effect on lowering the level of cholesterol in the blood

FRUIT CHEESECAKE

This high-protein dessert will be enjoyed by all the members of the family and it can be eaten by lacto-ovo vegetarians as it contains no gelatine.

MAKES 8 SLICES 305 calories each
PREPARATION 10 minutes
BAKING 45 minutes
COOLING About 3 hours

700 g (1½ lb) ricotta cheese
3 eggs, size 3
finely grated rind of 1 lemon
75 g (3 oz) light muscovado sugar
60 ml (4 tbsp) Greek strained yogurt
2 kiwi fruit, peeled and sliced, and 225 g
(8 oz) strawberries, hulled and sliced,
to decorate

BASE
50 g (2 oz) polyunsaturated margarine
25 g (1 oz) medium oatmeal
75 g (3 oz) plain wholemeal flour
40 g (1½ oz) light muscovado sugar
7.5 ml (1½ tsp) ground ginger

——— 1 ———

To make the base, melt the margarine in a saucepan and stir in the oatmeal, flour, sugar and ginger.

Cook gently for 1–2 minutes, stirring, until well mixed. Press on to the base of an 18 cm (7 inch) loose-bottomed cake tin. Bake at 180°C (350°F) mark 4 for 5 minutes.

——— 2 ———

Meanwhile, beat the cheese until smooth, then add the eggs, one at a time, blending in well. Add the lemon rind and sugar and mix together thoroughly.

——— 3 ———

Pour on the baked base, smooth the surface and continue baking for 20 minutes. Then carefully spoon the yogurt over the filling. Bake for a further 20 minutes.

——— 4 ———

Cool for about 3 hours in the tin. When cold, carefully remove cheesecake from the tin and serve decorated with kiwi fruit and strawberries.

GOODNESS GUIDE
MINERALS The cheese, yogurt and flour make this dish high in calcium which is necessary for strong bones and blood clotting. The protein and lactose found in the ricotta cheese help us to absorb the calcium more readily
FIBRE The wholemeal flour, oatmeal and fruit supply fibre

FRUIT CHEESECAKE

CHERRY ALMOND TART

CHERRY ALMOND TART

MAKES 8 SLICES 305 calories each
PREPARATION 10 minutes
BAKING 35 minutes
CHILLING 30 minutes

5 ml (1 tsp) cornflour
25 g (1 oz) blanched almonds, freshly grated
25 g (1 oz) light muscovado sugar
450 g (1 lb) fresh cherries, stoned
225 ml (8 fl oz) Greek strained yogurt and
15 ml (1 tbsp) brandy (optional), to serve

PASTRY
175 g (6 oz) plain wholemeal flour
75 g (3 oz) almonds, freshly grated
25 g (1 oz) light muscovado sugar
75 g (3 oz) polyunsaturated margarine

——— 1 ———

To make the pastry, place the flour, almonds and sugar in a bowl and rub in the margarine until the mixture resembles fine breadcrumbs. Add enough cold water to form into a dough. Chill for 30 minutes.

——— 2 ———

Roll out the dough on a lightly floured surface and use to line a 23 cm (9 inch) tart tin. Prick the pastry, line with greaseproof paper and fill with baking beans. Bake blind at 190°C (375°F) mark 5 for 15 minutes, then remove the beans and paper.

——— 3 ———

Sift the cornflour over the base of the tart. Sprinkle with the grated almonds and sugar and cover with the cherries. Bake for 20 minutes. Cool.

——— 4 ———

Stir the brandy, if using, into the Greek strained yogurt and serve with the tart.

GOODNESS GUIDE
PROTEIN The combination of almonds, flour and yogurt provides an excellent source of protein
FIBRE A good helping of fibre is supplied by the flour, almonds and cherries
VITAMINS The almonds, flour and yogurt are sources of B-complex vitamins

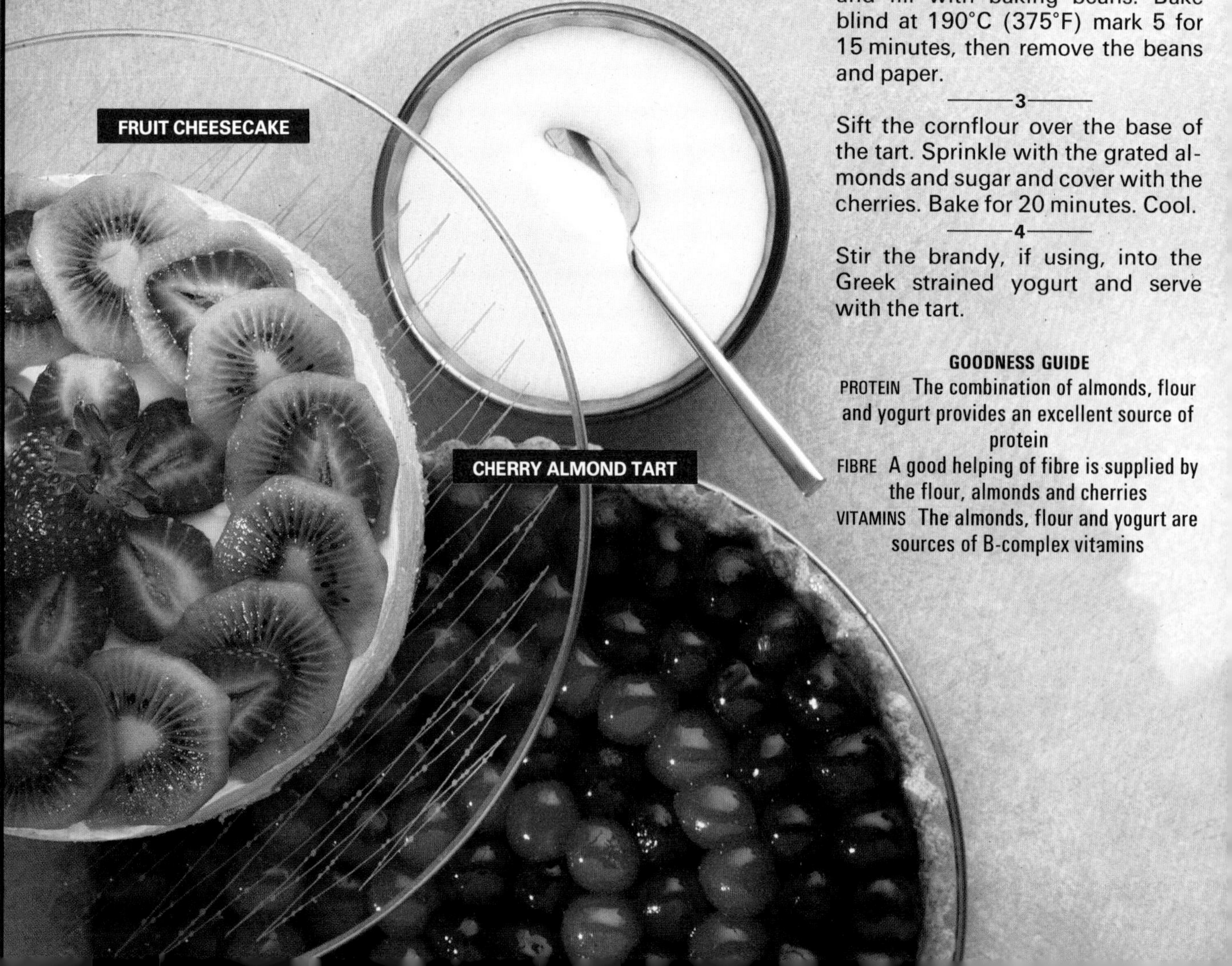

RICE RING WITH RASPBERRY SAUCE

SERVES 8 220 calories per serving
PREPARATION 15 minutes
COOKING 40 minutes
CHILLING 2 hours

1.1 litres (2 pints) semi-skimmed milk
140 g (4¾ oz) short grain brown rice, rinsed
75 g (3 oz) raisins, rinsed
grated rind of 1 lemon
7.5 ml (1½ tsp) ground cinnamon
25 g (1 oz) light muscovado sugar
30 ml (2 tbsp) Greek strained yogurt
15 ml (1 tbsp) powdered gelatine
40 g (1½ oz) blanched almonds, toasted and
coarsely chopped
raspberries, to garnish (optional)

RASPBERRY SAUCE
700 g (1½ lb) raspberries
50 g (2 oz) light muscovado sugar

PEANUT AND DATE SWEETS

RICE RING WITH RASPBERRY SAUCE

——— 1 ———

Lightly grease a 1.1 litre (2 pint) ring mould and set aside. Combine the milk, rice, raisins, lemon rind and cinnamon in a saucepan. Bring to the boil and simmer, partly covered, for 30 minutes, until almost tender.

——— 2 ———

Uncover the saucepan and simmer the rice mixture for a further 10 minutes. Remove from the heat and stir in the sugar and yogurt.

——— 3 ———

Pour about 45 ml (3 tbsp) of the rice liquid into a small bowl, sprinkle on the gelatine, and stir to dissolve. Pour back into the saucepan, add the nuts and mix well. Pour the rice mixture into the ring mould, shaking to remove air bubbles, and leave to cool. Chill for 2 hours or until set.

——— 4 ———

Meanwhile, make the sauce. Put the raspberries in a pan with the sugar and 15 ml (1 tbsp) of water. Cook, covered, until the raspberries are soft. Sieve and leave to cool.

——— 5 ———

Turn out the ring carefully on to a plate and fill the centre of the ring with raspberries, if wished. Serve sliced with the sauce poured over or around, or serve sauce separately in a jug.

PEANUT AND DATE SWEETS

These sweets are high in fibre and do not contain any refined sugar. Pack as a treat in a lunch box.

MAKES 20 45 calories each
PREPARATION 10 minutes
COOKING 5–10 minutes
CHILLING 1–2 hours

100 g (4 oz) stoned dates, rinsed
and chopped
50 g (2 oz) raisins, rinsed and
roughly chopped
30 ml (2 tbsp) orange juice
100 g (4 oz) low-fat soft cheese
30 ml (2 tbsp) crunchy natural peanut butter
5 ml (1 tsp) grated orange rind
60 ml (4 tbsp) finely chopped natural
roasted peanuts

——— 1 ———

Put the dates and raisins in a small non-stick pan with the orange juice. Cover and cook over a very low heat for 5–10 minutes until soft, stirring occasionally. Leave to cool.

——— 2 ———

Beat the cheese with the peanut butter and orange rind. Using a wooden spoon, mix in the date mixture and beat well. Chill for 15 minutes.

——— 3 ———

Shape the mixture into 20 small balls rolling lightly in the hands. Toss in the peanuts and place in sweet cases on a baking sheet. Chill until required.

GOODNESS GUIDE

PEANUT AND DATE SWEETS
MINERALS The cheese, dates and peanuts provide calcium. Iron is present in the dates, peanuts and raisins. All the ingredients provide potassium.

*RICE RING WITH
RASPBERRY SAUCE*
VITAMINS Brown rice, milk, yogurt and almonds provide B-complex vitamins. Raspberries are a good source of vitamin C

DESSERTS

RASPBERRY TOFU ICE CREAM

Tofu is made from ground soya beans and water and is extremely rich in protein. Buy it at Chinese grocers' or health food shops

MAKES 12 SLICES 80 calories each
PREPARATION 20 minutes
COOKING None
FREEZING 4–5 hours

625 g (1 lb 6 oz) tofu
1 egg, separated
100 g (4 oz) golden granulated sugar
90 ml (6 tbsp) Greek strained yogurt
few drops of vanilla essence
100 g (4 oz) raspberries
a few raspberries, to decorate

———1———

Drain excess liquid from the tofu. Place in a blender or food processor with the egg yolk and 75 g (3 oz) of the sugar and blend until smooth. Add the yogurt and vanilla essence and blend again briefly.

———2———

Pour the mixture into a freezer container and freeze for about 1 hour until beginning to set. Meanwhile, press the raspberries through a nylon sieve to make a purée.

———3———

Whisk the egg white until stiff and gradually whisk in the remaining sugar. Carefully fold in the purée.

———4———

Remove the tofu mixture from the freezer. Gently swirl in the raspberry mixture to create a marbled effect. Pour the mixture into a 900 g (2 lb) loaf tin and freeze until firm. To serve, dip the tin in hot water, then invert on to a serving plate. Slice and decorate with raspberries.

GOODNESS GUIDE
PROTEIN The egg, yogurt and tofu are rich in protein
VITAMINS The raspberries supply vitamin C
MINERALS There is a good supply of iron, potassium and calcium. The tofu provides magnesium which appears to protect the body against stress

SPICY CIDER GRANITA

SERVES 4 105 calories per serving
PREPARATION 2 minutes
COOKING 10 minutes
COOLING 30 minutes
FREEZING 4–5 hours

600 ml (1 pint) dry cider
2 pieces thinly pared orange rind
1 cinnamon stock
4 cloves
50 g (2 oz) light muscovado sugar
extra orange rind, to decorate

———1———

Put all the ingredients in a saucepan and very gently heat until nearly boiling, then set aside to cool for 30 minutes.

———2———

When quite cold, strain the liquid into a 600 ml (1 pint) freezer container and freeze for about 2 hours, until the mixture just begins to set around the edge.

———3———

Turn the mixture into a bowl and whisk to break up the granules. Return to the container and freeze until solid.

———4———

To serve, scrape spoonfuls of the mixture into bowls or glasses and decorate with the orange rind tied into knots.

GOODNESS GUIDE
VITAMINS The orange provides some vitamin C, which is necessary for healthy cells, blood vessels, bones, gums and teeth
MINERALS Oranges are a good source of potassium. The cider provides a little potassium too. The cider also supplies small amounts of other minerals

MIXED FRUIT BRULEE

SERVES 4 115 calories per serving
PREPARATION 30 minutes
COOKING 3 minutes
CHILLING 1 hour

100 g (4 oz) strawberries, hulled and halved
100 g (4 oz) raspberries
100 g (4 oz) redcurrants
30 ml (2 tbsp) blackcurrant liqueur
150 ml (5 fl oz) whipping cream
150 ml (5 fl oz) Greek strained yogurt
25 g (1 oz) golden granulated sugar

———1———

Mix the prepared fruit with the liqueur in a flameproof serving dish. Set aside.

———2———

Whip the cream until it forms soft peaks, then carefully fold in the yogurt. Spoon the mixture evenly over the fruit and smooth the surface. Cover and chill for at least 1 hour in the refrigerator.

———3———

To serve, sprinkle over the sugar and place under a preheated grill. Cook until brown and bubbling. Serve immediately.

GOODNESS GUIDE
VITAMINS Using fresh, uncooked fruit preserves the valuable vitamin C
MINERALS The fruit provide a range of minerals and all are high in potassium. Raspberries and redcurrants are high in iron and also supply calcium. Yogurt is rich in calcium
FIBRE The fruit is high in fibre

120

RASPBERRY TOFU ICE CREAM

MANGO AND PAPAYA SALAD

MANGO AND PAPAYA SALAD

SERVES 4   160 calories per serving
PREPARATION   15 minutes
COOKING   None
MACERATING   1 hour

2 ripe mangoes, peeled
2 ripe papayas, peeled and seeded
finely grated rind and juice of 1 lime
lime slices and fresh mint sprigs, to
decorate

——— 1 ———
Slice the mango flesh off the flat
stone, as neatly as possible, then cut
the flesh into long slices or equal-
sized cubes. Cut the papaya lengthways, then into neat slices or equal-
sized cubes.

——— 2 ———
Place the prepared fruit in a bowl
and add the lime rind and juice.
Gently toss together, then cover and
leave to macerate for 1 hour before
serving. Serve in individual bowls,
decorated with lime slices and fresh
mint sprigs.

GOODNESS GUIDE
VITAMINS This is a vitamin C-rich salad.
Mangoes and papaya are also major
contributors of vitamin A—a vitamin
essential for healthy skin and mucous
membranes and sharp vision in low-light
conditions
FIBRE Although both fruits are soft and
pulpy, they contribute excellent
amounts of fibre

MIXED FRUIT BRULEE

123

SPICY APPLE CRUMBLE

SERVES 4–6 405–270 calories
PREPARATION 15 minutes
COOKING 45 minutes

450 g (1 lb) cooking apples, peeled, cored
and sliced
50 g (2 oz) sultanas
25 g (1 oz) light muscovado sugar
10 ml (2 tsp) ground cinnamon

HONEY AND OAT TOPPING
50 g (2 oz) plain wholemeal flour
50 g (2 oz) plain flour
50 g (2 oz) polyunsaturated margarine
100 g (4 oz) porridge oats
45 ml (3 tbsp) clear honey

———1———
Mix the apples, sultanas, sugar and
cinnamon in an ovenproof dish. In
another bowl, mix the flours and rub
in the margarine, then add the oats
and honey.

———2———
Sprinkle over the top of the apples
and bake at 180°C (350°F) mark 4
for about 45 minutes until golden.

GOODNESS GUIDE
SUGAR Mixing sweet dried fruit with tarter
fresh fruit greatly reduces the amount of
added sugar required
FIBRE There is plenty of fibre in this
crumble from the fruit content and the oats
and wholemeal flour in the topping

CUSTARD SAUCE

SERVES 4 115 calories per serving
PREPARATION 2 minutes
COOKING 5 minutes

2 egg yolks
15 g (½ oz) cornflour
25 g (1 oz) light muscovado sugar
300 ml (½ pint) semi-skimmed milk
few drops vanilla essence

———1———
Beat together the egg yolks, cornflour and sugar.

———2———
Heat the milk until boiling and pour
on to the egg mixture. Return to the
saucepan and stir constantly over
a gentle heat until the custard
thickens. Add a few drops of vanilla
essence, stir and serve.

DATE AND FIG PUDDING

DATE AND FIG PUDDING

SERVES 4–6 335–225 calories
PREPARATION 10 minutes
STANDING 1 hour
STEAMING 1½ hours

pared rind and juice of 1 orange
100 g (4 oz) dried dates, chopped
100 g (4 oz) dried figs, coarsely chopped
50 g (2 oz) fresh root ginger, peeled and
finely shredded
25 g (1 oz) polyunsaturated margarine
25 g (1 oz) plain wholemeal flour
25 g (1 oz) plain flour
5 ml (1 tsp) baking powder
2 eggs, beaten
150 g (5 oz) fresh wholemeal breadcrumbs
orange slices, to garnish

ORANGE SAUCE
2 eggs, separated
25 g (1 oz) light muscovado sugar
grated rind and juice of 2 oranges

———1———
Lightly grease a 900 ml (1½ pint)
pudding basin.

———2———
Cut the orange rind into fine strips
1 cm (½ inch) long and mix with the
juice, dates, figs and ginger. Set
aside for 1 hour, stirring occasionally.

———3———
Add the margarine, flours, baking
powder, eggs and breadcrumbs to
the fruit mixture. Put in the basin.
Tie a double thickness of greaseproof paper over the top and steam
1½ hours.

———4———
Fifteen minutes before the end of
cooking, make the sauce. Whisk the
egg yolks with the sugar and rind in
a heatproof bowl over a pan of
boiling water until pale and creamy.
Warm the juice in another saucepan
and gradually add to the egg mixture
off the heat, whisking continuously.
Whisk the egg whites until stiff, then
fold in. Turn out the pudding on to a
serving dish and garnish with the
orange slices. Serve the pudding
with the orange sauce.

GOODNESS GUIDE
FIBRE Both dried dates and especially dried
figs are very high in fibre. With the
wholemeal breadcrumbs the fibre content is
high
SUGAR There is no added sugar in the
pudding; sweetness comes from the dried
fruits which are high in natural sugars

CUSTARD SAUCE
FAT The use of semi-skimmed milk in this
sauce instead of whole milk helps cut the
fat content
PROTEIN Both eggs and milk are especially
rich sources of protein

CUSTARD SAUCE

MINTY FRUIT SALAD

SPICY APPLE CRUMBLE

MINTY FRUIT SALAD

If mint is unavailable use ground cinnamon or freshly grated nutmeg.

SERVES 4   105 calories per serving
PREPARATION 10 minutes
COOKING None

100 ml (4 fl oz) unsweetened apple juice
1 red eating apple, cored and sliced
1 green eating apple, cored and sliced
2 ripe pears, sliced
3 satsumas, peeled and segmented
2 bananas, peeled and sliced
15 ml (1 tbsp) chopped fresh mint
fresh mint sprig, to decorate

—— 1 ——
Put the apple juice in a bowl and add the remaining ingredients.

—— 2 ——
Toss gently so all the ingredients are coated in the apple juice. Cover and chill until ready to serve.

GOODNESS GUIDE
FIBRE All these fruits provide plenty of fibre—even soft fruits such as orange and banana contain useful amounts
SUGAR Fruits add sweetness without having to add sugar. Apple juice makes a healthy low-sugar alternative to the syrups used in some fruit salads
VITAMINS This is rich in vitamin C

CAROB ROULADE

SERVES 4–6 285–190 calories per serving
PREPARATION 45 minutes
BAKING 10–12 minutes
SOAKING Overnight

3 eggs, size 2, separated
50 g (2 oz) light muscovado sugar
30 ml (2 tbsp) carob powder
40 g (1½ oz) hazelnuts in skins, coarsely ground
a small amount of caster or icing sugar (optional), to dust

APRICOT FILLING
50 g (2 oz) ready-to-eat dried apricots, rinsed and soaked overnight in 300 ml (½ pint) water
225 g (8 oz) low-fat soft cheese or natural set low-fat yogurt

———1———
Grease and line a 30.5 × 21.5 cm (12 × 8½ inch) Swiss roll tin with greaseproof paper and set aside.

———2———
Whisk together the egg yolks and sugar until very thick and creamy; then whisk in the carob powder. Whisk the egg whites until stiff. Fold 15 ml (1 tbsp) of the whites into the carob mixture with the ground hazelnuts, then evenly fold in the remaining egg whites.

———3———
Turn the mixture into the prepared tin and level the surface. Bake at 180°C (350°F) mark 4 for 10–12 minutes, until risen and just firm.

———4———
Turn out the sponge on to a sheet of greaseproof paper dusted very lightly with the caster or icing sugar. Carefully peel off the baking paper from the sponge, then roll up from the short side with the greaseproof paper inside. Cool on a wire rack.

———5———
To make the filling, stew the apricots in their soaking water for about 30 minutes, until soft and nearly all the liquid has evaporated. Drain off all but 15 ml (1 tbsp). Purée the apricots in a blender or food processor and leave to cool. Stir the cooled purée into the cheese or yogurt.

———6———
When the roulade is cold, unroll. Spread the apricot filling evenly over the top with a palette knife. Re-roll, carefully using the greaseproof paper as an aid to rolling. Slice.

KIWI FRUIT SORBET

Strawberries make a delicious and colourful accompaniment to this refreshing dessert.

SERVES 4 75 calories per serving
PREPARATION 15 minutes
COOLING 30 minutes
FREEZING 6 hours

50 g (2 oz) golden granulated sugar
6 kiwi fruit, plus 1, sliced, to decorate
2 egg whites

———1———
Chill a shallow freezer container. Place the sugar in a heavy saucepan and pour over 150 ml (¼ pint) water. Warm over a low heat until the sugar has dissolved, then simmer for 2 minutes to form a syrup. Remove from the heat and leave to cool for 30 minutes.

———2———
Thinly peel the kiwi fruit and halve. Place in a blender or food processor with the syrup and purée, then pass through a nylon sieve to remove the pips. Freeze for 2 hours, or until the mixture is half-frozen.

———3———
Whisk the egg whites until just stiff, then fold into the half-frozen syrup until it is an even texture. Cover the freezer container and freeze for 4 hours, until firm. Remove from the freezer just before serving. Spoon into glasses and decorate with slices of kiwi fruit.

GOODNESS GUIDE

KIWI FRUIT SORBET
VITAMINS Kiwi fruit is an excellent source of vitamin C, needed for healthy cells, gums and teeth. It also aids in the healing of wounds
FIBRE Some dietary fibre is provided by the kiwi fruit

CAROB ROULADE
MINERALS This dish is rich in minerals. Iron is provided by the eggs, apricots, nuts and carob. The yogurt provides calcium, as do the eggs, nuts and carob. All the ingredients contribute potassium, necessary for nerve impulse transmission
VITAMINS Apricots are noted for their high vitamin A content. The eggs and carob also supply vitamin A, essential for good vision in low light as well as healthy mucous cells

APPLE SLICES POACHED IN CIDER

RHUBARB BETTY

SERVES 4 180 calories per serving
PREPARATION 30 minutes
BAKING 30–40 minutes

450 g (1 lb) rhubarb, cut into 5 cm (2 inch) lengths
75 g (3 oz) light muscovado sugar
grated rind and juice of 1 orange
100 g (4 oz) fresh wholemeal breadcrumbs
2.5 ml (½ tsp) ground mixed spice
25 g (1 oz) polyunsaturated margarine

———1———
Lightly grease a 900 ml (1½ pint) ovenproof dish and set aside. Put the rhubarb in a large saucepan with 25 g (1 oz) of the sugar and the orange juice. Cover and simmer for 10 minutes, until just tender.

———2———
Mix the remaining sugar with the orange rind, breadcrumbs and mixed spice. Put half this mixture in the bottom of the prepared dish. Spoon the rhubarb mixture over the top, then cover with the remaining crumb mixture and dot with the margarine.

RHUBARB BETTY

KIWI FRUIT SORBET

CAROB ROULADE

———3———

Bake at 190°C (375°F) mark 5 for 30–40 minutes, until the top is crisp and browned. Serve hot.

MICROWAVE Put rhubarb, 25 g (1 oz) sugar and orange juice into a bowl. Cook, uncovered, 100% (High) 4–5 minutes. Follow step 2, placing breadcrumb and rhubarb mixtures into a microwave oven dish. Cook, uncovered, 100% (High) 4 minutes. Brown surface under a grill before serving if liked.

GOODNESS GUIDE
FIBRE A good amount of fibre is provided by the rhubarb and wholemeal breadcrumbs
VITAMINS Rhubarb is a source of vitamin C, which is further boosted by the orange juice. The breadcrumbs provide B-complex vitamins, which are essential for energy production from carbohydrates
MINERALS Rhubarb and the breadcrumbs are sources of potassium and calcium

---

APPLE SLICES POACHED IN CIDER

If you prefer, pour the hot, spiced cider over the apple slices in an ovenproof dish. Cover and cook at 180°C (350°F) mark 4 for 10–15 minutes.

SERVES 4 115 calories per serving
PREPARATION 10 minutes
COOKING 5–10 minutes

300 ml (½ pint) sweet cider, or dry cider mixed with 25 g (1 oz) light muscovado sugar
1 cinnamon stick
2 cloves
450 g (1 lb) eating apples
50 g (2 oz) sultanas (optional)

———1———

Pour the cider into a saucepan, add the cinnamon and cloves and bring slowly to the boil.

———2———

Quarter the apples, remove the cores, then slice and add to the hot cider, with the sultanas. Cover and simmer for 5–10 minutes, until tender. Remove the spices. Serve hot or cold.

MICROWAVE Put cider, cinnamon and cloves into a microwave bowl. Cover and cook 100% (High) 5 minutes. Prepare the apples, then add with the sultanas. Cover and cook 100% (High) 5 minutes.

GOODNESS GUIDE
FIBRE The apples supply pectin, a type of fibre beneficial to glucose absorption in the intestine
MINERALS The sultanas contribute some iron, needed for healthy blood cells. Both the apples and sultanas provide potassium; potassium helps the muscle cells of the body to function efficiently
VITAMINS Although eating apples are not extremely high in vitamin C, they do contribute a little

125

PINEAPPLE TART

SERVES 4 455 calories per serving
PREPARATION 25–30 minutes
BAKING 25–30 minutes
CHILLING 15 minutes

75 g (3 oz) plain wholemeal flour
100 g (4 oz) plain flour
75 (3 oz) polyunsaturated margarine, chilled
15 ml (3 tsp) light muscovado sugar
1 egg yolk
1 egg, size 2, beaten
300 ml (½ pint) semi-skilled milk
5 ml (1 tsp) vanilla essence
1 small pineapple about 700 g (1½ lb),
peeled, sliced, cored and segmented
30 ml (2 tbsp) reduced-sugar apricot jam
30 ml (2 tbsp) lemon juice

1

Place an 18 cm (7 inch) fluted flan ring on a baking sheet. Put the wholemeal flour and 75 g (3 oz) of the plain flour into a mixing bowl and rub in the margarine until the mixture resembles fine breadcrumbs. Stir in 5 ml (1 tsp) of the sugar.

2

Beat the egg yolk with 30 ml (2 tbsp) cold water and use about half of it to mix the flours and margarine to a firm but pliable dough. Knead on a lightly floured board until smooth, roll out and use to line the flan ring. Chill for 15 minutes.

3

Place a sheet of greaseproof paper over the base of the pastry, cover with baking beans and bake blind at 200°C (400°F) mark 6 for 15 minutes. Remove the baking beans and greaseproof paper, return to the oven and bake for a further 10 minutes or until the pastry case is cooked. Allow to cool, then remove the flan ring carefully and place the pastry case on a serving plate.

4

Put remaining 25 g (1 oz) flour in a small bowl. Add the remaining egg yolk and water mixture and the beaten egg. Beat well until smooth.

5

Warm the milk and gradually stir into the flour and egg mixture, then strain into a small saucepan and cook over a gentle heat for about 4 minutes, stirring until the pastry cream has thickened and is free from lumps. Remove from the heat and beat in the remaining sugar and the vanilla essence. Cool slightly, then pour into the pastry case. Leave until completely cold.

6

Arrange the sliced pineapple decoratively on top of the pastry cream. Heat the apricot jam and lemon juice together, sieve, then use to glaze the top of the tart. Leave for at least 5 minutes before serving.

GOODNESS GUIDE
PROTEIN The milk, egg and flours make this a high-protein dessert
VITAMINS Margarine and eggs are a source of vitamin D, which is necessary for calcium and phosphorous absorption
MINERALS This dish provides a good range of minerals, including phosphorous, which helps in the building of cell membranes

RASPBERRY AND BANANA BOMBE

PINEAPPLE TART

RASPBERRY AND BANANA BOMBE

SERVES 4 190 calories per serving
PREPARATION 20–25 Minutes
COOKING None
FREEZING 2–2½ hours

2 ripe bananas, peeled and sliced
juice of 1 lemon
40 g (1½ oz) light muscovado sugar
100 ml (4 fl oz) whipping cream
100 ml (4 fl oz) low-fat natural yogurt
225 g (8 oz) raspberries, thawed if frozen
1 egg white
extra raspberries, to decorate

———1———

Put a 600 ml (1 pint) bombe mould or pudding basin in the freezer to chill. Purée the bananas, half the lemon juice and 5 ml (1 tsp) of the sugar in a blender or food processor until smooth.

———2———

Whip the cream until thick and fold into the banana purée with the yogurt. Pour into a freezing container and freeze for about 1–1½ hours, until ice crystals form around the edge.

———3———

Meanwhile, dissolve the remaining sugar in 225 ml (8 fl oz) water, bring to the boil and boil gently for 5 minutes. Allow to cool. Purée the raspberries with the remaining lemon juice, then sieve into a bowl. Add the cooled syrup and pour into a freezing container. Freeze for 45 minutes or until half set.

———4———

Whisk the egg white until stiff, then fold into the raspberry sorbet. Freeze for 30 minutes or until almost set.

———5———

Line the chilled mould or basin with the banana ice cream, then fill the centre with the raspberry sorbet. Freeze for at least 1 hour or until firm.

———6———

Transfer to the refrigerator to soften for 30 minutes before serving. Turn out and serve, cut into wedges.

GOODNESS GUIDE

VITAMINS There is a high amount of vitamin C in the bananas and raspberries
FIBRE The fruit supplies quite a bit of fibre
FAT Although this is not a low-fat dessert, the fat content is lower than in traditional ice-cream bombes; the use of low-fat yogurt reduces the amount of cream needed

PASTA AND FRUIT PUDDING

PASTA AND FRUIT PUDDING

SERVES 4 220 calories per serving
PREPARATION 15 minutes
BAKING 45 minutes

75 g (3 oz) wholemeal macaroni
450 ml (¾ pint) semi-skimmed milk
1 cooking apple, peeled, cored, chopped
50 g (2 oz) raisins, rinsed
grated rind of 1 lemon
10 ml (2 tsp) light muscovado sugar
1 egg, separated

APPLE TOPPING
1 eating apple, peeled, cored, sliced
7.5 ml (½ tbsp) polyunsaturated margarine, melted

———1———

Lightly grease a 1.1 litre (2 pint) ovenproof serving dish and set aside. Put the macaroni and milk in a saucepan, bring to the boil, cover and simmer for 10 minutes. Remove from the heat. Add the apple, raisins, lemon rind and sugar, then beat in the egg yolk.

———2———

Whisk the egg white until stiff, then fold into the mixture. Pour into the prepared dish and bake at 180°C (350°F) mark 4 for about 30 minutes.

———3———

To make the topping, place the sliced apple in a decorative pattern over the pudding and brush with the melted margarine. Return to the oven for a further 10–15 minutes, until the apple slices are softened and golden brown. Serve hot.

MICROWAVE Put macaroni and milk into a microwave oven dish. Part cover and cook 100% (High) 5 minutes, then 60% (Medium) 9 minutes. Add apple, raisins, lemon rind, sugar and beat in egg yolk; fold in whisked white. Cook, uncovered, 100% (High) 4–5 minutes. Follow step 3 and cook, uncovered, 100% (High) 2 minutes. Place the dish under a pre-heated grill to brown the surface, if liked.

GOODNESS GUIDE

CARBOHYDRATE This dessert provides a great deal of energy in the form of complex carbohydrates. It is vital to consume enough carbohydrates so the body will not have to rely on protein for energy—when this occurs, the protein is unavailable for building tissues
PROTEIN The pasta, egg and milk are good sources of protein

BRANDIED FRUIT SALAD

Cut the pineapple and oranges over a plate to catch the juices, then add these to the salad. If liked, substitute apple juice for the brandy.

SERVES 4   250 calories per serving
PREPARATION 15 minutes
COOKING None
SOAKING At least 2 hours

50 g (2 oz) raisins, rinsed
50 ml (2 fl oz) brandy
juice of 2 oranges
2 oranges, peeled, segmented and cut into bite-sized pieces
2 red eating apples, cored and cut into bite-sized pieces
1 small pineapple, about 900 g (2 lb), peeled, cored and cut into bite-sized pieces
50 g (2 oz) hazelnuts, coarsely chopped and toasted
Greek strained yogurt, to serve

——— 1 ———

Place the raisins in a bowl, add the brandy and soak for at least 2 hours.

——— 2 ———

Put the orange juice and all the fruit in a serving bowl. Stir gently to mix. Add the raisins with any brandy left in the bowl and sprinkle the toasted hazelnuts over the top. Serve with Greek strained yogurt.

GOODNESS GUIDE

VITAMINS The fresh fruit provides vitamin C
MINERALS The raisins contribute iron and calcium. All the fruits provide potassium which is important in preserving the body's acid-alkaline balance

WHOLEMEAL SUMMER PUDDING

SERVES 6   130 calories per serving
PREPARATION 10 minutes
COOKING 2–3 minutes
CHILLING 6 hours or overnight

8 slices day-old wholemeal bread, crusts removed
225 g (8 oz) strawberries, hulled, halved if large
450 g (1 lb) mixed soft fruits such as redcurrants, raspberries, loganberries and stoned cherries
75 ml (5 tbsp) apple juice
25 g (1 oz) light muscovado sugar
Greek strained yogurt, to serve

——— 1 ———

Place 1 slice of bread in the base of a 900 ml (1½ pint) pudding basin. Reserve 2 slices of bread and use the remainder to line the sides of the basin, cutting them slightly to fit if necessary.

——— 2 ———

Put the fruit in a saucepan with the apple juice and sugar. Bring gently to the boil and cook for 2–3 minutes, until the fruit is slightly softened.

——— 3 ———

Fill the basin with the fruit, pressing it down well. Place the reserved bread on the top, cutting it to fit. Place a saucer on top of the pudding and weigh it down. Chill for at least 6 hours or overnight.

——— 4 ———

Just before serving, invert the pudding on to a plate. Serve with Greek strained yogurt.

MICROWAVE Complete step 1. Put the fruit into a bowl with 30 ml (2 tbsp) apple juice and sugar. Partly cover, cook 100% (High) 2–3 minutes, until slightly softened. Complete recipe.

GOODNESS GUIDE

FIBRE The use of wholemeal bread increases the fibre content of this dessert. The soft fruits also supply substantial fibre
MINERALS Potassium is contributed by all the ingredients. Potassium is an essential activator of some enzymes, particularly those involved in energy production. It also plays an important role in maintaining the body's fluid balance

HOT CAROB AND ALMOND SAUCE

SERVES 4   185 calories per serving
PREPARATION 10 minutes
COOKING 2–4 minutes

65 g (2½ oz) plain sweetened carob bar
300 ml (½ pint) semi-skimmed milk
30–45 ml (2–3 tbsp) fine oatmeal
25 g (1 oz) flaked almonds
chopped almonds, to garnish

——— 1 ———

Break the carob into small pieces and put in a heatproof bowl over a saucepan of simmering water. Stir until the carob melts.

——— 2 ———

Gradually stir the milk into the melted carob, then pour the mixture into a pan. Sprinkle in 30 ml (2 tbsp) of the oatmeal and bring gently to the boil, stirring constantly. Cook for 2–3 minutes until thickened.

——— 3 ———

If a thicker sauce is required, sprinkle in an extra 15 ml (1 tbsp) oatmeal and cook until the desired consistency is reached.

——— 4 ———

Stir in the flaked almonds and serve immediately. Serve with ice cream, garnished with the chopped almonds.

MICROWAVE Break carob pieces into a bowl. Add the milk and 30 ml (2 tbsp) fine oatmeal. Cook, uncovered, 100% (High) 3–4 minutes, whisking twice, until thickened. If a thicker sauce is required, add 45 ml (3 tbsp) oatmeal instead of 30 ml (2 tbsp). Stir in the almonds and serve immediately.

GOODNESS GUIDE

PROTEIN This is a high protein sauce
FIBRE Oatmeal, almonds and carob are all sources of fibre, necessary for healthy intestinal movement
VITAMINS All of the ingredients provide plenty of B-complex vitamins. B vitamins among their many other functions help the body to utilise energy from carbohydrates, proteins and fats

HOT CAROB AND ALMOND SAUCE

BRANDIED FRUIT SALAD

WHOLEMEAL SUMMER PUDDING

GRAPEFRUIT AND RUM POSSETS

This is a new healthy version of a very old English dessert which takes only minutes to prepare.

MAKES 4 245 calories each
PREPARATION 10 minutes
COOKING 3–4 minutes

45 ml (3 tbsp) clear honey
finely grated rind of ¼ grapefruit
juice of 2 grapefruit
30 ml (2 tbsp) dark rum
200 ml (7 fl oz) whipping cream
150 ml (5 fl oz) low-fat natural yogurt
peeled segments from 1 large grapefruit

———1———
Put the honey and grapefruit rind and juice into a saucepan and heat gently. Stir in the rum and keep warm over a low heat.

———2———
Whip the cream until thick peaks form, then whisk in the yogurt and the honey and grapefruit mixture.

———3———
Put a grapefruit segment into the bottom of each of 4 stemmed glasses and top with the warm posset. Decorate with the remaining grapefruit segments and serve.

MICROWAVE Put the honey, grapefruit rind and juice into a bowl. Cook, uncovered, 100% (High) 2 minutes until warm. Stir in the rum and keep warm. Whip the cream until thick, then whisk in the yogurt and the honey and grapefruit mixture. Put a grapefruit segment into the bottom of each glass and top with the warm posset. Decorate with the remaining grapefruit segments.

GOODNESS GUIDE
FAT Possets are traditionally made with all cream. The substitution of yogurt for half the cream reduces the overall fat content of this dish
VITAMINS The grapefruit provides a good helping of vitamin C
FIBRE Grapefruit provides a little fibre

DATE AND WALNUT SAVARIN

This dessert is low in refined sugar; the dates are naturally sweet.

SERVES 6 355 calories each
PREPARATION About 30 minutes
RISING 35–40 minutes
BAKING 30–35 minutes

20 g (¾ oz) fresh yeast, crumbled, or 12.5 ml (2½ tsp) dried yeast and 1.25 ml (¼ tsp) light muscovado sugar
67.5 ml (4½ tbsp) tepid semi-skimmed milk
75 g (3 oz) plain wholemeal flour
75 g (3 oz) plain flour
2.5 ml (½ tsp) salt
25 g (1 oz) light muscovado sugar
3 eggs, beaten
75 g (3 oz) polyunsaturated margarine
50 g (2 oz) walnut halves, chopped
75 g (3 oz) stoned dates, rinsed and chopped
60 ml (4 tbsp) clear honey
finely grated rind of ½ orange
45 ml (3 tbsp) unsweetened orange juice
30 ml (2 tbsp) brandy
Greek strained yogurt, to serve

———1———
Thoroughly grease a 20 cm (8 inch) savarin tin and set aside. Blend the fresh yeast with the milk. If using dried yeast, sprinkle into the milk with the sugar. Leave in a warm place for 15 minutes or until frothy.

———2———
Put the flours into a warm bowl and add the yeast mixture, salt, sugar, eggs, margarine, walnuts and dates. Beat well for 3 minutes until well blended, then pour into the savarin tin. Cover and leave to rise in a warm place for 35–40 minutes.

———3———
Bake at 200°C (400°F) mark 6 for 30–35 minutes, until golden brown.

———4———
Heat the honey, orange rind and juice. Stir in the brandy. Keep warm.

———5———
Turn the savarin out on to a wire rack placed over a baking tray, and pierce all over with a fine skewer. Spoon the syrup, and any that drips on to the baking tray, evenly over the hot savarin. Set aside to cool. Serve sliced, with Greek strained yogurt.

GOODNESS GUIDE
FIBRE A good amount of fibre is obtained from the flour, walnuts and dates
MINERALS The flour, eggs, nuts, milk and yogurt provide calcium, potassium, magnesium and zinc. Iron is present in the flour, nuts and eggs

FRUIT FREEZE

This refreshing dessert is similar to a sorbet mixture, but unlike a sorbet it is served while still soft and slushy.

SERVES 6 75 calories per serving
PREPARATION 10 minutes
COOKING None
FREEZING 2–3 hours

3 bananas peeled
juice of ½ lemon
300 g (10 oz) strawberries, hulled
1 egg white
200 ml (7 fl oz) unsweetened orange juice
175 g (6 oz) raspberries
strawberries and mint, to decorate

DATE AND WALNUT SAVARIN

1

Put the bananas, lemon juice and strawberries into a blender or food processor and purée until smooth.

2

Pour into a shallow freezerproof container and freeze for 2–3 hours or until solid.

3

Just before serving break up the frozen fruit pulp and blend it quickly in the blender or food processor with the egg white and orange juice until a frothy slush is formed. Fold in the raspberries.

4

Carefully pour the mixture into wide-bowled stemmed glasses and decorate with sliced strawberries and sprigs of fresh mint. Serve.

GOODNESS GUIDE

VITAMINS Freezing the fruit and fruit juice will slow down the enzymes which destroy vitamin C when it is exposed to the air. All the fruit and fruit juices provide plenty of vitamin C

FIBRE Good quantities of fibre are contained in the fruit

FRENCH FRUIT TART

If fresh peaches are not available canned peaches may be used instead.

MAKES 6 SLICES 305 calories each
PREPARATION 30 minutes
BAKING 20 minutes
CHILLING 30 minutes

100 g (4 oz) plain wholemeal flour
100 g (4 oz) plain flour
100 g (4 oz) polyunsaturated margarine
225 g (8 oz) strawberries, hulled
2 peaches, halved, stoned and sliced
2 kiwi fruit, peeled and sliced
30 ml (2 tbsp) clear honey
200 ml (7 fl oz) fresh orange juice
100 ml (2 tsp) powdered gelatine

1

Mix the flours together and rub in the margarine until the mixture resembles fine breadcrumbs. Add 15–30 ml (1–2 tbsp) chilled water and mix to a soft dough. Cover and chill for at least 30 minutes.

2

Roll out the pastry and use to line a 10 × 30 cm (4 × 12 inch) rectangular loose-bottomed tin. Line with grease-proof paper and baking beans and bake blind at 190°C (375°F) mark 5 for 15 minutes. Remove the paper and beans and bake for a further 5 minutes, then set aside to cool.

3

Arrange the fruit in an attractive pattern, in alternating bands of colour in the pastry case.

4

Mix together the honey and orange juice in a small pan over low heat. Place 30 ml (2 tbsp) hot water in a bowl and sprinkle over the gelatine. Stir until dissolved. Add to the orange juice mixture and cool until syrupy.

5

Spoon the glaze evenly over the fruits and leave until set. Serve sliced.

GOODNESS GUIDE

FIBRE Plenty of fibre is provided by the wholemeal flour and fruit

VITAMINS The fruits contain vitamin C in varying quantities. B-complex vitamins are present in the wholemeal flour

FRENCH FRUIT TART

FRUIT FREEZE

GRAPEFRUIT AND RUM POSSETS

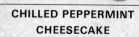

SUMMER FRUIT CRUMBLE

This is a high-fibre, low-sugar variation of the traditional pudding. The spices can be omitted, if liked. Replace the raspberries or strawberries with loganberries, blackberries or blueberries when in season.

SERVES 4   265 calories per serving
PREPARATION   10 minutes
BAKING   20–25 minutes

50 g (2 oz) polyunsaturated margarine
100 g (4 oz) plain wholemeal flour
25 g (1 oz) light muscovado sugar
5 ml (1 tsp) ground cinnamon
2.5 ml (½ tsp) mixed spice
25 g (1 oz) stoned dates, rinsed and finely chopped
15 g (½ oz) walnuts, chopped
225 g (8 oz) eating apples, cored and sliced
225 g (8 oz) raspberries or strawberries

———1———
Rub the margarine into the flour until the mixture resembles fine bread-crumbs. Stir in the sugar, cinnamon, mixed spice, dates and walnuts and mix thoroughly together.

———2———
Put the apples and berries into a 900 ml (1½ pint) pie dish. Spoon over the crumble mixture and press down lightly until smooth.

———3———
Bake at 200°C (400°F) mark 6 for 20–25 minutes, until the fruit is just tender. Serve hot with custard or low-fat natural yogurt.

MICROWAVE   Follow steps 1 and 2. Cook, uncovered, 100% (High) 7–8 minutes, turning the dish twice, until the fruit is tender.

GOODNESS GUIDE
FIBRE   The flour, dates, walnuts and fruit make this a high-fibre dish
MINERALS   Iron and calcium are supplied by the flour, nuts and raspberries. The flour, nuts and fruits all provide lots of potassium, which is needed for muscle contraction
VITAMINS   Vitamin C is mainly provided by the raspberries with extra supplied by the apples. The flour and nuts contribute B vitamins

BLACKCURRANT AND ROSE WATER MOUSSES

As an alternative, use redcurrants in this delicious light summer dessert.

SERVES 4   100 calories per serving
PREPARATION   20 minutes
COOKING   None
CHILLING   2–3 hours

200 ml (7 fl oz) Greek strained yogurt
290 g (10½ oz) can blackcurrants in unsweetened fruit juice, drained and juice reserved
5 ml (1 tsp) rose water, plus a few drops
15 ml (1 tbsp) powdered gelatine
1 egg white

———1———
Put the yogurt in a bowl. Add 90 ml (6 tbsp) of the juice from the can of blackcurrants and 5 ml (1 tsp) rose water. Beat well together.

———2———
Sprinkle the gelatine over 60 ml (4 tbsp) cold water in a heatproof bowl and leave to soak for 1 minute. Place over a pan of gently boiling water and stir until the gelatine is dissolved. Set aside to cool slightly, then stir into the yogurt mixture. Whisk the egg white until stiff and fold gently into the mixture.

———3———
Rinse the insides of 4 ramekin dishes under cold water and drain. Spoon in the yogurt mixture and level the surface. Chill for 2–3 hours or until set.

———4———
To serve, run a knife around the edge of each ramekin dish and turn out each mousse on to a plate. Carefully spoon the blackcurrants on top and sprinkle with a few drops of rose water. Serve immediately.

GOODNESS GUIDE
VITAMINS   Blackcurrants are very high in vitamin C. The yogurt is a source of B vitamins
MINERALS   The blackcurrants and yogurt provide potassium and calcium; the blackcurrants are also a source of iron
FIBRE   The blackcurrants are a valuable source of fibre

CHILLED PEPPERMINT CHEESECAKE

MAKES 6 SLICES   230 calories each
PREPARATION   20 minutes
COOKING   None
CHILLING   3–4 hours

100 g (4 oz) wholemeal digestive biscuits, crushed
15 ml (1 tbsp) carob powder
50 g (2 oz) polyunsaturated margarine
225 g (8 oz) curd cheese
30 ml (2 tbsp) light muscovado sugar
2 eggs, separated
5–7.5 ml (1–1½ tsp) peppermint essence
150 ml (5 fl oz) low-fat natural yogurt
15 ml (1 tbsp) powdered gelatine
carob powder, for dusting
fresh mint sprigs, to garnish (optional)

———1———
Lightly grease a 20 cm (8 inch) loose-based cake tin and set aside. Mix the crushed biscuits with the carob powder. Melt the margarine over a gentle heat and stir into the biscuit mixture. Press evenly over the base of the tin. Set aside.

———2———
Beat the curd cheese with the sugar, egg yolks, peppermint essence to taste and yogurt.

———3———
Sprinkle the gelatine over 45 ml (3 tbsp) cold water in a heatproof bowl and leave to soak for 1 minute. Place over a pan of gently boiling

CHILLED PEPPERMINT CHEESECAKE

BLACKCURRANT AND ROSE WATER MOUSSES

GOOSEBERRY AND PLUM TART

water and stir until the gelatine is dissolved. Remove from the heat and leave to cool slightly, then add to the cheese mixture.

———4———

Whisk the egg whites until stiff and fold lightly into the cheese mixture. Spoon on to the biscuit base and chill for 3–4 hours, until set.

———5———

Carefully unmould the cheesecake from the tin and dust the top with carob powder before serving. Garnish with fresh mint sprigs, if liked.

MICROWAVE Lightly grease a 20 cm (8 inch) loose-based tin. Mix biscuits and carob powder. Put margarine in a bowl; cook, uncovered, 100% (High) 45 seconds, to melt. Stir into biscuit mixture. Press evenly over tin base. Follow step 2. Put 45 ml (3 tbsp) water into a small bowl; sprinkle over gelatine. Cook, uncovered, 100% (High) 30–45 seconds and stir to dissolve gelatine. Cool, then stir into cheese mixture. Complete the recipe.

GOODNESS GUIDE

FAT Curd is a medium-fat cheese. Using this with low-fat yogurt substantially reduces the fat of traditional cheesecakes

GOOSEBERRY AND PLUM TART

MAKES 8 SLICES 150 calories each
PREPARATION 30 minutes
COOKING 30 minutes
CHILLING AND COOLING 3 hours

100 g (4 oz) plain wholemeal flour
2.5 ml ($\frac{1}{2}$ tsp) cream of tartar
1.25 ml ($\frac{1}{4}$ tsp) bicarbonate of soda
pinch of salt
50 g (2 oz) polyunsaturated margarine
45 ml (3 tbsp) light muscovado sugar
1 egg yolk
15 ml (1 tbsp) semi-skimmed milk
700 g (1$\frac{1}{2}$ lb) ripe plums, halved stoned and quartered
175 g (6 oz) ripe gooseberries, topped and tailed
30 ml (2 tbsp) ginger wine
5 ml (1 tsp) powdered gelatine

———1———

Lightly grease a 23 cm (9 inch) fluted loose-based flan tin or ring and set aside. Sift the flour, cream of tartar, bicarbonate of soda and salt into a bowl and add the bran from the sieve.

———2———

Rub in the margarine lightly. Stir in 15 ml (1 tbsp) sugar. Add the egg yolk and milk and mix to a smooth dough. Press into the tin, pressing up the sides to form a rim. Chill for 30 minutes.

———3———

Arrange the plum quarters skin side up in the flan case. Sprinkle with 15 ml (1 tbsp) sugar. Bake at 190°C (375°F) mark 6 for 30 minutes. Cool on a wire rack.

———4———

Meanwhile, put the gooseberries, wine and remaining sugar into a saucepan with 45 ml (3 tbsp) water. Simmer for 5 minutes and cool, then sieve.

———5———

Sprinkle the gelatine over 30 ml (2 tbsp) cold water and leave to soak for 1 minute. Place over a pan of gently boiling water and stir until the gelatine is dissolved. Cool slightly, then stir into the gooseberry mixture. Spoon the gooseberry glaze evenly over the plums and chill for about 2 hours.

GOODNESS GUIDE

VITAMINS The gooseberries supply vitamin C. The plums and gooseberries also provide some carotene
FIBRE This is a high-fibre dessert

INDIVIDUAL CABINET PUDDINGS

SERVES 4   200 calories per serving
PREPARATION   20 minutes
COOKING   About 40 minutes
STANDING   30 minutes

16 split almonds
8 natural glacé cherries, cut into quarters
50 g (2 oz) chopped mixed peel
2 eggs
15 ml (1 tbsp) clear honey
300 ml (½ pint) semi-skimmed milk
5 ml (1 tsp) vanilla essence
40 g (1½ oz) fresh wholemeal breadcrumbs

ORANGE SAUCE
150 ml (5 fl oz) low-fat natural yogurt
grated rind and juice of 1 orange
15–30 ml (1–2 tbsp) orange-flavoured
liqueur

——— 1 ———

Grease four 150 ml (¼ pint) dariole moulds or ramekins and line the bases with greaseproof paper. Place the almonds and half the cherries in the moulds to form a decorative pattern. Chop the remaining cherries, add to the mixed peel and set aside.

——— 2 ———

Whisk the eggs with honey. Warm the milk and beat into the eggs with the vanilla essence.

——— 3 ———

Divide the breadcrumbs, cherries and peel between the 4 moulds. Strain over the egg and milk mixture and leave to stand for 30 minutes.

——— 4 ———

Loosely cover each mould with a piece of foil. Place in a roasting pan half-filled with boiling water. Cook at 180°C (350°F) mark 4 for about 40 minutes, until set. Leave to cool for 5 minutes, then turn out.

——— 5 ———

To make the orange sauce, mix the yogurt with the orange rind and juice. Stir in the liqueur. Serve with the puddings.

MICROWAVE   Complete step 1. Whisk eggs with honey and vanilla essence. Cook milk 100% (High) 2 minutes, to warm. Whisk into egg mixture. Complete step 3. Loosely cover each ramekin and place in a dish half-filled with boiling water. Cook 7 minutes, rotating dishes once, until just set in centres. Complete recipe.

GOODNESS GUIDE
PROTEIN   The milk, eggs, yogurt and breadcrumbs make this a high-protein dish
FAT   The use of semi-skimmed milk and low-fat yogurt makes these cabinet puddings low in fat

PANCAKES WITH BLACKBERRY AND APPLE SAUCE

MAKES 12   105 calories each
PREPARATION   20 minutes
COOKING   About 30 minutes
STANDING   At least 30 minutes

50 g (2 oz) plain wholemeal flour
65 g (2½ oz) plain flour
15 g (½ oz) buckwheat flour
2 eggs, size 3
300 ml (½ pint) semi-skimmed milk
5 ml (1 tsp) sunflower oil
corn oil, for frying
vanilla ice cream, to serve
blackberries and apple slices, to decorate

FRUIT SAUCE
2 eating apples, cored and diced
225 g (8 oz) blackberries, thawed if frozen
25 g (1 oz) light muscovado sugar
2.5 ml (½ tsp) ground cinnamon

——— 1 ———

To make the batter, put the flours in a blender or food processor. Add the eggs, milk and sunflower oil. Blend until smooth. Pour into a bowl, cover and leave to rest for at least 30 minutes.

——— 2 ———

Meanwhile, combine the sauce ingredients in a small saucepan. Add 75 ml (5 tbsp) of water and bring to the boil. Stir and cook gently, covered for 5 minutes, until the fruit is soft.

SPICY APPLE AND APRICOT TURNOVERS

PANCAKES WITH BLACKBERRY AND APPLE SAUCE

3

Sieve the sauce into a bowl, then return to a clean saucepan and set aside while making the pancakes.

4

To cook the pancakes, lightly oil an 18 cm (7 inch) frying pan and heat. Using a small ladle, pour enough batter into the pan until the base is just covered, tilting the pan to spread the batter evenly. Cook each side over a high heat for about 1 minute. Place on a plate lined with absorbent kitchen paper. Continue making pancakes until all the batter is used. Stack them on top of each other and keep warm in a low oven.

5

Reheat the sauce. Place a scoop of ice cream on one half of each pancake and fold over. Pour about 15 ml (1 tbsp) sauce on each pancake and serve.

GOODNESS GUIDE

VITAMINS The flours, milk and eggs provide a good range of B vitamins. Blackberries are very rich in vitamin C

MINERALS The milk, eggs, fruit and flours make this dish high in potassium, which is needed for fluid balance in the cells

---

SPICY APPLE AND APRICOT TURNOVERS

MAKES 12 155 calories each
PREPARATION 30 minutes
BAKING 15–20 minutes

100 g (4 oz) ready-to-eat dried apricots, rinsed and chopped
1 large eating apple, peeled, cored and coarsely chopped
finely grated rind of 1 lemon
25 g (1 oz) sultanas
1.25 ml ($\frac{1}{4}$ tsp) ground cinnamon
2.5 ml ($\frac{1}{2}$ tsp) mixed spice
pinch of freshly grated nutmeg
25 g (1 oz) ground almonds
100 g (4 oz) plain wholemeal flour
100 g (4 oz) plain flour
pinch of salt
100 g (4 oz) polyunsaturated margarine
semi-skimmed milk and 30 ml (2 tbsp) light muscovado sugar, to glaze

1

Lightly grease a baking sheet and set aside. Put the apricots into a small saucepan and add 225 ml (8 fl oz) water. Bring to the boil, cover tightly and simmer for 15 minutes.

2

Add the apple, lemon rind, sultanas, cinnamon, mixed spice and nutmeg. Cook, covered, for about 10 minutes longer, stirring occasionally, until the liquid has been absorbed and the mixture is a soft pulp. Stir in the almonds and leave to cool.

3

To make the pastry, put the flours and salt into a bowl and rub in the margarine until the mixture resembles fine breadcrumbs. Add enough chilled water to form a smooth dough. Roll out thinly on a lightly floured surface to a 30 × 40 cm (12 × 16 inch) rectangle. Cut the pastry into 10 cm (4 inch) squares.

4

Put 15 ml (1 tbsp) fruit filling just off the centre of each square. Brush the edges lightly with water and fold over to form a triangle. Seal and crimp the edges.

5

Place the turnovers on the prepared baking sheet, glaze with the milk and sprinkle evenly with the sugar. Bake at 190°C (375°F) mark 5 for 15–20 minutes, until golden brown. Cool on a wire rack and serve warm or cold.

GOODNESS GUIDE

FIBRE The apricots, apple, almonds, flours and sultanas make this dessert high in fibre

MINERALS Iron, calcium and potassium are supplied by the apricots, sultanas, nuts and flours

SUGAR The natural sweetness of the fruit and nuts makes added sugar unnecessary

INDIVIDUAL CABINET PUDDINGS

RUM AND ORANGE SAVARIN

SERVES 4   360 calories per serving
PREPARATION   40 minutes
BAKING   20–25 minutes
RISING   30 minutes

150 ml ($\frac{1}{4}$ pint) semi-skimmed milk
50 g (2 oz) plain wholemeal flour
15 g ($\frac{1}{2}$ oz) fresh yeast or
7.5 ml (1$\frac{1}{2}$ tsp) dried yeast and
2.5 ml ($\frac{1}{2}$ tsp) light muscovado sugar
75 g (3 oz) plain flour
15 ml (1 tbsp) light muscovado sugar
1 egg, beaten
25 g (1 oz) polyunsaturated margarine
grated rind of 1 orange
30 ml (2 tbsp) clear honey, to glaze
100 g (4 oz) seedless green grapes, halved
2 oranges, peeled and segmented
2 bananas, peeled and sliced

ORANGE SYRUP
300 ml ($\frac{1}{2}$ pint) orange juice
30 ml (2 tbsp) honey
30 ml (2 tbsp) light rum

─────1─────
Lightly oil a 900 ml (1$\frac{1}{2}$ pint) ring mould and set aside. Warm the milk in a small saucepan. Pour into a large bowl and add 25 g (1 oz) of the wholemeal flour. Add the fresh yeast, or dried yeast and sugar, and mix. Leave in a warm place for about 20 minutes, until frothy.

─────2─────
Add the remaining wholemeal flour and the plain flour, sugar, egg, margarine and orange rind and beat for 3 minutes. Pour the savarin batter into the prepared ring mould and level the surface. The mixture should half fill the tin. Cover with a clean cloth and leave in a warm place for about 30 minutes, until the batter doubles in size, rising to the top of the tin.

─────3─────
Bake at 200°C (400°F) mark 6 for 20–25 minutes, until firm to the touch and golden brown. Cool for 5 minutes, then turn out on to a serving dish and prick the savarin all over with a fork so that it will readily absorb the orange syrup.

─────4─────
To make the syrup, heat the orange juice with the honey until dissolved. Stir in the rum, then pour the syrup over the savarin while the syrup is still warm. Leave the savarin to cool.

─────5─────
Warm the honey for the glaze and brush over the outside surface of the savarin. Mix together the grapes, oranges and bananas for the filling and pile into the centre of the savarin. Serve with low-fat natural yogurt, if liked.

GOODNESS GUIDE
FIBRE The fruit filling and wholemeal flour contribute a good amount of fibre
VITAMINS The fresh fruit provides a high amount of vitamin C, which is known to lower blood cholesterol levels
MINERALS The milk, flour and egg provide calcium, good quantities of which are essential for young children, pregnant and post-menopausal women

RUM AND ORANGE SAVARIN

RASPBERRY AND APPLE FLAN

MAKES 6 SLICES 205 calories each
PREPARATION 20 minutes
BAKING 30–40 minutes
CHILLING 30 minutes

225 g (8 oz) raspberries, thawed if frozen
3 dessert apples, peeled, cored and diced
45 ml (3 tbsp) light muscovado sugar
25 ml (1½ tbsp) cornflour
Greek strained yogurt, to serve

SPICY PASTRY
75 g (3 oz) plain wholemeal flour
75 g (3 oz) plain flour
10 ml (2 tsp) ground cinnamon
5 ml (1 tsp) mixed spice
65 g (2½ oz) polyunsaturated margarine,
chilled
semi-skimmed milk, to glaze

—— 1 ——

Put the raspberries and apples into a saucepan and cook gently over a medium heat for 10 minutes. Add the sugar and cook for a further 5 minutes.

—— 2 ——

Blend together cornflour and 30 ml (2 tbsp) cold water. Add to the pan and cook, stirring, until thickened. Leave to cool slightly.

—— 3 ——

Meanwhile, make the pastry. Put the flours, cinnamon and mixed spice into a bowl. Rub in the margarine and add 30–60 ml (2–4 tbsp) chilled water or just enough to form a soft dough. Chill for 30 minutes.

—— 4 ——

Roll out two-thirds of dough into a circle and line a 20.5 cm (8 inch) loose-bottomed flan tin. Spoon filling into tin and smooth surface.

—— 5 ——

Roll out the remaining pastry into an oblong about 20.5 cm (8 inches) long and cut into 1 cm (½ inch) strips. Twist the pastry strips and arrange over the filling in a lattice design. Seal the edges and brush the strips with a little milk to glaze.

—— 6 ——

Bake at 180°C (350°F) mark 4 for 30–40 minutes, until golden brown and cooked through. Cool slightly and remove from tin. Serve hot or cold with Greek strained yogurt.

MICROWAVE In step 1, put raspberries and apples into a micro-wave oven dish. Cover, cook 100% (High) 6 minutes, stirring once. Add sugar, cook, covered, 100% (High) 1 minute. In step 2, stir in blended cornflour, cook, uncovered, 100% (High) 2–2½ minutes. Follow step 3. For steps 4 and 5, line a pie plate with pastry, cover base with a double thickness of absorbent kitchen paper. Lay pastry strips on top. Place on an upturned dish and cook 100% (High) 4 minutes. Remove paper and pastry strips. Cook, uncovered, 4 minutes. Remove flan, return strips to cook 1½ minutes. Fill flan with fruit, arrange pastry strips on top. In step 6, cook finished flan 3–4 minutes to heat if serving hot.

GOODNESS GUIDE
FIBRE The wholemeal flour and the fruit, especially the raspberries, supply fibre
VITAMINS The fruit supplies vitamin C, which helps to maintain healthy tissues generally, and healthy skin, bones and teeth in particular
MINERALS The flours contain calcium, which is necessary for building strong bones. Calcium also has a role in nerve conduction and muscle contraction

RASPBERRY AND APPLE FLAN

5 LIGHT MEALS AND SNACKS

GRILLING AND BARBECUING

Grilling and barbecuing are increasingly popular—both are healthy ways to cook. Grilling is a good alternative to frying while barbecuing can be great fun—most people enjoy charcoal-grilled food cooked outdoors. In both methods the food is exposed directly to the heat: either a hot grill or an open fire. The food cooks quickly, is full of flavour and —most important—it is low in fat. Marinades add extra flavour.

Both barbecuing and grilling emphasise the natural flavour of food, which is usually—but not exclusively—meat or fish. The methods call for ingredients of a high quality and these are cooked in a simple, rather than sophisticated, way. Immediate exposure to high temperatures at the beginning of cooking seals in the flavour, and gives a good crisp texture to the food. As it cooks, most of the fat drips off, so only a small amount is left at the end of cooking time.

Extra flavour can be added to grilled and barbecued food by marinating and using basting sauces.

Marinades tenderise food before it is cooked. Most contain acid-based ingredients such as fruit juice, wine or vinegar; these help to break down the fibres of the food and soften it, which shortens the time needed for cooking.

Marinades can give a much more successful result than simple seasoning before cooking; because the flavours are so sharp, they can take the place of salt—a definite health advantage. In any case, salt should not be added to marinades for meat as it tends to draw out the juices.

USING MARINADES
Even food which needs a little tenderising—such as fish, lamb or young

GRILLING TIMES FOR MEAT AND SEAFOOD

		THICKNESS/ WEIGHT	DISTANCE FROM HEAT	RARE	MEDIUM	WELL DONE	
MEAT AND POULTRY							
Beef	steaks	1 cm ($\frac{1}{2}$ inch)	10 cm (4 inches)	3 minutes	5 minutes	9 minutes	turn once
	hamburgers	2 cm ($\frac{3}{4}$ inch)	10 cm (4 inches)	6 minutes	9 minutes	14 minutes	turn once
Chicken	skinned, boneless breast	150 g (5 oz)	7.5 cm (3 inches)	—	—	12–13 minutes	turn once
	leg	150 g (5 oz)	7.5 cm (3 inches)	—	—	15 minutes	turn once
	thigh	150 g (5 oz)	7.5 cm (3 inches)	—	—	14 minutes	turn once
Lamb	chump chop	150 g (5 oz)	7.5 cm (3 inches)	6 minutes	7 minutes	15 minutes	turn once
	loin chop	75–100 g (3–4 oz)	7.5 cm (3 inches)	5 minutes	6 minutes	12 minutes	turn once
	leg steak	175 g (6 oz)	7.5 cm (3 inches)	6 minutes	7 minutes	16 minutes	turn once
	kebabs	4 cm (1$\frac{1}{2}$ inch) cubes	5 cm (2 inches)	3 minutes	5 minutes	10 minutes	turn several times
Pork	loin chop	175 g (6 oz)	7.5 cm (3 inches)	—	—	12 minutes	turn once
	tenderloin	275 g (10 oz)	7.5 cm (3 inches)	—	—	18 minutes	turn once
Veal	chop	175–200 g (6–7 oz)	7.5 cm (3 inches)	—	—	17 minutes	turn once
SEAFOOD & SHELLFISH							
Cod	cutlet	175 g (6 oz)	10 cm (4 inches)	—	—	10 minutes	
	kebabs	2.5 cm (1 inch) cubes	10 cm (4 inches)	—	—	7 minutes	turn several times
Mackerel	double fillet	225 g (8 oz)	10 cm (4 inches)	—	—	5 minutes	
	whole, cleaned	275 g (10 oz)	10 cm (4 inches)	—	—	10 minutes	turn once
Plaice	fillet	150 g (5 oz)	10 cm (4 inches)	—	—	4 minutes	
Prawns	skewered with shell	45 g (1$\frac{3}{4}$ oz)	10 cm (4 inches)	—	—	5 minutes	turn several times
Scallops	skewered	25 g (1 oz)	10 cm (4 inches)	—	—	7 minutes	turn several times
Trout	whole, cleaned	275 g (10 oz)	10 cm (4 inches)	—	—	10 minutes	turn once

chicken—can benefit from marinating. The time recommended for marinating the food can vary from 1–24 hours, and the food should always be marinated in glass or enamel bowls without chips.

To get the best results, the entire surface should be covered. Meat can be cut into cubes so that it will absorb more flavour; larger pieces of meat and whole fish should have deep cuts scored in the surface so that the marinade can seep in.

Recipes for marinades often include generous amounts of oil. However, you can achieve just as successful a result by using a small quantity or omitting it altogether. If you do use oil, make sure it is an unsaturated oil such as olive, sunflower or corn.

Marinades can be made from a wide range of ingredients. These include fruit and vegetable juices; wine and vinegar; soy sauce (if possible, naturally fermented shoyu); honey.

COOKING TECHNIQUES

Many grilling and barbecuing recipes suggest basting the food with oil to prevent drying out during cooking. But to keep food low in fat, baste either with the marinade the food has marinated in or with a basting sauce which may contain such ingredients as fruit juice, tomato purée, wine or vinegar.

Apply the basting sauce with a natural bristle brush. Avoid plastic brushes as these could melt. A little oil should also be brushed on to the metal sheets or the barbecue grids to prevent sticking.

The golden rule in grilling and barbecuing is to start food on a high heat, then reduce and cook slowly so the inside is done before the outside is over-cooked.

Most meats, poultry and fish are suitable for grilling and barbecuing. Red meats should be tender, as the cooking time is not long enough to soften the fibres of tough cuts. Oily fish such as mackerel are ideal, as some of the fat melts into the flesh during cooking, keeping the fish moist, and the remainder drips out. White fish with firm flesh, such as halibut, are suitable for kebabs and can also be cooked whole.

On most barbecues and some grills you can use a spit to roast poultry and large joints of meat. Smaller pieces of meat or fish can be made into kebabs and threaded onto skewers which are laid on the grid. Frequent turning will guarantee that the food cooks evenly and the fat drips away.

SUCCESSFUL SAUCES

There is a great deal of mystique attached to making sauces, which is perhaps one of the reasons why so many of us reach for the packet variety. But these are high in salt, contain additives and colourings, and simply do not compare in flavour to home-made sauces. By learning how to make basic sauces you can banish the packets from your cupboard and have the satisfaction of coming up with your own variations.

In traditional cooking, sauces are often rich because ingredients such as butter, cream and wine are used for binding, thickening and flavouring. By substituting semi-skimmed milk and polyunsaturated margarine it is possible to make sauces in a much healthier way—avoiding the high-fat content that a sauce often adds to a meal.

Sauces may be sweet or savoury and are made for the following reasons: to add flavour to food or to contrast with a dish that may be bland; to add colour and spice to dishes to make them more appealing; to add moisture as well as flavour to dry food, and to improve the overall nutritional value of a dish. In British cooking there are some classic sauces which accompany roast meat: horseradish with roast beef, mint sauce with roast lamb, apple sauce with roast pork and bread sauce with poultry. Apart from giving a delicious blend of flavours, these sauces help counteract the richness of the meat.

ROUX-BASED SAUCES

White and brown sauces are both classics and form the basis of other variations. They can be made in different consistencies by varying the quantities of the ingredients to make sauces of a pouring, coating or binding consistency, depending on the dish they accompany.

White and brown sauces both have a base called a roux. Traditionally, a roux is made from butter, plain flour, milk or stock, but it is healthier to use polyunsaturated margarine, and semi-skimmed or skimmed milk or stock. Wholemeal flour—or half wholemeal, half plain—can also be used but the colour and texture will be slightly different than usual. The roux is made by melting the margarine, adding flour and cooking, and then adding liquid. For a white sauce the margarine and flour—the roux—is cooked but not coloured; made with plain flour the roux is white, but if made with wholemeal flour the sauce will have a slightly darker tone. For a brown sauce the roux is cooked until it is a deep golden brown.

LOW-FAT SAUCES

Healthy, fat-free sauces can be made successfully. For a 600 ml (1 pint) pouring sauce, the required ingredients are 25 g (1 oz) plain flour or 40 g (1½ oz) plain wholemeal flour and 568 ml (1 pint) semi-skimmed milk. Simply mix the flour with a little of the milk to form a paste. Heat the remaining milk and stir in the paste, then bring to the boil and cook for 10 minutes, stirring constantly to prevent lumps. To make a coating sauce, use 50 g (2 oz) plain flour or 75 g (3 oz) plain wholemeal flour.

USING A FOOD PROCESSOR

Sauces which are thickened with margarine and flour can also be made in a blender or food processor. The milk or stock is heated and then brought to the boil in a pan and set aside; the margarine and flour are placed in the food processor and processed until blended. The heated milk or stock is then added using the pulsing action—if your food processor does not have this action, simply turn it on and off—until the mixture is smooth. The mixture is then returned to the pan, brought to the boil and simmered for 5 minutes, stirring until smooth and thickened.

CORNFLOUR AND ARROWROOT

Successful sauces can be made very quickly using cornflour or arrowroot, both of which can be used instead of wheat flour; sauces made in this way have a lower fat content because margarine is not used. The required ingredients are 25 ml (1½ tbsp) cornflour or arrowroot to 300 ml (½ pint) liquid; a little of the liquid is blended with the cornflour or arrowroot, while the remainder of the liquid is boiled. The blended mixture is then added to the boiling liquid and stirred vigorously to prevent lumps from forming. The mixture is then cooked for three minutes, stirring constantly until the sauce has become thick.

Cornflour tends to give a sticky texture to a sauce, and it also makes it cloudy; arrowroot gives a sauce a clear, shiny gloss.

LIQUIDS IN SAUCES

Most white sauces are made with milk, wine or stock—or a combination of all three. Brown sauces need a meat stock or a stock made from vegetable water; miso (a paste made from soya beans) or naturally fermented shoyu can be added to flavour and colour sauces. If possible use home-made stock (see page 15) when making sauces.

THICK AND THIN GRAVIES
The most frequently made sauce is gravy. Thin gravy is traditionally served with roast beef. Make it by removing the fat from the roasting pan, leaving the residue and then adding 300 ml ($\frac{1}{2}$ pint) of hot stock or vegetable water. Stir until the mixture has boiled for 3–4 minutes and is a rich brown colour.

Thick gravy is made in the same way as thin gravy, but before adding the liquid, 15 ml (1 tbsp) of wholemeal or plain flour is added and blended thoroughly with the sediment to form a thick roux. The stock or vegetable water must be hot and added slowly to prevent lumps forming. The mixture must be stirred constantly until it thickens and browns, then cooked for 2–3 minutes before serving. Do not add seasoning or the flavour of the meat residues will be masked.

ALTERNATIVE SAUCES
Gravies, brown sauces and white sauces all have their place in healthy eating when served with discretion. There are also alternative ways to create delicious sauces which add extra flavour and contrasts as well as liquid to dishes.

Nouvelle cuisine is based on the new principles of healthy cooking in which fats and salts are reduced and flavours come from stocks, vegetables and fruit; the freshness of the ingredients is emphasised. Sauces made according to these principles often use low-fat yogurt, curd cheese and natural Quark for taste, texture and thickening, instead of butter and cream; often a sauce consists of a simple purée of vegetables or fruit. Most nouvelle cuisine sauces are made without the addition of flour.

BASIC WHITE SAUCE

Flavoured pouring sauces can be served with fish or vegetables; the coating sauce will bind savoury pies.

MAKES 600 ML (1 PINT)
45 CALORIES PER 50 ML (2 FL OZ)
PREPARATION 5 minutes
COOKING 10 minutes

**25 g (1 oz) polyunsaturated margarine
25 g (1 oz) plain flour
568 ml (1 pint) semi-skimmed milk
salt and pepper, to taste (optional)**

——1——
Melt the margarine in a saucepan over medium heat. Remove from the heat, add the flour and mix well.

Return to a low heat and cook for 1 minute without browning.

——2——
Remove from the heat and gradually add 300 ml ($\frac{1}{2}$ pint) milk, stirring constantly with a wooden spoon. Return to the heat and simmer for 2–3 minutes, stirring, until the mixture thickens and is smooth.

——3——
Remove from the heat and add the remaining milk, stirring well. Return to the heat, stirring constantly, and bring to the boil. Boil for a further 4 minutes. Season, if desired.

VARIATIONS
White Sauce for coating: Use 50 g (2 oz) polyunsaturated margarine and 50 g (2 oz) plain flour; prepare as above.

Parsley Sauce: Stir in 60 ml (4 tbsp) chopped fresh parsley with the seasoning.

Cheese Sauce: Stir in 50 g (2 oz) finely grated mature Cheddar cheese with the seasoning and cook until melted.

Onion Sauce: Add 2 skinned and finely chopped small onions at step 1 and cook over a low heat for 5 minutes, until soft, before adding the flour.

Mushroom Sauce: Cook 75 g (3 oz) sliced mushrooms in the margarine.

Caper Sauce: Stir in 15 ml (1 tbsp) capers and 10 ml (2 tsp) lemon juice.

PREPARING PERFECT PASTA

In Italian, the word pasta means dough and this describes it exactly —spaghetti, lasagne, tagliatelle and all the other pasta varieties are shaped from a dough of fine durum, a wheat that grows near the Mediterranean. Like rice and potatoes, pasta is one of the world's food staples and it occupies a prized position both in homely Italian cooking and in haute cuisine. High in carbohydrates, pasta is filling and nutritious—it is only fattening if it is served with a rich sauce.

The recent emphasis on the importance of eating grain-based foods, particularly those high in fibre, has changed people's attitude towards pasta. Rather than being considered fattening and unhealthy, pasta is now regarded as a highly nutritious food with a calorific content little more than that of bread. It is also a highly versatile ingredient to have in the store cupboard and it is exceptionally easy and quick to cook. Whether you buy pasta for convenience, or enjoy making it yourself, it is an ingredient no cook should be without.

The best pasta that you can buy is made from durum wheat, a high protein wheat with long, hard grains that grows in the United States and around the Mediterranean.

This wheat can either be ground to make a refined white flour or a wholemeal flour, and pasta made from both types is readily available. Ground durum wheat is not available commercially, but you can make delicious pasta at home using ordinary wholemeal flour.

The simplest type of bought pasta is made only from durum wheat flour and water, but other ingredients, such as olive oil or eggs, can be added to provide extra flavour or a slightly different texture. Pasta which is described as being *all'uovo* (with eggs) must have at least 4 eggs per 1 kg (2$\frac{1}{4}$ lb) flour.

Many health food shops also stock buckwheat spaghetti which is made from a mixture of buckwheat flour and wholemeal flour. It is a grey colour, generally thinner than standard spaghetti, with a softer texture and characteristic buckwheat flavour.

ADDING COLOUR
Coloured pasta makes extremely attractive dishes. The green, spinach pasta is the most readily available and it is usually made into lasagne or tagliatelle. Although at first made with only white durum flour, wholemeal varieties can now be bought from specialist shops. You can colour home-made pasta using tomato, spinach or beetroot purée. Infused saffron will give an attractive yellow colour to white pasta. You can also add chopped fresh mixed herbs to give a flecked appearance to either white or wholemeal pasta.

Most of the pasta sold in Britain is of the dried variety, but some specialist shops, particularly those specialising in Italian or Greek foods, and even some supermarkets, sell freshly-made pasta.

SHAPES AND SIZES
Some pasta is available ready-cooked

and in cans. This includes spaghetti and ravioli in tomato sauce. Very often you will find that canned pasta is very soft in texture as a result of the pre-cooking process.

Pasta can be made into many different shapes and sizes. Types of wholemeal pasta available include spaghetti, macaroni, tagliatelle or ribbons, rings, twists, shells and lasagne.

White pasta is also made into vermicelli, small bows, tubes for making cannelloni, stars and flowers.

Home-made pasta can be cut into ribbons rather like tagliatelle, and if you have a pasta-making machine you can make spaghetti. You can cut it into small squares or oblong pieces and make butterflies by pinching the centres of the oblong pieces together. For cap-shaped pieces, cut small rounds from a cylinder of dough and form them into caps by pressing your thumb into the centre.

Dried pasta can be kept in airtight containers for up to four months. Fresh pasta can be stored in a cool larder, but should be eaten within two days of making or purchasing.

NUTRITIOUS PASTA

Pasta is not the fattening food that it was once thought to be; 50 g (2 oz) pasta, weighed before cooking, contains around 165 calories. About 50 g (2 oz) uncooked weight of dried pasta will make a substantial portion for one person.

As with wholemeal bread, the wholemeal varieties of pasta are more nutritious than the white. The most widely available brand of wholemeal pasta per 100 g (4 oz) contains 10 g dietary fibre, 14 g protein, 4.6 mg iron, 0.4 mg thiamin. The equivalent weight of white pasta contains less fibre, 9 g protein 1.23 mg iron and 0.10 mg thiamin. The fat content of both types of pasta is very low.

COOKING TECHNIQUES

To cook pasta for a meal to serve four people you will need 2.3 litres (4 pints) water to 350 g (12 oz) pasta. Although it is standard practice to add 5 ml (1 tsp) salt to the water, the juice of half a lemon will work just as well. If you like your pasta to have a glossy texture, add 15–30 ml (1–2 tbsp) olive or corn oil. Bring the water to the boil, add the pasta and stir. Lower the heat and cook, uncovered, until the pasta is cooked through, but still firm—'al dente'. Never overcook pasta. Cooking times vary for different types of pasta. The average cooking time for most dried pasta is 12 minutes; freshly made pasta may only take half that time. During cooking, take small pieces of pasta from the pan from time to time to test for readiness. When the pasta is cooked, drain it in a sieve or colander. There is no need to rinse.

SERVING PASTA

Pasta can be served as an accompaniment, as a first course or as a salad, or it can be combined with other ingredients to make a substantial main meal. If it is to be served as an accompaniment, pasta is best if it is given some kind of light coating, such as grated Parmesan cheese. For a healthier alternative, try olive oil, crushed garlic and some finely-chopped walnuts or freshly-chopped herbs such as parsley, basil or sage. A little low-fat natural yogurt, mixed with tomato purée or other flavouring, can replace a cream sauce, and natural Quark can be substituted in a sauce usually made with cream cheese.

All types of fish go well with pasta. For quick main meals or first courses, try folding in flaked canned tuna fish or sardines. These fish also make ideal pasta salads, especially if some cooked haricot or cannellini beans are added.

Many traditional meat-based pasta dishes can be made solely with vegetable ingredients.

Make a Bolognese sauce with small brown lentils, a lasagne with cooked vegetables and chopped nuts, or fill home-made ravioli or cannelloni with a cheese or nut stuffing.

WHOLEMEAL PASTA

Fresh pasta is so quick to cook, it makes a nutritious and speedy meal.

MAKES 400 G (14 OZ)
70 CALORIES PER 25 G (1 OZ)
PREPARATION About 30 minutes
COOKING 3–5 minutes
STANDING 1–1½ hours

275 g (10 oz) plain wholemeal flour
2 eggs
15 ml (1 tbsp) olive oil

———1———
Put the flour into a bowl and make a well in the centre. Beat together the eggs, oil and 75 ml (5 tbsp) water. Mix into the flour using fingers or a fork, adding more water if necessary, until the dough is soft and pliable. Turn on to a lightly floured surface and knead for 5–10 minutes until smooth.

———2———
Alternatively, blend the eggs with the oil and 75 ml (5 tbsp) water in a food processor for about 30 seconds, add the flour and mix for about 1 minute.

———3———
Wrap the dough and leave to rest at room temperature for 30 minutes to 1 hour.

———4———
Divide the dough into 4 and roll one portion at a time, keeping the remainder wrapped. Roll out the dough on a lightly floured surface, turn it and roll again. Repeat turning and rolling until the dough is paper thin. Cover with a cloth and leave to dry for 30 minutes, turning over after 15 minutes.

———5———
To make tagliatelle, cut pasta into narrow strips. For lasagne, cut into 15 × 5 cm (6 × 2 inch) rectangles.

———6———
To cook fresh pasta, bring a large saucepan of water to the boil, add the pasta, stir and cook for 3–5 minutes, until just tender. Drain well, then serve.

TOMATO PASTA
Make the pasta as directed but substitute 30 ml (2 tbsp) tomato purée for 30 ml (2 tbsp) water.

SPINACH PASTA
Make the pasta as directed replacing 45 ml (3 tbsp) water with 45 ml (3 tbsp) spinach purée.

GOODNESS GUIDE
FIBRE Wholemeal pasta contains more than twice as much fibre as white pasta
VITAMINS B vitamins and vitamin E are present in the flour and eggs. The egg also contains vitamins A and D
MINERALS Wholemeal flour and eggs provide calcium, iron, potassium and zinc

SPINACH ROLL

CHICKEN STIR-FRY SALAD

TOASTED SEEDS

SAVOURY FRESH APRICOT DIP

SPINACH ROLL

MAKES 8 SLICES 215 calories each
PREPARATION 30 minutes
COOKING 25–30 minutes

450 g (1 lb) potatoes, scrubbed
700 g (1½ lb) fresh spinach, chopped, or
290 g (10.6 oz) packet frozen chopped
spinach
1 onion, skinned and grated
2 garlic cloves, skinned and crushed
45 ml (3 tbsp) tomato purée
175 g (6 oz) low-fat Cheddar cheese, grated
salt and pepper, to taste
50 g (2 oz) plain wholemeal flour
50 g (2 oz) plain flour
1 egg, beaten

———1———

Lightly grease a baking sheet and set aside. Cook the potatoes in boiling water for 20 minutes, or until tender. Drain and cool slightly, then peel. Mash well, turn into a bowl and leave to cool completely.

———2———

Meanwhile, put the spinach into a saucepan, cover and cook with just the water clinging to the leaves for about 5 minutes, until wilted. If using frozen spinach, cook, stirring, for about 10 minutes. Drain well.

———3———

Add the onion, garlic, tomato purée and 100 g (4 oz) cheese to the spinach. Add seasoning and mix well. Set aside.

———4———

Mix the flours into the mashed potato, then add the egg and seasoning. Mix well together and knead until smooth.

———5———

On a lightly floured surface, roll out the potato pastry to a 30 × 25 cm (12 × 10 inch) rectangle. Spread over the spinach mixture to within 0.5 cm (¼ inch) of the edges.

———6———

Starting with a short edge, roll up like a Swiss roll and place joinside down on the work surface. Cut into 8 chunky slices. Place the slices, flat side down, on the baking sheet and pat out lightly with a knife to form neat rounds, about 7 cm (3 inches) in diameter.

———7———

Sprinkle with the remaining grated cheese and bake at 190°C (375°F) mark 5 for 25–30 minutes, until cooked through and golden brown. Serve hot with a tomato salad.

TOASTED SEEDS

SERVES 4 110 calories per serving
PREPARATION 5 minutes
COOKING 3 minutes

45 ml (3 tbsp) pumpkin seeds
45 ml (3 tbsp) sunflower seeds
1 garlic clove, skinned and crushed
15 ml (1 tbsp) soy sauce, preferably
naturally fermented shoyu

───── 1 ─────

Put the pumpkin and sunflower seeds in a large saucepan and dry-fry over a medium heat for about 2 minutes, stirring constantly, until the seeds pop and 'jump' and colour.

───── 2 ─────

Add the garlic and soy sauce. Lower the heat and cook for 1 minute, stirring constantly, until thoroughly combined. Turn into a small serving bowl and serve warm or cold.

Variations can be made by mixing other spices with the cooked seeds.

SPICY TOASTED SEEDS

Stir in 1.25 ml ($\frac{1}{4}$ tsp) chilli powder and 2.5 ml ($\frac{1}{2}$ tsp) ground cumin and cook over low heat for 1 minute, stirring constantly

PAPRIKA TOASTED SEEDS

Stir in 5 ml (1 tsp) paprika and a large pinch of cayenne pepper and cook over low heat for 1 minute, stirring constantly

GOODNESS GUIDE

TOASTED SEEDS

MINERALS Seeds are rich in potassium, calcium, iron and zinc

VITAMINS Seeds provide B vitamins and vitamin E. Vitamin E is essential to protect the polyunsaturated fats present in the seeds from rancidity

FATS Seeds are a source of essential fatty acids

SPINACH ROLL

FIBRE This is a high-fibre dish, supplied by the potatoes, spinach, onion and wholemeal flour

MINERALS High quantities of iron, calcium, potassium and zinc are supplied. Zinc aids the action of enzymes responsible for mental and physical development and helps to heal wounds

CHICKEN STIR-FRY SALAD

SERVES 4 195 calories per serving
PREPARATION 15 minutes
COOKING 3–4 minutes
MARINATING 15 minutes

450 g (1 lb) boneless chicken breasts,
skinned and cut into very thin strips
10 ml (2 tsp) sesame oil
2 garlic cloves, skinned and crushed
2 cm ($\frac{3}{4}$ inch) piece fresh root ginger, peeled
and grated
45 ml (3 tbsp) soy sauce, preferably
naturally fermented shoyu
1 bunch of watercress, trimmed
$\frac{1}{2}$ head Chinese leaves, torn into
bite-size pieces
$\frac{1}{2}$ head curly endive, torn into
bite-size pieces
15 ml (1 tbsp) corn oil
pepper, to taste
radish roses and a dill sprig, to garnish

───── 1 ─────

Put the chicken strips in a bowl. Add the sesame oil, garlic, grated ginger and soy sauce. Stir well and leave to marinate for 15 minutes.

───── 2 ─────

Meanwhile, arrange the watercress, Chinese leaves and endive on a serving platter or individual plates.

───── 3 ─────

Heat the oil in a large frying pan or wok. Add the chicken mixture and cook over a high heat for 3–4 minutes, stirring constantly, until the chicken is cooked through.

───── 4 ─────

Spoon the mixture over the leaves, season and serve immediately, garnished with radish roses and a fresh dill sprig.

MICROWAVE Complete steps 1 and 2. Put oil into a bowl, cook, uncovered, 100% (High) 4 minutes. Add chicken strips. Cook, uncovered, 100% (High) 4 minutes, stirring three times, until cooked through. Complete recipe.

GOODNESS GUIDE

MINERALS The watercress and Chinese leaves are a rich plant source of iron and also provide a good helping of calcium

VITAMINS The fast cooking method of stir-frying prevents large losses of vitamins, particularly vitamin C and B vitamins

SAVOURY FRESH APRICOT DIP

SERVES 4 260 calories per serving
PREPARATION 5 minutes
COOKING 5–8 minutes
CHILLING 20 minutes

350 g (12 oz) fresh apricots, stoned
1 small onion, skinned and chopped
grated rind and juice of 1 lemon
15 ml (1 tbsp) white wine vinegar
30 ml (2 tbsp) chicken stock
1.25 ml ($\frac{1}{4}$ tsp) grated nutmeg
1 cinnamon stick
175 g (6 oz) low-fat soft cheese

TO SERVE

strips of wholemeal pitta bread
100 g (4 oz) cooked chicken meat, skinned
and cut into bite-size pieces
100 g (4 oz) cooked lean boned lamb, cut
into bite-size pieces
a selection of raw fresh vegetables:
cauliflower florets
cucumber, cut into chunks
red or green pepper, cut into strips
celery sticks, cut into strips
carrots, cut into strips
button mushrooms

───── 1 ─────

Put the apricots in a saucepan with the onion, lemon rind and juice, vinegar, stock and spices. Cover and cook gently for 5–8 minutes, until the apricots are tender.

───── 2 ─────

Discard the cinnamon stick and drain, reserving the liquid. Purée the apricots in a blender or food processor with 30 ml (2 tbsp) of the liquid, until smooth.

───── 3 ─────

Cream the cheese, then add the apricot purée and beat until well blended and smooth. Add more of the reserved liquid to make a good dipping consistency. Turn into a bowl, cover and chill for at least 20 minutes. Serve with a selection of bread, meat and vegetables.

GOODNESS GUIDE

PROTEIN The cheese, lamb and pitta bread provide protein

VITAMINS The cheese, lamb and pitta bread provide B vitamins

FIBRE The apricots, bread and vegetables make this dish high in fibre

CRAB-STUFFED AVOCADO

SERVES 4 370 calories per serving
PREPARATION 10 minutes
COOKING 10–15 minutes

2 ripe avocados
175 g (6 oz) fresh white crabmeat or 175 g
(6 oz) can crabmeat, drained and flaked
2 spring onions, trimmed and finely chopped
30 ml (2 tbsp) lemon juice
45 ml (3 tbsp) olive oil
pepper, to taste
5 ml (1 tsp) curry powder
45 ml (3 tbsp) fresh wholemeal breadcrumbs
15 ml (1 tbsp) grated Parmesan cheese

———1———

Cut the avocados in half, discard the stones and scoop out the flesh to within 0.25 cm ($\frac{1}{8}$ inch) of the skin. Place the avocado shells in a shallow ovenproof dish and set aside. Chop the avocado flesh into small cubes and place in a bowl.

———2———

Add the flaked crabmeat and spring onions. Put the lemon juice, olive oil, seasoning and curry powder in a screw-topped jar and shake until well blended. Pour the dressing over the crab mixture and toss well.

———3———

Pile the mixture into the avocado shells. Mix the breadcrumbs and Parmesan cheese together and sprinkle over the top of the avocados.

———4———

Bake at 200°C (400°F) mark 6 for 10–15 minutes or until the topping is crisp. Serve immediately with a seasonal salad.

MICROWAVE Complete steps 1, 2 and 3. Cook uncovered, 100% (High) 3–4 minutes, turning twice, until warmed through.

GOODNESS GUIDE

PROTEIN Crab is a low-fat source of protein
FAT Avocados are rich in polyunsaturated oil which contains essential fatty acids
VITAMINS Vitamin E is provided by the avocado which is also one of the rare plant sources of vitamin D. Vitamin E prevents oxidation of the polyunsaturated oil in the avocado

ONION QUICHE

MAKES 6 SLICES 270 calories each
PREPARATION 25 minutes
BAKING 50–60 minutes
CHILLING 30 minutes

75 g (3 oz) plain wholemeal flour
75 g (3 oz) plain flour
75 g (3 oz) polyunsaturated margarine
30 ml (2 tbsp) corn oil
3 onions, skinned and thinly sliced
6 spring onions, trimmed and cut diagonally
into 2.5 cm (1 inch) pieces
75 ml (5 tbsp) semi-skimmed milk
3 eggs, beaten
2.5 ml ($\frac{1}{2}$ tsp) cayenne pepper

———1———

Put the flours into a mixing bowl and rub in the margarine until the mixture resembles fine breadcrumbs. Mix to a firm but pliable dough with about 30 ml (2 tbsp) cold water. Knead on a lightly floured surface.

———2———

Roll out the dough and use to line a 20 cm (8 inch) loose-based flan tin. Chill for 30 minutes.

———3———

Place a sheet of greaseproof paper in the base of the flan case, cover with baking beans and bake at 200°C (400°F) mark 6 for 15 minutes. Remove the beans and paper, then bake 5 minutes more.

———4———

Meanwhile, heat the oil in a saucepan and cook the onions for 6–8 minutes, until transparent. Drain off the oil, then place the onions in the partially baked flan case.

———5———

Beat the semi-skimmed milk with the eggs and add the cayenne pepper. Pour into the partially baked flan case and bake for 25–30 minutes, until the filling is set and golden.

MICROWAVE Complete steps 1 and 2. Cover the pastry base with a double thickness of absorbent kitchen paper. Cook, uncovered, 100% (High) 4 minutes. Remove paper and cook 100% (High) 2 minutes, turning twice. Put the oil and onions into a bowl. Cover and cook 100% (High) 6 minutes. Place in the pastry case. Beat the milk, eggs and cayenne pepper together and pour over the onions. Cook, uncovered, 60% (Medium) 6–7 minutes turning the dish 3 times, until set. Serve hot or cold.

SMOKED CHICKEN SANDWICH

SERVES 4 195 calories per serving
PREPARATION 8 minutes

100 g (4 oz) smoked chicken meat, skinned
and chopped
45 ml (3 tbsp) medium dry white wine
15 ml (1 tbsp) low-fat natural yogurt
2 spring onions, trimmed and chopped
2.5 ml ($\frac{1}{2}$ tsp) ground mace
15 ml (1 tbsp) chopped fresh tarragon or
10 ml (2 tsp) dried
30 ml (2 tbsp) diced celery or cucumber
15 g ($\frac{1}{2}$ oz) polyunsaturated margarine
8 slices granary bread
1 lettuce leaf, shredded

———1———

Mix together the chicken, wine, yogurt, spring onions, mace and 10 ml (2 tsp) of the fresh tarragon or 7.5 ml (1$\frac{1}{2}$ tsp) dried. Then add the celery or cucumber and mix well.

———2———

Beat the remaining tarragon into the margarine and use to spread on the bread. Fill each sandwich with the prepared chicken mixture and shredded lettuce. To serve, cut each sandwich diagonally into 4.

GOODNESS GUIDE

CHICKEN SANDWICH

PROTEIN The chicken, yogurt and the granary bread provide protein. All the cells in the body require proteins which must be replaced daily
ENERGY All foods provide energy. It is best provided by complex carbohydrates and a little fat which enables the body to use protein fully

ONION QUICHE

PROTEIN The eggs, milk and flour provide protein
FIBRE Fibre is provided by the flours and by the onions
MINERALS Calcium is found in the eggs, milk and flour; the eggs also provide iron
VITAMINS The eggs and margarine provide vitamins A, D and E. Eggs, milk and flour provide vitamin B

144

ONION QUICHE

CRAB-STUFFED AVOCADO

SMOKED CHICKEN SANDWICH

145

SPICED POPCORN

SERVES 4 105 calories per serving
PREPARATION 5 minutes
COOKING 5 minutes

15 ml (1 tbsp) corn oil
50 g (2 oz) popping corn

CURRY MIX
5 ml (1 tsp) turmeric
5 ml (1 tsp) ground ginger
10 ml (2 tsp) ground coriander
2.5 ml ($\frac{1}{2}$ tsp) cayenne pepper
5 ml (1 tsp) ground fenugreek

CHILLI MIX
5 ml (1 tsp) chilli powder
5 ml (1 tsp) garlic powder
5 ml (1 tsp) ground cloves
7.5 ml (1$\frac{1}{2}$ tsp) paprika
5 ml (1 tsp) ground cumin

SESAME MIX
15 ml (1 tbsp) sesame seeds, toasted
2.5 ml ($\frac{1}{2}$ tsp) ground mace
5 ml (1 tsp) ground cinnamon
2.5 ml ($\frac{1}{2}$ tsp) ground cloves

—— 1 ——

Make one of the spice mixtures. Mix together all the spices for the Curry Mix or for the Chilli Mix. For the Sesame Mix, crush the sesame seeds to a powder in a pestle and mortar; mix with remaining spices.

—— 2 ——

To prepare the popcorn, heat the oil in a 3.4 litre (6 pint) saucepan with a tight-fitting lid. Add 3 kernels of the corn and heat with the lid on until the kernels pop.

—— 3 ——

Remove the pan from the heat and add the remaining corn. Cook, covered, over a medium heat for 2 minutes, shaking the pan, until the corn starts to pop. Reduce the heat slightly and continue to cook, still covered, shaking the pan, until the popping stops.

—— 4 ——

Remove from the heat and sprinkle the popcorn with one of the mixes. Replace the lid and shake vigorously to coat the popcorn. Serve hot.

GOODNESS GUIDE
FIBRE Corn provides a good supply of fibre
MINERALS Dried spices are a very concentrated supply of minerals: iron, calcium, potassium and zinc
VITAMINS Spices also contain concentrated sources of carotene and vitamin C. Carotene is converted into vitamin A in the body; it is important for dim-light vision

TUNA AND DILL CAKES

TUNA AND DILL CAKES

These are a healthy alternative to traditional fish cakes.

SERVES 4 390 calories per serving
PREPARATION 20 minutes
COOKING 30–35 minutes
CHILLING 15 minutes

225 g (8 oz) potatoes, scrubbed
15 g ($\frac{1}{2}$ oz) polyunsaturated margarine
30 ml (2 tbsp) low-fat natural yogurt
two 200 g (7 oz) cans tuna in brine, drained and flaked
40 ml (2$\frac{1}{2}$ tbsp) chopped fresh dill or 15 ml (1 tbsp) dried
15 ml (1 tbsp) grated onion
grated rind of 1 lemon
pepper, to taste
15 ml (1 tbsp) plain wholemeal flour
2 egg whites, beaten
75 g (3 oz) dried wholemeal breadcrumbs or rolled oats
45 ml (3 tbsp) mayonnaise
lemon wedges and fresh dill, to garnish

—— 1 ——

Cook the potatoes in boiling water for 20 minutes or until tender. Drain and peel, then add the margarine and 15 ml (1 tbsp) of the yogurt. Mash until smooth. Turn into a mixing bowl. Cool.

—— 2 ——

Add the tuna, 25 ml (1$\frac{1}{2}$ tbsp) of the fresh dill or 10 ml (2 tsp) dried dill, the onion, lemon rind and seasoning. Mix well. Cover and chill for about 15 minutes, until firm enough to handle.

—— 3 ——

Dust the work surface with the flour, then shape the tuna and potato mixture into 8 even-sized cakes. Dip into the egg white, then coat in the breadcrumbs. Place on a baking sheet and cook at 200°C (400°F) mark 6 for 10–15 minutes, until hot and crisp.

—— 4 ——

Meanwhile, mix the remaining yogurt and dill with the mayonnaise. Serve this sauce in a separate bowl with the cooked fish cakes. Garnish the fish cakes with lemon wedges and fresh dill.

GOODNESS GUIDE
PROTEIN The fish, egg, yogurt, breadcrumbs and potatoes combine to provide a high-protein dish
FIBRE The breadcrumbs (or oats) and potatoes supply fibre
VITAMINS Many B vitamins are present. The tuna provides vitamin B$_{12}$ for healthy red blood cells

146

SPICED POPCORN

PASTA WITH PESTO

**BAKED JACKET POTATOES
WITH PEANUT STUFFING**

PASTA WITH PESTO

PASTA WITH PESTO

SERVES 4 353 calories per serving
PREPARATION 5 minutes
COOKING 15 minutes

225 g (8 oz) wholemeal pasta, any shape
30 ml (2 tbsp) olive oil
1–2 garlic cloves, skinned
about 7 g ($\frac{1}{4}$ oz) fresh basil leaves and stems
50 g (2 oz) pine nuts
25 g (1 oz) Parmesan cheese, grated
semi-skimmed milk, to blend
100 g (4 oz) low-fat curd cheese
pepper, to taste
fresh basil, to garnish
Parmesan cheese, preferably freshly grated,
to serve

———1———

Cook the pasta in a large saucepan of boiling water for 10–12 minutes, until just tender.

———2———

Meanwhile, make the pesto. Put the oil, garlic, basil, pine nuts and Parmesan cheese in a blender or food processor. Add a little milk to moisten the mixture and blend to a thick purée. Transfer to a bowl. Stir in curd cheese and seasoning.

———3———

Drain the pasta, return to the pan and stir in the pesto. Cook, stirring, for 1–2 minutes over a very low heat. Thin the sauce with a little more milk, if needed. Garnish with basil and serve with Parmesan cheese.

MICROWAVE Put the pasta into a bowl with 600 ml (1 pint) boiling water. Cook, uncovered, 100% (High) 8–10 minutes. Cover and leave in the bowl. Complete step 2. Drain pasta and return to the bowl. Stir in the pesto sauce. Cook, uncovered, 100% (High) 2 minutes, stirring twice and adding more milk if wished. Complete recipe.

GOODNESS GUIDE
FIBRE Wholemeal pasta supplies a good serving of fibre unlike pasta made from refined flour
VITAMINS A range of B vitamins are provided by the pasta, pine nuts and cheeses
MINERALS Nuts, pasta and cheese supply potassium; nuts and pasta provide iron and calcium; cheese provides calcium

BAKED JACKET POTATOES WITH PEANUT STUFFING

SERVES 4 415 calories per serving
PREPARATION 5 minutes
COOKING 1 hour

4 baking potatoes, about 250 g (9 oz) each, scrubbed and pricked
100 g (4 oz) raw peanuts
1 green pepper, cored, seeded and chopped
few sprigs of fresh parsley
50 g (2 oz) mature Cheddar cheese, roughly chopped
pepper, to taste
2.5 ml ($\frac{1}{2}$ tsp) hot chilli powder
semi-skimmed milk, to blend

———1———

Bake the potatoes at 220°C (425°F) mark 7 for 50–60 minutes, until tender.

———2———

Meanwhile, place the peanuts on a baking sheet at the top of the oven and cook for 10 minutes, or lightly brown them in an ungreased, thick-based saucepan on a low heat for about 5 minutes, shaking the pan.

———3———

Purée the green pepper, parsley, cheese, seasoning and chilli powder in a blender or food processor with enough milk to make a very thick purée. Add the toasted peanuts and blend so that the nuts are chopped but not ground. Check the seasoning, adding more if wished. The filling can be left cold or gently heated.

———4———

To serve, split the baked potatoes down the centre and spoon in the stuffing mixture. If wished, place the stuffed potatoes under the grill for a few minutes to brown the filling. Serve with a seasonal salad.

MICROWAVE Spread the peanuts on a browning sheet. Cook, uncovered, 100% (High) 6 minutes, stirring twice. Arrange the pricked potatoes on absorbent kitchen paper. Cook, uncovered, 100% (High) 20 minutes, rearranging twice until tender. Complete the recipe.

GOODNESS GUIDE
PROTEIN The peanuts, cheese and potatoes provide protein. The combination of proteins in the peanuts and cheese is equivalent to the protein supplied by lean beef
FIBRE The peanuts and potatoes make this a high-fibre dish
MINERALS Peanuts contain good quantities of iron and calcium. The cheese is rich in calcium

TUNA AND BEAN SALAD WITH ORANGE DRESSING

SERVES 4 270 calories per serving
PREPARATION 20 minutes
COOKING 4–5 minutes

2 oranges
**100–150 g (4–5 oz) fresh spinach, cos
lettuce or endive leaves, rinsed and dried**
½ small onion, skinned and thinly sliced
**200 g (7 oz) can tuna in brine, well drained
and flaked**
100 g (4 oz) button mushrooms, sliced
**400 g (14 oz) can cannellini beans, drained
and rinsed**
**8 black olives and 5 ml (1 tsp) chopped fresh
parsley, to garnish**

ORANGE DRESSING
juice of 1 orange
150 ml (5 fl oz) low-fat natural yogurt
1 garlic clove, skinned and crushed
15 ml (1 tbsp) soya oil

——— 1 ———

Thinly pare the rind from the oranges
and cut into thin strips. Remove all
white pith from the oranges and
segment them. Set aside. Blanch the
rind in boiling water for 4–5 minutes,
drain and reserve.

——— 2 ———

Arrange the leaves, onion and orange
on a platter. Mix the tuna, mushrooms and beans together.

——— 3 ———

To make the dressing, mix together
the juice, yogurt, garlic, oil and salt
and pepper. Pour half over the tuna
bean mixture and toss lightly.

——— 4 ———

Pile the tuna on the serving platter
and garnish with the olives, parsley
and orange rind. Pour over the remaining dressing before serving.

GOODNESS GUIDE

FIBRE The beans and the vegetables supply
a good helping of fibre
VITAMINS Tuna is a rich source of vitamin D,
which aids the body's absorption of calcium
MINERALS Both the tuna and the beans
provide iron, which is needed for healthy
blood cells. The yogurt supplies calcium,
essential for healthy bones and
muscle contraction

EGG AND SPROUT SALAD

*The toasted sesame seeds, sesame
oil and the nuts give this dish an
unusual flavour and texture.*

SERVES 4 200 calories per serving
PREPARATION 25 minutes
COOKING None

4 eggs, hard-boiled
100 g (4 oz) tofu or low-fat soft cheese
2 tomatoes, skinned, seeded and chopped
15 ml (1 tbsp) sesame seeds, toasted
pinch of garlic or onion salt
pepper, to taste
225 g (8 oz) alfalfa sprouts or beansprouts
5 ml (1 tsp) sesame oil
15 ml (1 tbsp) soya oil
30 ml (2 tbsp) cider vinegar
**25 g (1 oz) unsalted cashew nuts, toasted
and chopped**
30 ml (2 tbsp) chopped fresh parsley

——— 1 ———

Remove the egg shells, cut the eggs
in half lengthways, gently scoop out
the yolks and place in a mixing
bowl. Reserve the egg whites.

——— 2 ———

Add the tofu or cheese, tomatoes,
sesame seeds and seasoning to the
egg yolks and mix well. Fill the egg
whites and then mould more filling
on top to give a whole egg shape.
Chill until ready to serve.

——— 3 ———

Toss together the sprouts, oils, vinegar and nuts, season and arrange
on a salad platter. Arrange the eggs
on top, sprinkle with the parsley and
serve.

GOODNESS GUIDE

PROTEIN Eggs, cheese, tofu and nuts are all
high in protein
VITAMINS The sprouting of beans increases
their vitamin C content, making them as
rich as oranges in vitamin C. The sprouts
also supply B vitamins, including B_{12},
which is otherwise found only in animal
products and helps proper nervous system
functioning and aids in the formation of red
blood cells

EGG AND SPROUT SALAD

CHICKEN AND WALNUT STUFFED ONIONS

The onion centres can be used in salads or sandwich fillings if they are chopped, wrapped tightly and stored in the refrigerator.

SERVES 4   250 calories per serving
PREPARATION   40 minutes
COOKING   1½ hours

50 g (2 oz) brown rice
4 large Spanish onions, each about 275 g
(10 oz), skinned
150 g (5 oz) cooked chicken meat, skinned
and finely chopped
50 g (2 oz) walnuts, finely chopped
15 ml (1 tbsp) lemon juice
5 ml (1 tsp) ground coriander
5 ml (1 tsp) mixed dried herbs
salt and pepper, to taste

CHEESE SAUCE
5 ml (1 tsp) instant vegetable stock granules
10 ml (2 tsp) cornflour
150 ml (¼ pint) semi-skimmed milk
30 ml (2 tbsp) low-fat soft cheese
50 g (2 oz) low-fat Cheshire cheese, grated
5 ml (1 tsp) ground coriander
30 ml (2 tbsp) chopped fresh parsley

—————1—————

Cook the rice in a saucepan of boiling water for about 30 minutes or until tender. Meanwhile, place the onions in a large saucepan of boiling water to cover and simmer gently for 20 minutes. Drain, reserving the liquid. Set aside to cool slightly. Drain the rice.

—————2—————

Mix together the chicken, rice, walnuts, lemon juice, coriander, herbs and seasoning.

—————3—————

Scoop out and discard a spoonful of the centre of each onion, and pack in the filling.

—————4—————

Place the onions in a casserole or ovenproof serving dish large enough to hold them upright and add 600 ml (1 pint) of the reserved cooking liquid. Cover and cook at 190°C (375°F) mark 5 for 1½ hours, basting occasionally. Drain the juices into a saucepan and keep the onions hot.

—————5—————

To make the sauce, stir the vegetable stock granules into the juices and simmer until reduced to 150 ml (¼ pint). Mix the cornflour with the milk and add to the pan. Bring slowly to the boil, stirring continuously, and cook for 2 minutes. Reduce the heat and stir in the cheeses, coriander and parsley. Cook very gently for 5 minutes, then pour over the onions and serve.

GOODNESS GUIDE
FIBRE The onions, rice and nuts
contribute fibre
VITAMINS Onions are a source of vitamin C,
with extra contributed by the parsley and
coriander. A range of B-complex vitamins
are provided by the rice, nuts, chicken,
cheese and semi-skimmed milk

CHICKEN AND WALNUT STUFFED ONIONS

TUNA AND BEAN SALAD WITH ORANGE DRESSING

CARAWAY CHEESE STRAWS

MAKES ABOUT 30 40 calories each
PREPARATION 35–40 minutes
BAKING 12–15 minutes
STANDING 1 hour

50 g (2 oz) plain flour
50 g (2 oz) plain wholemeal flour
75 g (3 oz) polyunsaturated margarine
5 ml (1 tsp) lemon juice
1 egg, size 6, beaten
60 ml (4 tbsp) grated Parmesan cheese
5–10 ml (1–2 tsp) caraway seeds
pepper, to taste

———1———

Put the flours into a bowl and rub in the margarine. Add the lemon juice and 45–60 ml (3– tbsp) chilled water and mix to a soft dough.

———2———

Turn the dough on to a lightly floured surface and roll out to a rectangle about 38 × 12.5 cm (15 × 5 inches). Fold the bottom third of the pastry up over the centre third, and bring the top third of the pastry down. Wrap in cling film and chill 15 minutes.

———3———

Repeat the rolling and folding process twice more. Stand for 15 minutes in between. Chill the dough for a further 15 minutes. Meanwhile, lightly grease a baking sheet.

———4———

Roll the dough out to a 30.5 cm (12 inch) square and cut in half. Brush one piece of pastry with beaten egg and sprinkle with half the Parmesan cheese, caraway seeds and pepper.

———5———

Top with the second piece of dough and roll the two together gently. Glaze with the beaten egg and sprinkle with the remaining cheese.

———6———

Cut into 1 cm (½ inch) wide strips. Twist each one 3 or 4 times and place on the baking sheet.

———7———

Bake at 220°C (425°F) mark 7 for 12–15 minutes, until golden. Carefully transfer to a wire rack to cool.

FRUITED CHEESE SALAD

A refreshing salad full of goodness—its low-fat dressing has no oil or egg yolk, just juice and the seasonings.

SERVES 4 180 calories per serving
PREPARATION 15–20 minutes
COOKING None

225 g (8 oz) green cabbage, finely shredded
4 courgettes, shredded or coarsely grated
350 g (12 oz) cottage cheese
100 g (4 oz) black grapes, halved and seeded
2 eating apples, quartered, cored and sliced
2 oranges, peeled and segmented
1 bunch watercress, trimmed and divided into small sprigs

ORANGE AND HERB DRESSING
90 ml (6 tbsp) unsweetened orange juice
1.25 ml (¼ tsp) grated nutmeg
salt and pepper, to taste
30 ml (2 tbsp) finely chopped fresh parsley
15 ml (1 tbsp) snipped fresh chives
1 garlic clove, skinned and crushed

———1———

Mix the shredded cabbage and courgettes together in a bowl. To make the dressing, mix together all the ingredients in another bowl.

CARAWAY CHEESE STRAWS

FRUITED CHEESE SALAD

2

Add all but 15 ml (1 tbsp) of the dressing to the shredded vegetables and toss together. Spoon the shredded vegetables on to a shallow dish or platter.

3

Make 4 hollows in the vegetables and spoon in the cottage cheese. Arrange the grapes, apples, oranges and watercress sprigs over and around the vegetables. Spoon over the remaining dressing and serve.

GOODNESS GUIDE

FIBRE Cabbage, courgettes, grapes, apples, oranges and watercress supply this dish with plenty of fibre
FAT This salad is low in fat, as the dressing does not contain oil and cottage cheese is only 4% fat
VITAMINS The fruit and vegetables all contribute to the high C content of the salad

FRUIT AND NUT MUNCH

This is a good snack to keep on hand as a healthy alternative to sweets and biscuits during the day.

MAKES 450 G (1 LB)
70 CALORIES PER 25 G (1 OZ)
PREPARATION 10 minutes
COOKING 3–4 minutes

100 g (4 oz) ready-to-eat dried apricots, rinsed and chopped
100 g (4 oz) ready-to-eat dried stoned prunes, rinsed and chopped
50 g (2 oz) plump dried figs, chopped
25 g (1 oz) dried banana flakes
50 g (2 oz) unsalted cashew nuts
25 g (1 oz) shelled pumpkin seeds
25 g (1 oz) shelled sunflower seeds
25 g (1 oz) natural roasted peanuts

1

Mix together the apricots, prunes, figs and banana flakes. Lightly toast the cashew nuts, pumpkin seeds, sunflower seeds and peanuts under a hot grill for 3–4 minutes.

2

Add the seeds and nuts to the fruit and stir well. Set aside to cool completely, then store in an airtight container.

GOODNESS GUIDE

CARAWAY CHEESE STRAWS
FIBRE Wholemeal flour has about three times as much fibre as plain
MINERALS The egg and flours contain iron and there is calcium in the cheese and flours
PROTEIN Parmesan is a very high protein cheese; with the eggs and flour as well, these contain a great deal

FRUIT AND NUT MUNCH
FIBRE This is a very high fibre snack; all the ingredients supply some in greater or lesser amounts
SUGAR The natural sweetness of the dried fruit is sufficient to satisfy any sweet tooth without having to add any sugar

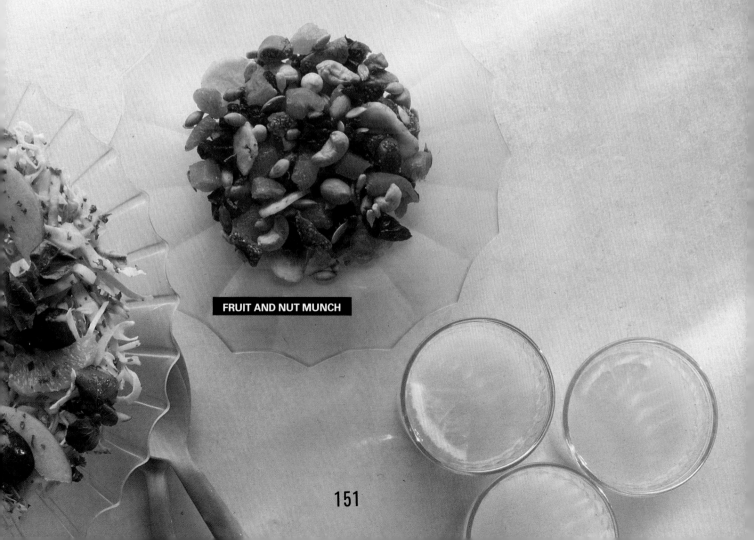

FRUIT AND NUT MUNCH

LUNCHEON SALAD

SERVES 4 185 calories per serving
PREPARATION 15 minutes
COOKING None

225 g (8 oz) cold cooked chicken meat,
skinned and cut into small cubes
75 g (3 oz) pickled dill cucumber, cut into
small cubes
1 orange, rind finely grated and reserved,
pith removed and segmented
10 ml (2 tsp) chopped fresh parsley
225 g (8 oz) cottage cheese, sieved
pepper, to taste
100 g (4 oz) Webb's Wonder or Iceberg
lettuce, shredded
25 g (1 oz) blanched almonds, toasted

———1———
Put the chicken and cucumber into a
bowl, then add the orange rind and
parsley. Stir in the cottage cheese
and add the pepper.
———2———
Arrange the lettuce on a serving
platter and place the chicken mixture on top. Place the orange segments around the chicken mixture.
Scatter the almonds over the chicken
mixture and serve.

GOODNESS GUIDE

LUNCHEON SALAD
FIBRE The vegetables and nuts provide fibre
FAT The skinned chicken and cottage
cheese are low in fat. No high-fat salad
dressing is used
PROTEIN Protein is contributed by the
chicken, cheese and almonds which provide
good amounts
VITAMINS B-complex vitamins are provided
by the chicken, cheese and almonds

AUBERGINE DIP
MINERALS The cheese is a source of
calcium, necessary for strong bones and
teeth, nerve conduction and blood clotting
FIBRE The vegetables provide a good
helping of fibre
VITAMINS All the vegetables provide vitamin
C, but the tomatoes are the richest source.
Vitamin C requirements rise during
times of stress

AUBERGINE DIP

*This unusual dip, served with
chunks of fresh pineapple and
melon, would also be a welcome
addition to any party buffet table.*

SERVES 4 40 calories per serving
PREPARATION 25 minutes
COOKING 30–40 minutes

1 aubergine, about 225 g (8 oz)
1 garlic clove, skinned and crushed
1 fresh green chilli, seeded and chopped
150 g (5 oz) low-fat soft cheese
15 ml (1 tbsp) lemon juice
pepper, to taste
100 g (4 oz) tomatoes, finely chopped
fresh sage sprigs, to garnish
bread sticks, cut into 7.5 cm (3 inch) pieces,
toasted wholemeal bread and small chunks
of fresh pineapple and melon, to serve

———1———
Prick the aubergine in several places
with a fork and place on a baking
sheet. Cook the aubergine at 200°C
(400°F) mark 6 for about 30–40

LUNCHEON SALAD

AUBERGINE DIP

minutes or until the skin starts to wrinkle and the flesh feels soft.

——— 2 ———

Set the aubergine aside for about 20 minutes or until cool enough to handle. Peel, discarding the skin, stalk and any charred flesh. Chop the aubergine coarsely.

——— 3 ———

Put into a blender or food processor together with the garlic, chilli, cheese and lemon juice, and purée until smooth. Transfer to a small bowl. Add pepper and mix in the tomatoes.

——— 4 ———

To serve, place the dip in a small serving bowl and garnish with sprigs of sage. On a separate serving platter arrange the pieces of bread sticks, toasted wholemeal bread and the fresh pineapple and melon.

MICROWAVE Prick aubergine and place on absorbent paper. Cook, uncovered, 100% (High) 3–4 minutes, turning twice. Complete recipe.

EGG FRIED RICE

Crunchy cashew nuts provide a pleasing contrast to the rice in this Oriental-style dish.

SERVES 4   315 calories per serving
PREPARATION 6 minutes
COOKING About 30 minutes

150 g (5 oz) brown rice
30 ml (2 tbsp) corn oil
1 egg, beaten
3 celery sticks, trimmed and finely chopped
6 spring onions, trimmed and chopped
100 g (4 oz) whole green beans, cut into 2.5 cm (1 inch) pieces
100 g (4 oz) peeled cooked prawns
10 ml (2 tsp) grated fresh root ginger
15 ml (1 tbsp) soy sauce, preferably naturally fermented shoyu
pepper, to taste
50 g (2 oz) unsalted cashew nuts

——— 1 ———

Cook the rice in boiling water for about 25 minutes, or until tender. Drain well and set aside. Heat the oil in a large frying pan, pour in the egg and stir for 2–3 seconds.

——— 2 ———

Add the cooked rice, celery, spring onions, green beans, prawns, ginger, soy sauce and seasoning. Cook quickly, stirring continuously, for 3–5 minutes or until all the ingredients are heated through and mixed.

——— 3 ———

Sprinkle on the cashew nuts and cook a further 2 minutes, until the vegetables are just tender. Serve.

GOODNESS GUIDE

FIBRE Lots of fibre is contributed by the brown rice, fresh vegetables and nuts
VITAMINS Brown rice is a good source of B vitamins, especially thiamine, which is needed for growth and healthy nerves and muscles
MINERALS Iron, calcium, potassium and zinc are provided by the rice, prawns, egg and nuts
PROTEIN Prawns are a low-fat source of protein

EGG FRIED RICE

VEGETABLE FRITTERS

SPICY BARLEY PEPPERS

MUSHROOM AND LENTIL PASTIES

VEGETABLE FRITTERS

These fritters are shallow fried, but they can also be cooked in a deep-fat fryer at 180°C (350°F) for 3 minutes each.

SERVES 4 380 calories per serving
PREPARATION 15 minutes
COOKING 10–15 minutes
STANDING 1 hour

⅓ cauliflower, finely chopped
1 courgette, finely diced
50 g (2 oz) mushrooms, finely diced
1 celery stick, trimmed and finely diced
1 carrot, scrubbed and finely diced
½ red pepper, cored, seeded and finely diced
60 ml (4 tbsp) corn or olive oil
red pepper rings, to garnish

BATTER
1 egg
1 egg, separated
50 g (2 oz) plain wholemeal flour
50 g (2 oz) buckwheat flour
150 g (5 oz) strong plain flour
300 ml (½ pint) semi-skimmed milk
15 ml (1 tbsp) sunflower oil

TAHINI SAUCE
15 ml (1 tbsp) tahini
20 ml (4 tbsp) lemon juice
30 ml (2 tbsp) low-fat natural yogurt
1 garlic clove, skinned and crushed
salt and pepper, to taste

——1——
To make the batter, put the whole egg, egg yolk, flours, milk and sunflower oil in a blender or food processor and blend until smooth. Pour into a bowl. Set aside to rest for 1 hour.

——2——
Meanwhile, make the sauce. Place the tahini, lemon juice, yogurt and garlic in a blender or food processor and blend until smooth. Add 15 ml (1 tbsp) cold water and blend again. Season. Set aside.

——3——
Whisk the egg white until stiff and fold into the batter. Add all the vegetables and mix.

——4——
Heat the oil in a large frying pan. Drop dessertspoonfuls of the batter into the pan, spacing well apart.

——5——
Press the fritters down to flatten, then cook for 2 minutes, until lightly brown. Turn over and cook for a

further 2 minutes, until lightly brown. Remove with a fish slice.

—6—

Place the cooked fritters on an oven-proof plate lined with absorbent kitchen paper. Keep warm in the oven at 170°C (325°F) mark 3, while making the remaining fritters. Serve the fritters hot with the Tahini sauce.

GOODNESS GUIDE

VITAMINS Conserve the vitamin C in the vegetables by preparing them just before cooking and eating the fritters as soon as they are made. The egg, flours, milk and tahini provide plenty of B-complex vitamins. Vitamin A is supplied by the egg and carotene by some of the vegetables
PROTEIN A good amount of protein is supplied by the egg, tahini, flours, milk and yogurt

---

MUSHROOM AND LENTIL PASTIES

MAKES 8 205 calories each
PREPARATION 1½ hours
BAKING 20–25 minutes
CHILLING 30 minutes

50 g (2 oz) green lentils, rinsed
600 ml (1 pint) vegetable stock
100 g (4 oz) plain wholemeal flour
100 g (4 oz) plain flour
100 g (4 oz) polyunsaturated margarine
2.5–3.75 ml (½–¾ tsp) cayenne pepper
5 ml (1 tsp) mustard powder
15 ml (1 tbsp) sesame seeds
1 onion, skinned and chopped
1 carrot, scrubbed and chopped
1 celery stick, trimmed and chopped
100 g (4 oz) mushrooms, chopped
10 ml (2 tsp) chopped fresh thyme or
5 ml (1 tsp) dried
10 ml (2 tsp) chopped fresh sage or
5 ml (1 tsp) dried
sage leaves, to garnish

—1—

Put the lentils in a pan with the stock. Bring to the boil. Cover and simmer for 1 hour or until soft.

—2—

Meanwhile, put the flours in a bowl and rub in the margarine until the mixture resembles fine breadcrumbs. Stir in 1.25 ml (¼ tsp) cayenne, the mustard, sesame seeds and about 45 ml (3 tbsp) cold water to make a smooth, pliable dough.

—3—

Knead the dough well, then cover and chill for 30 minutes in the refrigerator.

—4—

Drain the lentils, reserving the cooking liquid. Purée the lentils in a blender or food processor with 45 ml (3 tbsp) of the liquid until smooth. Put in a bowl and set aside while preparing the vegetables.

—5—

Blanch the onion, carrot, celery and mushrooms in boiling water for 2 minutes. Drain and add to the lentil purée. Add the remaining cayenne to taste, the thyme and sage. Moisten, if necessary, with more of the reserved cooking liquid.

—6—

Thinly roll out the pastry dough on a lightly floured surface, then cut into eight 11 cm (4½ inch) rounds. Divide the filling between the rounds. Dampen the edges with cold water, then bring the edges of the pastry together across the top to form a seam. Crimp. Place on baking sheets and bake at 200°C (400°F) mark 6 for 20–25 minutes or until the pastry is cooked and golden brown. Serve the pasties hot or cold, garnished with sage leaves.

GOODNESS GUIDE

PROTEIN The combination of lentils, seeds and flour forms a balanced protein which the body can utilise fully for protein replacement and growth
MINERALS The lentils, seeds and flour provide calcium, iron, zinc and potassium
FIBRE The lentils, flour, seeds and vegetables provide fibre

SPICY BARLEY PEPPERS

Whatever the colour of the peppers you buy, whether green, red, yellow or even black, choose those that are firm to the touch and have shiny skins.

SERVES 4 240 calories per serving
PREPARATION 10 minutes
COOKING 40 minutes

15 ml (1 tbsp) groundnut, sunflower or olive oil
½ onion, skinned and chopped
1 large garlic clove, skinned and crushed
0.5 cm (¼ inch) piece fresh root ginger, peeled and finely chopped

5 ml (1 tsp) garam masala
1.25 ml (¼ tsp) turmeric
2.5 ml (½ tsp) cayenne pepper
175 g (6 oz) pot barley
450 ml (¾ pint) vegetable stock
100–150 g (4–6 oz) haddock fillet, skinned
2.5 ml (½ tsp) black peppercorns
15 ml (1 tbsp) lemon juice
2 parsley sprigs
15 ml (1 tbsp) tomato purée
50 g (2 oz) frozen petits pois
salt and pepper, to taste
2 red peppers, cored, halved lengthways and seeded
2 green peppers, cored, halved lengthways and seeded
fresh coriander sprigs, to garnish

—1—

Heat the oil in a saucepan, add the onion and cook, stirring, for 5 minutes, until soft. Add the garlic and continue cooking for 1 minute, then add the ginger, garam masala, turmeric and cayenne and stir for about 30 seconds. Add the barley and stir to coat well in the spice mixture. Pour in the stock and simmer, half covered, for 15 minutes.

—2—

Meanwhile, half fill a saucepan with cold water and add the haddock, peppercorns, lemon juice and parsley sprigs. Bring to a simmer and gently poach for 4–5 minutes. Drain the fish and allow to cool slightly, then flake, discarding any bones. Set aside.

—3—

Mix the tomato purée with 150 ml (¼ pint) hot water. Add to the barley mixture and continue cooking for 10 minutes. Stir in the petits pois and seasoning and continue cooking, half covered, for a further 5 minutes.

—4—

Meanwhile, place the peppers in a steamer and steam for 7 minutes. Lightly mix the fish into the barley mixture. Spoon the mixture into the peppers and steam for a further minute. Garnish with fresh sage leaves and serve hot.

GOODNESS GUIDE

FIBRE Pot barley is less refined than pearl barley and therefore provides more fibre and vitamins
VITAMINS The barley and fish are sources of B-complex vitamins and the vegetables and spices supply carotene and vitamin C

EGGS FLORENTINE

This tasty and nutritious light meal is high in protein. Serve with an onion and tomato salad

SERVES 4 280 calories per serving
PREPARATION 15 minutes
COOKING 20 minutes

450 g (1 lb) fresh spinach, stalks removed, or 225 g (8 oz) frozen chopped spinach
5 ml (1 tsp) grated nutmeg
45 ml (3 tbsp) low-fat natural yogurt
pepper, to taste
6 eggs, hard-boiled and shelled
25 g (1 oz) polyunsaturated margarine
15 g ($\frac{1}{2}$ oz) plain wholemeal flour
15 g ($\frac{1}{2}$ oz) plain flour
2.5 ml ($\frac{1}{2}$ tsp) mustard powder
225 ml (8 fl oz) semi-skimmed milk
40 g (1$\frac{1}{2}$ oz) Canadian Cheddar or Red Leicester cheese, grated

——— 1 ———
Cook fresh spinach, with just the water clinging to the leaves, for about 5 minutes, until wilted. If using frozen spinach, cook, stirring, for about 10 minutes. Drain well, pressing out all excess water.

——— 2 ———
Purée the spinach in a blender or food processor with 2.5 ml ($\frac{1}{2}$ tsp) nutmeg, 15 ml (1 tbsp) yogurt and the seasoning.

——— 3 ———
Spread over the base of a 1.1 litre (2 pint) capacity ovenproof dish. Arrange the eggs carefully on top of the spinach. Set aside.

——— 4 ———
Melt the margarine in a small sauce-pan, stir in the flours and mustard and cook for 1 minute. Remove from the heat and gradually stir in the milk. Return to the heat and cook, stirring, for 2–3 minutes or until thickened. Remove from the heat and add the remaining nutmeg and yogurt and the cheese. Stir until the cheese has melted.

——— 5 ———
Coat the eggs completely with the sauce. Bake at 180°C (350°F) mark 4 for 20 minutes, until the top is golden brown and bubbly. Serve.

MICROWAVE Put spinach into a bowl. Cover and cook 100% (High) 6–7 minutes, until cooked. Drain and blend with seasoning, 2.5 ml ($\frac{1}{2}$ tsp) nutmeg and 15 ml (1 tbsp) yogurt. Put in base of dish and arrange eggs on top. Put margarine in bowl, cook, uncovered, 30 seconds, to melt. Stir in flours and mustard, cook, uncovered, 30 seconds. Gradually stir in milk, cook, uncovered, 3 minutes, until thickened, stirring twice. Stir in remaining nutmeg, yogurt and cheese. Coat eggs with sauce. Cook, uncovered, 8–9 minutes, until heated through. Brown surface under grill, if liked.

GOODNESS GUIDE
FIBRE The spinach and flour supply fibre
VITAMINS AND MINERALS The spinach provides vitamin C and the B vitamin folic acid. The vitamin C helps with the absorption of iron present in the eggs, flour and spinach

SUMMER BEAN SALAD

EGGS FLORENTINE

SOUSED HERRINGS

SERVES 4 435 calories per serving
PREPARATION 15 minutes
COOKING 45 minutes
CHILLING At least 1 hour

4 herrings, about 275 g (10 oz) each, cleaned
and boned
10 ml (2 tsp) chopped fresh dill or 5 ml
(1 tsp) dried dill weed
pepper, to taste
1 onion, skinned and thinly sliced
6 black peppercorns
4 bay leaves
150 ml (¼ pint) cider vinegar
150 ml (¼ pint) unsweetened apple juice
slices of granary bread, to serve
fresh dill sprigs, to garnish

——— 1 ———

Remove the heads, tails and fins from the herrings and as many small bones as possible. Sprinkle the flesh with dill and seasoning.

SOUSED HERRINGS

——— 2 ———

Roll up each herring, starting from the tail end, and secure with wooden cocktail sticks. Put in a large oven-proof dish in a single layer and add the onion, peppercorns and bay leaves. Pour over the vinegar and unsweetened apple juice.

——— 3 ———

Cover and cook at 180°C (350°F) mark 4 for 45 minutes or until cooked through.

——— 4 ———

Set aside to cool in the cooking liquid, turning the herrings occasionally, then chill for at least 1 hour.

——— 5 ———

To serve, remove the herrings with a slotted spoon, shaking off any excess liquid, and discard the cocktail sticks. Serve with granary bread.

MICROWAVE Prepare herrings, secure with wooden cocktail sticks. Arrange in a dish with onion, peppercorns, bay leaves, 75 ml (3 fl oz) vinegar and 75 ml (3 fl oz) apple juice. Cover, cook 100% (High) 5–6 minutes, turning dish twice, until cooked. Cool in cooking liquid then chill for 1 hour. Complete recipe.

SUMMER BEAN SALAD

SERVES 4 300 calories per serving
PREPARATION 10–15 minutes
COOKING 15–20 minutes

2 corn on the cob
225 g (8 oz) runner beans, trimmed and
sliced
100 g (4 oz) shelled fresh or frozen peas
45 ml (3 tbsp) olive oil
15 ml (1 tbsp) cider vinegar
15 ml (1 tbsp) clear honey
10 ml (2 tsp) whole grain mustard
2.5 ml (½ tsp) paprika
215 g (7½ oz) can red kidney beans, drained
and rinsed
225 g (8 oz) can butter beans, drained
and rinsed
2–3 spring onions, trimmed and
finely chopped
45 ml (3 tbsp) chopped fresh coriander
or parsley
salt and pepper, to taste

——— 1 ———

Cook the corn on the cob in a large saucepan of boiling water for 8–10 minutes, until tender. Remove, rinse under cold water and set aside.

——— 2 ———

Add the runner beans to the water, bring back to the boil, then simmer for 3–4 minutes, until just tender. Remove with a slotted spoon and rinse under cold running water.

——— 3 ———

Add the peas to the water, bring back to the boil and simmer for 5 minutes for fresh peas, or 3–5 minutes if using frozen, until tender. Drain and rinse.

——— 4 ———

Put the oil, vinegar, honey, mustard and paprika in a salad bowl and whisk until thick.

——— 5 ———

Strip the corn kernels off the cobs with a sharp knife and add to the dressing. Add the runner beans, peas, kidney and butter beans, spring onions and coriander. Toss well to mix, then season to taste. Cover and chill until ready to serve.

MICROWAVE Put corn on the cob into a bowl with 90 ml (6 tbsp) water. Cover and cook 100% (High) 8–9 minutes. Remove, rinse in cold water and drain. Cool. Add runner beans to water in bowl. Cover and cook 100% (High) 5 minutes. Add peas, cover and cook 100% (High) 3–4 minutes, until tender. Complete recipe.

GOODNESS GUIDE

SUMMER BEAN SALAD

FIBRE Fibre is supplied by the pulses, beans, peas and sweetcorn. Fibre is necessary to prevent constipation and diverticulosis (an intestinal disorder which develops as a result of difficulty in moving waste food along the gut)

PROTEIN Plenty of protein is provided by the legumes. Serve with grain products such as rice or bread to balance the protein

SOUSED HERRINGS

VITAMINS Herrings, like all oily fish, are a valuable source of the fat-soluble vitamin D. Food sources of this vitamin are vital for those people who do not spend much time in the sun

PROTEIN Herrings are a valuable source of easily digested protein

FAT The oils in fish are believed to be beneficial in preventing heart attacks

GRANARY TORPEDO ROLLS

The addition of red pepper and carrots adds a crunchy texture to the filling and makes a nutritionally balanced snack.

SERVES 4 420 calories per serving
PREPARATION 15 minutes
COOKING None

150 g (5 oz) Caerphilly cheese, crumbled
½ red pepper, cored, seeded and
finely chopped
1–2 carrots, scrubbed and grated
15 ml (1 tbsp) mayonnaise
pepper, to taste
4 long granary rolls or 2 French
granary loaves
a little cress, to garnish

Mix together the cheese, red pepper, carrots, mayonnaise and seasoning. Just before serving, split the rolls lengthways and divide the filling between the rolls. Sprinkle the cress on top and serve.

GOUDA-BAKED POTATOES

This easy-to-make snack can be turned into a more substantial meal by serving with a seasonal salad.

SERVES 4 365 calories per serving
PREPARATION 20 minutes
COOKING 1¼ hours

4 large potatoes, scrubbed
15 ml (1 tbsp) corn oil
1 celery stick, trimmed and finely chopped
50 g (2 oz) button mushrooms, chopped
5 ml (1 tsp) chopped fresh thyme, or 1.25 ml
(¼ tsp) dried
4 stuffed olives, sliced
30 ml (2 tbsp) semi-skimmed milk
175 g (6 oz) mature Gouda cheese, grated
pepper, to taste

——— 1 ———

Prick the potatoes and bake at 200°C (400°F) mark 6 for about 1 hour, until tender.

——— 2 ———

Meanwhile, heat the oil in a small saucepan. Add the celery and gently cook for about 5 minutes, until slightly softened. Add the mushrooms and thyme. Cook for 5 minutes.

——— 3 ———

Cut the potatoes in half and scoop out the flesh into a bowl, without damaging the potato skins. Mash the potato with a fork. Stir in the celery mixture, olives, milk, three-quarters of the cheese and seasoning. Mix well.

——— 4 ———

Pile the mixture back into the potato shells and sprinkle with the remaining cheese.

——— 5 ———

Return the potatoes to the oven and bake for about 15 minutes, until the cheese has melted.

MICROWAVE Prick potatoes and put on absorbent paper. Cook 100% (High) 18–20 minutes, rearranging 4 times. Put the oil and celery into a bowl. Cover and cook 100% (High) 2 minutes. Add mushrooms and thyme. Cook, uncovered, 100% (High) 1 minute. Follow steps 3 and 4. Cook filled potatoes 100% (High) 3 minutes, or until hot and cheese has melted.

GOODNESS GUIDE

PROTEIN The cheese and potatoes provide a good source of protein
CARBOHYDRATE Potatoes provide very low-fat carbohydrate for energy
FIBRE The vegetables, and especially the potato skins, provide fibre
MINERALS Gouda cheese is a rich source of calcium

GRANARY TORPEDO ROLLS

GOUDA-BAKED POTATOES

FOUR CHEESE PIZZA

Four types of Italian cheese—Mozzarella, Dolcelatte, ricotta and Parmesan, all made from cow's milk—provide a dish rich in protein, calcium and vitamins.

SERVES 4 375 calories per serving
PREPARATION 30 minutes
COOKING 25–30 minutes
RISING 30 minutes

5 ml (1 tsp) light muscovado sugar
5 ml (1 tsp) dried yeast
100 g (4 oz) plain wholemeal flour
100 g (4 oz) strong white flour
5 ml (1 tsp) salt
10 ml (2 tsp) sunflower oil
fresh basil leaves, to garnish

TOMATO SAUCE
400 g (14 oz) can chopped tomatoes
5 ml (1 tsp) dried oregano
15 ml (1 tbsp) tomato purée
pepper, to taste

CHEESE TOPPING
100 g (4 oz) Mozzarella cheese, thinly sliced
50 g (2 oz) Dolcelatte cheese, chopped
100 g (4 oz) ricotta cheese, crumbled
45 ml (3 tbsp) grated Parmesan cheese

FOUR CHEESE PIZZA

——1——
Lightly grease a baking sheet and set aside. To make the dough, dissolve the sugar in 150 ml (¼ pint) tepid water. Sprinkle over the yeast. Leave in a warm place for about 15 minutes, until frothy.

——2——
Mix the flours and salt in a bowl. Add the yeast liquid and oil. Mix to a soft dough.

——3——
Turn out the dough on to a floured surface and knead for 5 minutes. Return the dough to the bowl and cover with a clean cloth. Leave to rise in a warm place for 30 minutes, or until doubled in size.

——4——
Meanwhile, place all the sauce ingredients in a saucepan and bring to the boil. Reduce the heat and simmer, uncovered, for 15–20 minutes, until the sauce is thick and pulpy. Remove from the heat and leave to cool.

——5——
Quickly knead the risen dough, then roll out to a 25 cm (10 inch) round and place on the baking sheet. Fold up dough edges slightly to form rim.

——6——
Spread the sauce over the dough to within 1 cm (½ inch) of the edge. Arrange the Mozzarella, Dolcelatte and ricotta cheeses evenly over the sauce. Finish with a topping of Parmesan cheese.

——7——
Bake at 200°C (400°F) mark 6 for 25–30 minutes, until the cheese has melted and the dough is golden brown. Serve the pizza piping hot, garnished with basil leaves.

GOODNESS GUIDE

FOUR CHEESE PIZZA
FIBRE The wholemeal flour and tomatoes provide fibre
MINERALS The cheeses are a source of calcium and the flours provide calcium and iron
VITAMINS The cheeses provide B vitamins and the tomatoes, vitamins A and C. The vitamin C in the tomatoes increases iron absorption

GRANARY TORPEDO ROLLS
VITAMINS Fresh, uncooked vegetables are the best source of vitamin C, which is necessary for a healthy immune system
MINERALS These rolls provide iron and calcium
FIBRE Although not so high in fibre as wholemeal rolls, the granary rolls, along with the vegetables, do provide some fibre

PRAWN-CHEESE SANDWICHES

You can use other bread combinations for this recipe, including pumpernickel with light rye or granary bread.

MAKES 4 315 calories each
PREPARATION 20 minutes
COOKING None

100 g (4 oz) low-fat soft cheese
1 punnet mustard and cress, trimmed
10 ml (2 tsp) Worcestershire sauce
100 g (4 oz) peeled cooked prawns
60 ml (4 tbsp) mayonnaise
15 ml (1 tbsp) tomato purée
2 or 3 drops Tabasco sauce or to taste
8 slices dark pumpernickel bread
4 slices light pumpernickel bread
polyunsaturated margarine for spreading
3 tomatoes, sliced
$\frac{1}{4}$ cucumber, thinly sliced

———1———
Mix together the cheese, mustard and cress and Worcestershire sauce in a bowl.

———2———
In another bowl, mix together the prawns, mayonnaise, tomato purée and Tabasco sauce.

———3———
Lightly spread one side of each slice of bread with the margarine. Place 4 slices of the dark pumpernickel on a board, divide the cheese filling between the slices and spread evenly. Cover with the tomato slices.

———4———
Top with the light pumpernickel, slices, spread side up. Spread with the prawn mixture and cover with the cucumber slices.

———5———
Top with the remaining dark pumpernickel slices, spread side down. Cut each into quarters, secure with wooden cocktail sticks and serve.

GOODNESS GUIDE
FIBRE Pumpernickel is a whole-grain rye bread and is high in fibre
PROTEIN Prawns, pumpernickel and low-fat soft cheese are good sources of protein
VITAMINS AND MINERALS Rye flour is rich in folic acid, biotin, iron and zinc

VEGETABLE PASTA SALAD

This crunchy salad is almost a meal in itself. It can be made in advance and stored, covered, in the refrigerator.

SERVES 4 560 calories per serving
PREPARATION 10 minutes
COOKING 10–12 minutes

225 g (8 oz) pasta shells (use spinach and tomato, if available)
225 g (8 oz) frozen sweetcorn kernels
200 g (7 oz) can tuna fish, well drained
1 red pepper, cored, seeded and diced
4 celery sticks, trimmed and sliced
90 ml (3 fl oz) olive oil
30 ml (2 tbsp) white wine vinegar
1 garlic clove, skinned and crushed
15 ml (1 tbsp) whole grain mustard
salt and pepper, to taste
50 g (2 oz) toasted flaked almonds
paprika, to taste
watercress sprigs, to garnish

———1———
Cook the pasta in lightly salted boiling water for 5–8 minutes, then add the sweetcorn and boil for a further 5 minutes, until the pasta is just tender. Drain and rinse under cold water. Set aside until cold.

———2———
Mix together with the tuna fish, red pepper and celery in a large bowl.

———3———
In another bowl, whisk together the oil, vinegar, garlic and mustard. Season and add to the pasta salad. Mix thoroughly.

———4———
Transfer to a serving dish. Scatter over the flaked almonds and sprinkle over a little paprika. Garnish with watercress sprigs.

GOODNESS GUIDE
CARBOHYDRATE Pasta is an excellent carbohydrate energy source
VITAMINS The vegetables are rich in vitamin C and the tuna fish contributes vitamins D and B complex
FIBRE All the vegetables contribute fibre to this dish

RED BEAN QUICHE

MAKES 6 SLICES 410 calories each
PREPARATION 20 minutes
BAKING 30 minutes
CHILLING 30 minutes

100 g (4 oz) plain flour
100 g (4 oz) plain wholemeal flour
100 g (4 oz) polyunsaturated margarine
6 stuffed olives, sliced, and basil sprigs, to garnish

BEAN FILLING
25 g (1 oz) polyunsaturated margarine
1 small onion, skinned and chopped
1 garlic clove, skinned and crushed
50 g (2 oz) button mushrooms, sliced
5 ml (1 tsp) dried mixed herbs or basil
400 g (14 oz) can red kidney beans, drained and rinsed
3 tomatoes, sliced
150 ml ($\frac{1}{4}$ pint) semi-skimmed milk
2 eggs
salt and pepper, to taste
65 g ($2\frac{1}{2}$ oz) can anchovy fillets, well drained and cut in half lengthways

———1———
Put the flours into a bowl, add the margarine and rub in until the mixture resembles fine breadcrumbs. Add 30 ml (2 tbsp) chilled water and mix to form a stiff dough.

———2———
Knead on a lightly floured work surface and roll out into a circle to line a 20.5 cm (8 inch) flan dish. Chill for 30 minutes.

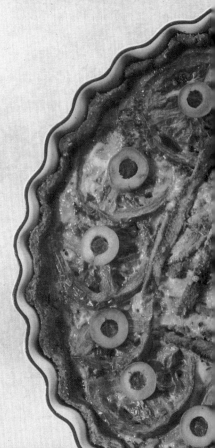

3

Prick the base with a fork, cover with greaseproof paper and baking beans. Bake blind at 200°C (400°F) mark 6 for 10–15 minutes, until set. Remove the paper and beans, then return to the oven and bake for a further 5 minutes to crisp.

4

To make the filling, melt the margarine, add the onion and garlic and cook for 5 minutes, until soft. Add the mushrooms and herbs and cook for a further 3 minutes. Remove from the heat, stir in the beans and mix well. Transfer to the pastry case and cover with the tomatoes.

5

Whisk together the milk, eggs and seasoning, then pour into the dish. Bake at 200°C (400°F) mark 6 for 30 minutes. Arrange the anchovies in a lattice design over the top and bake for another 10 minutes. Garnish with the olives and basil. Serve warm or cold.

MICROWAVE Follow steps 1 and 2, lining a 22–23 cm ($8\frac{1}{2}$–9 inch) plate or dish with pastry. Press double thickness absorbent paper over base. In step 3, cook 100% (High) 3 minutes, remove paper and cook 3 minutes, until pastry base is dry. In step 4, put margarine, onion and garlic into a bowl. Cover and cook 3 minutes, until onion is soft. Add mushrooms and herbs, cover and cook $1\frac{1}{2}$ minutes. Complete step 4. In step 5, pour in egg mixture and cook 60% (Medium) 15 minutes, until just set, turning plate several times. Arrange anchovies on top after 12 minutes. Stand 2–3 minutes, then garnish with olives and basil. Serve warm or cold.

GOODNESS GUIDE

FIBRE Beans, wholemeal flour, mushrooms, onions and tomatoes are good sources of fibre

PROTEIN Beans, eggs and milk are good sources of protein

MINERALS Beans are rich in calcium, potassium, magnesium, iron and zinc

VEGETABLE PASTA SALAD

RED BEAN QUICHE

PRAWN-CHEESE SANDWICHES

161

WARM CHICKEN LIVER AND BREAD SALAD

On cold days, warm salads make an interesting change from the traditional chilled variety. If you want more colour and crunch, add chopped celery and replace some of the chick-peas with red kidney beans.

SERVES 4   470 calories per serving
PREPARATION   15–20 minutes
COOKING   None

two 400 g (14 oz) cans chick-peas, rinsed and well drained
1 large green pepper, cored, seeded and cut into thin strips
½ cucumber, seeded and chopped
2 firm tomatoes, quartered
1 small onion, skinned and sliced
15 ml (1 tbsp) chopped fresh mint or 7.5 ml (1½ tsp) dried
15 ml (1 tbsp) coarsely chopped fresh parsley
1 garlic clove, skinned and crushed
2 slices wholemeal bread

25 g (1 oz) polyunsaturated margarine
225 g (8 oz) chicken livers, trimmed and chopped
15 ml (1 tbsp) olive oil

DRESSING
45 ml (3 tbsp) olive oil
juice of 2 limes or lemons
salt and pepper, to taste

———1———
Put the chick-peas into a bowl with the other vegetables, herbs and garlic, if using.

———2———
Heat the margarine in a frying pan and add the chicken livers with 15 ml (1 tbsp) olive oil. Cook for about 4 minutes, until cooked through and evenly coloured but still slightly pink in the centre.

———3———
Meanwhile, toast the bread slices for 2 minutes, until lightly golden.

———4———
To make the dressing, mix the 45 ml (3 tbsp) olive oil with the lime juice and seasoning. Stir the dressing into the salad ingredients.

———5———
Break or chop the toasted bread into pieces and add to the salad bowl, then add the cooked chicken livers and their pan juices. Quickly toss the salad until well mixed and serve.

GOODNESS GUIDE
FIBRE There are substantial quantities of fibre in the bread, vegetables and chick-peas
MINERALS The chicken livers are a good source of iron and other minerals
VITAMINS Chicken livers are rich in A and B vitamins, particularly B_{12}. There are also A vitamins and plenty of C in the vegetables, especially when eaten raw

WARM CHICKEN LIVER AND BREAD SALAD

SPICY NUT MIX

Serve this spicy nut mix at a party instead of crisps or other high-fat snacks. Garam masala is a combination of ground spices used in Asian cooking. It is available from supermarkets and specialist grocers.

MAKES ABOUT 225 G (8 OZ)
170 CALORIES PER 25 G (1 OZ) SERVING
PREPARATION 5 minutes
COOKING 12–15 minutes

75 g (3 oz) shelled fresh peanuts with skins
left on
50 g (2 oz) cashew nuts
25 g (1 oz) flaked almonds
50 g (2 oz) walnut halves, coarsely chopped
30 ml (2 tbsp) sunflower oil
5 ml (1 tsp) caraway seeds
2.5 ml ($\frac{1}{2}$ tsp) paprika
1.25 ml ($\frac{1}{4}$ tsp) garlic powder
1.25 ml ($\frac{1}{4}$ tsp) garam masala
pinch of ground turmeric

——— 1 ———

Mix all the nuts together. Mix the oil with the seeds and seasonings and stir into the nuts, making sure they are evenly coated.

——— 2 ———

Spread the nuts out evenly on a baking sheet, and bake at 190°C (375°F) mark 5 for 12–15 minutes, until they are a rich golden colour.

——— 3 ———

Drain the nuts on absorbent kitchen paper and leave them to cool completely. Once they are cold, store them in an airtight jar.

MICROWAVE Follow step 1. Spread nuts on a large plate, cook 100% (High) 6–7 minutes, stirring the mixture every 2 minutes.

GOODNESS GUIDE
PROTEIN The protein in peanuts complements the walnuts, almonds and seeds so that the high protein content is more efficiently used by the body
MINERALS Nuts and seeds are rich in iron, calcium, potassium and zinc
FIBRE This nut mix is extremely high in fibre

SOUFFLEED RAREBITS

Easy to make, these are a delicious variation of the traditional Welsh rarebit, with a delightful piquant taste.

SERVES 4   235 calories per serving
PREPARATION 10–15 minutes
COOKING About 25 minutes

4 slices wholemeal bread
15 g ($\frac{1}{2}$ oz) polyunsaturated margarine, plus
a little extra for spreading
15 ml (1 tbsp) poppy seeds
15 ml (1 tbsp) plain flour
150 ml ($\frac{1}{4}$ pint) semi-skimmed milk
5 ml (1 tsp) Dijon mustard
5 ml (1 tsp) Worcestershire sauce
100 g (4 oz) Edam or Gouda cheese, grated
2 eggs, separated
tomato wedges and watercress sprigs,
to garnish

——— 1 ———

Spread the slices of bread lightly with margarine. Sprinkle each slice with poppy seeds and bake at 190°C (375°F) mark 5 for 5 minutes.

——— 2 ———

Melt 15 g ($\frac{1}{2}$ oz) margarine in a saucepan, stir in the flour and cook for 1 minute.

——— 3 ———

Gradually stir in the milk and bring to the boil. Stir over a low heat until the sauce has thickened. Remove from the heat.

——— 4 ———

Beat in the mustard, Worcestershire sauce, grated cheese and egg yolks.

——— 5 ———

Whisk the egg whites until stiff, then fold into the cheese mixture.

——— 6 ———

Spoon the mixture on top of each slice of bread and return to the oven for a further 15 minutes, until puffed and golden. Serve immediately, garnished with the tomato wedges and watercress sprigs.

GOODNESS GUIDE
PROTEIN The combination of cheese, semi-skimmed milk, eggs, wholemeal bread and poppy seeds makes a light dish which is very high in protein
FAT Semi-skimmed milk and a relatively low-fat cheese make a reduced fat alternative to the usual Welsh rarebit
FIBRE Wholemeal bread boosts the fibre content

SPICY NUT MIX

SOUFFLEED RAREBITS

AVOCADO AND CHICK-PEA SALAD

Quark is used in this recipe with semi-skimmed milk, to make a low-fat dressing. Use Quark in recipes calling for full-fat soft cheese.

SERVES 4 250 calories per serving
PREPARATION About 10 minutes
COOKING None

1 avocado
15 ml (1 tbsp) lemon juice
450 g (1 lb) fresh young spinach, with stalks removed, finely sliced
100 g (4 oz) red cabbage, finely shredded
400 g (14 oz) can chick-peas, drained and rinsed
1 slice wholemeal bread, toasted and diced
2 eggs, hard-boiled and sliced
paprika, to taste

LEMON DRESSING
juice of ½ lemon
50 g (2 oz) natural Quark
100 ml (4 fl oz) semi-skimmed milk
30 ml (2 tbsp) snipped fresh chives or parsley
salt and pepper, to taste

———1———
To make the dressing, place the lemon juice, Quark and milk in a bowl and whisk until smooth. Add the herbs, reserving some for garnish, and season. Set aside.

———2———
Peel the avocado, discard the stone and dice. Coat with the lemon juice to prevent discoloration.

———3———
Mix together the spinach and red cabbage and arrange over a large serving platter. Arrange the avocado around the edge of the platter.

———4———
Pile the chick-peas in the centre of the spinach and scatter the toast around them. Arrange the egg slices on top and sprinkle over a little paprika.

———5———
To serve, spoon a little of the dressing over the chick-peas, and garnish with the reserved snipped chives. Serve the remaining dressing separately.

GOODNESS GUIDE
PROTEIN The combination of chick-peas and wholemeal bread, plus the eggs and natural Quark makes this salad high in protein
MINERALS The salad is rich in iron and calcium
VITAMINS There are ample quantities of vitamin C in this salad, which is important in helping the body absorb iron

HADDOCK QUICHE

MAKES 6 SLICES 290 calories each
PREPARATION 30 minutes
COOKING 40 minutes
CHILLING 30 minutes

75 g (3 oz) plain flour
75 g (3 oz) plain wholemeal flour
pinch of salt
100 g (4 oz) polyunsaturated margarine
225 g (8 oz) fresh haddock fillets
100 g (4 oz) smoked haddock fillets
1 onion, skinned and chopped
150 ml (¼ pint) semi-skimmed milk
1 egg
15 ml (1 tbsp) chopped fresh parsley
25 g (1 oz) mature Cheddar, grated

———1———
Put flours and salt into a bowl, then rub in 75 g (3 oz) of the margarine until mixture resembles fine breadcrumbs. Add 25 ml (1 fl oz) chilled water and mix to make a soft dough. Add a little extra water if necessary.

———2———
Knead the dough on a lightly floured surface. Roll out and line a 20.5 cm (8 inch) loose based flan tin. Chill 30 minutes.

AVOCADO AND CHICK-PEA SALAD

HADDOCK QUICHE

3

Meanwhile, place the fish in a saucepan with just enough water to cover. Bring to the boil and simmer gently 10 minutes. Drain, discard the skin and any bones and flake the fish into small pieces.

4

Melt the remaining 25 g (1 oz) margarine in a saucepan, add the onion and cook gently 3–5 minutes, until soft. Add the fish and heat through.

5

Spoon the filling into the flan case. Whisk together the milk, egg and parsley and pour over the fish. Sprinkle the cheese on top. Cook at 190°C (375°F) mark 5 for about 40 minutes, until the filling is set.

GOODNESS GUIDE

PROTEIN The fish and dairy produce provide a high-protein dish

FAT The strong flavour of mature Cheddar means less goes further, and using semi-skimmed milk keeps the fat content low

---

AUBERGINE AND BEAN GRATIN

A hearty filling makes these aubergines substantial enough for a vegetarian meal if served with a salad.

SERVES 4 110 calories per serving
PREPARATION 20 minutes
COOKING 5 minutes

2 medium aubergines
15 g (½ oz) polyunsaturated margarine
1 onion, skinned and chopped
1 garlic clove, skinned and crushed
100 g (4 oz) button mushrooms
225 g (8 oz) can cannellini beans, drained and rinsed
2 tomatoes, chopped
pepper, to taste
30 ml (2 tbsp) grated Parmesan cheese
parsley sprigs, to garnish

1

Cut the ends off the aubergines and cook in boiling water for about 10 minutes, until tender.

2

Cut the aubergines in half lengthways and scoop out the flesh, leaving a 0.5 cm (¼ inch) shell. Finely chop flesh and reserve shells.

3

Melt the margarine, add the onion, garlic and chopped aubergine flesh and cook gently for 5 minutes.

4

Add mushrooms, beans, tomatoes and seasoning.

5

Stuff the aubergine shells with the prepared mixture and sprinkle with Parmesan cheese. Cook under a grill for 4–5 minutes, until heated through. Garnish and serve.

MICROWAVE Omit step 1. Cut the aubergines in half lengthways, scoop out flesh, leaving a border, chop roughly and put in a bowl with the onion, garlic and tomatoes. Cover and cook at 100% (High) 3 minutes. Stir in the mushrooms, beans and seasoning. Cover and cook 1 minute. Fill the shells with the mixture and sprinkle with the cheese. Lay cling film loosely on top, then cook 8–9 minutes, rearranging twice, until the shells are tender. Stand 3–4 minutes.

GOODNESS GUIDE

PROTEIN Pulses such as cannellini beans are the richest source of vegetable protein

VITAMINS Tomatoes are a very good source of vitamins A and C

FIBRE Beans and aubergines are high in fibre

AUBERGINE AND BEAN GRATIN

ARTICHOKE AND TUNA PANCAKES

SPINACH AND CHEESE QUICHE WITH CRISP POTATO CRUST

BROCCOLI AND MUSHROOM PASTIES

166

SPINACH AND CHEESE QUICHE WITH CRISP POTATO CRUST

The potato crust can be prepared in advance and stored, covered, in the refrigerator.

MAKES 6 SLICES 120 calories each
PREPARATION About 20 minutes
BAKING About 1 hour

275 g (10 oz) trimmed spinach leaves,
finely shredded
3 eggs
225 g (8 oz) ricotta cheese
100 g (4 oz) low-fat soft cheese
30 ml (2 tbsp) grated Parmesan cheese
5 ml (1 tsp) grated nutmeg
finely grated rind of 1 lemon
juice of $\frac{1}{2}$ lemon
pepper, to taste
50 ml (2 fl oz) semi-skimmed milk
paprika, for sprinkling

CRISP POTATO CRUST
100 g (4 oz) plain wholemeal flour
50 g (2 oz) polyunsaturated margarine
100 g (4 oz) potatoes, scrubbed and
finely grated
$\frac{1}{2}$ small onion, skinned and grated
salt and pepper, to taste
5 ml (1 tsp) corn oil

———1———

To make the crust, put the flour in a bowl and rub in the margarine until the mixture resembles fine breadcrumbs. Squeeze the grated potatoes well, to remove as much excess moisture as possible. Add to the flour mixture with the onion and seasoning. Mix to a firm dough.

2

With lightly floured fingers, thinly press the dough over the base and sides of a 20 cm (8 inch) flan tin or dish. Bake at 200°C (400°F) mark 6 for 20 minutes. Brush with the corn oil and bake for a further 10 minutes, until the crust is crisp.

3

Meanwhile, place the spinach in a steamer over boiling water. Cover tightly and steam for 1 minute, until just tender. Set aside.

4

Beat together the eggs, ricotta cheese, low-fat soft cheese, half the Parmesan cheese, the nutmeg, lemon rind and juice, seasoning and milk until smooth. Add the spinach and gently mix.

5

Reduce the oven to 180°C (350°F) mark 4. Spoon the spinach and cheese mixture into the cooked crust and level the surface. Sprinkle over the remaining Parmesan cheese and paprika. Bake for 30–35 minutes, until lightly coloured and set. Serve warm or cold.

GOODNESS GUIDE

PROTEIN The cheeses, eggs, flour and potatoes make this dish high in protein
VITAMINS The spinach supplies carotene. The eggs and margarine supply vitamin A. The cheeses, milk, eggs and flour provide plenty of B-complex vitamins

---

ARTICHOKE AND TUNA PANCAKES

Serve these nutritious pancakes with a green salad or wholemeal rolls.

MAKES 8 155 calories each
PREPARATION 20 minutes
COOKING 40 minutes

50 g (2 oz) fine oatmeal
50 g (2 oz) plain flour
1 egg
300 ml (½ pint) semi-skimmed milk
groundnut oil, for cooking
chives, to garnish

ARTICHOKE AND TUNA FILLING
25 g (1 oz) polyunsaturated margarine
1 shallot, skinned and finely chopped
25 g (1 oz) plain wholemeal flour
300 ml (½ pint) semi-skimmed milk
200 g (7 oz) can tuna in brine, drained and flaked

---

100 g (4 oz) can artichoke hearts, drained and chopped
15 ml (1 tbsp) lemon juice
15 ml (1 tbsp) snipped fresh chives
salt and pepper, to taste

1

Mix the oatmeal and flour in a bowl. Make a well in the centre and add the egg. Gradually add half the milk, beating well to form a smooth batter. Stir in the remaining milk.

2

Brush a little oil over the base of a 20 cm (8 inch) non-stick frying pan. Pour in a little batter, swirling the pan to coat the base thinly. Cook on each side for about 2 minutes, until golden brown. Remove from the pan on to a warmed plate, cover with foil and keep warm. Repeat with the remaining batter to make 7 more pancakes.

3

Melt the margarine in a saucepan, add the shallot and cook for about 5 minutes, until softened. Stir in the flour and cook for 1 minute. Gradually add the milk, stirring well, until the sauce is thick and smooth. Simmer for 2 minutes.

4

Fold the tuna and artichokes into the sauce with the lemon juice, chives and seasoning. Gently heat through. Fill the pancakes with this mixture and serve hot, garnished with chives.

GOODNESS GUIDE

VITAMINS Tuna and egg are excellent sources of vitamins D and E. It is important to obtain good sources of dietary vitamin D in the dark winter months as there is insufficient sunlight for us to generate vitamin D through our skins
PROTEIN The flours, oatmeal, egg and milk provide a good serving of protein
FIBRE The flours, oatmeal and artichokes supply fibre

BROCCOLI AND MUSHROOM PASTIES

The pumpkin seeds, flours and vegetables make these pasties high in fibre. Serve them with a salad.

MAKES 4 735 calories each
PREPARATION 15 minutes
BAKING About 30 minutes
CHILLING 30 minutes

---

50 g (2 oz) unsalted shelled pumpkin seeds, finely ground
100 g (4 oz) plain wholemeal flour
175 g (6 oz) plain flour
175 g (6 oz) polyunsaturated margarine
fresh coriander, to garnish

BROCCOLI AND MUSHROOM FILLING
100 g (4 oz) broccoli, cut into florets
100 g (4 oz) mushrooms, sliced
40 g (1½ oz) frozen sweetcorn kernels, thawed
25 g (1 oz) polyunsaturated margarine
15 g (½ oz) plain wholemeal flour
15 g (½ oz) plain flour
225 ml (8 fl oz) semi-skimmed milk
2.5–5 ml (½–1 tsp) grated nutmeg
pepper, to taste

1

Lightly grease a baking sheet and set aside. Put the pumpkin seeds and flours into a mixing bowl. Rub in the margarine until the mixture resembles fine breadcrumbs. Mix to a smooth and pliable dough with about 60–75 ml (4–5 tbsp) cold water. Knead well. Wrap and chill for 30 minutes.

2

Cover the broccoli and mushrooms with boiling water. Leave for 2 minutes, then drain well. Mix in the sweetcorn kernels.

3

Melt the margarine in a small saucepan, stir in the flours and cook for 2 minutes. Remove from the heat and gradually stir in the milk, then return to the heat and cook, stirring, for 2–3 minutes or until the sauce thickens. Cook for a further 1 minute. Stir in the nutmeg and seasoning. Mix in the vegetables. Leave to cool.

4

Roll out the dough on a lightly floured surface and cut into four 18 cm (7 inch) rounds. Divide the filling between the rounds. Dampen the edges with cold water, fold over to form a seam and pinch together. Place on the prepared baking sheet. Bake at 200°C (400°F) mark 6 for 25 minutes or until the pastry is cooked and golden brown. Serve hot or cold.

GOODNESS GUIDE

VITAMINS The broccoli and sweetcorn supply carotene. B-complex vitamins are contributed by the flour, milk and mushrooms. Broccoli is a very rich source of vitamin C

TOFU SPREAD

Tofu is made from soya bean curd. Serve this spread on wholemeal bread or as a dip with any combination of fresh vegetables.

SERVES 4   120 calories per serving
PREPARATION   20 minutes
COOKING   None
CHILLING   About 1 hour

400 g (14 oz) tofu
1 garlic clove, skinned and finely chopped
25 ml (1½ tbsp) olive oil
7.5 ml (1½ tsp) tomato purée
5 ml (1 tsp) Dijon mustard
salt and pepper, to taste
4 spring onions, green leaves, discarded, finely chopped
15 ml (1 tbsp) chopped fresh parsley
1.25 ml (¼ tsp) dried thyme
6 fresh basil leaves, finely sliced

——— 1 ———

Put the tofu into a blender or food processor and blend until smooth. Add the garlic, olive oil, tomato purée and mustard. Mix. Season.

——— 2 ———

Transfer to a bowl and add the spring onions, parsley, thyme and basil, stirring until evenly mixed. Cover and chill at least 1 hour.

GOODNESS GUIDE

PROTEIN Tofu is an excellent source of high-quality, low-fat protein which the body can utilise efficiently for protein replacement
MINERALS Tofu contributes calcium and iron
CHOLESTEROL Tofu is cholesterol-free. The lecithin it contains helps to prevent a build-up of cholesterol deposits in blood vessels

CHICK-PEA AND TUNA SALAD

SERVES 4   340 calories per serving
PREPARATION   About 30 minutes
COOKING   1½ hours
SOAKING   Overnight

250 g (9 oz) dried chick-peas, soaked overnight
½ red pepper, cored, seeded and cut into thin strips
½ yellow pepper, cored, seeded and cut into thin strips
15 ml (1 tbsp) chopped fresh tarragon or 5 ml (1 tsp) dried
endive leaves, stoned black olives and capers, to garnish

TUNA DRESSING

200 g (7 oz) can tuna in brine, well drained
½ small onion, skinned and chopped
7.5 ml (1½ tsp) tarragon mustard
15 ml (1 tbsp) tarragon vinegar
1 garlic clove, skinned and crushed
salt and pepper, to taste
50 ml (2 fl oz) olive oil

——— 1 ———

Drain the chick-peas and put into a large saucepan of water. Boil for 10–15 minutes, drain, then cover with fresh water. Bring to the boil again, lower the heat, cover and simmer for 1½ hours, until tender. Drain and keep warm.

——— 2 ———

To make the dressing, mash the tuna to a fine paste, then beat in the onion, mustard, vinegar, garlic and seasoning. Whisk in the oil until the mixture emulsifies.

——— 3 ———

Put the warm chick-peas into a serving bowl with the peppers. Pour the dressing over and toss well. Sprinkle over the tarragon. Garnish and serve.

GOODNESS GUIDE

PROTEIN Chick-peas and tuna fish contribute good amounts of protein. Eating bread with the salad will increase the protein value of the chick-peas
VITAMINS Red and yellow peppers are good sources of vitamins A and C, both of which are necessary for healthy skin. The vitamin C also makes the iron in the chick-peas more available to the body

BROCCOLI AND TOMATO SOUFFLE

Low-fat natural yogurt replaces the traditional flour base in this light soufflé. It can also be made with puréed spinach.

SERVES 4   190 calories per serving
PREPARATION   30 minutes
COOKING   50 minutes

450 g (1 lb) broccoli, trimmed
salt and pepper, to taste
grated nutmeg, to taste
150 ml (5 fl oz) low-fat natural yogurt
3 egg yolks, size 2
4 egg whites, size 2
2 tomatoes, thinly sliced
15 ml (1 tbsp) finely grated Parmesan

——— 1 ———

Lightly grease a 1.7 litre (3 pint) soufflé dish and set aside. Chop the broccoli stalks and place in a saucepan with the florets on top. Add about 2.5 cm (1 inch) of boiling water, cover and simmer for about 15 minutes, until tender. Drain. Place in a blender or food processor and purée. Add seasoning and nutmeg.

——— 2 ———

Add the yogurt and egg yolks to the broccoli purée and mix well. Whisk the egg whites until stiff, then fold into the mixture.

——— 3 ———

Pour half the mixture into the soufflé dish. Arrange a layer of sliced tomatoes in the middle, then top with the remaining broccoli mixture. Sprinkle with the cheese.

——— 4 ———

Cook at 180°C (350°F) mark 4 for about 50 minutes, until golden brown on top, well risen and firm to touch but still slightly wobbly in the middle. Serve at once.

GOODNESS GUIDE

VITAMINS Eggs provide vitamin D, which is important to absorb calcium for strong bones. Vitamin D is manufactured in the skin during exposure to sunlight, so it is important to have vitamin D in your diet if you are seldom in the sun
MINERALS Broccoli is a good source of calcium and iron. Iron is necessary for healthy red blood cells which carry oxygen around the body

TOFU SPREAD

CHICK-PEA AND TUNA SALAD

BROCCOLI AND TOMATO SOUFFLE

CHEESE FONDUE

Quick to prepare, fondues are an informal way of entertaining.

SERVES 4   490 calories per serving
PREPARATION 10 minutes
COOKING 10 minutes

300 ml ($\frac{1}{2}$ pint) dry white wine
10 ml (2 tsp) lemon juice
100 g (4 oz) Gruyère cheese, grated
275 g (10 oz) Edam cheese, grated
100 g (4 oz) mature Cheddar cheese, grated
30 ml (2 tbsp) kirsch
25 ml (1$\frac{1}{2}$ tbsp) cornflour
1.25 ml ($\frac{1}{4}$ tsp) grated nutmeg
granary toast, cubed
a selection of raw or hot, lightly cooked
fresh vegetables, such as:
large French beans, trimmed
cauliflower florets
carrots, scrubbed and cut into bite-sized
pieces
small radishes
broccoli florets
button mushrooms
cucumbers, cut into chunks
courgettes, cut into chunks
celery sticks, trimmed and thickly chopped

1
Put the wine and lemon juice into a saucepan and bring almost to the boiling point. Add the cheeses and stir over a low heat until melted.

2
Blend together the kirsch and cornflour. Add to the cheese mixture. Stir carefully with a wooden spoon until the mixture thickens and coats the back of the spoon. Add the nutmeg.

3
To serve, pour into a fondue pot or heatproof serving dish set on a wire rack or trivet over a small warming candle. Use skewers or fondue forks for dipping the bread cubes and vegetables into the sauce.

MICROWAVE In step 1, put wine and lemon juice in a bowl. Cover and cook 100% (High) 3 minutes, until hot. Add cheeses, blended cornflour and kirsch. Cook 60% (Medium) 8–9 minutes, until thickened and smooth, stirring every minute. Add nutmeg. Follow step 3.

GOODNESS GUIDE
VITAMINS The vegetables are a good source of vitamin C; cheese contains A and B complex
FAT The distinctive tastes of mature Cheddar and Gruyère mean that a little goes a long way; Edam contains less fat and keeps the overall fat content down

CHEESE FONDUE

BEAN TABOULEH

Tabouleh is a traditional Middle Eastern dish. It is made with burghul wheat which is available at health food shops. This substantial salad is a variation on the classic recipe and fish can be substituted for the chicken.

SERVES 4 425 calories per serving
PREPARATION 15 minutes
COOKING None
SOAKING 35–40 minutes

150 g (5 oz) burghul wheat
15 ml (1 tbsp) sesame or sunflower seeds
400 g (14 oz) can red kidney beans, drained and rinsed
4 spring onions, finely chopped
1 garlic clove, skinned and crushed
15 ml (1 tbsp) chopped fresh tarragon or 5 ml (1 tsp) dried
60 ml (4 tbsp) olive oil
juice of 1 lemon
salt and pepper, to taste
175 g (6 oz) cooked chicken meat, skinned and chopped
small cabbage or lettuce leaves

——— 1 ———

Soak the burghul wheat in cold water for 35–40 minutes or until soft. Drain off the excess liquid, pressing the burghul to squeeze out the moisture. This can be done by putting the drained burghul into a clean tea towel and lightly squeezing the towel.

——— 2 ———

While the wheat is soaking, put the sesame or sunflower seeds in a heavy-based frying pan or saucepan over medium heat for about 2 minutes, stirring constantly, until the seeds are lightly toasted.

——— 3 ———

Mix together the prepared burghul, drained kidney beans, chopped spring onions, garlic, tarragon and sesame seeds.

——— 4 ———

Mix the olive oil with the lemon juice and seasoning, then stir into the burghul wheat and beans. Mix in the cooked chicken and place the tabouleh on a bed of small cabbage leaves to serve.

GOODNESS GUIDE

PROTEIN Vegetable protein is usually deficient in one or more components. In this dish the burghul and beans balance out each other's deficiencies, which means the body can take full advantage of the high protein content
FIBRE The beans, burghul and seeds make the tabouleh a very rich source of dietary fibre

BEAN TABOULEH

171

MONKFISH AND PRAWN TERRINE

This can be made in advance and stored, covered, in the refrigerator.

SERVES 4 195 calories per serving
PREPARATION 20 minutes
COOKING 45 minutes
COOLING 1 hour

450 g (1 lb) monkfish fillet, skinned
60 ml (4 tbsp) chopped fresh dill or
30 ml (2 tbsp) dried
50 ml (2 fl oz) dry white wine
1 egg white, size 2
salt and pepper, to taste
100 g (4 oz) peeled cooked prawns, thawed
if frozen and chopped
small bunch of fresh watercress,
finely chopped
4 tomatoes, skinned, seeded and
finely chopped
1 garlic clove, skinned and crushed
150 ml (5 fl oz) low-fat natural yogurt
unpeeled cooked prawns. to garnish

———1———
Lightly oil a 450 g (1 lb) loaf tin and set aside. Place the monkfish, chopped dill, wine, egg white and seasoning in a blender or food processor and purée until smooth. In another bowl, mix the prawns and watercress together.

———2———
Spread half the monkfish purée in the base of the prepared loaf tin. Sprinkle over the prawns and watercress, then spread the remaining purée over the top. Smooth with a knife, then cover with foil.

———3———
Put the dish in a roasting pan with enough boiling water to come half way up the side. Cook at 200°C (400°F) mark 6 for 45 minutes or until firm. Drain off any liquid, then leave to cool for 1 hour.

———4———
Meanwhile, make the tomato sauce. Put the tomatoes and garlic in a small saucepan and simmer for 10 minutes, stirring occasionally. Mix in the yogurt and seasoning, then leave the mixture to cool.

———5———
Turn out the terrine on to a serving dish and garnish with the unpeeled cooked prawns. Cut into slices and serve with the tomato sauce.

MICROWAVE Lightly oil a microwave oven loaf tin and set aside. Complete steps 1 and 2. Put tin into a dish with enough boiling water to come half way up the side. Cover the terrine. Cook 60% (Medium) 10 minutes, turning dish twice. Complete step 3. Put tomatoes and garlic into a bowl and cook, uncovered, 100% (High) 5 minutes. Complete step 4 and step 5 of the recipe.

GOODNESS GUIDE

FAT Both monkfish and prawns are low-fat sources of protein. The sauce is also low in fat

VITAMINS The monkfish is a good source of B vitamins which, among other functions, help the body utilise energy from carbohydrates

MINERALS Prawns are rich in potassium, calcium, iron and zinc

MONKFISH AND PRAWN TERRINE

MARINATED STEAK SALAD

This warm salad should be eaten as soon as it is ready, otherwise the heat from the steak and rice will speed the loss of vitamin C in the raw vegetables. Marinades should contain an acid such as lemon juice; this helps to tenderise the meat. Marinate for at least 3 hours for flavour absorption.

SERVES 4   200 calories per serving
PREPARATION   20 minutes
COOKING   35 minutes
MARINATING   3 hours or overnight

225 g (8 oz) lean rump steak, trimmed of excess fat, cut in 5 cm (2 inch) long narrow strips
1 garlic clove, skinned and crushed
15 ml (1 tbsp) soy sauce, preferably naturally fermented shoyu
15 ml (1 tbsp) lemon juice
5 ml (1 tsp) finely grated fresh root ginger
2 spring onions, trimmed, chopped
30 ml (2 tbsp) dry red wine
pepper, to taste
75 g (3 oz) brown rice
2.5 ml ($\frac{1}{2}$ tsp) corn oil
100 g (4 oz) button mushrooms, halved
1 red pepper, cored and seeded
1 bunch of watercress, trimmed, or
100 g (4 oz) fresh spinach leaves

———1———

Place the steak strips in a glass, ceramic or stainless steel bowl with the garlic, soy sauce, lemon juice, ginger, spring onions, wine and seasoning. Stir. Cover and marinate in the refrigerator for 3 hours or overnight, stirring occasionally.

———2———

Put the rice in 450 ml ($\frac{3}{4}$ pint) boiling water. Cover and simmer for 30 minutes or until tender and the liquid has been absorbed. Place in a serving bowl and keep warm.

———3———

Lightly brush a heavy-based frying pan or wok with the oil and heat.

Pour in the meat and marinade, then the mushrooms. Cook, stirring constantly, over a medium heat for 1 minute. Cover and simmer for a further 5 minutes. Remove from the heat and set aside to cool slightly.

———4———

Meanwhile, cut the red pepper into long narrow strips and add to the rice with the watercress or fresh spinach. Stir in the meat and mushroom mixture. Check the seasoning, adding a little more soy sauce, if liked. Serve immediately.

GOODNESS GUIDE

PROTEIN Meat provides high levels of protein, which is essential for tissue replacement and carrying nutrients in and out of cells
FIBRE The brown rice and vegetables provide some fibre
VITAMINS Steak and brown rice are a source of valuable B vitamins which have various functions, including releasing energy from proteins, fats and carbohydrates

MARINATED STEAK SALAD

LEEK PANCAKES

MAKES 8 230 calories each
PREPARATION 25 minutes
COOKING About 45 minutes

100 g (4 oz) plain wholemeal flour
1 egg
300 ml ($\frac{1}{2}$ pint) semi-skimmed milk
salt and pepper, to taste
15 ml (1 tbsp) snipped fresh chives
15 ml (1 tbsp) sunflower oil
3 leeks, trimmed and cut into thin strips
25 g (1 oz) polyunsaturated margarine
100 g (4 oz) button mushrooms, sliced
30 ml (2 tbsp) chopped fresh parsley
15 ml (1 tbsp) chopped sunflower seeds
50 g (2 oz) Gouda cheese, grated
15 ml (1 tbsp) grated Parmesan cheese

WATERCRESS–ANCHOVY SAUCE

1 bunch watercress, chopped
4 anchovy fillets, well drained
10 ml (2 tsp) capers
75 ml (3 fl oz) olive oil
1 garlic clove, skinned and crushed
grated rind and juice of $\frac{1}{2}$ lemon
30 ml (2 tbsp) vegetable stock

———1———

Put the flour into a bowl and make a well in the centre, then add the egg and half the milk and beat until smooth. Beat in remaining milk, add seasoning and chives.

———2———

Lightly grease an 18 cm (7 inch) frying pan or crêpe pan with the sunflower oil, tilting the pan to coat base and sides. Pour off surplus.

———3———

Pour in just enough batter to coat the base. Cook for 1–2 minutes, until light brown, then turn and cook on the other side. Make 8 pancakes.

———4———

Cook the leeks in the margarine until soft. Add the mushrooms and cook 2 minutes more, then stir in parsley, sunflower seeds and seasoning.

———5———

Lay the pancakes out flat and divide the prepared filling between them, then roll up. Arrange the pancakes in a greased shallow ovenproof dish.

———6———

To make the sauce, put the watercress, anchovy fillets, capers and half the olive oil in a blender or food processor and purée until smooth. Gradually blend in the remaining olive oil, garlic, lemon juice and rind. Add a little vegetable stock to give a smooth pouring consistency. Put in a saucepan and heat through gently.

———7———

Pour the sauce over pancakes and sprinkle with the cheeses. Bake at 190°C (375°F) mark 5 for 20 minutes, or until crisp and golden.

SEAFOOD SPAGHETTI

SERVES 4 500 calories per serving
PREPARATION 10 minutes
COOKING 15 minutes

350 g (12 oz) wholemeal spaghetti
3 spring onions, chopped
300 ml ($\frac{1}{2}$ pint) dry white wine
2 egg yolks
100 g (4 oz) natural Quark
175 g (6 oz) cooked white fish, skinned boned and flaked
100 g (4 oz) fresh or canned shelled mussels
100 g (4 oz) fresh or canned shelled cockles
salt and pepper, to taste

———1———

Cook the spaghetti in a large saucepan of fast-boiling lightly salted water for about 10 minutes.

———2———

Meanwhile, put the spring onions and white wine into a saucepan and simmer very gently for 3–4 minutes, without allowing the wine to evaporate too much. Remove from the heat and whisk in the egg yolks, one at a time, and the natural Quark.

———3———

Drain the pasta, then spoon into a serving dish and keep warm. Return the wine sauce to the heat and add the white fish, mussels and cockles. Heat through gently and season. Spoon the sauce over the pasta.

GOODNESS GUIDE

SEAFOOD SPAGHETTI

MINERALS Shellfish are a good source of iron and calcium and other important minerals such as iodine and zinc
FAT High in protein, white fish and shellfish are very low in fat, especially the saturated type. Quark is also low in fat.

LEEK PANCAKES

FIBRE Cooking with wholemeal flour instead of white is an easy way of substantially increasing fibre intake
FAT Using semi-skimmed milk and lower fat Gouda keeps the amount in check

STUFFED VEGETABLES

Protein-rich taramasalata can be used instead of hummus.

SERVES 4 180 calories per serving
PREPARATION 25 minutes
COOKING None

2 celery sticks, trimmed
8 button mushrooms
12 cherry tomatoes
$\frac{1}{2}$ cucumber
60–75 ml (4–5 tbsp) hummus
1 red pepper, cored, seeded and finely chopped
225 g (8 oz) curd cheese
15 ml (1 tbsp) low-fat natural yogurt
salt and pepper, to taste
15 ml (1 tbsp) fresh snipped chives
50 g (2 oz) chopped nuts, toasted
shredded spinach, to serve

———1———

Prepare the vegetables. Cut each celery stick into 4 equal lengths, crossways. Neatly remove the stalks from the mushrooms. Cut a thin slice from the stalk end of each tomato and carefully hollow out the centre. Cut the cucumber into 8 thick rings and carefully hollow out the seeds.

———2———

Mix together the hummus and red pepper, then use the mixture to fill the mushroom cups and tomatoes.

———3———

Mix the cheese with the yogurt, seasoning, chives and chopped nuts and use to fill the celery and cucumber. Make a bed of shredded spinach on a serving platter and arrange the stuffed vegetables decoratively on the top.

GOODNESS GUIDE

FAT Curd cheese has far less fat than many soft cheeses. Using curd cheese and yogurt helps to keep the fat content low
FIBRE All the vegetables and nuts supply fibre
MINERALS Nuts and spinach are rich in iron and other minerals
VITAMINS The vegetables, especially the spinach, provide a lot of A and C

SEAFOOD SPAGHETTI

STUFFED VEGETABLES

LEEK PANCAKES

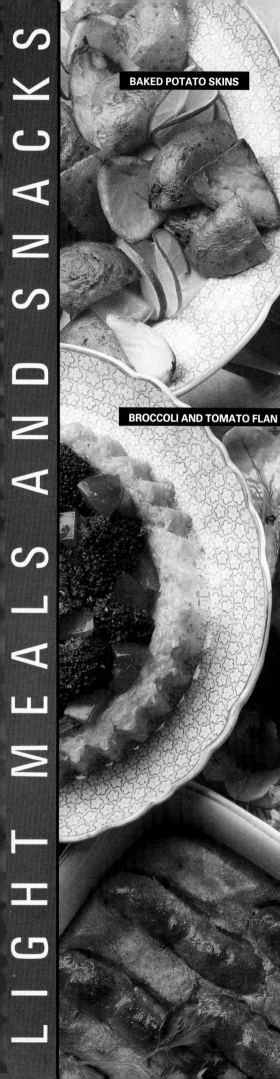

BAKED POTATO SKINS

BROCCOLI AND TOMATO FLAN

TOFU PRAWN TOASTS

TOAD IN THE HOLE

SERVES 4   415 calories per serving
PREPARATION 10 minutes
COOKING 40–50 minutes

15 ml (1 tbsp) corn oil
8 low-fat sausages, uncooked
50 g (2 oz) self-raising wholemeal flour
50 g (2 oz) self-raising flour
1 egg
300 ml ($\frac{1}{2}$ pint) semi-skimmed milk
10 ml (2 tsp) chopped fresh mixed herbs or
2.5 ml ($\frac{1}{2}$ tsp) dried
salt and pepper, to taste

——————1——————

Place the oil in an ovenproof dish
and heat at 220°C (425°F) mark 7
for 2–3 minutes, until hot. Arrange
the sausages in the dish and cook
for 10 minutes.

——————2——————

Meanwhile, put the flours in a bowl
and make a well in the centre. Whisk
together the egg and milk, then pour
into the well and gradually mix in
the flours to make a smooth batter.
Stir in the herbs and seasoning.

——————3——————

Pour the batter over the sausages
and cook for 30–40 minutes, until
the batter is crisp and well risen.
Serve at once.

GOODNESS GUIDE

FAT Using low-fat sausages and semi-
skimmed milk considerably reduces the fat
content of this dish
MINERALS The sausages, egg and flours
provide iron and calcium. The milk is also
rich in calcium
FIBRE The flour and the breadcrumbs in the
sausage add fibre

TOAD IN THE HOLE

BROCCOLI AND TOMATO FLAN

SERVES 4 230 calories per serving
PREPARATION 15 minutes
COOKING About 1¼ hours

100 g (4 oz) brown rice
50 g (2 oz) Cheddar cheese, grated
50 g (2 oz) Mozzarella cheese, grated
1 egg
salt and pepper, to taste
250 g (8 oz) broccoli spears
5 tomatoes, coarsely chopped
15 ml (1 tbsp) chopped fresh basil

———1———

Put the rice in a saucepan of 450 ml (¾ pint) boiling water. Cover and simmer for 30 minutes or until tender, and the liquid has been absorbed. Leave to cool.

———2———

Lightly grease a 20 cm (8 inch) loose-based flan tin. Combine the rice, cheeses, egg and seasoning. Press the mixture into the tin and cook at 190°C (375°F) mark 5 for 30 minutes or until firm to the touch.

———3———

Meanwhile, steam the broccoli over boiling water for 7–8 minutes, until just tender.

———4———

Carefully remove the rice crust from the flan tin and slide it on to a baking sheet. Arrange the broccoli in the flan case. Spread the tomatoes over and sprinkle with the basil and seasoning. Return to the oven to bake for a further 5 minutes. Serve hot.

MICROWAVE Put rice in bowl with 350 ml (12 fl oz) boiling water. Part cover. Cook 100% (High) 4 minutes, then 60% (Medium) 20 minutes. Drain. Cool. In step 2 spread mixture in flan dish. Cook 100% (High) 4 minutes. Cook broccoli in 60 ml (4 tbsp) water 5 minutes. Drain and arrange over rice crust. Spread tomatoes over, sprinkle with basil and seasoning. Cook 3 minutes. Serve from dish.

GOODNESS GUIDE

MINERALS The brown rice, egg yolk and cheeses contain chromium, an important trace mineral which is responsible for promoting transport of glucose into cells and its uptake by tissue and muscles
FIBRE The brown rice and vegetables provide plenty of fibre

BAKED POTATO SKINS

Use the scooped out potato from the skins in another dish, such as Potato Scones (page 251).

SERVES 4 115 calories per serving
PREPARATION 10 minutes
COOKING About 1¼ hours

4 large baking potatoes, about 225 g (8 oz) each, scrubbed and pricked
40 g (1½ oz) polyunsaturated margarine, melted
1 lime, cut into thin slices, to garnish
Greek strained yogurt, to serve

SPICY TOMATO SAUCE
100 g (4 oz) ripe tomatoes, coarsely chopped
2 spring onions, trimmed and chopped
juice of ½ lime
15 ml (1 tbsp) chopped fresh parsley
2.5 ml (½ tsp) dried oregano
few drops of Tabasco sauce

———1———

Bake the potatoes at 190°C (375°F) mark 5 for about 1 hour or until they are just tender.

———2———

Meanwhile, combine the ingredients for the sauce and put into a serving bowl. Cover and refrigerate until needed.

———3———

Remove the potatoes from the oven and allow them to cool slightly, until you can handle them, then cut them into quarters lengthways. Cut each quarter in half crossways. Scoop the potato from the skins, leaving a layer of potato about 0.25 cm (⅛ inch) thick on the skins. Brush the skins on both sides with the margarine and arrange them in a single layer on a baking sheet.

———4———

Increase the oven temperature to 240°C (475°F) mark 9 and bake the potato skins for 12–15 minutes, until crisp and just beginning to brown.

———5———

Serve hot, garnished with lime slices, with the sauce and yogurt.

MICROWAVE Arrange potatoes on absorbent paper. Cook 100% (High) 18–20 minutes, rearranging twice, until potatoes are just tender. Complete step 2. Leave the potatoes to cool slightly. Complete step 3, arranging the skins on a rack. Cook 100% (High) 8–10 minutes, turning over and rearranging twice until crisp.

TOFU PRAWN TOASTS

MAKES 14 30 calories each
PREPARATION 5 minutes
COOKING 4 minutes

225 g (8 oz) firm tofu
5 ml (1 tsp) sesame seeds
a few unpeeled prawns and watercress, to garnish

PRAWN TOPPING
175 g (6 oz) cooked peeled prawns, thawed if frozen
2 spring onions, trimmed and finely chopped
5 ml (1 tsp) grated fresh root ginger
10 ml (2 tsp) soy sauce, preferably naturally fermented shoyu
5 ml (1 tsp) corn oil
salt and pepper, to taste

———1———

Place all the topping ingredients in a blender or food processor and blend until they form a smooth paste.

———2———

Cut the tofu into fourteen 2.5 × 5 cm (1 × 2 inch) slices. Cook under the grill for about 1 minute or until just beginning to brown, then turn and cook for a further minute.

———3———

Spread the prawn paste over the tofu slices and sprinkle with sesame seeds. Cook under the grill until the sesame seeds are golden brown. Serve hot, garnished with prawns and watercress.

GOODNESS GUIDE

TOFU PRAWN TOASTS
PROTEIN The tofu, sesame seeds and prawns provide plenty of protein
MINERALS The sesame seeds, prawns and some kinds of tofu are rich in calcium, which is necessary for building and maintaining bones and teeth. Calcium is deposited as calcium phosphate within the bone and teeth tissue

BAKED POTATO SKINS
FIBRE The potato skins and other vegetables provide plenty of fibre. The fibre absorbs water in the intestine enabling the easy passage of waste products. Therefore it is important to ensure a good fluid intake. Low-fibre diets can result in such disorders as hiatus hernia, diverticulosis, appendicitis and haemorrhoids

ASPARAGUS TART

NOODLES AND CRISP VEGETABLES

ASPARAGUS TART

SERVES 4   350 calories per serving
PREPARATION   30 minutes
BAKING   20 minutes

100 g (4 oz) plain wholemeal flour
50 g (2 oz) polyunsaturated margarine
225 g (8 oz) potatoes, scrubbed
and quartered
225 g (8 oz) fresh asparagus, trimmed
and scraped
15 g (½ oz) polyunsaturated margarine
4 eggs, lightly beaten
50 g (2 oz) low-fat soft cheese

———1———

Lightly oil an 18 cm (7 inch) flan tin and set aside. Place the flour in a bowl and rub in the margarine until the mixture resembles fine bread-crumbs. Gradually add about 15 ml (1 tbsp) chilled water to make a soft dough, then knead lightly for a few seconds.

———2———

Roll out the dough on a lightly floured surface and use to line the prepared tin. Flute the edges. Place a sheet of greaseproof paper and baking beans over the pastry and bake blind at 200°C (400°F) mark 6 for 15 minutes. Remove the beans and greaseproof paper from the pastry shell and bake for a further 5 minutes. Place on a rack to cool.

———3———

Meanwhile, place the potatoes and asparagus in a small, deep sauce-pan of boiling water so that the asparagus tips are above the water. Cover tightly and return to the boil. Reduce the heat and cook for 15 minutes.

———4———

Melt the margarine in a small frying pan, add the eggs and scramble until they are just setting. Remove from the heat and stir in the cheese and seasoning to taste.

———5———

Drain the vegetables. Chop the potatoes and the ends of the aspara-gus stalks, reserving the tips, and add to the eggs.

———6———

Fill the baked tart shell with the egg mixture, and top with the asparagus tips, halved lengthways and cut to fit the tart top as necessary. Serve the tart warm or cool.

POTTED CHEESE WITH HERBS

This dish is best made a day or two before eating, to allow time for the flavours to blend.

SERVES 4   115 calories per serving
PREPARATION   40 minutes
COOKING   None
CHILLING   At least 1 hour

225 g (8 oz) low-fat soft cheese
or natural Quark
75 g (3 oz) low-fat Cheshire cheese,
finely grated
2.5 ml (½ tsp) ground mace or grated nutmeg
30 ml (2 tbsp) red or white wine
45 ml (3 tbsp) snipped fresh chives or
trimmed and chopped spring onions, or
chopped fresh herbs such as thyme, sage,
marjoram, basil, parsley or dill
pepper, to taste
2 eating apples
15 ml (1 tbsp) lemon juice
2 large carrots, scrubbed and
cut into sticks
4 large celery sticks, trimmed and
cut into sticks
wholemeal crispbread or thin
wholemeal toast

———1———

Place the soft cheese in a mixing bowl. Add the Cheshire cheese, mace, wine, herbs and seasoning and mix well with a fork. Transfer the mixture to a serving dish or 4 small individual bowls. Cover with aluminium foil and chill until ready to serve.

———2———

Core and slice the apples, then gently toss in the lemon juice to prevent discoloration. Arrange with the carrot and celery sticks on a large platter or individual dishes around the potted cheese. Serve the cheese mixture with slices of crispbread or thin toast.

GOODNESS GUIDE

PROTEIN Cheese provides valuable protein
FAT The use of low-fat cheese makes the overall fat content of this dish quite low
MINERALS The cheese provides calcium, essential for healthy bones and muscle contraction

178

BAKED JACKET POTATOES WITH HUMMUS

POTTED CHEESE WITH HERBS

NOODLES AND CRISP VEGETABLES

SERVES 4 245 calories per serving
PREPARATION 15 minutes
COOKING 20 minutes

225 g (8 oz) wholemeal noodles, such as
soba buckwheat noodles or wholemeal
fettucine
5 ml (1 tsp) corn oil
2 onions, skinned and thinly sliced
100 g (4 oz) carrots, scrubbed and
thinly sliced
450 g (1 lb) mixed fresh vegetables, such as
turnips, mushrooms, cabbage, fennel,
peppers, swedes or broccoli florets,
thinly sliced
75 g (3 oz) frozen or fresh peas, or
mange-tout
15 ml (1 tbsp) soy sauce, preferably
naturally fermented shoyu
15 ml (1 tbsp) dry sherry
dash of chilli oil
(optional)

——————1——————

Cook the noodles according to the
instructions on the packet and drain
well. Heat the oil in a large frying
pan or wok. Add the onions and
carrots and cook over a medium heat
for 5 minutes, stirring occasionally
until the onions are soft.

——————2——————

Add the remaining vegetables, soy
sauce and 30 ml (2 tbsp) water.
Raise the heat, and cover the pan
when the mixture begins to sizzle.
Cook gently for 5 minutes, stirring.

——————3——————

Add the noodles, sherry and chilli
oil, if using. Stir the mixture over a
medium heat for 2–3 minutes to
reheat the noodles. Serve at once.

GOODNESS GUIDE

NOODLES AND CRISP VEGETABLES
MINERALS The noodles are a source of
calcium for strong bones, and of iron, which
is needed for healthy red blood cells

ASPARAGUS TART
FIBRE The wholemeal flour, potatoes and
asparagus provide fibre
PROTEIN The eggs, cheese, flour and
potatoes provide ample protein
VITAMINS The eggs and margarine contain
the fat-soluble vitamins A, D and E, all of
which can be stored by the body and are
needed in small amounts

BAKED JACKET POTATOES WITH HUMMUS

SERVES 4 335 calories per serving
PREPARATION 5 minutes
COOKING 50 minutes

4 potatoes, about 225 g (8 oz) each,
scrubbed
75 g (3 oz) low-fat soft cheese
225 g (8 oz) hummus
salt, to taste

——————1——————

Pierce each potato with a metal
skewer. Place on a baking sheet
and cook at 220°C (425°F) mark 7
for 45–50 minutes, until soft and
cooked through.

——————2——————

Meanwhile, stir the cheese into the
hummus and season, if liked. Cut a
cross in the top of each potato and
spoon in the hummus mixture. Serve
at once with a crunchy salad.

MICROWAVE Place pierced potatoes
on absorbent paper. Cook,
uncovered, 100% (High)
15–20 minutes, rearranging twice,
until cooked. Stir cheese into
hummus and season, if liked. Fill
each cut potato with hummus
mixture.

GOODNESS GUIDE

FIBRE Baked jacket potatoes and hummus
provide a great deal of fibre. One type of
the fibre aids easy movement of food
through the intestinal tract, and the other
helps control the blood's sugar absorption
VITAMINS B vitamins are present in the
hummus, cheese and potatoes. The
potatoes provide vitamin C, which helps
maintain healthy tissues

179

TUNA CHEESECAKE

Most people are familiar with sweet cheesecakes, but a savoury one is rather unusual. Serve for lunch, or as part of a cold buffet.

MAKES 6 SLICES 270 calories per slice
PREPARATION 15 minutes
BAKING None
CHILLING 3–4 hours

100 g (4 oz) savoury wheatmeal biscuits, crushed
50 g (2 oz) polyunsaturated margarine, melted
thin lemon wedges, slices of hard-boiled egg and chopped fresh parsley, to garnish

FILLING
225 g (8 oz) curd cheese or cottage cheese, sieved
2 eggs, separated
150 ml (5 fl oz) low-fat natural yogurt
100 g (4 oz) canned tuna in brine, well drained
2.5 ml ($\frac{1}{2}$ tsp) anchovy essence
2.5 ml ($\frac{1}{2}$ tsp) curry powder
15 g ($\frac{1}{2}$ oz) powdered gelatine
60 ml (4 tbsp) chicken or vegetable stock
1 egg, size 2, hard-boiled and chopped pepper, to taste

———1———
Mix the biscuits with the margarine and press the mixture evenly over the base of a 20.5 cm (8 inch) loose-bottomed flan tin. Cover while making the filling.
———2———
Beat the curd cheese with the egg yolks, yogurt, tuna, anchovy essence and curry powder.
———3———
Place the gelatine and stock in a small heatproof bowl and stand in a saucepan of simmering water. Stir until the gelatine is dissolved.
———4———
Add the gelatine to the cheese mixture and mix well. Stir in the chopped egg and season. Whisk the egg whites until stiff and fold in. Pour the mixture into the tin, level the surface, cover with cling film and chill for 3–4 hours, until set.
———5———
Carefully loosen the sides of the tin and gently ease out the cheesecake. Slide off the base on to a serving plate and garnish with lemon wedges, hard-boiled egg and parsley. Serve at once.

SPINACH ROULADE

A savoury roulade looks very impressive. 'Resting' the egg sponge for a few minutes makes the rolling-up easier.

MAKES 8 SLICES 130 calories each
PREPARATION 25 minutes
BAKING 20–25 minutes

700 g (1$\frac{1}{2}$ lb) fresh spinach, rinsed
pinch of grated nutmeg
4 eggs, separated
finely grated rind of $\frac{1}{2}$ lemon
salt and pepper, to taste
unpeeled cooked prawns, to garnish

PRAWN FILLING
100 g (4 oz) curd cheese
30 ml (2 tbsp) low-fat natural yogurt
75 g (3 oz) peeled cooked prawns chopped

SAUCE
60 ml (4 tbsp) mayonnaise
60 ml (4 tbsp) low-fat natural yogurt
15 ml (1 tbsp) chopped fresh dill or
5 ml (1 tsp) dill weed

———1———
Grease and line a 33 × 23 cm (13 × 9 inch), Swiss roll tin with grease-proof paper. Set aside.
———2———
Cook the spinach in just the water clinging to its leaves until just tender. Drain thoroughly, pressing the spinach to remove excess moisture. Chop the spinach finely and mix with the nutmeg, egg yolks, grated lemon rind and seasoning.
———3———
Whisk the egg whites until stiff but not dry, then fold into the spinach mixture. Spread evenly in the prepared tin. Bake at 190°C (375°F) mark 5 for about 20–25 minutes or until well risen and set. Cool in the tin for a few minutes.
———4———
Invert the cooked 'cake' on to a sheet of lightly greased greaseproof paper. Remove the tin and lining paper. Beat together the curd cheese, yogurt, prawns and seasoning. Spread evenly over the 'cake'. Roll up as for a Swiss roll. Wrap the roll in the greaseproof paper and set aside until cool.
———5———
Mix together the mayonnaise, yogurt, dill and seasoning to make the sauce. Garnish the roulade with unpeeled prawns. Serve sauce separately.

ANCHOVY SPREAD

Soaking the anchovies in milk will draw out the salt. If you still find the flavour too strong, you can dilute it by adding a little natural yogurt.

SERVES 4 150 calories per serving
PREPARATION 10 minutes
COOKING None
SOAKING 30 minutes

8 anchovy fillets, well drained
semi-skimmed milk, for soaking
24 plump black olives, stoned
30 ml (2 tbsp) capers
15 ml (1 tbsp) chopped walnuts
grated rind and juice of 1 lemon
30 ml (2 tbsp) olive oil
1 garlic clove, skinned and crushed
pepper, to taste
low-fat natural yogurt, to taste (optional)
parsley sprig, to garnish
1 wholemeal French loaf (see page 228), sliced and toasted, to serve

———1———
Soak the anchovy fillets for 30 minutes in just enough semi-skimmed milk to cover. Drain and pat dry. Discard the milk.
———2———
Put the olives, anchovy fillets, capers, walnuts, lemon rind and juice, olive oil and garlic into a food processor or blender and purée until smooth. Add seasoning. For a milder flavour, add a little yogurt.
———3———
Spoon into a small dish and garnish with a parsley sprig. Serve with toasted French bread.

GOODNESS GUIDE

ANCHOVY SPREAD
MINERALS Anchovies are rich in calcium and magnesium, vital for building bones and for muscle and nerve activity

SPINACH ROULADE
VITAMINS This dish is rich in a wide variety of vitamins; C from the spinach and D from the eggs aid the absorption of certain minerals
MINERALS The egg yolk supplies iron, used in the formation of haemoglobin, which transports oxygen around the body

CORNISH PASTIES

*Make sure that the pieces of beef
are cut into small cubes, so they
finish cooking at the same time as
the vegetables.*

MAKES 4 660 calories each
PREPARATION 30 minutes
BAKING 55–60 minutes

1½ quantities Basic pastry (see page 104)
1 small carrot, scrubbed and finely chopped
½ red pepper, cored, seeded and
finely chopped
30 ml (2 tbsp) chopped fresh parsley
15 ml (1 tbsp) chopped walnuts
225 g (8 oz) stewing steak, cut into
small cubes
1 small leek, trimmed and finely chopped
salt and pepper, to taste
1 egg, beaten
sesame seeds, to decorate

———1———
Lightly grease a baking sheet. Roll
out the pastry on a lightly floured
surface and cut out 4 circles using
an 18 cm (7 inch) plate as a guide.
———2———
Mix the carrot, pepper, parsley,
walnuts, beef and leek together,
then season.
———3———
Glaze the rim of each pastry circle
with a little of the beaten egg and
divide the filling among the pastry
circles. Pull up the pastry edges over
the filling and crimp with your
fingers to seal. Place on the baking
sheet. Glaze with the remaining egg
and sprinkle with the sesame seeds.
———4———
Bake at 200°C (400°F) mark 6 for
15 minutes, then at 180°C (350°F)
mark 4 for a further 40–45 minutes
or until cooked. Serve hot or cold.

GOODNESS GUIDE

CORNISH PASTIES
MINERALS Beef is rich in easily-absorbed
iron. Vitamin C in the vegetables makes the
iron in the pastry flour and walnuts more
available to the body

TUNA CHEESECAKE
VITAMINS Tuna is an especially rich source
of vitamin D, which is extremely important
in absorbing calcium. It also supplies plenty
of B vitamins

TUNA CHEESECAKE

SPINACH ROULADE

ANCHOVY SPREAD

CORNISH PASTIES

181

6 SIDE DISHES AND SALADS

RAW FOODS

In the early part of this century, Dr Max Bircher-Benner, one of the pioneers of nutritional science, first proved that raw fruits and vegetables in the diet aid digestion and are positively beneficial to health. Today, raw foods are used by some doctors to treat a variety of complaints, ranging from cancer to diabetes; some advocates even believe that a raw food diet is capable of slowing the aging process. Make raw foods a substantial part of your diet by gradually increasing your intake, so that the body becomes accustomed to them—the experience should be enjoyable and the benefits healthy.

The average Western diet relies heavily on heating food: it is either cooked at home or during processing by food manufacturers. The reasons for cooking are to soften the texture of food, to destroy any harmful micro-organisms which may be present—particularly in foods of animal origin—and, in the case of processing carried out by food manufacturers, to prolong shelf life.

A raw food diet consists of at least 70 per cent raw fruit and vegetables, with the remaining 30 per cent consisting of grains—cooked or sprouted—seeds, nuts, dried fruit, dairy products and occasional items of cooked poultry, meat or fish. People who have followed this diet claim that they feel exceptionally well, with higher than average levels of energy and stamina. Raw food diets are used by some physicians and naturopaths to treat conditions such as obesity, high blood pressure, allergies, maturity onset diabetes and cancer.

NUTRITIONAL VALUE
Raw foods contain proteins, fats, carbohydrates, vitamins, minerals and, in the case of plants, fibre; fibre is valuable because it has a wide range of protective properties.

Raw vegetables and fruit continue to respire—exchange oxygen and carbon dioxide—even after they are harvested, and their enzymes continue to control chemical reactions. It is these living enzymes which are of particular benefit to the digestive system.

Enzymes are made up of different types of protein and are responsible for the initiation and control of chemical reactions in living matter. Proteins are made of chains of 22 different amino acids, eight of which are essential to the body; we are unable to manufacture these amino acids ourselves. Heating proteins results in changes to these amino acid chains; their natural properties change and in some cases are completely destroyed.

Most of us include a certain amount of raw food in our diet—fresh fruit and occasionally salads, although very often these are only eaten in the summer. However, a raw food dish which is increasingly popular is muesli.

MUESLI
Muesli is a raw dish of uncooked grains mixed with dried fruit and nuts. The original muesli was made popular in 1904 by the Swiss physician Dr Max Bircher-Benner who used it as part of a healing regime in his clinics in Switzerland, where it is used to this day.

Dr Bircher-Benner was introduced to the basis of the dish by a Swiss shepherd. The 70-year-old man was preparing his evening meal which consisted of a kind of raw porridge made from coarsely milled wheat soaked in milk and sweetened with honey, with which he ate a fresh apple. The shepherd explained that if he ate the porridge without the apple it lay heavily on his stomach and he did not feel so well nourished. Further investigation revealed that the man's meal was not uncommon in that part of Switzerland and that meals, especially in the evening, consisted of various raw cereals together with milk straight from the cow, fresh fruit and sometimes nuts.

Bircher-Benner devised his muesli along the same principles: a mixture of oatmeal and milk and a large apple or berries. The protein value of the combination of the oats and milk is equivalent to that of an egg, which is considered to contain protein of the highest quality. The muesli is also rich in carbohydrates, fibre, vitamins and minerals, together with a little fat for essential fatty acids.

SALADS
Dr Bircher-Benner recommended eating a raw salad before any cooked food at every meal to aid digestion. Try to get into the habit of serving an interesting and colourful salad made from a mixture of fruit and vegetables with main meals.

Wash the ingredients well and prepare the salad just before serving to retain all the goodness and prevent destruction of vitamin C. Make a point of occasionally serving a large salad as a main meal and include a variety of fruit and vegetables, seeds, nuts and grains. Exciting starters, soups and desserts can be made entirely from raw ingredients; light meals consisting of cheese and vegetable dips served with different breads, fruit and vegetable drinks are also tasty.

FOODS TO TREAT WITH CAUTION
It is wise to cook meats, poultry and fish because they are products which putrify quickly and the bacteria which cause putrification can be very harmful. However, there is evidence to show that when heated, the proteins in meat bind chemically to some minerals and so make them unavailable to the body.

Chicken eggs can be eaten raw; in fact many of us eat them raw in real mayonnaise, egg nogs and flips, and in sorbets.

The whites of all raw eggs should be eaten sparingly as egg white contains avidin, a substance which binds with the B vitamin biotin and prevents its absorption into the blood. A biotin deficiency can give rise to anaemia, nausea and muscular pain. It is not wise to eat the raw eggs of duck or other water fowl. This is because these eggs are often laid near brackish water and may be infected with bacteria.

Pulses—dried beans and peas—should never be eaten raw, although they can be sprouted; sprouting changes pulses into growing plants with active enzymes.

RICE AND OTHER GRAINS

In many parts of the world, grains form the staple food. They provide protein, carbohydrate, a little polyunsaturated fat, fibre, vitamins and minerals. Combined with other sources of protein such as pulses, nuts and seeds, the protein content is comparable to animal protein without the saturated fat content.

Rice is divided into three groups: long, medium and short grain. Both long and short grain rice are readily available; traditionally long grain rice is used for savoury dishes and short grain for rice puddings and other desserts. Medium grain rice can also be purchased and can be used equally well for main dishes or for desserts. Brown rice is the grain in its natural state as it retains the outer bran covering. White rice has been milled and polished to remove the bran layer. 'Easy-cook' rice has been steam-treated before the husk is removed, which helps retain some of these nutrients by carrying them into the centre of the grain. Wild rice is not a grain but the seeds of a grass which grows wild in the United States. It is expensive.

Nutritionally, brown rice is infinitely superior to white, as the milling process inevitably removes much of the goodness along with the all-important fibre content. Cooked brown rice contains 25 per cent more protein than white rice and is higher in calcium, iron, phosphorus, thiamine, riboflavin and niacin. Brown rice is an excellent source of B vitamins, important for energy production and for a healthy nervous system. Rice is a great energy producer, high in carbohydrates and very low in fat. It is gluten-free and, therefore, valuable for those suffering from a gluten allergy. It is also the easiest grain to digest and one of the first solid foods suitable for infants who are being weaned. You can produce wholefood baby rice either by grinding brown rice grains to a powder before cooking or milling the cooked grain to form a smooth paste.

COOKING WITH BROWN RICE

Brown rice should always be washed before cooking. This is necessary because rice should not be rinsed after cooking if the nutrients are to be retained. Allow 50 g (2 oz) uncooked rice per person as an accompaniment and 40–50 g (1½–2 oz) when mixed with other ingredients; as a general rule use two parts water or other liquid to one part rice. Brown rice takes slightly longer to cook than white but can replace white in any recipe. As a basic method, place the grain in a saucepan of boiling water, then cover and simmer on a very low heat for 30 minutes or until all the liquid has been absorbed and the rice is 'al dente'. There is no need to add salt to the cooking water.

Rice can also be cooked in the oven. Pour boiling water on to the rice, then cover the casserole with foil and a lid and place in the centre of a pre-heated oven at 180°C (350°F) mark 4. Cook for approximately 1 hour or until all the liquid has been absorbed.

Cooked rice is best eaten immediately but it will keep in a sealed container in the fridge for up to five days and can be frozen for up to six months. Reheat in a pan with a little water or sauté in a polyunsaturated oil with onion and/or spices. Possible uses for rice include: paella; risotto; pilaff; fried rice; salads; rice moulds and loaves; as an accompaniment for vegetable, meat or fish dishes; savoury stuffings for tomatoes and peppers and, of course, rice pudding.

WHEAT

Wheat is widely used in this country in the form of flour. Cooked wheat grains, or berries, are delicious in savoury dishes and salads; wheat is also available in flakes, for use as a breakfast cereal, and cracked, when it is often called burghul or bulgur wheat.

Burghul wheat has been partially cooked and only needs soaking in boiling water (allow 1½ cups of water per cup of grain) or a very short cooking time (2 cups water per cup of grain, simmer for 12 minutes). It can be used in place of rice in savoury dishes or in salads such as tabouleh, which is traditionally flavoured with fresh mint, lemon juice, olive oil and crushed garlic or spring onions.

Couscous—made from semolina, the hard part of wheat—is similar to burghul wheat but has been processed more.

Wheat has a high gluten content, so it gives the desired elasticity to bread dough. People with food allergies however, may not be able to tolerate this and should use grains such as millet, rice, rye and corn which have a much lower gluten content or are gluten-free.

MILLET AND BUCKWHEAT

Millet is used mainly as birdseed. It is, however, a good food, with a very high iron content and is one of the best sources of laetrile (vitamin B_{17}) in addition to supplying thiamine and many trace minerals.

Millet, like many whole grains, benefits from being lightly dry roasted to bring out the flavour before adding boiling water and cooking as rice. This is best done in a heavy pan or a non-stick pan over a medium heat; stir continuously until the grain changes colour and there is a nutty fragrance. Alternatively, dry roast in the oven.

Pot barley is nutritionally superior to husked, polished pearl barley as it still contains the nutrient-laden outer covering. It thickens soups and stews.

Buckwheat is actually a seed rather than a grain. It is rich in iron and has a good range of B vitamins. It is also a useful source of phosphorus and calcium. Buckwheat flour can be used to make pasta, pancakes and biscuits. In Russia it is used to prepare kasha, a type of porridge, but it can also be added to savoury dishes. It combines well with most vegetables.

Cooking times and liquid ratios for different grains are as follows:

Pot barley—1 part grain to 3 or 4 parts water; 50–60 minutes

Buckwheat—1 part buckwheat to 2½–3 parts water; 20 minutes

Millet—1 part grain to 2½–3 parts water; 20 minutes.

CORN, RYE AND OATS

Other grains, such as corn, rye and oats are not normally cooked in this way. All can be used as flours in baking, usually combined with wholemeal flour, and added to breads, cakes, biscuits, pancakes and muffins.

Corn or maize is most often eaten as sweetcorn, popcorn or yellow cornmeal (polenta) in both savoury and sweet dishes and baking. White cornflour, used to thicken sauces and gravies, is simply the starch of the grain and has little nutritional value.

Rye flour is used extensively in the delicious black breads and pumpernickel of northern Europe. Rye is a source of potassium, vitamin E, magnesium, silicone and unsaturated fatty acids.

Porridge oats are, of course, a traditional breakfast cereal; oat groats (if available) or rolled oats offer delicious and wholesome alternatives.

SALAD DRESSINGS

Fresh vegetables and fruit, rich in vitamins and minerals, can be transformed into exciting salads by the addition of a piquant dressing. Whether served separately or combined with the ingredients, a dressing not only adds flavour to a salad, it also enhances appearance, prevents oxidation and helps digestion.

The range of dressings that you can make includes oil-based dressings, mayonnaise and—as a low-fat alternative—yogurt-based and fruit juice-based dressings. However, one particular dressing will not necessarily complement every salad, and an indifferent dressing—one that is too oily, too sharp, or too strongly-flavoured—will ruin a salad by masking the flavour of the ingredients.

OIL-BASED DRESSINGS

Oil-based dressings are an emulsion, formed by mixing together two liquids—usually oil and vinegar. When the oil and vinegar are shaken or whisked the particles of each are dispersed and temporarily bind together. Mustard and garlic, added to the oil and vinegar, speed up the emulsifying process. If the dressing settles the emulsion will break down and the oil will rise to the top.

Ideally, a dressing should be made just before use, but large quantities can be made in advance and stored in a sealed container in the refrigerator; the dressing will keep for several weeks.

French dressing and vinaigrette are the classic oil-based dressings; the main distinction between the two is that vinaigrette contains a higher proportion of vinegar. To make oil-based dressings

in the healthiest way possible, the oil should be chosen carefully and should be high in polyunsaturates. Avoid blended vegetable oils as these may be high in saturated fat and have a poor flavour. Cold-pressed oils, which are produced by pressing nuts, seeds or fruit to extract the oil, are preferable to solvent-extracted oils, where heat or chemicals are used.

Sesame seed, grapeseed, safflower and sunflower oils are all excellent for salad dressings; each has its own distinctive flavour. Olive oil is considered to be the most superior salad oil, but it is expensive; a combination of olive oil and sunflower is a healthy, but economical, culinary compromise.

The flavour of an oil-based dressing depends on the seasoning; while the classic seasonings for French dressing are freshly ground pepper, rock salt and mustard, the substitution of freshly chopped herbs such as mint, dill, fennel, chives, tarragon or crushed garlic, will alter the character of the dressing.

VINEGARS

Oil-based dressings always contain some form of acid, usually vinegar or lemon juice. As a general guide, the quantity of vinegar to oil is usually one part vinegar to three or four parts oil, although this varies according to taste. Avoid adding too much vinegar to a salad dressing as it will spoil the flavour of the ingredients.

The strength of the vinegar depends on the food from which it is made and will affect the quality of the dressing. Malt vinegar, which is made from malted

grain, is very harsh and should be avoided. Wine or cider vinegars are preferable, while herb or spice vinegars are interesting and make a subtle contribution to a dressing. However, commercially prepared herb or spice vinegars are expensive. You can make your own by adding fresh herbs such as tarragon, rosemary or fennel, or spices such as cinnamon or cloves, to a bottle of wine vinegar. Seal the bottle tightly and leave for at least three weeks before using.

Apart from vinegar, other ingredients can be added to a salad dressing to provide the acid base. Lemon, orange or tomato juice are all rich in vitamin C and are interesting alternatives, as is a combination of lemon juice and naturally fermented shoyu.

MAYONNAISE

Mayonnaise can be served as an accompaniment to a dish or used to bind salad ingredients together. It is made from eggs or egg yolks, oil and a small quantity of liquid—lemon juice, wine vinegar or warm water.

Unlike oil-based dressings, mayonnaise is a stable emulsion that has a thick, smooth consistency. Its stability is due to the substance known as lecithin, present in egg yolk, which acts as an emulsifying agent. To make mayonnaise successfully, the eggs and oil should be at room temperature—this speeds up the emulsifying process. The oil must be added slowly to the egg yolk; curdling,

---

VINAIGRETTE DRESSING

MAKES 150 ML ($\frac{1}{4}$ PINT)
100 CALORIES PER 15 ML (1 TBSP)
PREPARATION 5 minutes

30 ml (2 tbsp) vinegar
120 ml (8 tbsp) sunflower or olive oil
2.5 ml ($\frac{1}{2}$ tsp) whole grain or Dijon mustard
salt and pepper, to taste

Place the ingredients in a screw-topped jar or a bowl and shake or whisk until well blended. Store covered in the refrigerator for up to 3 months, and shake well each time before using.

MAYONNAISE DRESSING

These dressings are quick to make and add interest to a variety of salads.

MAKES 150 ML ($\frac{1}{4}$ PINT)
95 CALORIES PER 15 ML (1 tbsp)
PREPARATION 5 minutes

1 egg
2.5 ml ($\frac{1}{2}$ tsp) Dijon mustard
7.5 ml ($1\frac{1}{2}$ tsp) white wine vinegar
salt and pepper, to taste
150 ml ($\frac{1}{4}$ pint) olive oil

Put the egg, mustard, vinegar and seasoning in a blender or food processor and blend for 30 seconds. With the blender still running, add the oil slowly until it is all combined and the mixture is thick. Store in a covered jar in the refrigerator for up to 1 week.

YOGURT DRESSING

MAKES 150 ML ($\frac{1}{4}$ PINT)
10 CALORIES PER 15 ML (1 TBSP)
PREPARATION 5 minutes

150 ml (5 fl oz) low-fat natural yogurt
10 ml (2 tsp) white wine vinegar
5 ml (1 tsp) clear honey
10 ml (2 tsp) chopped fresh mint
salt and pepper, to taste

In a small bowl, mix together the yogurt, vinegar, honey and mint with a fork. Season.

VARIATION Omit the mint and add 1 small garlic clove, skinned and crushed.

GOODNESS GUIDE

VITAMINS The yogurt supplies some B vitamins, riboflavin in particular, which helps release energy from food
MINERALS Calcium for muscle contraction and strong bones is provided by the yogurt
PROTEIN The egg in the Mayonnaise Dressing provides some protein

or breaking up of the emulsion, will occur if it is added too quickly. While personal preference will dictate the choice of oil, for a healthy mayonnaise it should be high in polyunsaturates because egg yolks contain both cholesterol and saturated fat.

The seasoning added to the mayonnaise will provide piquancy. Freshly ground black pepper is essential; salt and sugar are not necessary if the combination of seasonings is correct. Crushed garlic, freshly chopped herbs, grated horseradish, Tabasco sauce, tomato purée, olives, capers or pimientoes are all full of flavour and will add interest to the mayonnaise. Experiment with flavours, but remember that the salad dressing should blend with and complement all the other flavours that are used in the salad.

YOGURT-BASED DRESSINGS
Yogurt-based dressings are a refreshing and healthy alternative to mayonnaise, and contain less than half the calories of egg-based mayonnaise. Yogurt-based dressings are quick and easy to prepare; the taste and texture of yogurt is perfect for salads. Low-fat natural yogurt contains less than 2 per cent fat and should be used for the base, while a little clear honey will take the edge off the yogurt's slightly acidic flavour if it is not to your taste. Season as for French dressings.

An alternative to yogurt as a base for a healthy, low-fat dressing is to substitute tomato juice for the oil. Seasoned with herbs or crushed garlic, it provides a low-calorie alternative to an oil-based dressing and is also rich in vitamin C.

COMMERCIAL SALAD DRESSINGS
Commercial salad dressings, whether of the vinaigrette or mayonnaise type, tend to be expensive. They usually contain additives such as glycerol monsterate, which acts as an emulsifying agent, modified starch which thickens the dressing but may produce an unpleasant consistency, and sugar, salt, preservatives and colouring agents. Homemade, additive-free dressings are cheaper and much more healthy.

FRESH FRUIT SALADS
Fresh fruit salads are refreshing and are a perfect way to end a heavy meal or use up quantities of fruit. The juice in a fruit salad should be light; the best are made from the natural juices of the fruit used in the salad. Sugar need not always be added, but if a sweetener is required, use a small quantity of light muscovado sugar or clear honey. Using fruit which is fully ripe reduces the need to add sweeteners because it contains glucose and fructose which are natural sweeteners.

Fruits which have a pale flesh and a low acid content such as apples, bananas and pears will go brown when cut and exposed to the air. The juice which forms the base of the fruit salad should therefore contain citric acid; it is present in lemon, lime and orange juice and slows discoloration.

For special occasions soak fruit salad ingredients in a small quantity of dry white wine or 30 ml (2 tbsp) of an orange-flavoured liqueur. To enjoy any fresh fruit salad at its best, store it tightly covered in the refrigerator until just before serving.

PULSES—HIGH VALUE

Versatile and delicious, extremely inexpensive and highly nutritious, pulses should form a part of any healthy, well-balanced diet.

Pulse is a collective term for the edible seeds of the legume family—beans, peas and lentils. These can be preserved by drying and reconstituted by soaking and cooking, and it is generally the dried vegetable that we are referring to when we use the term pulses.

PROTEIN RICH
Pulses are a very rich source of a number of essential nutrients. Their protein content—a good 20 per cent or more on average—puts them on a par with meat but with none of the fat and at a fraction of the cost. (Soya beans are the exception: more than 30 per cent protein, they are also about 20 per cent fat, although largely of the unsaturated type.) These figures need qualifying slightly. The protein from vegetables is generally not regarded as being of the same quality as that from animal sources.

Proteins are made up of amino acids and animal protein contains all the essential amino acids and in the right proportions for the protein to be used by the body. By contrast, the protein in pulses and other vegetables is often deficient in one or more amino acid. However, by combining different vegetables these deficiencies can be balanced out.

Serving bean soup with a wedge of wholemeal bread is an example of this type of combination; eating the beans with a cereal product can release up to one third more protein. Combinations of this sort will provide complete protein, equivalent to the protein in meat and other animal foods.

ENERGY FOOD
Pulses are a good source of a number of the B group of vitamins, such as thiamine and niacin, which help the

PULSES—PREPARATION TIMES						
	ADUKI BEANS	**BLACK-EYE BEANS**	**BUTTER BEANS**	**CANNELLINI BEANS**	**CHICK-PEAS**	**FLAGEOLETS**
Soaking time	8–12 hours	8–12 hours	8–12 hours	8–12 hours	8–12 hours	8–12 hours
Basic cooking	30minutes	45 minutes	50 minutes	$1\frac{1}{2}$ hours	$1\frac{1}{2}$ hours	$1\frac{1}{4}$ hours
Pressure cooking	15 minutes	12 minutes	17 minutes	25 minutes	20 minutes	14 minutes
	HARICOT BEANS	**LENTILS**	**MUNG BEANS**	**RED KIDNEY BEANS**	**SOYA BEANS**	**SPLIT PEAS**
Soaking time	8–12 hours	None	8–12 hours	8–12 hours	8–12 hours	None
Basic cooking	$1\frac{1}{4}$ hours	1 hour	30 minutes	50 minutes	$1\frac{1}{2}$ hours	45 minutes
Pressure cooking	18 minutes	15 minutes	10 minutes	17 minutes	25 minutes	15 minutes

NOTE: All beans should be boiled rapidly for 10–15 minutes before start of cooking

185

body to release energy from foods, or folic acid, which is essential for the formation of new body cells. They also provide useful amounts of a variety of important minerals such as calcium, zinc, potassium and phosphorus. They are high in iron, although iron is less well absorbed from pulses than from animal foods. However, serving pulse dishes with vegetables such as peppers or spring greens, or adding the juice of a lemon during cooking will supply the vitamin C to aid the iron absorption.

Just as important, dried beans, peas and lentils are rich in dietary fibre, particularly the fibres which are associated with reducing the amount of fat the body absorbs from food.

PREPARATION AND COOKING

Many people are put off using pulses by what they see as an elaborate and time-consuming process of preparation and cooking. In fact the actual preparation is quite straightforward and it is easy to put together wholesome and appetising dishes. (*See* chart, page 185.)

When soaked and cooked the beans will roughly double in size and weight; 350 g (12 oz) dried weight should be enough for a main dish for four.

OILS FOR COOKING

Oils for cooking are produced from a wide range of seeds, nuts and fruit— sunflower, safflower, groundnut and corn are just some of the oils that can be found on most supermarket shelves. With so many to choose from, selecting the most suitable oil can be a daunting task. Here we explain the differences between many of those that are available, and point you in the direction of the healthiest.

Oils are highly nutritious. They help to carry the fat soluble vitamins A, D, E and K around the body. These vitamins are essential to the healthy functioning of the body—they assist in metabolic processes, help to maintain body temperature and protect tissues and nerves. When eaten with other foods, oils help to ensure a slow, steady digestion.

Like all fatty foods, oils are high in calories and should be consumed in moderation. Some oils are healthier than others—those high in polyunsaturates are the ones to opt for.

TYPES OF OIL

The following is a guide to many of the oils that are available. While some are sold in supermarkets, others may only be found in health food shops or delicatessens.

Almond oil is colourless and has a delicate flavour; it is made by pressing sweet almonds, which have an oil content of 50–60 per cent and are high in polyunsaturates. Almond oil may be used in mayonnaise, particularly when mayonnaise is served with seafood; it is also used in the manufacture of confectionery for oiling moulds.

Coconut oil has a high level of saturated fat—approximately 75 per cent. For health reasons, it is not generally recommended, but its particular flavour does lend itself to some Caribbean and Indian dishes. If coconut oil is called for in a recipe, try to limit the amount used.

Corn oil is one of the most popular oils, as it is economical and highly versatile. It is made from pressed sweetcorn kernels and is deep yellow in colour. Corn oil is suitable for deep frying and quick shallow frying; it can also be substituted for margarine when making pastry.

Cottonseed oil is used as a pure oil in the United States both for cooking and for salads. In Britain it is used as an ingredient in blended oils and margarines.

Groundnut (or peanut or arachide) oil is pale in colour with a very mild flavour. It is suitable for salads, stir-frying and deep frying.

Mustard oil is used in Indian cooking, particularly for making hot pickles. It has a strong flavour which diminishes as it is heated; for this reason, mustard oil is not used as part of a cold dressing. Mustard oil can be bought in Asian grocers' shops; it is an expensive oil.

Olive oil is the finest cooking oil. With its unique flavour it is used for salad dressings and also as a dressing for cooked vegetables and pasta. It can be used in mayonnaise, although some people find its flavour too strong for this. It is excellent for shallow frying but, because of its low smoking temperature, it is not suitable for deep frying.

Two types of olive oil are produced, virgin and pure. Virgin olive oil is made from the pulp of high-grade fruit without the stone and is never deodorised or bleached; it is green in colour with a rich flavour and is the more expensive of the two types. Pure olive oil is produced by pressing fruit, stone and pith and is yellow without as rich a flavour.

Rape-seed oil is not used as a pure oil but is commonly an ingredient in margarines and blended cooking oils; it is also found in some curry pastes. Rape-seed oil is high in monounsaturated fats. One of its constituents is a fatty acid called eracic acid which, when fed to animals in large quantities, causes adverse changes in the circulatory system. For this reason, EEC and British regulations limit the amount of eracic acid in edible oils and foods to 50 per cent of the total fat content.

Safflower oil has a polyunsaturated fat content of 75 per cent and is a good source of vitamin E. With its mild flavour it is excellent for salad dressings and mayonnaise. However, it is not suitable for deep frying.

Sesame oil has a deep amber colour and pronounced nutty flavour. It can be used for stir-frying, sautéing and in salad dressings. It is also often used in Chinese cooking as a final garnish and to add gloss to a dish. Sesame oil is one of the more expensive oils.

Soya oil has either a light amber or pale green colour and a heavy texture; it may also have a slightly fishy flavour. It can be used for stir-frying and in salad dressings; it is often used as a constituent of blended oils, margarines and commercial salad dressings. It is composed of 55 per cent polyunsaturated fat, 25 per cent monounsaturated and 10 per cent saturated.

Sunflower oil is one of the most popular oils. It has a mild flavour, light texture and pale yellow colour; it is suitable for all types of salad dressing, including mayonnaise. Commercially it is used for margarines and some salad dressings.

Walnut oil is an expensive oil with a fine, nutty flavour. It is used in salad dressings, and for moistening cooked vegetables and pasta.

Blended oils usually include soya, rape and cottonseed. Blended oils should be avoided because they are high in saturated fats; in addition, their flavour is generally poor.

REFINED AND UNREFINED OILS

Most oils that are available in the supermarket have been refined as part of their manufacturing process. When oils are first pressed, they contain minerals and vitamins which include lecithin and a natural preservative, usually vitamin E. Most of these nutrients are chemically removed in the refining process, which lengthens the oil's shelf life. If an oil is unrefined, this will be marked on the label. A further process that the oil may go through is that of winterising, a chilling process that prevents the oil becoming cloudy in cold conditions.

COLD PRESSED OILS

The best oils are 'cold pressed' which means that the nut, seed or fruit is not subjected to heat to extract the oil. In cold-pressing the nut or seed is pressed by a screw or press, to produce a highly-coloured, richly-flavoured oil that is excellent for salad dressings.

Most other oils are solvent extracted. In this process a chemical solvent is added either to the complete nut or seed or to the residue left from cold pressing. The oil dissolves into the solvent which then evaporates. Most solvent extracted oils are then refined.

BUYING AND STORING OILS

Oils can be bought in containers of varying sizes. If you use a great deal of one particular type it may be economical to buy it in 5 litre (9 pint) cans and pour it into smaller bottles as required. Oils should be stored in a cool, dark place; in these conditions unrefined oils will keep for up to six months, and refined oils for up to one year.

Essential fatty acids are so-called because they are necessary in the diet. Linoleic acid is the most important of these—without it, the body cannot make fats properly. Linoleic and linolenic acids are converted into another essential fatty acid, arachidonic acid. This is important for fat formation, proper growth, healthy skin and the manufacture of the hormones which regulate the body's use of cholesterol. Vegetable oils such as corn oil and soya bean oil contain linoleic acid; linseed oil contains linolenic acid.

ESSENTIAL FATTY ACIDS
(g per 100 g)

Oil	Saturated	Monounsaturated	Polyunsaturated	linoleic	linolenic
Coconut	75.9	7.0		1.8	0.0
Corn	17.2	30.7		50.0	1.6
Olive	14.7	73.0		11.0	0.7
Groundnut (peanut)	19.7	50.1		29.0	0.8
Safflower	10.7	13.2		75.0	0.5
Sunflower	13.7	33.3		52.0	0.3

USING OILS

The following guide shows which oils are suitable for different cooking methods.

FOR DEEP FRYING corn and groundnut oil

FOR SHALLOW FRYING corn, groundnut, soya and olive oil

FOR STIR-FRYING corn, groundnut, soya and sesame oil

FOR CAKES AND PASTRIES corn oil

The following oils are particularly suitable for making salad dressings and mayonnaise:
olive, safflower, sunflower, sesame, soya, walnut and groundnut oil.
Almond oil is only suitable for making mayonnaise.

HERB OILS

Give piquancy to salad dressings by adding herbs to good quality oils.

MAKES 300 ML (½ PINT) HERB OIL
110 CALORIES PER 15 ML (1 TBSP)

4 sprigs fresh thyme
4 sprigs fresh tarragon
4 sprigs fresh marjoram
300 ml (½ pint) sunflower, groundnut (peanut), safflower or mild-flavoured olive oil

———1———

Put the herb sprigs into a glass jar and pour in the oil. Cover with a non-corrosive top. Leave the jar in a cool place for 2 weeks, shaking once a day.

———2———

Strain the oil, pressing down hard on the herbs sprigs. Taste, and if the flavour is not sufficiently strong, add more herbs and repeat the process.

———3———

Pour the flavoured oil into a bottle and seal tightly. The oil may be used immediately and is best used within 2 months.

VARIATIONS

• Most fresh herbs can be used to flavour oil. Others that are most suitable include rosemary, fennel, savory, sage and basil. Use the same method as in the above recipe.

• For chilli oil, use 12 dried chillis bruised but not sliced.

• You can also mix herbs and spices to make oils. Try 6 thyme sprigs plus 15 ml (1 tbsp) coriander seeds, bruised but not crushed.

• For lemon oil, use the thinly pared rind of 1 lemon.

• Chopped or slivered garlic can be added to any of the above.

GOODNESS GUIDE

FAT Sunflower and safflower oils are high in polyunsaturates, and groundnut and olive oils are monounsaturated, so the saturated fat content of these oils is low. Oils are a source of essential fatty acids necessary for the production of some hormones

STUFFED COURGETTES

Gruyère cheese complements the walnuts as it has a nut-like flavour.

SERVES 4 185 calories per serving
PREPARATION 10 minutes
COOKING 20 minutes

8 small courgettes, trimmed and halved lengthways
100 g (4 oz) sweetcorn kernels
50 g (2 oz) Gruyère cheese, grated
50 g (2 oz) walnuts, finely chopped
walnut halves, to garnish (optional)

——— 1 ———
Carefully scoop out the flesh from the courgettes. Finely chop the flesh and reserve the shells. Put the flesh in a saucepan with the sweetcorn and gently cook over a low heat for 10 minutes. Stir in the cheese and walnuts and cook for a further 2 minutes.

——— 2 ———
Put the mixture in a blender or food processor and purée until smooth. Fill each courgette shell with the stuffing and lay them in a baking tin. Pour in 150 ml ($\frac{1}{4}$ pint) water and cover with foil.

——— 3 ———
Cook at 190°C (375°F) mark 5 for 10 minutes or until the courgettes are just tender. Serve immediately, garnished with walnut halves.

GOODNESS GUIDE

STUFFED COURGETTES
FIBRE The courgettes, sweetcorn and walnuts make this a high-fibre dish
PROTEIN The cheese, walnuts and sweetcorn all provide protein
VITAMINS B vitamins are present in the cheese, sweetcorn and walnuts. The courgettes provide vitamin C, necessary for healthy connective tissue

ONION BHAJIS (Far Right)
FAT These onion bhajis are lower in fat than when made using the traditional recipe
FIBRE Wholemeal flour provides fibre. The onion also supplies a little fibre
MINERALS Calcium and iron are supplied by the egg, flour and spices. The milk also supplies calcium

FRENCH BEAN CRUMBLE

When adding the dried herbs crumble them in your fingers to release their full aroma and flavour.

SERVES 4 115 calories per serving
PREPARATION 15 minutes
COOKING 15 minutes

75 g (3 oz) fresh wholemeal breadcrumbs
50 g (2 oz) blanched almonds, finely chopped
30 ml (2 tbsp) chopped fresh parsley
1.25 ml ($\frac{1}{4}$ tsp) dried sage
1.25 ml ($\frac{1}{4}$ tsp) dried rosemary
1.25 ml ($\frac{1}{4}$ tsp) dried thyme
225 g (8 oz) French beans, topped and tailed

——— 1 ———
Mix together the breadcrumbs, almonds, parsley, sage, rosemary and thyme and toast under a medium grill for about 9–10 minutes, until golden brown. Place in the serving dish. Set aside and keep warm.

——— 2 ———
Cook the beans in boiling water for 4–5 minutes or until just tender. Drain the beans and mix with the breadcrumbs. Serve immediately.

STUFFED COURGETTES

FRENCH BEAN CRUMBLE

GOODNESS GUIDE

FRENCH BEAN CRUMBLE

VITAMINS Fresh parsley and beans provide vitamins A and C. B vitamins are present in the breadcrumbs and almonds

PROTEIN The breadcrumbs and almonds provide a good balance of protein

FIBRE All of the ingredients contribute fibre, making this a high fibre dish, necessary for healthy bowel movements

ROSTI

FIBRE Leaving the skins on the potatoes greatly increases the fibre content

FAT Only a little oil is used in this dish and all the vegetables are very low in fat

VITAMINS The potato and onion provide vitamin C needed for healthy connective tissue like bone cartilage

---

ROSTI

Try this nutritious version of the traditional Swiss fried potato dish, made with grated potato.

SERVES 4 130 calories per serving
PREPARATION 20 minutes
COOKING 30–35 minutes

450 g (1 lb) potatoes, scrubbed and grated
1 onion, skinned and grated
45 ml (3 tbsp) chopped fresh parsley
1.25 ml ($\frac{1}{4}$ tsp) grated nutmeg
salt and pepper, to taste
15 ml (1 tbsp) oil
parsley sprig, to garnish

——— 1 ———

Thoroughly mix together the potatoes, onion, parsley, nutmeg and seasoning.

——— 2 ———

Heat the oil in a large non-stick frying pan and add the potato mixture, patting it down to form a firm cake.

——— 3———

Cook very gently for about 15 minutes on each side until firm and golden. If the Rosti breaks up a bit when you turn it don't worry, as it is easy to pat back into shape with a wooden spoon. Remove from the pan and serve immediately.

ONION BHAJIS

MAKES 16 40 calories each
PREPARATION 5 minutes
COOKING 16–24 minutes

5 ml (1 tsp) corn oil
50 g (2 oz) self-raising wholemeal flour
50 g (2 oz) self-raising flour
10 ml (2 tsp) ground coriander
10 ml (2 tsp) ground cumin
5 ml (1 tsp) turmeric
2.5–5 ml ($\frac{1}{2}$–1 tsp) chilli powder
1 egg
150 ml ($\frac{1}{4}$ pint) semi-skimmed milk
2 large Spanish onions, skinned and chopped
fresh coriander and onion rings, to garnish

——— 1 ———

Lightly grease a non-stick frying pan; set aside. Sift the flours and spices into a bowl, and add the bran from the sieve. Add the egg, and half the milk and beat until smooth. Beat in the remaining milk and mix in the onions.

——— 2———

Heat the pan, then drop in dessertspoonfuls of the mixture. Cook until bubbles burst on the surface. Turn over. Allow 2–3 minutes each side. Cook remaining mixture.

ROSTI

ONION BHAJIS

MANGE-TOUT SALAD

SERVES 4 115 calories per serving
PREPARATION 8 minutes
COOKING 5–6 minutes

**grated rind and juice of 1 orange
450 g (1 lb) mange-tout
4 spring onions, chopped
10 ml (2 tsp) chopped fresh mint
5 outer leaves of Cos lettuce, shredded
1 orange, peeled and segmented
150 ml (5 fl oz) low-fat natural yogurt
pepper, to taste
10 ml (2 tsp) sesame seeds, toasted**

———1———

Put half the grated orange rind and all of the juice into a saucepan with the mange-tout, spring onions, mint and 45 ml (3 tbsp) water. Cover, bring to the boil and cook for 4 minutes. Add the lettuce and cook for 1–2 minutes or until the mange-tout are tender but still crisp.

———2———

Drain, then arrange the vegetables on a serving platter. Set aside to cool.

———3———

To make the dressing, cut each orange segment into 4. Put into a small bowl and add the remaining orange rind, the yogurt and season-ing. Mix well. Spoon the dressing over the prepared salad and sprinkle with the sesame seeds.

MICROWAVE To toast sesame seeds, spread on a plate, cook, uncovered, 100% (High) 5 minutes, stirring once. Put half the orange rind and all the juice into a bowl with mange-tout, spring onions, mint, 45 ml (3 tbsp) water. Cover, cook 100% (High) 7–8 minutes, stirring twice, until just tender. Stir in lettuce, cover, cook 100% (High) ½ minute. Complete recipe.

GOODNESS GUIDE

FIBRE The mange-tout provide lots of fibre; extra fibre is supplied by the orange and sesame seeds

VITAMINS Vitamin C is present in all the vegetables. B vitamins, especially riboflavin, are contributed by the yogurt. Riboflavin is essential for fertility, growth, healthy skin and eyes

WALNUT COLESLAW

Caraway seeds are traditionally thought of as a natural anti-flatulence agent, which may explain their popularity in cabbage-based dishes.

SERVES 4 210 calories per serving
PREPARATION 10 minutes
COOKING 2–3 minutes

**350 g (12 oz) mixed white cabbage and Chinese leaves, finely shredded
50 g (2 oz) walnuts, chopped
1 pear, cored and diced
75 g (3 oz) grapes, halved
10 ml (2 tsp) caraway seeds, lightly toasted and crushed**

SOURED CREAM DRESSING

**150 ml (5 fl oz) soured cream
10 ml (2 tsp) clear honey
2.5 ml (½ tsp) mustard powder
salt and pepper, to taste
15 ml (1 tbsp) cornflour
juice of 1 lemon**

———1———

To make the dressing, mix the cream, honey, mustard, seasoning and cornflour to a paste with 15 ml (1 tbsp) cold water. Put the mixture in the top of a double saucepan over simmering water. Stir constantly for 2–3 minutes, then add the lemon juice, stirring well. Set aside to cool.

———2———

Mix the white cabbage, Chinese leaves, walnuts, diced pear and grapes in a bowl. Add the dressing, either warm or cold, and toss well. Sprinkle over caraway seeds. Serve.

GOODNESS GUIDE

VITAMINS The cabbage, Chinese leaves, pear and grapes provide good sources of vitamin C. The walnuts are a good source of B vitamins and vitamin E

MINERALS Chinese leaves and caraway seeds are high in calcium, magnesium and iron. The vegetables, fruit, nuts and seeds also provide potassium which is essential for the body's fluid balance

MANGE-TOUT SALAD

WALNUT COLESLAW

GREEN BEAN SALAD

SERVES 4 140 calories per serving
PREPARATION 10 minutes
COOKING 5–8 minutes

grated rind of 1 lemon
fresh basil sprig
pepper, to taste
100 g (4 oz) shelled broad beans
100 g (4 oz) small whole French
beans, trimmed
100 g (4 oz) runner beans, trimmed and cut
diagonally into 5 cm (2 inch) pieces
2 shallots, skinned and finely chopped
10 ml (2 tsp) chopped fresh basil
30 ml (2 tbsp) lemon juice
60 ml (4 tbsp) olive oil
15 ml (1 tbsp) sunflower seeds

——— 1 ———

Put half the lemon rind, the basil
sprig, seasoning and 300 ml (½ pint)
water in a saucepan. Bring to the
boil, then add the broad beans,
French beans, runner beans and
shallots. Cover and simmer for 5–8
minutes, until the beans are tender
but still crisp.

——— 2 ———

Drain, discarding the basil sprig.
Arrange the vegetables on a serving
platter and leave to cool.

——— 3 ———

To make the dressing, put the remaining lemon rind, the chopped
basil, lemon juice, olive oil and
seasoning into a screw-topped jar.
Shake well until blended. Pour over
the beans and sprinkle with the
sunflower seeds.

MICROWAVE Put half lemon rind,
basil sprig, seasoning and 100 ml
(4 fl oz) boiling water into a bowl
with prepared beans and shallots.
Cover, cook 100% (High) 7–8
minutes, stirring once, until beans
are tender but still crisp. Drain and
discard basil sprig. Arrange on
serving dish. Complete recipe.

GOODNESS GUIDE

GREEN BEAN SALAD

VITAMINS AND MINERALS The beans provide
vitamin C and iron. The vitamin C present in
the beans helps the body to absorb the iron
more readily; iron is involved with the
transport of oxygen in our blood

ORANGE AND ONION SALAD

VITAMINS The fresh vegetables and oranges
provide a good supply of vitamin C. Vitamin
C is essential for healthy skin and wound
healing
FIBRE The vegetables and fruit supply a
good helping of fibre

ORANGE AND ONION SALAD

SERVES 4 140 calories per serving
PREPARATION 10 minutes
COOKING None

2 heads of chicory, separated into leaves
3 large oranges, peeled and cut into
very thin slices
1 Spanish onion, skinned and thinly sliced
12 black olives, stoned

ORANGE DRESSING
45 ml (3 tbsp) orange juice
45 ml (3 tbsp) olive oil
15 ml (1 tbsp) chopped fresh tarragon
pepper, to taste

——— 1 ———

Place the chicory leaves on a serving
platter and arrange the orange slices
and onion rings on top. Decorate
with the olives.

——— 2 ———

To make the dressing, put the
orange juice in a small bowl.
Gradually beat in the olive oil, tarragon and seasoning. Pour over the
prepared salad. Leave to stand for 5
minutes before serving to allow
flavours to blend.

ORANGE AND ONION SALAD

GREEN BEAN SALAD

CURRIED OKRA

Okra (ladies' fingers or gumbo) come from Africa and are eaten either fresh, cooked, canned or dried. They can be used to thicken soups and stews or eaten as a vegetable on their own.

SERVES 4   80 calories per serving
PREPARATION   15 minutes
COOKING   20 minutes

225 g (8 oz) potatoes, scrubbed and cut into fingers
10 ml (2 tsp) corn oil
2 garlic cloves, skinned and crushed
½ fresh green chilli, seeded and cut into 4 pieces
1 large onion, finely chopped
2.5 ml (½ tsp) turmeric
2.5 ml (½ tsp) garam masala
225 g (8 oz) okra, ends barely trimmed
1 tomato, cut into wedges, to garnish

———1———
Put the potatoes in a small saucepan and add boiling water to a depth of 0.5 cm (¼ inch). Cover and simmer for 10 minutes.

———2———
Meanwhile, heat half the oil in a thick-based saucepan and cook the garlic and chilli over a low heat for 2 minutes. Add the onion, cover the pan and cook for 6 minutes. Stir in the turmeric and garam masala and cook for a further 2 minutes.

———3———
Drain the potatoes, reserving the cooking water. Add to the onion-spice mixture with the okra and remaining oil. Stir for 1 minute, then increase the heat and add the potato cooking water. Cover and simmer for 5–6 minutes, until the okra are just tender but still bright green. Serve hot, garnished with tomato.

GOODNESS GUIDE
FIBRE The potatoes, okra and other vegetables provide large amounts of fibre
MINERALS Okra is a good source of calcium, magnesium and potassium. Potassium is needed for proper fluid balance in the cells
VITAMINS Okra is high in vitamin C and together with the other vegetables and spices provides a good helping

AUBERGINE PARMESAN

SERVES 4   120 calories per serving
PREPARATION   4 minutes
COOKING   25 minutes

45 ml (3 tbsp) corn oil
2 large aubergines, cut into rings 1 cm (½ inch) thick
pepper, to taste
10 ml (2 tsp) chopped fresh marjoram or 5 ml (1 tsp) dried
30 ml (2 tbsp) fresh wholemeal breadcrumbs
15 ml (1 tbsp) grated Parmesan cheese
fresh marjoram, to garnish

———1———
Lightly grease a 900 ml (1½ pint) ovenproof dish with 5 ml (1 tsp) of the oil and set aside

———2———
Blanch the aubergines in boiling water for 3 minutes and drain well. Brush the slices on both sides with the remaining oil. Put in layers in the dish, sprinkling each layer with seasoning and marjoram.

———3———
Mix the breadcrumbs and Parmesan cheese together. Sprinkle over the aubergines. Bake at 190°C (375°F) mark 5 for 25 minutes, until the aubergines are tender and the topping crisp. Serve hot. Garnish with fresh marjoram.

MICROWAVE Complete step 1. Put aubergine into a bowl with 300 ml (½ pint) boiling water. Cover, cook 100% (High) 6 minutes, stirring twice. Drain well. Brush slices on both sides with oil. Layer in the casserole, sprinkle with seasoning and marjoram. Mix breadcrumbs and Parmesan and sprinkle over aubergine. Cover, cook 100% (High) 10 minutes, turning casserole once, until aubergine is tender. Brown surface under a preheated grill if liked.

GOODNESS GUIDE
FIBRE Fibre is supplied by the aubergine and wholemeal breadcrumbs
PROTEIN The cheese and breadcrumbs provide a little protein
VITAMINS The cheese and breadcrumbs provide some B vitamins which help the body utilise energy from our food. The aubergine and fresh marjoram are a source of some vitamin C

BANANA SALAD

Nuts, raisins, coconut and banana are well known partners; combine these with the other ingredients and you have an exotic salad which can be eaten year round.

SERVES 4   274 calories per serving
PREPARATION   10 minutes
COOKING   None

1 grapefruit
3 bananas
50 g (2 oz) flaked almonds, roasted
50 g (2 oz) raisins, rinsed
4 small baby carrots, scrubbed and thinly sliced
15 ml (1 tbsp) white wine vinegar
45 ml (3 tbsp) olive oil
5 ml (1 tsp) clear honey
pepper, to taste
1 Cos lettuce heart, separated
15 ml (1 tbsp) unsweetened flaked coconut

———1———
Peel the grapefruit over a bowl to catch all the juices. Divide the flesh into segments and dice.

———2———
Peel and thinly slice the bananas and toss in the grapefruit juice until well coated. Drain, reserving the juice, then put the bananas in a bowl with the grapefruit segments, almonds, raisins and carrots.

———3———
Put the reserved grapefruit juice, vinegar, oil, honey and seasoning in a screw-topped jar and shake well until blended. Pour over the salad and toss together.

———4———
Place the lettuce leaves on a serving platter or in a salad bowl and arrange the salad on top. Sprinkle with the flaked coconut and serve immediately.

GOODNESS GUIDE
FIBRE The vegetables, fruit and nuts provide a good supply of fibre, for healthy bowel movements
VITAMINS Vitamin C is present in the fresh fruit and vegetables. Vitamin C is water-soluble and cannot be stored in the body; some is required every day
MINERALS The dried fruit and nuts are a source of iron, and all the fruit and vegetables provide potassium. Potassium is needed for proper fluid balance in the cells

BANANA SALAD

AUBERGINE PARMESAN

CURRIED OKRA

HUNGARIAN MUSHROOMS

This piquant side dish is the perfect accompaniment to cold roast meat such as pork, chicken or beef.

SERVES 4 35 calories per serving
PREPARATION 10 minutes
COOKING 5 minutes

1 small onion, skinned and grated
60 ml (4 tbsp) tomato juice
350 g (12 oz) button mushrooms, halved or quartered, depending on size
7.5 ml (1½ tsp) paprika
celery salt and pepper, to taste
45 ml (3 tbsp) Greek strained yogurt
chopped fresh parsley, to garnish

——— 1 ———

Cook the onion gently in the tomato juice for 1 minute, stirring occasionally. Add the mushrooms and cook over high heat for 2 minutes, tossing or stirring frequently.

——— 2 ———

Add the paprika and celery salt and pepper to taste and mix well. Stir in the yogurt. Heat through very gently for 1–2 minutes. Serve sprinkled with parsley.

MICROWAVE Put onion and tomato juice into a bowl. Cover and cook 100% (High) 2 minutes. Add mushrooms, paprika, celery salt and pepper. Cover and cook 100% (High) 1½ minutes. Add yogurt and cook, uncovered, 100% (High) 1 minute. Turn into serving dish, garnish and serve immediately.

GOODNESS GUIDE

MINERALS One serving of the mushrooms in this dish will provide nearly 10 per cent of the daily recommended amount of iron and a high amount of potassium. Iron helps form the oxygen-carrying substance in the red blood cells
VITAMINS The tomato juice provides some vitamin A, and all the vegetables provide vitamin C. The yogurt supplies some B vitamins

MINTED PEAS WITH CUCUMBER

If fresh peas are not available, this dish can be made with frozen peas; cook them in the minimum of boiling water until just tender.

SERVES 4 110 calories per serving
PREPARATION 15 minutes
COOKING 22 minutes

350 g (12 oz) shelled fresh peas
25 g (1 oz) polyunsaturated margarine
½ cucumber, peeled and diced
10 ml (2 tsp) orange juice
15 ml (1 tbsp) chopped fresh parsley
15 ml (1 tbsp) chopped fresh mint, or 7.5 ml (1½ tsp) dried
15 ml (1 tbsp) chopped fresh lemon thyme, or 7.5 ml (1½ tsp) dried
salt and pepper, to taste

——— 1 ———

Cook the peas in boiling water for 15 minutes, or until nearly tender but still crunchy. Drain well.

HUNGARIAN MUSHROOMS

MINTED PEAS WITH CUCUMBER

194

2

Return to the pan with the margarine, cucumber and orange juice. Cover tightly and cook gently for a further 5 minutes, stirring frequently.

3

Add the herbs and seasoning and cook for a further 2 minutes, stirring occasionally. Serve hot.

MICROWAVE Put fresh peas into a bowl with 45 ml (3 tbsp) water. Cover and cook 100% (High) 5 minutes. Drain well. Return to bowl with margarine, cucumber, orange juice, herbs and seasoning. Cook, uncovered, 100% (High) 4 minutes.

GOODNESS GUIDE

VITAMINS Peas are a good source of vitamin A, which is needed for dim-light vision and healthy skin and hair. It also provides vitamin C, as well as some B-complex vitamins such as thiamine, riboflavin and niacin

FAT The only added fat is the polyunsaturated margarine, so this dish is quite low in fat

---

NORMANDY BEANS

To make the apple purée, slit a small eating apple around the middle and bake in an ovenproof dish at 200°C (400°F) mark 6 for 45 minutes, or cook in the microwave oven at 60% (Medium) for 5 minutes. Set aside to cool, then remove and discard the skin and core. Purée in a blender or food processor or mash by hand.

SERVES 4 45 calories per serving
PREPARATION 10 minutes
COOKING 10 minutes

350 g (12 oz) French beans, cut into 2.5 cm (1 inch) pieces
1 spring onion, chopped
45 ml (3 tbsp) unsweetened apple purée
15 ml (1 tbsp) French dressing
5 ml (1 tsp) chopped fresh parsley
25 g (1 oz) flaked almonds, toasted
salt and pepper, to taste

1

Cook the beans in boiling water for about 5 minutes, or until tender but still crunchy. Drain, return to pan.

2

Add the spring onion, apple purée and French dressing. Toss over a high heat for about 1 minute, then cover and cook over a gentle heat for 2–3 minutes, stirring occasionally. Add the parsley, almonds and seasoning and serve.

MICROWAVE Put prepared beans into a bowl with 60 ml (4 tbsp) water. Cover and cook 100% (High) 7 minutes. Drain well. Return to bowl with spring onion, apple purée and French dressing. Cook, uncovered, 100% (High) 2–3 minutes. Complete the recipe.

GOODNESS GUIDE

VITAMINS The beans provide vitamin A and a little vitamin C. Almonds are a good source of B-complex vitamins, which are involved in energy production from carbohydrates, fats and proteins

---

NORMANDY BEANS

BEANSPROUT SALAD

SERVES 4 180 calories per serving
PREPARATION 15 minutes
COOKING None
CHILLING Up to 30 minutes

25 ml (1½ tbsp) soy sauce, preferably
naturally fermented shoyu
45 ml (3 tbsp) apple juice
30 ml (2 tbsp) sunflower or safflower oil
pepper, to taste
few drops lemon juice
450 g (1 lb) fresh beansprouts
175 g (6 oz) carrots, scrubbed and grated
1 crisp eating apple, cored and grated
60 ml (4 tbsp) finely chopped naturally
roasted peanuts

———1———

In a large bowl, mix together the soy
sauce, apple juice, oil, seasoning
and a few drops of lemon juice. Add
the beansprouts, carrots and apple
and mix thoroughly.

———2———

Sprinkle the nuts over the salad and
mix well. Cover and chill for up to 30
minutes, until ready to serve.

GOODNESS GUIDE

VITAMINS Sprouted beans are high in
vitamin C and also provide B vitamins
FAT Sunflower and safflower oils are good
sources of essential fatty acids
FIBRE The salad is high in fibre
PROTEIN Peanuts are full of protein

FLORENCE FENNEL SALAD

*The fennel bulb, with its strong
aniseed flavour, is known as
Florence fennel to distinguish it
from the herb fennel.*

SERVES 4 125 calories per serving
PREPARATION 20 minutes
COOKING None

1 red pepper, cored, seeded and very
thinly sliced
1 fennel bulb, halved and very thinly sliced
1 small onion, skinned and very thinly sliced
½ crisp green lettuce
75 g (3 oz) feta cheese, broken into cubes
3 stoned black olives, sliced

MUSTARD DRESSING
1 garlic clove, skinned and crushed
2.5 ml (½ tsp) whole grain mustard
30 ml (2 tbsp) sunflower or safflower oil
30 ml (2 tbsp) cider vinegar
salt and pepper, to taste
5 ml (1 tsp) chopped fresh parsley

———1———

Combine the crushed garlic, mustard,
sunflower or safflower oil, cider
vinegar, seasoning and chopped
parsley in a mixing bowl and whisk
well. Add the sliced red pepper,
fennel and onion and toss to coat.

———2———

Line a salad bowl with the lettuce
leaves and pile the fennel mixture on
top. Scatter over the cheese and
olives and serve.

GOODNESS GUIDE

FIBRE The vegetables provide lots of fibre
VITAMINS This is a vitamin-rich salad, with
A in the pepper, C in all the fresh
vegetables, and B-complex vitamins in the
feta cheese. Vitamin C is highest in raw
fresh fruit and vegetables. Among the many
functions of vitamin C, it is necessary for a
healthy immune system and for healthy
tissues. Vitamin A assists in the formation
and maintenance of healthy hair, skin and
mucous membranes

WATERCRESS AND ORANGE SALAD WITH WALNUT DRESSING

*This versatile salad is a good
accompaniment to grilled chicken
or fish, as well as being a
substantial lunch salad for two
persons.*

SERVES 4 160 calories per serving
PREPARATION 10 minutes
COOKING None

1 bunch watercress
¼ head endive, divided into leaves
2 oranges, peeled and segmented
2 slices granary or wholemeal bread, cubed
50 g (2 oz) walnuts
15 ml (1 tbsp) soya oil
100 g (4 oz) set low-fat natural yogurt
salt and pepper, to taste

———1———

Arrange the watercress, endive and
orange segments in a salad bowl.
Scatter over the bread cubes.

———2———

Put the walnuts, oil, yogurt and
seasoning into a blender or food
processor and blend for 2–3
minutes, to give a thick, fairly
smooth dressing. Spoon over the
salad. Toss and serve immediately.

GOODNESS GUIDE

MINERALS Watercress and walnuts provide
iron and calcium
PROTEIN Yogurt and walnuts are both good
sources of protein
VITAMINS Watercress and oranges supply
vitamins A and C. Watercress supplies folic
acid for healthy red blood cells. Walnuts
supply B vitamins

WATERCRESS AND ORANGE SALAD
WITH WALNUT DRESSING

FLORENCE FENNEL SALAD

BEANSPROUT SALAD

SUMMER VEGETABLES WITH YOGURT

Peas are delicious with yogurt, so when mange-tout are unavailable, add fresh garden peas, or frozen, and use basil instead of mint to flavour.

SERVES 4 80 calories per serving
PREPARATION 10 minutes
COOKING About 10 minutes

225 g (8 oz) carrots, scrubbed and cut into
4 cm (1½ inch) long narrow sticks
100 g (4 oz) spring onions, trimmed and cut
into 1 cm (½ inch) lengths
225 g (8 oz) mange-tout, trimmed
150 ml (5 fl oz) low-fat natural yogurt
pepper, to taste
15 ml (1 tbsp) chopped fresh mint
mint sprig, to garnish

———1———

Place the carrots in a steamer over a saucepan of gently simmering water and steam for 5 minutes. Add the spring onions and mange-tout and steam for a further 5 minutes or until cooked and tender.

———2———

Heat the yogurt in a saucepan over a very low heat for just 1 minute. Add the steamed vegetables, seasoning and chopped mint, and toss to coat thoroughly. Turn into a serving dish, garnish with a mint sprig and serve.

MICROWAVE Place the carrots in a bowl with 75 ml (3 fl oz) water. Cover and cook 100% (High) 5 minutes. Add onion and mange-tout, cover and cook 100% (High) 5 minutes. Drain thoroughly. Place the yogurt, mint and vegetables in the bowl, toss to coat, cover and cook 100% (High) 2 minutes. Turn into a serving dish, garnish with a mint sprig and serve at once.

GOODNESS GUIDE

FIBRE The carrots and spring onions provide a good deal of fibre
VITAMINS All the vegetables contain vitamin C. The carrots are also an excellent source of vitamin A, which is needed for proper bone growth and maintaining healthy skin and hair
MINERALS The spring onions supply calcium and iron, and the yogurt provides calcium

FENNEL AND POTATO BAKE

This side dish makes a good accompaniment to beef and poultry dishes.

SERVES 4 265 calories per serving
PREPARATION 10 minutes
COOKING 1¾ hours

25 g (1 oz) polyunsaturated margarine
700 g (1½ lb) potatoes, scrubbed
1 fennel bulb, trimmed
1.25 ml (¼ tsp) grated nutmeg
salt and pepper, to taste
300 ml (½ pint) semi-skimmed milk
25 g (1 oz) mature Cheddar cheese,
finely grated

———1———

Lightly grease a 1.7 litre (3 pint) shallow ovenproof dish with a little of the margarine and set aside.

———2———

Cut the potatoes and fennel into very thin slices. Layer, reserving one-third of the potato slices, in the prepared dish, sprinkling each layer with the nutmeg and seasoning. Pour the milk over.

———3———

Arrange the reserved potato slices in a neat overlapping layer on top. Melt the remaining margarine and brush over the potatoes.

SUMMER VEGETABLES WITH YOGURT

FENNEL AND POTATO BAKE

———4———

Cover the dish with aluminium foil and cook at 180°C (350°F) mark 4 for 1 hour. Remove the foil. Sprinkle the grated cheese over the top and cook for a further 45 minutes, until golden and tender. Serve hot.

MICROWAVE Melt the margarine and complete step 2, adding some melted margarine between the layers. Pour milk over. Arrange the rest of the potato slices on top and brush with remaining margarine. Cover and cook 100% (High) 20 minutes, until tender. Sprinkle cheese on top and cook, uncovered, 100% (High) 2 minutes. Brown top under a grill, if liked.

GOODNESS GUIDE
PROTEIN The potatoes and cheese provide protein

FIBRE The fennel and potatoes with their skins on provide a good amount of fibre

VITAMINS Vitamin C is supplied by the potatoes and fennel, and B-complex vitamins by the milk and cheese

MINERALS The milk and cheese are good sources of calcium

LEMON BROCCOLI WITH PINE NUTS

Pine nuts are available at health food shops and specialist grocers. To toast them, place on a tray under the grill and shake until they are just browned.

SERVES 4 130 calories per serving
PREPARATION 5 minutes
COOKING 15 minutes

350 g (12 oz) broccoli, trimmed and cut into florets
25 g (1 oz) polyunsaturated margarine
100 ml (4 fl oz) chicken stock
10 ml (2 tsp) cornflour
30 ml (2 tbsp) lemon juice
40 g (1½ oz) pine nuts, toasted

———1———

Steam the broccoli over a saucepan of gently boiling water, or cook in simmering water, until tender.

———2———

Meanwhile, melt the margarine in the stock in a small non-stick pan and bring to the boil. Blend the cornflour with the lemon juice and stir into the mixture. Bring back to the boil, stirring continuously. Cook for 2 minutes, until smooth and shiny, then stir in the pine nuts.

———3———

Drain the broccoli and arrange in a serving dish. Pour the lemon sauce over and serve at once.

MICROWAVE Put the broccoli into a bowl with 100 ml (4 fl oz) water. Cover and cook 100% (High) 7 minutes. Put the margarine into a bowl with blended cornflour and lemon juice and boiling stock. Cook, uncovered, 100% (High) 1½ minutes, whisking twice. Add the toasted pine nuts to sauce. Complete the recipe.

GOODNESS GUIDE
MINERALS Broccoli is valuable as a source of iron and calcium

VITAMINS The vitamin C in the broccoli and lemon juice enables the iron to be converted into a form which is more easily absorbed by the intestines. Broccoli is also a rich source of vitamin A and of riboflavin, a B-complex vitamin that helps maintain mucous membranes

SALT Use home-made stock to keep this dish low in salt

LEMON BROCCOLI WITH PINE NUTS

STIR-FRIED ASPARAGUS

Take advantage of the lower prices while the British asparagus season is at its height to make this unusual vegetable dish. The lightly toasted sesame seeds sprinkled over the asparagus gives a nutty flavour to this deliciously simple dish.

SERVES 4 60 calories per serving
PREPARATION 15 minutes
COOKING 3 minutes

25 ml (1½ tbsp) sesame seeds
450 g (1 lb) fresh asparagus
30 ml (2 tbsp) corn oil
6 spring onions, trimmed and finely chopped
pepper, to taste
5 ml (1 tsp) grated fresh or bottled horseradish

———1———

Put the sesame seeds on a baking tray and lightly toast at 200°C (400°F) mark 6 for 8–10 minutes. Set aside.

———2———

Discard the woody end of the asparagus spears and scrape the stalks to remove any coarse scales. Cut the asparagus diagonally into 2.5 cm (1 inch) pieces.

———3———

Heat the oil in a frying pan or wok, add the asparagus and spring onions and cook, stirring, for 1 minute. Season with pepper and horseradish and sprinkle in the sesame seeds. Cook briskly for a further 1–2 minutes. Do not overcook the asparagus; it should be very crunchy. Serve hot or cold.

GOODNESS GUIDE

FIBRE The sesame seeds, asparagus and onions provide a good amount of fibre
VITAMINS Asparagus contains carotene, which is converted to vitamin A in the body. Absorption of vitamin A is dependent on the presence of a small amount of fat or oil in the diet
FAT The sesame seeds and corn oil contain essential fatty acids that help the transport of vitamin A into the body from the intestinal tract

SUCCOTASH

SERVES 4 120 calories per serving
PREPARATION 10 minutes
COOKING 15 minutes

200 ml (⅓ pint) vegetable stock
2 small fresh corns on the cob, or
175 g (6 oz) frozen sweetcorn kernels
225 g (8 oz) shelled fresh broad beans
1 small onion, skinned and finely chopped
150 g (5 oz) low-fat soft cheese
45 ml (3 tbsp) low-fat natural yogurt
10 ml (2 tsp) chopped fresh basil or
5 ml (1 tsp) dried
salt and pepper, to taste
fresh basil leaves, to garnish

———1———

Bring the vegetable stock to a boil in a saucepan. Meanwhile, using a sharp knife, remove the kernels from the corn cobs, cutting lengthways down the cobs. Discard the cobs.

———2———

Place the fresh corn kernels in another saucepan with the broad beans and onion. Pour the boiling stock over, bring back to the boil, then lower the heat and cook gently for 8–10 minutes, until the vegetables are just tender. If using frozen corn, add it to the other vegetables halfway through cooking.

———3———

Meanwhile, beat the cheese until creamy, then stir in the yogurt, basil and seasoning.

———4———

Drain the vegetables and return them to the saucepan. Add the cheese and yogurt mixture to the vegetables and reheat gently, stirring continuously, for 2–3 minutes. Serve hot, garnished with the fresh basil leaves.

STIR-FRIED ASPARAGUS

MICROWAVE Put fresh corn kernels, beans, onion and stock into a bowl with 150 ml (¼ pint) water. Cover and cook 100% (High) 6–7 minutes. If using frozen corn, add halfway through cooking. Follow step 3, then drain vegetables and return to bowl. Add the cheese and yogurt mixture to the vegetables and cook, uncovered, 100% (High) 2–3 minutes.

GOODNESS GUIDE

PROTEIN The low-fat cheese and yogurt provide protein which is further enhanced by the protein present in the corn and beans

VITAMINS Fresh broad beans are a source of vitamin C, as are the corn on the cob and onions

FIBRE A high amount of fibre is supplied by the corn, beans and onion

PARMESAN TOMATOES

These tomatoes are a fitting accompaniment to pasta dishes

SERVES 4 55 calories per serving
PREPARATION 20 minutes
GRILLING 3–4 minutes

4 large tomatoes, halved
1 garlic clove, skinned and cut into thin slivers
5 ml (1 tsp) chopped fresh oregano or 2.5 ml (½ tsp) dried
pepper, to taste
25 ml (1½ tbsp) fresh wholemeal breadcrumbs
15 ml (1 tbsp) grated Parmesan cheese
watercress sprigs, to garnish

——— 1 ———

Stud the tomato halves with the garlic slivers and sprinkle over the oregano and seasoning. Leave to stand for 15 minutes, then remove the garlic, if preferred.

——— 2 ———

Mix the wholemeal breadcrumbs with the Parmesan cheese and then sprinkle the mixture over the tops of the tomatoes.

——— 3 ———

Cook under a moderate grill for 3 minutes, then increase the heat to high and cook for a further 30 seconds, until the topping on the tomatoes is crisp and golden brown. Garnish with the watercress sprigs and serve immediately.

GOODNESS GUIDE

VITAMINS Tomatoes are noted for their high content of vitamins A and C. Vitamin A helps maintain healthy skin. Some B-complex vitamins, which are needed for energy production in the body, are provided by the cheese and breadcrumbs

FIBRE The wholemeal breadcrumbs and tomatoes provide some fibre

SUCCOTASH

PARMESAN TOMATOES

201

STRAWBERRY AND CUCUMBER SALAD

This attractive and refreshing fruit and vegetable combination is the perfect summertime accompaniment to cold meats.

SERVES 4   40 calories per serving
PREPARATION 10 minutes
COOKING None
CHILLING 15 minutes

1 small cucumber
10 ml (2 tsp) chopped fresh mint
pepper, to taste
200 ml ($\frac{1}{3}$ pint) unsweetened apple juice
225 g (8 oz) strawberries, hulled
mint sprigs, to garnish

——— 1 ———

With the prongs of a fork, scrape down the sides of the cucumber to make a ridged effect. Slice very thinly and lay in a shallow dish. Sprinkle with the chopped mint and seasoning. Pour 150 ml ($\frac{1}{4}$ pint) of the apple juice over. Chill for 15 minutes.

——— 2 ———

Slice the strawberries if large; otherwise, cut them in half. Put into a small bowl and pour the remaining apple juice over. Chill for 15 minutes.

——— 3 ———

Drain the cucumber and strawberries and arrange them attractively on a serving dish. Garnish with mint.

GOODNESS GUIDE
VITAMINS The strawberries and cucumber provide good amounts of vitamin C. Besides its other roles, vitamin C helps combat allergic responses and aids in the formation of collagen, a protein found in bones and tendons
FIBRE The cucumber and strawberries provide some fibre

SPINACH SALAD

If liked, this tasty and colourful spinach salad can be given a garnish of wholemeal croûtons sprinkled on the top.

SERVES 4   150 calories per serving
PREPARATION 10 minutes
COOKING 3 minutes

450 g (1 lb) young spinach leaves, stems
removed and well washed
75 g (3 oz) button mushrooms, sliced
60 ml (4 tbsp) olive oil
6 spring onions, trimmed and chopped
1 small red pepper, cored, seeded and
chopped
5 ml (1 tsp) French mustard
5 ml (1 tsp) light muscovado sugar
pepper, to taste
30 ml (2 tbsp) white wine vinegar

——— 1 ———

Tear the spinach leaves into small pieces and put into a salad bowl with the mushrooms. Mix together. Chill while preparing the dressing.

——— 2 ———

Put the oil into a small saucepan and heat gently. Add the spring onions and red pepper and cook for 2 minutes. Remove from the heat.

——— 3 ———

Stir in the mustard, sugar and seasoning, then add the vinegar. Return to the heat and cook gently, until nearly boiling. Pour the dressing immediately over the prepared salad, toss and serve.

MICROWAVE Follow step 1. Put oil into a bowl and cook, uncovered, 100% (High) 3 minutes. Add onions and red pepper and cook, uncovered, 100% (High) 2 minutes. Stir in mustard, sugar, seasoning and vinegar. Cook, uncovered, 100% (High) 1 minute. Complete the recipe.

GOODNESS GUIDE
VITAMINS Spinach, like all dark green leafy vegetables, is a source of folic acid, a water-soluble B vitamin. Lack of this vitamin can lead to anaemia, especially in pregnant women, and nerve degeneration. The spinach and red pepper contain carotene
FIBRE The vegetables supply a high amount of fibre

BURGHUL WHEAT SALAD

SERVES 4   175 calories per serving
PREPARATION 10 minutes
COOKING None
SOAKING 30 minutes

100 g (4 oz) burghul wheat
50 g (2 oz) currants, rinsed
6 spring onions, trimmed and chopped
3 tomatoes, diced
juice of 1 orange
30 ml (2 tbsp) chopped fresh parsley
15 ml (1 tbsp) chopped fresh mint
pepper, to taste
30 ml (2 tbsp) olive oil
orange segments and mint sprigs, to garnish

——— 1 ———

Put the burghul wheat in a bowl, cover with cold water and leave to soak for 30 minutes. Drain through a clean piece of muslin or cloth and squeeze well to remove all the water.

——— 2 ———

Return the wheat to the rinsed-out bowl. Add the currants, spring onions and tomatoes and mix together well.

——— 3 ———

Blend together the orange juice, parsley, mint and pepper. Gradually add the olive oil, beating until well blended. Pour over the wheat mixture and leave for 5 minutes.

——— 4 ———

Transfer the salad to a serving dish and garnish with the orange segments and mint sprigs.

GOODNESS GUIDE
FIBRE High fibre is provided by the wheat, currants and vegetables. Choosing such salads is an easy way to increase fibre intake
VITAMINS Wheat supplies B-complex vitamins, which are used to obtain energy from food. Vitamin C is present in all the fresh vegetables and herbs

SPINACH SALAD

BURGHUL WHEAT SALAD

STRAWBERRY AND CUCUMBER SALAD

SAUTEED POTATOES WITH HERBS

Fresh herbs and olive oil give a sunny Mediterranean flavour to this potato side dish.

SERVES 4 275 calories per serving
PREPARATION 10 minutes
COOKING 10–15 minutes

900 g (2 lb) potatoes, scrubbed
30 ml (2 tbsp) corn oil
15 ml (1 tbsp) olive oil
fresh herb sprigs, such as rosemary, thyme and oregano
4 spring onions, white and green parts chopped separately
15 ml (1 tbsp) chopped fresh herbs

————1————

Boil the potatoes in their skins for 10 minutes. Drain and leave to cool. Cut into 1 cm ($\frac{1}{2}$ inch) slices.

————2————

Heat the oils with the sprigs of herbs in a large frying pan. Add the sliced potatoes to the pan and cook over a moderate heat for 10–15 minutes, turning until they are crisp and golden brown. Five minutes before the end of cooking time add the chopped white parts of the spring onions and cook with the potatoes.

————3————

Drain the potatoes on absorbent kitchen paper and remove the sprigs of herbs. Transfer to a warm serving dish and sprinkle with the chopped fresh herbs and reserved spring onion tops.

MICROWAVE Slice uncooked potatoes and put in a dish with 90 ml (3 fl oz) water and cover. Cook 100% (High) 12–13 minutes, stirring 2 or 3 times. Drain. In step 2, put oils and herbs into the cleaned dish and cook 100% (High) 4 minutes. Add potatoes and cook, uncovered, 2 minutes, stirring twice, then add onion and cook a further 2 minutes, stirring once. Complete as recipe.

GOODNESS GUIDE
SALT Excessive salt intake is widely felt to cause high blood pressure and contribute to strokes. This recipe uses herbs and spring onions, rather than salt, to flavour the potatoes
FIBRE Leaving the skins on the potatoes raises the fibre content

FLAGEOLETS IN ROSEMARY SAUCE

Dried green flageolets are available from health food shops. This substantial side dish makes an excellent vegetable accompaniment to roast lamb.

SERVES 4 270 calories per serving
PREPARATION 5 minutes
COOKING About 1$\frac{1}{2}$ hours
SOAKING Overnight

225 g (8 oz) dried green flageolet beans, soaked overnight, drained and rinsed
1 garlic clove, skinned
2 fresh rosemary sprigs
40 g (1$\frac{1}{2}$ oz) polyunsaturated margarine
1 onion, skinned and finely chopped
25 g (1 oz) plain flour
150 ml ($\frac{1}{4}$ pint) semi-skimmed milk
salt and pepper, to taste

————1————

Cover the beans with water and boil for 10–15 minutes, then drain. Place the beans in the rinsed-out saucepan with 750 ml (1$\frac{1}{4}$ pints) water and bring to the boil. Skim any scum from the surface, then add the garlic and 1 rosemary sprig. Cover and simmer for about 1$\frac{1}{4}$ hours, until the beans are tender. Drain, reserving the cooking liquid but discarding the garlic and rosemary.

————2————

Heat the margarine in a saucepan and cook the onion gently for 5 minutes, until soft. Stir in the flour, then the milk. Add 200 ml (7 fl oz) of the cooking liquid and bring to the boil, stirring, until thickened. Add seasoning and the remaining sprig of rosemary.

————3————

Stir in the beans and simmer for 2–3 minutes or until heated through. Serve hot.

GOODNESS GUIDE
PROTEIN The combination of beans and milk is excellent for efficient use of the high protein content
FIBRE Flageolet beans are a very good source of fibre, which stimulates the smooth, efficient working of the bowels
FAT Semi-skimmed milk is used to lower the fat content

SPICED AUBERGINES

The rich, creamy taste of the aubergines is complemented by the tomato and spices in this dish. Serve with poultry.

SERVES 4 130 calories per serving
PREPARATION 15 minutes
COOKING 20–30 minutes

45 ml (3 tbsp) corn oil
700 g (1$\frac{1}{2}$ lb) aubergines, cubed
2 onions, skinned and chopped
1 garlic clove, skinned and crushed
2.5 ml ($\frac{1}{2}$ tsp) ground coriander
2.5 ml ($\frac{1}{2}$ tsp) ground cumin
400 g (14 oz) can chopped tomatoes
15 ml (1 tbsp) chopped fresh coriander or parsley, to garnish

————1————

Heat the oil in a large saucepan and cook the aubergines and onions for 5 minutes, stirring occasionally. Add the garlic and spices and cook, stirring, for 2 minutes.

————2————

Add the tomatoes to the pan with their juice and bring to the boil, stirring. Cover and simmer for 20–30 minutes, until the aubergines are tender. Serve hot with chopped coriander or parsley sprinkled over.

MICROWAVE Put the oil, aubergines and onions in a deep bowl, cover and cook 100% (High) 4 minutes, stirring once. Add the garlic and spices and cook, covered, 100% (High) 4 minutes. In step 2, add the tomatoes, then cover and cook 100% (High) 8–10 minutes, stirring 2 or 3 times. Complete as the recipe.

GOODNESS GUIDE
MINERALS Although only a small amount of coriander is used it is extremely rich in a number of minerals including potassium, which is necessary for the transmission of nerve impulses and muscle contractions
SALT With the strong flavouring supplied by the spices there is no need for any salt to be added

BRAISED CHICORY

SERVES 4   40 calories per serving
PREPARATION   5 minutes
COOKING   5–10 minutes

4 large heads of chicory
300 ml (½ pint) vegetable stock
grated rind and juice of 1 orange
salt and pepper, to taste
grated nutmeg, to taste
25 g (1 oz) hazelnuts, coarsely chopped

———1———

Cut the chicory in half lengthways and place in a saucepan. Pour over the stock, orange rind and juice, seasonings and nuts. Bring to the boil, cover, lower the heat and simmer for 5–10 minutes, until the chicory is tender but still crisp.

———2———

Drain the chicory, reserving the cooking liquid, place in a serving dish and keep warm. Reduce the cooking liquid over a high heat to about 150 ml (¼ pint) and pour over the chicory. Serve hot.

MICROWAVE   Follow step 1, putting the chicory into a dish with the orange rind and juice, 90 ml (3 fl oz) of the stock, seasonings and nuts. Cover and cook 100% (High) 6–8 minutes, rearranging chicory twice. Follow step 2 but do not reduce the cooking liquid.

GOODNESS GUIDE

VITAMINS   The orange juice provides a useful amount of vitamin C. As well as its role in the heating process and for general body maintenance, vitamin C is very effective in eliminating toxins from the system

FAT   Braising the chicory in stock rather than water and fat, the more traditional method, greatly reduces the fat content of this dish

SPICED AUBERGINES

FLAGEOLETS IN ROSEMARY SAUCE

SAUTEED POTATOES WITH HERBS

BRAISED CHICORY

205

APPLE AND RED CABBAGE SALAD

Apple and red cabbage are traditionally served as a hot accompaniment to roast pork. Here they are combined to make a cold, crispy salad which is delicious with cold meats or on its own with cheese and wholemeal bread.

SERVES 4   120 calories per serving
PREPARATION   10 minutes
COOKING   None

250 g (9 oz) red cabbage, finely shredded
2 spring onions, cut into 5 cm (2 inch) lengths and shredded
1 orange, peeled and segmented
1 dessert apple
50 g (2 oz) raisins, rinsed

ORANGE DRESSING
45 ml (3 tbsp) sunflower oil
grated rind and juice of 1 small orange
1.25 ml ($\frac{1}{4}$ tsp) dry mustard
salt and pepper, to taste

———1———

To make the dressing, place all the ingredients in a large serving bowl and mix well.

———2———

Add the red cabbage, spring onions and orange. Cut the apple into quarters, remove the core and slice very thinly into the bowl. Add the raisins and gently toss the salad so all the ingredients are coated with the dressing.

GOODNESS GUIDE

VITAMINS Water-soluble vitamins such as vitamin C are not stored by the body in any quantity and need to be consumed regularly to avoid a deficiency. Vitamin C is easily destroyed during the preparation of food; eating the fruit and vegetables raw in this recipe preserves their substantial C content

NUTTY PILAFF

If you don't want to mould the rice into a ring, simply stir the walnuts into the pilaff at the end of step 2 and serve.

SERVES 4   300 calories per serving
PREPARATION   10 minutes
COOKING   30 minutes

15 ml (1 tbsp) corn oil
1 onion, skinned and chopped
225 g (8 oz) brown rice
600 ml (1 pint) vegetable or chicken stock
5 cm (2 inch) cinnamon stick
1 bay leaf
salt and pepper, to taste
50 g (2 oz) walnut halves, coarsley chopped
shredded lettuce, to serve

———1———

Heat the oil in a saucepan and cook the onion for 5 minutes, stirring, until lightly brown. Add the rice and cook, stirring, for 1 minute. Pour in the stock and add the cinnamon stick, bay leaf and seasoning.

———2———

Bring to the boil, cover, lower the heat and simmer for 30 minutes, until the rice is tender and all the stock has been absorbed. Discard the cinnamon stick and bay leaf.

———3———

To mould the rice, lightly grease a 900 ml (1$\frac{1}{2}$ pint) ring mould and place the chopped walnuts in the bottom. Spoon the cooked rice into the mould on top of the nuts and press down well.

———4———

Run the tip of a sharp knife around the edge of the mould. Place a warmed serving plate on top and invert the mould and plate, giving a sharp shake halfway over. Remove the mould. Garnish the centre with shredded crisp lettuce and serve.

———5———

If prepared in advance, cover with foil and reheat at 180°C (350°F) mark 4 for 20 minutes.

GOODNESS GUIDE

PROTEIN Rice and nuts complement each other well, balancing out each other's deficiencies so that the body can better use their protein content
FIBRE Large amounts of fibre are contributed by the rice and nuts; each serving supplies about 20 per cent of the recommended daily intake

MUSHROOM AND YOGURT SALAD

Because mushrooms have such a high water content they should not be soaked in water or they will shrivel up. Choose ones with firm white caps and just use a damp piece of absorbent kitchen paper to wipe clean.

SERVES 4   100 calories per serving
PREPARATION   20 minutes
COOKING   None

225 g (8 oz) mushrooms, sliced
30 ml (2 tbsp) olive oil
grated rind and juice of 1 lemon
1 garlic clove, skinned and crushed
4–6 spring onions, thinly sliced
1 red or green pepper, cored, seeded and cut into thin strips
150 ml (5 fl oz) low-fat natural yogurt
60 ml (4 tbsp) semi-skimmed milk
15 ml (1 tbsp) chopped fresh parsley
15 ml (1 tbsp) finely shredded fresh mint or basil (optional)
salt and pepper, to taste
25 g (1 oz) walnut halves, roughly chopped
finely shredded spinach, to garnish

———1———

Place mushrooms in a bowl. Sprinkle over the olive oil, lemon rind and juice and garlic. Toss and leave to marinate for 5 minutes. Add the onions and pepper.

———2———

Thin the yogurt with the milk and add the herbs and seasoning. Pour the yogurt dressing over the vegetables and toss well. Stir in the walnuts. Cover and chill until required. Garnish with the spinach and serve.

GOODNESS GUIDE

PROTEIN The yogurt is higher in protein than milk. The milk, mushrooms and walnuts also contribute to the protein content of the dish.
FIBRE A fair amount of fibre is supplied by all the vegetables and the walnuts
FAT Low-fat yogurt and semi-skimmed milk are used in the dressing to provide a creamy texture without giving the dish a high-fat content

MUSHROOM AND YOGURT SALAD

APPLE AND RED CABBAGE SALAD

NUTTY PILAFF

BROCCOLI AND TOMATO SALAD

The salad uses a colourful and unusual combination of vegetables which are available at most times of the year.

SERVES 4 75 calories per serving
PREPARATION 15 minutes
COOKING None

175 g (6 oz) broccoli, divided into florets
225 g (8 oz) tomatoes, sliced
6 radishes, sliced
100 g (4 oz) sweetcorn kernels,
cooked if frozen
chopped fresh parsley, to garnish

TOMATO DRESSING
100 g (4 oz) tomatoes, skinned and seeded
1 garlic clove, skinned and crushed
pepper, to taste
150 ml (5 fl oz) low-fat natural yogurt
15 ml (1 tbsp) tomato purée

———1———

Put the broccoli florets into boiling water and cook for 3 minutes. Drain and cool.

———2———

Arrange the tomatoes on an oval platter. Add the broccoli around the outside edge of the tomatoes and place the radish slices on top of the tomatoes. Place the sweetcorn kernels in the centre.

———3———

To make the dressing, place the tomatoes in a blender of food processor with the garlic, pepper, yogurt and tomato purée and blend until smooth. Serve the dressing separately.

GOODNESS GUIDE
FIBRE A substantial amount of fibre is supplied by all the vegetables, particularly the sweetcorn, which is a very rich source
MINERALS The yogurt and broccoli contain calcium; each serving supplies about 20 per cent of the recommended adult daily intake

CHICORY AND APPLE SALAD

Cheese and apple are a traditional combination; this is a rather different way of serving them.

SERVES 4 120 calories per serving
PREPARATION 15 minutes
COOKING None

1 large red eating apple, cored and diced
1 large green eating apple, cored and diced
juice of $\frac{1}{2}$ orange
225 g (8 oz) chicory, trimmed and
sliced into rings
100 g (4 oz) black grapes, halved and seeded

BLUE CHEESE DRESSING
50 g (2 oz) Roquefort or Danish Blue cheese
150 ml (5 fl oz) low-fat natural yogurt
10 ml (2 tsp) chopped fresh dill or
5 ml (1 tsp) dill weed

———1———

Place the apples in a salad bowl with the orange juice and toss until thoroughly coated. Add the chicory and grapes and mix together well.

———2———

To make the dressing, beat the cheese until smooth, then gradually add the yogurt, beating well until completely blended. Mix in the dill. Pour the dressing over the salad ingredients and stir well.

GOODNESS GUIDE
FAT Using a small amount of a strong-flavoured cheese mixed with low-fat yogurt keeps the overall fat content low
FIBRE The chicory and fruit provide a substantial amount of fibre. Fruit generally, especially soft fruit, is an extremely rich source that is often overlooked

PEPPER SALAD

Removing the skins from the peppers makes them more digestible. The colour mix in this salad is very attractive—most large supermarkets stock a variety of peppers, including the yellow.

SERVES 4 80 calories per serving
PREPARATION 20 minutes
COOKING None

2 red peppers
1 green pepper
1 yellow pepper
15 ml (1 tbsp) white wine vinegar
30 ml (2 tbsp) corn oil
5 ml (1 tsp) clear honey
pepper, to taste
10 ml (2 tsp) chopped fresh parsley
10 ml (2 tsp) sesame seeds, toasted

———1———

Place the peppers under a hot grill and cook for about 10–15 minutes, turning frequently until the skins are shrivelled and partially blackened.

———2———

Peel the peppers under cold running water and then cut in half, discarding the core and seeds. Cut into 2.5 cm (1 inch) pieces and place in a serving bowl.

———3———

Put the vinegar, oil, honey, pepper and parsley in a screw top jar and shake vigorously until well blended.

———4———

Pour over the peppers and sprinkle with the toasted sesame seeds just before serving.

GOODNESS GUIDE
VITAMINS Peppers and parsley are exceptionally high sources of vitamin C. They are also rich in carotene, which plays an important role in maintaining healthy skin and mucous membranes
MINERALS As well as providing fibre, sesame seeds are rich in calcium, iron and zinc

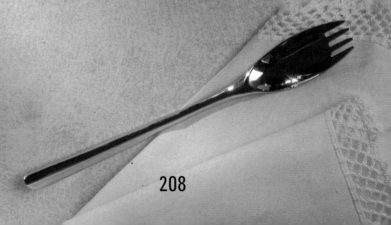

CAULIFLOWER SALAD

Raw carrots and cauliflower give a very crunchy texture; use an English or German mustard to vary the taste and strength of the dressing.

SERVES 4 130 calories per serving
PREPARATION 10 minutes
COOKING None

6 spring onions
1 small cauliflower, divided into florets
100 g (4 oz) carrots, scrubbed and thinly sliced
12 stuffed green olives, sliced

MUSTARD DRESSING
5 ml (1 tsp) Dijon mustard
5 ml (1 tsp) light muscovado sugar
30 ml (2 tbsp) tarragon vinegar
45 ml (3 tbsp) corn oil
pepper, to taste

———1———

Cut the tops from the spring onions and reserve. Chop the white part into 2.5 cm (1 inch) pieces and place in a salad bowl with the remaining vegetables.

———2———

To make the dressing, cream together the mustard and sugar, then gradually beat in the vinegar and corn oil. Season and continue beating until well blended.

———3———

Add the dressing to the vegetables and toss until well mixed. Scatter over the reserved spring onion tops just before serving.

GOODNESS GUIDE
VITAMINS This salad is rich in vitamins, with A from the carrots and olives and C from all the fresh vegetables. Vitamin C is easily destroyed—boiling a cauliflower reduces its vitamin content by half—so eating the ingredients raw greatly enhances their food value

BROCCOLI AND TOMATO SALAD

CHICORY AND APPLE SALAD

CAULIFLOWER SALAD

PEPPER SALAD

209

BRAISED CELERY

Smetana is a thick low-fat soured milk product. If unavailable, Greek strained yogurt is a good alternative.

SERVES 4 95 calories per serving
PREPARATION 10 minutes
COOKING 1 hour

1 large head celery, trimmed, separated and rinsed
1 onion, skinned and chopped
15 ml (1 tbsp) chopped fresh parsley
salt and pepper, to taste
900 ml (1½ pints) chicken or vegetable stock
150 ml (5 fl oz) smetana, to serve (optional)
fresh parsley sprigs, to garnish

———— 1 ————
Cut the celery in half crossways and place in an ovenproof dish. Sprinkle over the onion and parsley, season and add just enough stock to cover.
———— 2 ————
Cook at 190°C (375°F) mark 5 for 1 hour. Serve hot with smetana and garnish with parsley.

MICROWAVE Follow step 1, adding only 150 ml (¼ pint) stock. In step 2, cover and cook 100% (High) 15–17 minutes until just tender, turning the celery twice. Complete step 2.

GOODNESS GUIDE

BRAISED CELERY
FIBRE Celery is rich in fibre
VITAMINS The celery provides a good helping of vitamin C, which is also supplied by the onion
MINERALS Celery contains a number of essential minerals, particularly potassium, phosphorus and a small amount of iron

MUSHROOM RISOTTO
FIBRE This risotto is rich in fibre from the brown rice and sweetcorn as well as the red pepper and the spring onions
FAT This is low in fat, with just a little polyunsaturated margarine added
PROTEIN The chicken stock, brown rice and mushrooms all supply protein

MUSHROOM RISOTTO

This risotto is a nutritionally balanced dish and would be an excellent accompaniment for a simple roast chicken.

SERVES 4 320 calories per serving
PREPARATION 15 minutes
COOKING 40 minutes

25 g (1 oz) polyunsaturated margarine
1 onion, skinned and chopped
225 g (8 oz) brown rice
450 ml (¾ pint) hot chicken or vegetable stock
150 ml (¼ pint) dry white wine
1 red pepper
50 g (2 oz) frozen sweetcorn kernels
salt and pepper, to taste
1 bunch spring onions, cut in half crossways
225 g (8 oz) button mushrooms, quartered
15 g (½ oz) grated Parmesan cheese

———— 1 ————
Melt the margarine in a large saucepan, add the onion and rice and cook for 3–5 minutes, until the rice is opaque. Add the stock and wine, cover and cook over a low heat for 25 minutes.

BRAISED CELERY

MUSHROOM RISOTTO

———— 2 ————

Core, seed and dice the red pepper, then add with the sweetcorn and simmer for a further 10 minutes, until the liquid is absorbed.

———— 3 ————

Season to taste, stir in the spring onions and mushrooms and cook for 5 minutes more. Serve hot with a little Parmesan cheese sprinkled over the top.

MICROWAVE In step 1, put margarine in a bowl and cook 100% (High) 30–45 seconds to melt. Add onion and rice and cook 2 minutes, stirring once. Add hot stock and wine. Cover and cook 2 minutes until bubbling, then cook 60% (Medium) 10 minutes. In step 2, add pepper and sweetcorn. Cover and cook 60% (Medium) 25 minutes, until rice is tender. In step 3, stir in spring onions and mushrooms, cover and cook 100% (High) 3 minutes until mushrooms are hot. Complete step 3.

CHILLIED PEAS

This is a spicy and unusual way of preparing peas and would go particularly well with any grilled meat or oily fish.

SERVES 4 90 calories per serving
PREPARATION 10 minutes
COOKING 25 minutes

2 onions, skinned and chopped
400 g (14 oz) can tomatoes
1 garlic clove, skinned and crushed
10 ml (2 tsp) mild chilli powder
450 g (1 lb) frozen peas
30 ml (2 tbsp) tomato purée
pepper, to taste
onion rings, to garnish

———— 1 ————

Put the onions, tomatoes with their juice, garlic and chilli powder into a saucepan. Bring to the boil, lower the heat and simmer for 15 minutes, crushing the tomatoes occasionally.

———— 2 ————

Add the peas, tomato purée and pepper to taste. Cook for a further 5 minutes until the peas are just tender, then serve, garnished with thinly sliced onion rings.

MICROWAVE Follow step 1, putting ingredients in a bowl. Cover and cook 100% (High) 8 minutes, until boiling and vegetables tender, stirring twice. In step 2, add frozen peas and tomato purée, season. Cover and cook 7 minutes, until peas are just tender. Garnish dish with onion rings and serve.

GOODNESS GUIDE

VITAMINS This dish is rich in A and C, in particular with A from the tomatoes and tomato purée and C from all the vegetables. Vitamin A is needed for healthy skin and hair
FAT With none added, this side dish is very low in fat
FIBRE The vegetables contribute a useful helping of fibre

CHILLIED PEAS

WARM CUCUMBER WITH HERBS

WINTER SALAD

WARM CUCUMBER WITH HERBS

Although the cucumber pieces are sprinkled with salt to extract the bitterness, rinsing them thoroughly afterwards removes the salt.

SERVES 4 120 calories per serving
PREPARATION 10 minutes
COOKING 10 minutes

1 cucumber
25 g (1 oz) polyunsaturated margarine
1 small onion, skinned and finely chopped
15 ml (1 tbsp) chopped fresh dill or 7.5 ml
(½ tbsp) dried dill weed
2.5 ml (½ tsp) light muscovado sugar
salt and pepper, to taste
60 ml (2½ fl oz) Greek strained yogurt
chopped fresh dill or dill weed, to garnish

———1———
Score the skin of the cucumber with a fork. Cut into 5 cm (2 inch) lengths, then cut into quarters.

———2———
Scoop out the seeds, then put the cucumber in a colander and sprinkle with salt. Cover with a plate, weigh down, and leave to drain for 30 minutes. Rinse thoroughly and pat dry with absorbent paper.

———3———
Melt the margarine in a large frying pan. Add the onion and cook gently for 5 minutes, until soft.

———4———
Add the cucumber with the dill, sugar and seasoning. Cook for 5 minutes. Remove from the heat and stir in the yogurt. Garnish with the dill and serve.

GOODNESS GUIDE
SALT Flavouring the cucumber with dill eliminates the need for added salt
FAT Using Greek strained yogurt and a small amount of margarine is preferable to high-fat creamy sauces
VITAMINS Cucumber and the onions provide vitamin C

WINTER SALAD

Even in winter, when there is a lack of fresh produce, it is possible to make nutritious and flavourful salads from the vegetables available.

SERVES 4 75 calories per serving
PREPARATION 10 minutes
COOKING None

225 g (8 oz) fresh spinach, stalks removed and finely shredded
50 g (2 oz) white cabbage, finely shredded
1 bulb fennel, finely shredded
lemon twist, to garnish

DRESSING
15 ml (1 tbsp) olive oil
15 ml (1 tbsp) safflower oil
5 ml (1 tsp) Dijon mustard
juice of ½ lemon

BRUSSELS SPROUT SALAD

1

Place the shredded spinach, white cabbage and fennel in a bowl and mix together.

2

Whisk together the olive oil, safflower oil, Dijon mustard and the lemon juice until smooth. Add the dressing to the shredded vegetables and toss well. Garnish with a twist of lemon and serve at once.

GOODNESS GUIDE
VITAMINS This salad is full of vitamin C and B group vitamins—especially since the ingredients are eaten raw. Shredding the vegetables just before use helps preserve the vitamin C content of the vegetables
FAT The oils in the dressing are low in saturated fats and a healthy alternative to most commercial salad dressings

---

BRUSSELS SPROUT SALAD

Olive oil is high in monounsaturates and low in saturated fat. Although it is expensive, it is used here for its unique flavour.

SERVES 4   240 calories per serving
PREPARATION 15 minutes
COOKING None

75 ml (3 fl oz) olive oil
45 ml (3 tbsp) white wine vinegar
2 garlic cloves, skinned and crushed
15 ml (1 tbsp) clear honey
salt and pepper, to taste
350 g (12 oz) Brussels sprouts, trimmed and finely sliced
90 ml (6 tbsp) chopped fresh parsley
50 g (2 oz) shelled sunflower seeds
paprika, to garnish

1

Put the oil, vinegar, garlic and honey in a bowl and whisk until smooth. Add seasoning.

2

Put the sprouts and parsley in a large bowl, add the dressing and 25 g (1 oz) of the sunflower seeds and mix well.

3

Transfer the mixture to a serving bowl and sprinkle a little paprika and the remaining sunflower seeds over it. Serve immediately.

GOODNESS GUIDE
FIBRE The sprouts and sunflower seeds provide fibre in this crisp salad
VITAMINS Brussels sprouts supply A, some B and C—which is also provided by the parsley. The sunflower seeds contain some B vitamins as well as E
MINERALS Sprouts are a good source of calcium, magnesium and some iron

MIDDLE-EASTERN TOMATOES

If the bottoms of the tomatoes are very bumpy, cut a very thin piece from each one in order to make it stand upright.

SERVES 4 70 calories per serving
PREPARATION 15 minutes
COOKING None

4 large beefsteak tomatoes
60 ml (4 tbsp) hummus
15 ml (1 tbsp) chopped fresh coriander
50 g (2 oz) button mushrooms, chopped
30 ml (2 tbsp) shelled young broad beans, cooked and cooled
salt and pepper, to taste
watercress sprigs, to garnish

———1———

Cut a thin slice from the top of each tomato, reserving the slices, and carefully hollow out the centres with a teaspoon. Briefly drain the tomatoes cut side down on absorbent kitchen paper.

———2———

Chop the reserved tomato slices and mix with the hummus, coriander, mushrooms, broad beans and seasoning. Spoon the mixture into the hollowed tomatoes and serve garnished with watercress sprigs.

GOODNESS GUIDE

VITAMINS Tomatoes are a good source of carotene and vitamin C. Vitamin C is also contributed by the mushrooms and broad beans. Hummus provides some B-complex vitamins and vitamin E
MINERALS Hummus provides calcium, zinc and iron and, together with the other ingredients, supplies potassium
FIBRE Fibre is provided by the tomatoes, hummus, mushrooms and broad beans

RUSSIAN-STYLE POTATO SALAD

Cook the beetroot with the root and 5 cm (2 inches) of stalk intact. The skin will rub off easily when you remove the root and stalk.

SERVES 4 240 calories per serving
PREPARATION 20 minutes
COOKING 12–14 minutes

450 g (1 lb) potatoes, scrubbed and diced
2 carrots, scrubbed and diced
½ small cauliflower, broken into small florets
75 g (3 oz) shelled fresh peas or frozen peas, thawed
2 cooked beetroot, skinned and diced
1 small onion, skinned and chopped
45–60 ml (3–4 tbsp) mayonnaise
60 ml (4 tbsp) low-fat natural yogurt
10 ml (2 tsp) lemon juice
2 gherkins, chopped
6 stuffed olives, chopped
salt and pepper, to taste
watercress sprigs and chopped red pepper, to garnish

———1———

Cook the potatoes and carrots in a little boiling water for 5 minutes. Add the cauliflower florets and cook for a further 4 minutes. Add the peas and continue cooking for a further 3–5 minutes or until all the vegetables are just tender, but still firm.

———2———

Drain the vegetables and refresh in cold water, then drain again. Set aside to cool for about 10 minutes.

———3———

Meanwhile, put the beetroot and onion into a bowl and add the mayonnaise, yogurt, lemon juice, gherkins and olives. Mix well.

———4———

Add the vegetables and seasoning and toss together, until the ingredients are coated. Serve surrounded by watercress sprigs and sprinkled with chopped red pepper.

GOODNESS GUIDE

FIBRE The unpeeled potatoes and the other vegetables provide plenty of fibre
VITAMINS All the fresh vegetables contribute vitamin C
FAT The fat content of the mayonnaise dressing is reduced by mixing in some low-fat yogurt

AVOCADO AND PEANUT SALAD

The peanuts and the avocado provide a range of amino acids, making this salad a good source of protein.

SERVES 4 205 calories per serving
PREPARATION 10 minutes
COOKING None

½ small head of curly endive, separated into sprigs
2 oranges, peeled and segmented
30 ml (2 tbsp) natural roasted peanuts
¼ cucumber, halved, seeded and chopped
45 ml (3 tbsp) orange juice
15 ml (1 tbsp) olive oil
salt and pepper, to taste
1 garlic clove, skinned and crushed
15 ml (1 tbsp) chopped fresh mint
1 ripe avocado

———1———

Put the endive into a bowl and add the orange segments, peanuts and chopped cucumber.

———2———

In another bowl, mix the orange juice with the olive oil, seasoning, garlic and chopped mint.

———3———

Peel, halve and stone the avocado, then cut into thin slices. Toss gently in the dressing, then add with the dressing to the salad bowl. Toss lightly together and serve.

GOODNESS GUIDE

VITAMINS This salad is packed with vitamins. Carotene is contributed by the avocado, oranges and endive, and vitamin C is provided by all the vegetables and fruit. The peanuts supply B-complex vitamins, and the avocado is a source of vitamin E, which helps in the formation of muscles and other tissues

MIDDLE-EASTERN TOMATOES

RUSSIAN-STYLE POTATO SALAD

AVOCADO AND PEANUT SALAD

NUT-TOPPED VEGETABLES

Buy packets of broken cashew nuts; they are cheaper than whole nuts.

SERVES 4   100 calories per serving
PREPARATION   10 minutes
COOKING   8 minutes

1 cauliflower, cut into florets
225 g (8 oz) green beans, topped and tailed
50 g (2 oz) cashew nuts, finely chopped
15 ml (1 tbsp) finely chopped fresh parsley
grated rind of 1 lemon
15 ml (1 tbsp) lemon juice

————1————

Steam the cauliflower and beans over simmering water for about 8 minutes or until just tender.

————2————

Meanwhile, place the cashew nuts under a medium grill. Toast, shaking the grill pan occasionally to turn the nuts over, until golden brown.

————3————

Turn the cauliflower and beans into a serving dish and sprinkle over the nuts, parsley and lemon rind and juice. Serve immediately.

MICROWAVE Put cauliflower and beans into a bowl with 75 ml (3 fl oz) water. Cover and cook (100% (High) 10–12 minutes, stirring twice, until tender. Drain well. Spread nuts on a plate and cook 100% (High) 6 minutes, stirring once, until browned. Serve cauliflower and beans sprinkled with nuts, parsley, lemon rind and juice.

GOODNESS GUIDE

VITAMINS Cauliflower, green beans, parsley and lemon juice are rich in vitamin C. Vitamin C acts as an antihistamine in the prevention of allergic reactions. The cashew nuts are rich in some B-complex vitamins, especially thiamine and riboflavin. Cauliflower, green beans, parsley and cashew nuts provide carotene. Cashews also supply vitamin E

BABY MARROW IN BUTTERMILK SAUCE

This recipe can be made with marrow or courgettes and is equally good and nutritious with either.

SERVES 4   70 calories per serving
PREPARATION   5 minutes
COOKING   8 minutes

1 marrow, about 450 g (1 lb), halved, seeded and cut into 0.5 cm ($\frac{1}{4}$ inch) slices, or
450 g (1 lb) courgettes, sliced
25 ml (1$\frac{1}{2}$ tbsp) corn oil
30 ml (2 tbsp) finely chopped onion
1 garlic clove, skinned and crushed
1.25 ml ($\frac{1}{4}$ tsp) paprika
150 ml ($\frac{1}{4}$ pint) vegetable stock
15 ml (1 tbsp) plain wholemeal flour
150 ml ($\frac{1}{4}$ pint) buttermilk
15 ml (1 tbsp) chopped fresh dill or
7.5 ml ($\frac{1}{2}$ tbsp) dried
salt and pepper, to taste

————1————

Steam the marrow for 3–5 minutes, until just tender.

————2————

Meanwhile, heat the oil in a saucepan. Add the onion and gently cook for 2 minutes, until soft, then add the garlic and continue cooking for 1 minute. Add the paprika and stir. Add the vegetable stock, Cover and gently cook for 5 minutes.

————3————

In a bowl, mix together the flour and buttermilk until smooth. Pour the stock on to the mixture and stir well, then return it to the pan and cook, stirring, for 2 minutes, until thickened. Add the marrow, then stir in the dill and seasoning. Cook for 1 minute to heat through. Serve.

GOODNESS GUIDE

FAT Buttermilk is made from skimmed milk, so it is very low in fat
VITAMINS The milk and flour supply B-complex vitamins which, among other functions, help the body to utilise energy from carbohydrates. The marrow provides some carotene and vitamin C
PROTEIN The buttermilk and flour provide protein

CURRIED LENTILS

SERVES 4   280 calories per serving
PREPARATION   5 minutes
COOKING   1 hour

15 ml (1 tbsp) corn oil
1 small onion, skinned and finely chopped
1 garlic clove, skinned and thinly sliced
10 ml (2 tsp) ground cumin
5 ml (1 tsp) turmeric
10 ml (2 tsp) ground coriander
1 small dried red chilli, crushed (optional)
2 cardamom pods, bruised
175 g (6 oz) red lentils
25 g (1 oz) desiccated coconut
salt, to taste
tomato wedges, to garnish

————1————

Heat the oil in a saucepan, add the onion and garlic and cook about 3 minutes, until softened. Add the spices and cook for 2–3 minutes, stirring constantly.

————2————

Add the lentils and 450 ml ($\frac{3}{4}$ pint) water. Cover and simmer gently for about 1 hour or until the lentils are soft but not completely mushy.

————3————

Stir in the coconut and seasoning. Garnish with tomato wedges and serve hot.

MICROWAVE Put oil, onion and garlic into a bowl. Cover and cook 100% (High) 3 minutes, until softened. Stir in spices, cook, uncovered, 100% (High) 1 minute. Add lentils and 450 ml ($\frac{3}{4}$ pint) boiling water. Cover and cook 100%(High) 20–25 minutes, stirring twice, until lentils are soft. Stir in coconut and seasoning. Complete recipe.

GOODNESS GUIDE

MINERALS Lentils are rich in iron and zinc and also provide fair amounts of calcium and magnesium. Magnesium is necessary for a healthy heart and appears to protect the body in stressful situations. The spices are also concentrated sources of minerals. The lentils, vegetables and spices provide potassium
FIBRE The lentils, coconut and vegetables are high in fibre

COURGETTE SALAD

This allspice and lemon dressing also goes well with grated carrots.

SERVES 4   205 calories per serving
PREPARATION   15 minutes
COOKING   None

450 g (1 lb) courgettes, grated or shredded
50 g (2 oz) walnut halves, finely chopped
lemon twist and fresh parsley or coriander
sprig, to garnish

LEMON ALLSPICE DRESSING
60 ml (4 tbsp) sunflower oil
30 ml (2 tbsp) white wine vinegar
5 ml (1 tsp) ground allspice
finely grated rind and juice of $\frac{1}{2}$ lemon
salt and pepper, to taste

———1———
To make the dressing, put all the ingredients in a screw-topped jar and shake until well blended.
———2———
Place the courgettes in a bowl and add the walnuts. Toss gently until well mixed. Briefly shake the dressing, then pour over the courgettes and toss well. Garnish with a lemon twist and parsley sprig and serve.

GOODNESS GUIDE
VITAMINS Courgettes provide good quantities of carotene, vitamin C and the B vitamin folic acid. Walnuts are rich in a range of vitamins, including vitamin B_6 and folic acid in particular. Vitamin C helps to convert folic acid into its active form in the liver. Folic acid deficiency leads to a type of anaemia where red blood cells fail to mature and have a short life span

NUT-TOPPED VEGETABLES

BABY MARROW IN BUTTERMILK SAUCE

COURGETTE SALAD

CURRIED LENTILS

GLAZED ONIONS IN CIDER

The tiny onions in this dish are coated in a cider and honey sauce. They are particularly good served with plain grilled meat or chicken. Other vegetables such as carrots or turnips may also be cooked in this way.

SERVES 4 95 calories per serving
PREPARATION 10 minutes
COOKING 25–30 minutes

550 g (1¼ lb) pickling onions or shallots, skinned
150 ml (¼ pint) dry cider
10 ml (2 tsp) clear honey
15 g (½ oz) polyunsaturated margarine
5 ml (1 tsp) cornflour
snipped fresh chives, to garnish
pepper, to taste

———1———

Blanch the onions in boiling water for 2 minutes, then drain well. Return the onions to the saucepan and add the cider, the honey and the margarine. Cover the pan and cook gently for 20–25 minutes, until the onions are tender.

———2———

Blend the cornflour with 15 ml (1 tbsp) water to make a paste, then add to the pan and bring to the boil, stirring. Reduce the heat and simmer gently for 2 minutes, stirring continuously, until slightly thickened.

———3———

Turn the onions and sauce into a serving dish and sprinkle liberally with snipped chives and seasoning. Serve hot.

GOODNESS GUIDE

FIBRE The onions provide fibre which is effective in countering constipation
VITAMINS A little vitamin C is contributed by the onions in this dish
MINERALS The onions supply potassium which complements sodium in the body. Potassium is essential for the healthy functioning of the nerves

HERBED TWICE-BAKED POTATOES

These potatoes may be cooked and filled ahead, and reheated when required. The herbs may be varied according to taste.

SERVES 4 270 calories per serving
PREPARATION 10–15 minutes
COOKING 1½ hours

4 large potatoes, scrubbed
30 ml (2 tbsp) chopped fresh mixed herbs, such as chives, parsley, marjoram and basil
3 spring onions, trimmed and chopped
100 g (4 oz) natural Quark
2 tomatoes, finely chopped
salt and pepper, to taste
50 g (2 oz) low-fat Cheddar cheese, grated
extra fresh herb sprigs and tomato slices, to garnish

———1———

Prick the potatoes all over with a fork. Bake at 200°C (400°F) mark 6 for 50–60 minutes, until tender

———2———

Cut a thin slice horizontally from the top of each potato, then carefully scoop out most of the potato into a bowl, leaving shells about 0.5 cm (¼ inch) thick.

———3———

Mix the potato with the herbs, onions, Quark, chopped tomatoes and seasoning. Spoon the mixture back into the potato shells and place in a shallow ovenproof dish.

———4———

Sprinkle the filling with the grated cheese and return to the oven to bake for 25 minutes, until lightly golden. Garnish each potato and serve at once.

MICROWAVE Prick potatoes, arrange on absorbent paper. Cook 100% (High) 15–20 minutes, rotating twice, until tender. Complete steps 2, 3. Sprinkle over grated cheese. Cook 100% (High) 5 minutes.

GOODNESS GUIDE

PROTEIN The cheese and potatoes provide protein
VITAMINS The cheese is a source of B-complex vitamins and the vegetables and herbs provide vitamin C. The tomatoes and herbs are a source of carotene which is converted by the body into active vitamin A. Vitamin A aids dim-light vision

SAUERKRAUT AND APPLE HOTPOT

For variety, half the vegetable stock can be replaced with unsweetened apple juice.

SERVES 4 130 calories per serving
PREPARATION 10 minutes
COOKING 1 hour

15 ml (1 tbsp) corn oil
1 large onion, skinned and chopped
1 potato, scrubbed and chopped
1 carrot, scrubbed and sliced
450 g (1 lb) jar sauerkraut
2 eating apples, cored and chopped
2.5–5 ml (½–1 tsp) dill or caraway seeds
150 ml (¼ pint) vegetable stock
10 ml (2 tsp) clear honey
pepper, to taste

———1———

Heat the oil in a flameproof casserole, add the onion, potato and carrot and cook for 4 minutes, stirring frequently.

———2———

Add the sauerkraut, apples, dill seeds and stock. Stir well, then add the honey and seasoning.

———3———

Cover and cook at 180°C (350°F) mark 4 for 1 hour, until the carrot and onion are tender. Stir well and serve hot.

MICROWAVE Put oil, onion, potato, carrot into a dish. Cover. Cook 100% (High) 4 minutes, stirring once. Stir in sauerkraut, apples, dill seeds, boiling stock, honey, seasoning. Cover, Cook 100% (High) 10 minutes, stirring twice, until carrot is tender. Stir well. Serve hot.

GOODNESS GUIDE

FIBRE The vegetables provide plenty of fibre
VITAMINS Some vitamin C is supplied by the fresh vegetables and the apples
FAT Very little oil has been used in this dish which means that the fat content is low

SAUERKRAUT AND APPLE HOTPOT

GLAZED ONIONS IN CIDER

HERBED TWICE-BAKED POTATOES

SIDE DISHES AND SALADS

CHINESE ORANGE SALAD

Oranges contain vitamin C, which helps the body properly absorb the iron that is provided by the watercress.

SERVES 4–6 90–60 calories per serving
PREPARATION 15 minutes
COOKING None

½ head Chinese leaves, shredded
100 g (4 oz) fresh beansprouts
3 heads chicory, thinly sliced
3 oranges, peeled and segmented
1 bunch spring onions, chopped
1 bunch watercress, trimmed

ORANGE DRESSING
finely shredded rind of 1 orange
15 ml (1 tbsp) orange juice
5 ml (1 tsp) Dijon mustard
15 ml (1 tbsp) white wine vinegar
30 ml (2 tbsp) sunflower oil

———1———
To make the dressing, mix together the orange rind, juice and mustard, then add the vinegar and slowly beat in the oil.

———2———
Mix together the salad ingredients and pour the dressing over. Toss gently and serve at once.

GOODNESS GUIDE
VITAMINS Bransprouts, cabbage, oranges and watercress all add up to a salad that is rich in vitamin C as well as other vitamins—especially since all the ingredients are being eaten raw
FIBRE The vegetables and the fruit are a good source of fibre
FAT The salad dressing is quite low in fat

PEPPERY BEAN SALAD

Finely diced peppers add extra flavour to this healthy salad. Cannellini and butter beans could also be used.

SERVES 4 200 calories per serving
PREPARATION 20 minutes
CHILLING 15 minutes
COOKING None

1 red pepper
1 green pepper
200 g (7 oz) can red kidney beans, drained and rinsed
400 g (14 oz) can chick-peas, drained and rinsed
5 spring onions, finely chopped

DRESSING
1 garlic clove, skinned and crushed
10 ml (2 tsp) whole grain French mustard
10 ml (2 tsp) lemon juice
30 ml (2 tbsp) olive oil

———1———
Spear the peppers with a fork and hold over a gas burner or under a hot grill. Turn until black all over.
———2———
Remove the skins and seeds from the peppers under cold running water. Drain well and dice, then mix together with the beans, chick-peas and onions.
———3———
Mix together the garlic, mustard and lemon juice and blend in the oil. Pour over the beans and mix well. Cover and chill for at least 15 minutes.

GOODNESS GUIDE
PROTEIN Pulses are very high in protein
MINERALS The beans and peas contain useful quantities of iron and other minerals such as potassium
FIBRE The peppers, kidney beans and chick-peas are high in fibre

CURRIED APPLE COLESLAW

A healthy variation on traditional coleslaw, this combines crunchy textures with a creamy curried dressing.

SERVES 4 114 calories per serving
PREPARATION 10 minutes
COOKING None

½ medium white cabbage, finely shredded
4 celery sticks, chopped
2 red eating apples, thinly sliced
8 radishes, trimmed and sliced
1 bunch spring onions, trimmed and chopped
10 ml (2 tsp) caraway seeds for topping

CREAMY CURRY DRESSING
5 ml (1 tsp) curry powder
45 ml (3 tbsp) mayonnaise
45 ml (3 tbsp) low-fat natural yogurt
30 ml (2 tbsp) lemon juice

To make the dressing, mix together the curry powder, mayonnaise, yogurt and lemon juice. Place the salad ingredients in a bowl and pour the dressing over. Toss gently, then sprinkle with the caraway seeds. Serve at once.

GOODNESS GUIDE
FAT Mixing the mayonnaise with yogurt makes this coleslaw low in fat, compared with the traditional version
VITAMINS The salad ingredients and lemon juice are a rich source of vitamin C
FIBRE The vegetables, seeds and fruit combine to provide a very good helping of fibre

CHINESE ORANGE SALAD

PEPPERY BEAN SALAD

CURRIED APPLE COLESLAW

7 HEALTHY BAKING

However enjoyable the outcome may be there is much about traditional baking—the high saturated fat content, the amount of sugar added—that tends to break the guidelines for a better diet. But cakes, biscuits, bread, scones and pastries can all be produced that are not only good to eat but good for you too. We look at the ingredients and techniques for the best and healthiest results.

Many of the ingredients used in traditional baking are neither very wholesome nor very nutritious. Recipes call for butter, lard and hard margarine, all of them high in the saturated fats that we are particularly recommended to cut down on. While white flour is perfectly nutritious with, for example, a very worthwhile protein content, an awful lot of the goodness of the grain is lost in the refining process. White sugar has no nutritional value except calories.

But there is a healthier approach to baking using alternative ingredients and methods. It allows you to cut down on all fats, especially saturated ones, as well as the amount of sugar added. And by using whole grain flours and dried fruit with other healthy ingredients, you can substantially increase the vitamins and minerals available and, especially, the fibre content of the food you prepare.

All these alternative ingredients are just as easy to use for results that match those of traditional recipes in terms of flavour, texture and appearance.

WHOLE GRAIN GOODNESS
The healthiest type of flour to use for all baking is wholemeal flour. Light brown in colour and rather coarser than plain white flour, it is made from the whole of the wheat grain. To produce white flour, most of the outer fibrous layers—the bran and the sprouting section, the germ—are removed from the grain before it is ground.

However, the bran and germ are very rich in a wide range of essential nutrients. With far more dietary fibre, more B vitamins and vitamin E, and more of the essential minerals such as copper, magnesium and zinc, wholemeal flour is unquestionable the best for health.

Wholemeal flour can replace white flour in any recipe or, when a lighter result is required, it can be mixed with plain or self-raising white flour. Breads, scones and biscuits will be slightly different in texture to those made with white flour. Sponge cakes will not be quite so light but many people find them far more appetising. The wholemeal flour makes a rich, moist cake that is full of flavour and, unlike conventional sponge cakes which often need jam, cream, sugar and so on, it will taste very good served plain.

For variety, rye and barley flours can be used; again, these should be made from the whole of the grain. Rye flour has a strong flavour and a fairly heavy texture so it is best to use one half rye mixed with one half plain flour, or a quarter of rye with three-quarters of wholemeal. Barley flour is excellent when used alone for biscuits and pastries; for breads and cakes it is better mixed with other flours. One quarter of oatmeal can also be added to bread and scone recipes. Rolled oats are good mixed with wheat flour for making biscuits such as flapjacks.

CUTTING BACK THE FAT
All the guidelines for a healthier diet recommend cutting down on fat intake, particularly the hard, saturated fats. Certainly, in most baking recipes polyunsaturated margarine can be substituted for butter. Corn or groundnut oil—both high in polyunsaturates—can replace lard, butter or hard margarine in scones and tea breads; use 30 ml (2 tbsp) of oil for every 25 g (1 oz) of other fat. Corn oil can also be used in cakes.

For sponge cakes, the fat can be replaced by a mixture of half corn oil and half natural orange juice, in the proportions above: 15 ml (1 tbsp) each of oil and juice in place of every 25 g (1 oz) of butter used in the recipe. The mixture is then made in a similar way to a batter. The flour, raising agent and any additional sweetener are put into a bowl and the oil, orange juice and eggs put into a well in the centre and beaten in.

To cut down on the overall fat content, both semi-skimmed and skimmed milk can be used to replace full-cream milk in most recipes. For scones, try using natural yogurt—low-fat ideally—or buttermilk, instead of the traditional sour milk.

ALTERNATIVE SWEETENERS
One of the most notable features of the healthier approach to baking is the types of sugar and other sweeteners that are used. There is no sugar that is *good* for you—in nutritional terms it provides nothing but calories. But the raw brown sugars such as Barbados or muscovado, which are slightly less refined and have traces of minerals and vitamins, are considered more desirable. They also have a richer flavour than white sugar.

Both light and dark muscovado sugars are available, the light being suitable for sponge-type cakes and the dark for more flavoured teabreads. These sugars can be rather lumpy, in which case it is best to sieve them before use.

Molasses, the uncrystallised syrup from raw sugar, can be used as a sweetener; in nutritional terms it is superior to the other sugars with, for example, a significant iron content, and it has only about two-thirds the calories of white sugar. It does have quite a powerful flavour and is best suited to ginger cakes, fruit cakes and the like.

Honey is also much favoured in baking as an alternative to white sugar. While it does contain traces of vitamins and minerals they are present in such tiny amounts as to have no practical significance. It does, however, have a delicious flavour and it can be used in smaller quantities—replace the sugar in a recipe with, at most, three-quarters that amount of honey.

For baking, clear honey tends to be easier to handle than the thicker varieties. And a tiny amount brushed on top of loaves and buns makes a pretty glaze.

Whenever possible, by far the best approach is to use the natural sweetness of fruit, in which the sugar content comes packaged with vitamins, minerals and dietary fibre. Dried fruit, in particular, in which the goodness is concentrated by the removal of water, is a first-rate source of fibre. Fruit such as raisins, sultanas, currants, dried apricots and chopped dates can be added to scones, flavoured breads and teabreads, or the fruit can be mixed in a blender or food processor with the other ingredients for use in many other recipes. (For further information on sugar, see *Alternative Sweeteners,* page 105.)

ADDITIONAL INGREDIENTS

Both fresh and dried yeasts are available for bread making. Neither is nutritionally better than the other and which type you use is a matter of preference and availability. As a general rule, use half the amount of dried yeast as you would of fresh.

There is no need to add sugar to fresh yeast in order to make it work quickly. Warm water is quite sufficient; one-third boiling water to two-thirds cold gives the right temperature of tepid water. Dried yeast needs a pinch of sugar if it is to work within 20 minutes.

Fresh yeast wrapped in cling film can be stored in the refrigerator for up to a week, or stored in the freezer for up to three months. Frozen fresh yeast can be used without thawing, if necessary. It just needs a few minutes in the tepid water before adding to the flour mixture.

The raising agents baking powder and baking soda can destroy some of the vitamins and minerals in wholemeal flour, but not significantly, and they do provide a pleasant texture and appearance.

For chocolate-like cake or topping, carob is a very useful alternative to cocoa products. Made from the carob or locust bean, it is rich in B vitamins and minerals such as iron, as well as fibre. While carob does have a quite high natural sugar content there is generally less than in cocoa and it is far lower in fat. Carob comes either in powder form to be used like cocoa powder or made up into bars which can be used like chocolate. The bars are often sold with sugar added, so check the label.

Chopped nuts add flavour and texture to all baked goods, both sweet and savoury, and they are rich in protein and other nutrients. Spices and herbs will add flavour and in many recipes they can replace some of the salt or the sugar.

The few eggs used in baking will do no harm but if, because of a special diet for example, you want to cut down, replace each egg with 60 ml (4 tbsp) natural yogurt. Tofu, a soft, white soya bean curd, can also be used.

WHOLEMEAL BREAD

Kibbled wheat is the name given to whole pieces of cracked wheat.

MAKES TWO 900 g (2 lb) LOAVES WITH
20 SLICES PER LOAF
115 CALORIES PER SLICE
PREPARATION 40 minutes
BAKING 40–50 minutes
RISING 90 minutes

1.4 kg (3 lb) plain wholemeal flour
10 ml (2 tsp) salt
40 g (1½ oz) fresh yeast, crumbled, or 22.5 ml
(4½ tsp) dried
10 ml (2 tsp) clear honey
1 egg, beaten, to glaze
kibbled wheat for sprinkling (optional)

———1———

Lightly grease and flour two 900 g (2 lb) loaf tins and set aside. Put the flour and salt in a warmed bowl, mix well and set aside.

———2———

Blend the fresh yeast and honey with 300 ml (½ pint) tepid water. If using dried yeast, sprinkle it into 300 ml (½ pint) tepid water with the honey then leave in a warm place for 15 minutes, until frothy.

———3———

Make a well in the centre of the flour and pour in the yeast liquid. Mix well to form a firm dough, adding more tepid water if needed.

———4———

Return the dough to the bowl and cover with a clean cloth. Leave in a warm place for about 1 hour or until the dough has doubled in size.

———5———

To knock back the dough, turn out on to a lightly floured surface and knead well for 10 minutes to remove any air bubbles. Divide into 2 equal pieces, then shape each into a loaf. Place in the loaf tins. Cover and leave in a warm place to rise for about 30 minutes, until the loaves have almost doubled in size.

———6———

Brush the tops with the beaten egg and sprinkle over the kibbled wheat, if using. Bake at 220°C (425°F) mark 7 for 40–50 minutes, until cooked through. The base of each loaf should sound hollow when gently tapped. Remove from the tins and cool on a wire rack.

GOODNESS GUIDE

FIBRE Wholemeal bread is an excellent source of fibre—with nearly three times as much fibre as white bread—and is a good, basic staple of a healthy diet
VITAMINS Bread contains B vitamins and vitamin E and, again, wholemeal bread contains a larger amount than white

WHOLEMEAL BREAD

CHOLLA

MAKES 15 SLICES 112 calories each
PREPARATION 30 minutes
BAKING 15–20 minutes
RISING 1–1½ hours

15 g (½ oz) fresh yeast or 7.5 ml (½ tsp) dried
and 2.5 ml (½ tsp) light muscovado sugar
225 g (8 oz) plain wholemeal flour
225 g (8 oz) strong plain flour
1 egg, beaten
5 ml (1 tsp) semi-skimmed milk
25 ml (1½ tbsp) poppy seeds

——— 1 ———

Blend the fresh yeast with 150 ml (¼ pint) of tepid water and leave to stand in a warm place for 15 minutes. If using dried yeast, dissolved the sugar in the water, sprinkle the yeast over and leave for 10 minutes, until frothy.

——— 2 ———

Mix the flours together and leave in a very warm place until warmed through. Add the yeast liquid, egg and about 150 ml (¼ pint) of tepid water and mix to a smooth dough. Turn out on to a lightly floured board and knead for 5 minutes.

——— 3 ———

Put into a large bowl and cover, then leave to rise in a warm place for 25–35 minutes, until doubled.

——— 4 ———

Turn out on to a floured surface, flatten firmly to knock out all the air bubbles and knead again for 5 minutes. Return to bowl, cover with a clean cloth and leave to rise a further 25–35 minutes. Lightly grease a baking sheet and set aside.

——— 5 ———

Turn out, knock out the air bubbles and knead again until smooth. Divide the dough into three pieces and shape into 3 strips, each 25.5 cm (10 inches) long. Pinch the 3 strips together at one end and plait. Pinch the plait firmly at the other end. Place on baking sheet, cover and leave in warm place 15 minutes.

——— 6 ———

Brush lightly with the milk and sprinkle with seeds. Bake at 230°C (450°F) mark 8 for 15–20 minutes or until the bread sounds hollow when the base is tapped. Cool.

GOODNESS GUIDE
VITAMINS Bread is rich in energy-producing vitamin B complex

CRUMPETS

These crumpets are superior to those commercially produced as they contain nutritious wholemeal flour.
MAKES 4 255 calories each
PREPARATION 20–30 minutes
BAKING About 10 minutes
RISING 30–45 minutes

100 g (4 oz) plain wholemeal flour
100 g (4 oz) plain flour
1.25 ml (¼ tsp) salt
15 g (½ oz) fresh yeast or 7.5 ml (1½ tsp) dried
and 5 ml (1 tsp) clear honey
350 ml (12 fl oz) semi-skimmed milk, warmed
15–30 ml (1–2 tbsp) corn oil

——— 1 ———

Put the wholemeal and plain flours into a large mixing bowl, add the salt and leave in a warm place until warmed through.

——— 2 ———

Blend the fresh yeast with the milk. If using dried yeast, mix the honey with the milk, sprinkle the dried yeast on top and leave for 10–15 minutes, until frothy.

——— 3 ———

Make a well in the centre of the flour, pour in the yeast liquid and mix to a smooth batter. Cover with a clean cloth and leave to rise in a warm place for 30–45 minutes.

——— 4 ———

With a little of the oil, lightly grease a griddle or heavy-based frying pan and crumpet rings or plain metal 10 cm (4 inch) pastry cutters. Heat the griddle or frying pan until hot, place the crumpet rings on, then pour the batter inside the rings to a depth of 1 cm (½ inch). Cook until set and the bubbles on top have burst. Remove the rings, turn and cook the other sides for 1 minute.

GOODNESS GUIDE
FIBRE Because crumpets are traditionally made with all plain flour, the addition of wholemeal flour greatly improves the fibre content
FAT Using semi-skimmed instead of whole milk and a small amount of oil reduces the overall fat content
VITAMINS Yeast is a good source of B vitamins as are the flour and milk

OATCAKES

GINGERBREAD

MAKES 12 SQUARES 164 calories each
PREPARATION 10–12 minutes
BAKING 40–45 minutes

100 g (4 oz) ready-to-eat dried apricots, rinsed and chopped
100 g (4 oz) plain wholemeal flour
100 g (4 oz) plain flour
5 ml (1 tsp) ground cinnamon
15 ml (1 tbsp) ground ginger
25 g (1 oz) light muscovado sugar
100 g (4 oz) polyunsaturated margarine
100 g (4 oz) molasses
5 ml (1 tsp) bicarbonate of soda
150 ml (¼ pint) semi-skimmed milk, warmed
1 egg, size 2, beaten
25 g (1 oz) blanched almonds, split

——— 1 ———

Pour boiling water over the apricots and leave for 5 minutes, then drain. Lightly grease and line a 27 × 18 cm (10¾ × 7 inch) baking tin with greased greaseproof paper and set aside.

CHOLLA

GINGERBREAD

CRUMPETS

OATCAKES

2

Mix the wholemeal and plain flours and spices together in a mixing bowl with the sugar and apricots. Melt the margarine and molasses in a small saucepan, then add to the dry ingredients and beat well.

3

Dissolve the bicarbonate of soda in the milk and gradually beat into the mixture. Add the egg and beat to form a smooth batter. Pour the batter into the baking tin, sprinkle with the almonds and bake at 180°C (350°F) mark 4 for 40–45 minutes, until cooked through. Cool in the tin before turning out.

GOODNESS GUIDE

MINERALS Molasses is rich in minerals — iron, calcium and potassium, among others. The dried apricots provide calcium and iron too

FIBRE Substantial amounts of fibre are contributed by the wholemeal flour, apricots and almonds. These help control the absorption of sugar into the blood

---

MAKES 18 95 calories each
PREPARATION 10 minutes
BAKING 15–20 minutes

50 g (2 oz) plain wholemeal flour
50 g (2 oz) plain flour
2.5 ml ($\frac{1}{2}$ tsp) bicarbonate of soda
2.5 ml ($\frac{1}{2}$ tsp) cream of tartar
1.25 ml ($\frac{1}{4}$ tsp) salt
225 g (8 oz) medium oatmeal
50 g (2 oz) polyunsaturated margarine
15 ml (1 tbsp) clear honey
75 ml (3 fl oz) semi-skimmed milk

1

Lightly grease 2 baking sheets and set aside. Sift the flours into a mixing bowl with bicarbonate of soda, cream of tartar and salt, adding the bran left in the sieve. Stir in the oatmeal, then rub in margarine. Add honey and enough milk to make a firm dough.

2

On a lightly floured surface, roll out the dough to a 0.25 cm ($\frac{1}{8}$ inch) thickness, then cut into rounds with a 7.5 cm (3 inch) plan biscuit cutter. Reroll and recut until all the dough is used up.

3

Place the rounds on the baking sheets and bake at 190°C (375°F) mark 5 for 15–20 minutes or until firm to the touch. Cool for a few minutes on the baking sheets, then transfer to a wire rack to cool.

MICROWAVE In step 1, lightly grease 2 microwave trays. Follow recipe to step 3. Cook the oatcakes in two batches, uncovered, 60% (Medium) 6 minutes, turning the trays twice, until the oatcakes are entirely dry on the surface. Transfer to a wire rack to cool completely.

GOODNESS GUIDE

MINERALS Both the oatmeal and the flours are good sources of calcium. In addition to the role calcium plays in building healthy bones and teeth, it is essential to the normal working of muscles and clotting of blood

FIBRE The wholemeal flour and oatmeal contribute large amounts of fibre

ALMOND SHORTBREAD

This old-fashioned favourite with a healthy difference is delicious as a snack or for afternoon tea.

MAKES 8 WEDGES   345 calories each
PREPARATION   10–15 minutes
BAKING   40 minutes

100 g (4 oz) plain wholemeal flour
100 g (4 oz) plain flour
25 g (1 oz) unblanched almonds, chopped
75 g (3 oz) ground almonds
75 g (3 oz) light muscovado sugar
2.5 ml ($\frac{1}{2}$ tsp) ground ginger
225 g (8 oz) polyunsaturated margarine
10 ml (2 tsp) icing sugar (optional)

——— 1 ———

Put all the ingredients, except the icing sugar, in a bowl. Work together quickly to form a smooth dough.

——— 2 ———

Press into a 22–23 cm (8½–9 inch) fluted loose-bottomed flan tin. Mark into 8 wedges by scoring lightly on the top.

——— 3 ———

Bake at 180°C (350°F) mark 4 for about 40 minutes, until pale golden. Cut into 8 wedges and leave in the tin to cool. Dust lightly with the icing sugar before serving, if desired.

DATE AND FIG TEABREAD

This teabread has a moist texture and keeps very well—it actually improves in flavour after 2 or 3 days.

MAKES 12 SLICES   205 calories each
PREPARATION   10–15 minutes
BAKING   1¼ hours

75 g (3 oz) polyunsaturated margarine
100 g (4 oz) light muscovado sugar
2 eggs, size 2, beaten
finely grated rind of 1 lemon
225 g (8 oz) plain wholemeal flour
12.5 ml (2½ tsp) baking powder
60 ml (4 tbsp) low-fat natural yogurt
75 g (3 oz) fried stoned dates, chopped
75 g (3 oz) dried figs, chopped
50 g (2 oz) walnut halves, chopped

——— 1 ———

Grease and line a 900 g (2 lb) loaf tin and set aside. Beat together the margarine and sugar until light and fluffy. Gradually beat in the eggs and the lemon rind, adding a little flour if the mixture starts to curdle.

——— 2 ———

Sieve together the remaining flour and baking powder and mix into the creamed mixture, adding the bran left in the sieve. Add the yogurt and stir in the fruit and nuts. Place in the tin and level the top.

——— 3 ———

Bake at 170°C (325°F) mark 3 for 1–1¼ hours. Test with a fine skewer —if it comes out clean the bread is cooked through.

——— 4 ———

Cool for about 10 minutes in the tin, then turn out on a wire rack. Once cold, wrap tightly in aluminium foil or cling film before storing.

MICROWAVE For steps 1 and 2, grease and line a 900 g (2 lb) loaf dish. Put all ingredients together in a bowl, beat until evenly mixed without undue beating. Place in the dish and level the top. In step 3, cook 100% (High) 9–10 minutes until just set on the centre surface, turning the dish 3 or 4 times. Follow step 4.

ALMOND SHORTBREAD

HEALTHY BAKING

GRANARY BREAD

Sugar is added to the dried yeast to help it start growing, but this is not necessary if using fresh yeast.

MAKES 12 SLICES   141 calories each
PREPARATION   40 minutes
RISING $1\frac{1}{2}$–$1\frac{3}{4}$ hours
BAKING   35–40 minutes

15 g ($\frac{1}{2}$ oz) fresh yeast, or 7.5 ml ($1\frac{1}{2}$ tsp)
dried yeast and 2.5 ml ($\frac{1}{2}$ tsp) light
muscovado sugar
225 g (8 oz) plain wholemeal flour
225 g (8 oz) granary flour
pinch of salt
20 g ($\frac{3}{4}$ oz) polyunsaturated margarine
1 egg, beaten, to glaze
15–30 ml (1–2 tbsp) cracked wheat

1

Crumble the fresh yeast into 300 ml ($\frac{1}{2}$ pint) tepid water and stir until dissolved. If using dried yeast, sprinkle it into the tepid water mixed with the sugar and leave until frothy.

2

Mix together the flours in a large mixing bowl. Add the salt and rub in the margarine.

3

Make a well in the centre of the flour mixture and add yeast liquid. Mix to a dough. Turn out on to a lightly floured surface and knead for 5 minutes, until elastic and smooth. Put into a large bowl and cover with a clean cloth. Leave in a warm place for about 1 hour or until the dough is double in size. Meanwhile, lightly grease a baking sheet and set aside until required.

4

Turn out the dough on to a lightly floured surface and knead briefly. Shape into a neat, round ball and flatten slightly. Place on the baking sheet and cover. Leave to rise in a warm place for 30–40 minutes or until the dough is double in size and risen to the top of the bowl.

5

Glaze with the egg and sprinkle with cracked wheat. Bake at 230°C (450°F) mark 8 for 35–40 minutes, until the bread is well-risen, golden and hollow sounding when tapped on the bottom. Cool on a wire rack.

GOODNESS GUIDE

ALMOND SHORTBREAD

FIBRE The wholemeal flour and almonds contribute a very high fibre content to the shortbread

FAT The saturated butter used in traditional shortbread is replaced here with polyunsaturated margarine

PROTEIN Protein is present in the wholemeal flour and almonds

DATE AND FIG TEABREAD

FIBRE The teabread is rich in fibre which is provided by the wholemeal flour, dates, figs and walnuts

VITAMINS B vitamins, which help the body use food energy, are supplied by the dried fruit and eggs

GRANARY BREAD

FIBRE Although granary flour does not provide as much fibre as wholemeal flour, this is still a very high-fibre bread

VITAMINS Granary flour supplies a range of B vitamins and a little E

MINERALS The bread contains minerals including calcium and iron

DATE AND FIG TEABREAD

GRANARY BREAD

227

CAROB BROWNIES

These brownies are lighter than the traditional chocolate variety—and healthier, too.

MAKES 16 110 calories each
PREPARATION 20 minutes
BAKING 15 minutes

75 g (3 oz) plain carob bar
50 g (2 oz) polyunsaturated margarine
100 g (4 oz) light muscovado sugar
1 egg
25 g (1 oz) plain wholemeal flour
50 g (2 oz) plain flour
2.5 ml ($\frac{1}{2}$ tsp) baking powder
5 ml (1 tsp) vanilla essence
2.5 ml ($\frac{1}{2}$ tsp) salt
50 g (2 oz) walnut halves, chopped

———1———

Lightly grease and line a 20.5 cm (8 inch) square cake tin. Break the carob into pieces and put in a bowl with the margarine and sugar. Place the bowl over a pan of boiling water until the carob melts. Remove from the heat.

———2———

Sift together the flours and baking powder. Add to the bowl with any bran left in the sieve and the remaining ingredients. Mix well. Turn into the tin and spread evenly.

———3———

Bake at 180°C (350°F) mark 4 for 15 minutes, until slightly risen and shiny on top. Remove from oven and cool in tin. Cut into 16 squares. Store in an airtight container.

MICROWAVE Follow step 1, but put only carob and margarine in a bowl. Cook 100% (High) 45–60 seconds, until melted. Stir well. Follow step 2, adding sugar with other ingredients. Complete step 2. In step 3, cook 4$\frac{1}{2}$–5 minutes, until the surface is just set, turning the dish 4 times. Stand 5 minutes, then turn out on to a wire rack to cool.

GOODNESS GUIDE
FIBRE Carob is a good source of gummy fibre, which helps reduce the absorption of fat
VITAMINS Carob contains three B vitamins—thiamine, riboflavin and niacin. The walnuts supply some B vitamins and some vitamin E
MINERALS Iron and calcium are supplied by the carob and walnuts, and the walnuts also supply zinc

SESAME CRACKERS

Keep a batch of these easy-to-make biscuits on hand for a high-protein snack or lunch-box filler.

MAKES 20 80 calories each
PREPARATION 15 minutes
BAKING 15 minutes

100 g (4 oz) plain wholemeal flour
100 g (4 oz) plain flour
2.5 ml ($\frac{1}{2}$ tsp) baking powder
2.5 ml ($\frac{1}{2}$ tsp) bicarbonate of soda
45 ml (3 tbsp) sesame seeds
15 ml (1 tbsp) light muscovado sugar
45 ml (3 tbsp) sunflower oil
50 g (2 oz) polyunsaturated margarine

———1———

Lightly grease a baking sheet and set aside. Sift together the flours, baking powder and bicarbonate of soda, adding any bran left in the sieve. Stir in the sesame seeds and sugar. Add the oil, margarine and 25 ml (1$\frac{1}{2}$tbsp) water. Mix to a smooth dough. Roll out on a lightly floured surface to about 0.5 cm ($\frac{1}{4}$ inch) thick.

———2———

Cut out the biscuits with a 7.5 cm (3 inch) cutter. Place on the baking sheet and bake at 200°C (400°F) mark 6 for 15 minutes or until firm and slightly risen. Remove from the oven and stand for 1 minute before transferring to a wire rack to cool.

MICROWAVE In step 1, grease 3 sheets of greaseproof paper to fit cooker base. Complete step 1. Follow step 2 and arrange cut-out biscuits in circles, 7 each on 2 separate sheets of paper, 6 on the third sheet. Cook one sheet at a time 60% (Medium) 4 minutes, until biscuits look dry on the surface, turning paper every minute. Stand 5 minutes, then slide biscuits on to wire rack to cool.

GOODNESS GUIDE
FIBRE Dietary fibre is contributed by the wholemeal flour and seeds
PROTEIN Sesame seeds are rich in protein
MINERALS The seeds and flours are good sources of potassium, calcium, magnesium and iron
VITAMINS Significant amounts of B vitamins, specially thiamine and niacin, are provided by the seeds and flours

FRENCH LOAF

Serve this wholesome bread with soups or salads or use to make delicious jumbo filled sandwiches.

MAKES 14 SLICES
110 CALORIES PER SLICE
PREPARATION 20 minutes
BAKING 30 minutes
RISING 1$\frac{1}{2}$ hours

25 g (1 oz) fresh yeast, crumbled, or 10 ml (2 tsp) dried and 2.5 ml ($\frac{1}{2}$ tsp) light muscovado sugar
225 g (8 oz) plain wholemeal flour
225 g (8 oz) plain flour
5 ml (1 tsp) salt
a little semi-skimmed milk, to glaze

———1———

Lightly grease a large bowl and a baking sheet and set aside. Blend the fresh yeast with 300 ml ($\frac{1}{2}$ pint) tepid water. If using dried yeast, sprinkle it into the tepid water with the sugar. Leave in a warm place for 15 minutes, until frothy.

———2———

Put the flours and salt into a warmed bowl, stir in the yeast mixture and mix to a smooth dough, adding extra tepid water, if necessary. Turn out on to a lightly floured work surface and knead for 5 minutes or until very smooth and elastic.

———3———

Place in the oiled bowl, cover with a clean cloth and leave in a warm place for 1 hour or until doubled in size.

———4———

Turn out on to a lightly floured surface and knead for 5 minutes. Roll into a sausage shape about 38 cm (15 inches) long and place on the baking sheet. Cover with a clean cloth and leave for 30 minutes, until well risen.

———5———

Lightly glaze the dough with a little milk. Bake at 200°C (400°F) mark 6 for 30 minutes or until light golden and the loaf sounds hollow when tapped on the bottom. Place on a wire rack to cool.

GOODNESS GUIDE
FIBRE High fibre is provided by the wholemeal flour
MINERALS This loaf provides more potassium and zinc than traditional all-white French breads

PASSION CAKE

MAKES 8 SLICES 340 calories each
PREPARATION 20 minutes
BAKING 35 minutes

100 g (4 oz) polyunsaturated margarine
100 g (4 oz) light muscovado sugar
1.25 ml ($\frac{1}{4}$ tsp) ground cinnamon
1.25 ml ($\frac{1}{4}$ tsp) grated nutmeg
grated rind of 1 orange
2 eggs, beaten
65 g ($2\frac{1}{2}$ oz) plain wholemeal flour
65 g ($2\frac{1}{2}$ oz) plain flour
7.5 ml ($1\frac{1}{2}$ tsp) baking powder
5 ml (1 tsp) salt
75 g (3 oz) carrots, scrubbed and grated
25 g (1 oz) walnut halves, chopped

FILLING AND TOPPING
450 g (1 lb) low-fat soft cheese
100 g (4 oz) walnut halves, chopped, plus
extra to decorate
225 g (8 oz) can unsweetened pineapple,
drained and finely chopped

——— 1 ———

Lightly grease and flour two 18 cm
(7 inch) sandwich tins. Beat the margarine and sugar together until light
and creamy. Beat in the cinnamon,
nutmeg and orange rind.

——— 2 ———

Add the eggs a little at a time,
beating well after each addition and
adding a little of the plain flour if the
mixture starts to curdle. Sift together
the flours, baking powder and salt,
adding the bran in the sieve. Fold
into the egg mixture.

——— 3 ———

Fold in the grated carrots, walnuts
and 15 ml (1 tbsp) warm water.
Divide the mixture between the tins
and bake at 190°C (375°F) mark 5
for 35 minutes or until the sides of
the cakes come away from the tins
slightly. Turn out and cool on a rack.

——— 4 ———

Beat the cheese until creamy, then
fold in the nuts. Add the pineapple
to one-quarter of the cheese and use
to sandwich the cakes together.
Spread the remaining cheese over
the top and sides. Decorate.

GOODNESS GUIDE
FIBRE Carrots, walnuts and wholemeal flour
all provide dietary fibre
PROTEIN The protein in the flours is
completed by that in the eggs
VITAMINS The carrots provide vitamins C
and A. Some of the C, though, will be
destroyed by the baking powder

CAROB BROWNIES

SESAME CRACKERS

FRENCH LOAF

PASSION CAKE

LIGHT RYE BREAD

CARROT CORNBREAD

SPICY TEA BUNS

APRICOT AND PEANUT SCONES

CARROT CORNBREAD

MAKES 9 PIECES 110 calories each
PREPARATION 15 minutes
BAKING 40 minutes

100 g (4 oz) cornmeal
100 g (4 oz) self-raising wholemeal flour
12.5 ml (2½ tsp) baking powder
75 g (3 oz) curd cheese
350 ml (12 fl oz) semi-skimmed milk
2.5 ml (½ tsp) salt
100 g (4 oz) carrots, scrubbed and finely grated
polyunsaturated margarine, to serve

———1———
Lightly grease and line the bottom of a shallow 18 cm (7 inch) square baking tin.

———2———
Sift together the cornmeal, the flour and baking powder, adding the bran left in the sieve. Blend together the cheese, milk and salt. Stir the carrot into the flour, then gradually stir in the milk mixture.

———3———
Pour the mixture into the tin and bake at 190°C (375°F) mark 5 for 40 minutes or until pale golden.

———4———
Turn out and serve warm. Cut into squares and spread with margarine.

230

APRICOT AND PEANUT SCONES

The apricots and peanuts add flavour and sweetness to these scones without extra sugar or salt.

MAKES 10 160 calories each
PREPARATION 10 minutes
BAKING 15 minutes

100 g (4 oz) self-raising flour
100 g (4 oz) plain wholemeal flour
5 ml (1 tsp) baking powder
50 g (2 oz) polyunsaturated margarine, chilled
50 g (2 oz) ready-to-eat dried apricots, rinsed and finely chopped
40 g (1½ oz) natural roasted peanuts shelled and with or without skins, coarsely chopped
1 egg, size 2, beaten
30 ml (2 tbsp) Greek strained yogurt
60 ml (4 tbsp) semi-skimmed milk
30 ml (2 tbsp) cracked wheat

———1———

Sift the flours and baking powder into a bowl, adding any bran left in the sieve. Rub in the margarine until the mixture resembles fine bread-crumbs, then mix in the apricots and the peanuts.

———2———

Mix the egg with the yogurt and 45 ml (3 tbsp) of the milk. Add to the dry ingredients and mix to a fairly soft dough.

———3———

Turn the dough out on to a lightly floured surface and roll out to about 2 cm (¾ inch) thick. With a round pastry cutter, stamp out ten 5 cm (2 inch) rounds.

———4———

Place on non-stick, or lightly greased, baking sheets, allowing room for spreading. Lightly brush the tops with the remaining milk and sprinkle with the cracked wheat.

———5———

Bake at 190°C (375°F) mark 5 for 15 minutes, until risen and golden brown. Serve warm, or cool.

GOODNESS GUIDE

CARROT CORNBREAD

FAT Using curd cheese and semi-skimmed milk reduces the amount of fat in the cornbread

APRICOT AND PEANUT SCONES

FIBRE The scones are rich in fibre from the flour, cracked wheat, apricots and peanuts

SPICY TEA BUNS

MAKES 12 180 calories each
PREPARATION 1 hour
BAKING 15–20 minutes
RISING 1 hour 15 minutes

15 ml (1 tbsp) clear honey
350 ml (12 fl oz) semi-skimmed milk
15 ml (1 tbsp) dried yeast
225 g (8 oz) plain wholemeal flour
225 g (8 oz) plain flour
salt, to taste
5 ml (1 tsp) ground mixed spice
5 ml (1 tsp) ground cinnamon
25 g (1 oz) polyunsaturated margarine
50 g (2 oz) sultanas
50 g (2 oz) mixed peel, rinsed and chopped
a little extra honey, to glaze

———1———

Lightly grease a baking sheet. Warm the milk and mix the honey with 175 ml (6 fl oz) of the milk and sprinkle on the yeast. Stir well and stand in a warm place 10–15 minutes, until frothy.

———2———

Place flours in a bowl with the salt and spices; rub in the margarine.

———3———

Make a well in the centre and pour in the yeast with the remaining milk. Mix well, turn out on to a lightly floured surface and knead until smooth and soft.

———4———

Lightly oil the mixing bowl and place the dough back in it, turning over once. Cover and leave in a warm place for about 1 hour, until double in size.

———5———

Knock back and place on a lightly floured surface; knead in the fruit. Divide the dough into 12 even-sized pieces. Knead into small bun shapes and place on the baking sheet.

———6———

Leave to prove for about 15 minutes, then glaze each with a little honey. Bake at 200°C (400°F) mark 6 for 15–20 minutes or until they are a rich golden brown and sound hollow when tapped on the bottom.

GOODNESS GUIDE

SPICY TEA BUNS

FIBRE These tea buns are rich in fibre, provided by the wholemeal flour and the dried fruit

LIGHT RYE BREAD

FAT The small amount of margarine makes the bread low-fat

LIGHT RYE BREAD

MAKES 10 SLICES 175 calories each
PREPARATION 1 hour
BAKING 40–45 minutes
RISING 1¼ hours

15 ml (1 tbsp) clear honey
15 ml (1 tbsp) dried yeast
225 g (8 oz) rye flour
225 g (8 oz) plain wholemeal flour
2.5 ml (½ tsp) salt
15 ml (1 tbsp) caraway seeds
25 g (1 oz) polyunsaturated margarine
a little semi-skimmed milk to glaze and a few extra caraway seeds

———1———

Mix the honey with 175 ml (6 fl oz) tepid water and sprinkle on the yeast. Stir well and stand in a warm place for 10–15 minutes, until frothy.

———2———

Place the flours in a bowl with the salt and caraway seeds. Rub in the margarine.

———3———

Make a well in the centre of the bowl and pour in the yeast with another 175 ml (6 fl oz) tepid water. Mix well to form a firm but sticky dough. Turn out on to a floured surface and knead until smooth.

———4———

Lightly oil the mixing bowl and place the dough back in it, turning it over once. Cover with a damp cloth and leave to rise in a warm place for about 1 hour or until double in size. Lightly grease a baking sheet and set aside.

———5———

Knock back the dough. Place on a lightly floured surface and knead.

———6———

Shape into an oblong sausage and place on the baking sheet. Leave to prove for about 15–20 minutes, until the dough increases in bulk by a quarter to a half. Glaze with a little semi-skimmed milk and sprinkle with the extra seeds.

———7———

Bake at 200°C (400°F) mark 6 for 40–45 minutes or until golden brown and hollow-sounding when tapped. Cool on a wire rack.

WHOLEMEAL ROCK BUNS

These healthy wholemeal rock buns are ideal for afternoon tea or as a lunch box filler.

MAKES 10 180 calories each
PREPARATION 10 minutes
BAKING 15 minutes

225 g (8 oz) self-raising wholemeal flour
100 g (4 oz) polyunsaturated margarine, chilled
2.5 ml (½ tsp) ground cinnamon
100 g (4 oz) light muscovado sugar
100 g (4 oz) dried mixed fruit, rinsed
1 egg, beaten
25 ml (1½ tbsp) milk

———1———

Lightly grease a baking sheet and set aside. Put the flour into a bowl. Rub in the margarine until the mixture resembles fine breadcrumbs.

———2———

Stir in the cinnamon, sugar and dried fruit. Add the beaten egg and milk and mix together to form a stiff mixture. Form into 10 mounds and place on the baking sheet.

———3———

Bake at 200°C (400°F) mark 6 for 15 minutes or until golden and cooked through. Cool on a wire rack.

MICROWAVE Complete steps 1 and 2, but do not add the milk. Arrange mounds round a plate with space between each. Cook, uncovered, 100% (High) 7–9 minutes, turning plate three times, until buns are just firm all over. Cool on a wire rack.

GOODNESS GUIDE

WHOLEMEAL ROCK BUNS
FIBRE The wholemeal flour and dried fruit provide plenty of fibre. It is important to drink lots of fluid during the day as fibre absorbs extra water, and it is this combination which aids the movement of food through the intestine
PROTEIN The egg, milk and wholemeal flour provide protein

OAT BREAD
FIBRE The wholemeal flour and oats provide different forms of fibre, all of which are good for health
VITAMINS The flours and oatmeal provide B vitamins

OAT BREAD

MAKES 8 SLICES 230 calories each
PREPARATION 15 minutes
BAKING 45 minutes
SOAKING 1 hour
RISING 2 hours

175 g (6 oz) medium oatmeal
300 ml (½ pint) semi-skimmed milk
150 g (5 oz) plain wholemeal flour
150 g (5 oz) strong plain flour
2.5 ml (½ tsp) salt
1 sachet easy blend dried yeast
50 g (2 oz) polyunsaturated margarine
30 ml (2 tbsp) clear honey
beaten egg, to glaze
10 ml (2 tsp) medium oatmeal, for sprinkling

———1———

Lightly grease a 15 cm (6 inch) round deep cake tin and set aside. Put the oatmeal into a bowl, add the milk and stir well, then leave to soak for 1 hour.

———2———

Put the flours into a large bowl. Add the salt and yeast. Melt the margarine in a saucepan and mix with the honey. Add to the flours, together with the soaked oatmeal mixture. Mix well together.

———3———

Turn the dough on to a lightly floured surface and knead well, until firm. Shape into a ball, place in a large bowl and cover with a clean cloth. Leave to rise for about 1½ hours or until doubled in size.

———4———

Turn the dough on to a lightly floured surface and knead well. Shape the dough into a ball, then place in the greased cake tin. Press down firmly to cover the base of the tin. Slash the surface of the dough with a sharp knife to form a criss-cross pattern. Cover with a clean cloth and leave to prove for about 30 minutes or until the dough has risen to the top of tin.

———5———

Brush the surface of the dough with beaten egg and sprinkle with the remaining oatmeal. Bake at 220°C (425°F) mark 7 for 30 minutes. Cover the surface of the loaf with foil, reduce the oven temperature to 170°C (325°F) mark 3 and continue baking for a further 15 minutes. Remove from the tin and leave to cool on a wire rack.

OAT BREAD

FARMHOUSE TEABREAD

MAKES 12 SLICES 185 calories each
PREPARATION 15 minutes
BAKING 1¼ hours

75 g (3 oz) polyunsaturated margarine
100 g (4 oz) light muscovado sugar
3 eggs, beaten
150 g (5 oz) plain wholemeal flour
100 g (4 oz) self-raising flour
7.5 ml (1½ tsp) baking powder
2 green eating apples, peeled, cored and grated
75 g (3 oz) ready-to-eat dried apricots, rinsed and chopped
finely grated rind of 1 small orange
30 ml (2 tbsp) orange juice
low-fat soft cheese, to serve

———1———

Lightly grease the base and sides of a 900 g (2 lb) loaf tin and line with greaseproof paper. Cream the margarine and sugar together until soft. Gradually, add the eggs and beat.

232

VIENNESE FINGERS

WHOLEMEAL ROCK BUNS

FARMHOUSE TEABREAD

<hr />2<hr />

Stir in the flours and baking powder and mix well until combined. Add the grated apples, chopped apricots, orange rind and enough orange juice to give the mixture a soft dropping consistency.

<hr />3<hr />

Turn the mixture into the prepared tin and level the surface. Bake at 190°C (375°F) mark 5 for 45 minutes, then cover with foil to prevent the cake over-browning. Continue baking for a further 30 minutes, until well risen, golden brown and cooked through. Cool on a wire rack. Serve sliced and spread with low-fat soft cheese.

GOODNESS GUIDE

FIBRE The wholemeal flour, apples and apricots make this teabread high in fibre, necessary for healthy intestines

PROTEIN The eggs and flour provide plenty of protein

MINERALS The eggs, flours and apricots provide iron and calcium

VITAMINS B vitamins are provided by eggs, flour and cheese

VIENNESE FINGERS

Wholemeal flour and nuts makes these fingers higher in fibre than traditional Viennese biscuits.

MAKES 15 100 calories each
PREPARATION 15 minutes
BAKING 10–12 minutes

100 g (4 oz) polyunsaturated margarine
25 g (1 oz) light muscovado sugar
a few drops of vanilla essence
50 g (2 oz) plain wholemeal flour
50 g (2 oz) plain flour
1.25 ml ($\frac{1}{4}$ tsp) baking powder
60 g ($2\frac{1}{2}$ oz) unsweetened plain carob bar
15 g ($\frac{1}{2}$ oz) chopped nuts, toasted

<hr />1<hr />

Lightly grease a baking sheet and set aside. Cream the margarine and sugar together until soft and fluffy. Stir in the vanilla essence, flours and baking powder and mix well, until thoroughly combined.

<hr />2<hr />

Place the mixture in a piping bag fitted with a large star tube and pipe into 15 fingers, about 7.5 cm (3 inches) long, on the baking sheet.

<hr />3<hr />

Bake at 190°C (375°F) mark 5 for 10–12 minutes, until lightly browned and cooked. Cool on a wire rack.

<hr />4<hr />

Break the carob bar into a heatproof bowl, place over a saucepan of simmering water and melt the carob, stirring occasionally, until smooth.

<hr />5<hr />

Dip the ends of the biscuits in melted carob and sprinkle both ends of each biscuit with chopped toasted nuts. Leave to set on grease-proof paper.

GOODNESS GUIDE

VITAMINS The flours, nuts and carob are sources of important B vitamins

MINERALS The flours, nuts and carob supply iron, calcium, magnesium and potassium. Magnesium is an essential constituent of all cells and helps with the functioning of some enzymes

POPPYSEED TEABREAD

MAKES 20 SLICES 125 calories each
PREPARATION 25 minutes
BAKING 30 minutes
RISING 1 hour

1 sachet easy blend dried yeast
350 g (12 oz) strong plain wholemeal flour
5–10 ml (1–2 tsp) ground cinnamon
50 g (2 oz) polyunsaturated margarine
30 ml (2 tbsp) clear honey
2 eggs, lightly beaten
150 ml (¼ pint) tepid semi-skimmed milk

FILLING
100 g (4 oz) poppyseeds
25 g (1 oz) walnut halves, chopped
30 ml (2 tbsp) honey
5 ml (1 tsp) grated orange rind
30 ml (2 tbsp) orange juice
few drops of vanilla essence (optional)

— 1 —

Grease a baking sheet and set aside. Mix the yeast, flour, cinnamon, margarine, honey and eggs, reserving some egg to glaze. Add enough milk to give a soft, kneadable dough. Knead for 8 minutes on a floured surface. Cover with clean tea-cloth.

— 2 —

In a blender or food processor, grind all but 15 ml (1 tbsp) of the poppyseeds with just enough water to enable the machine to work. Place the poppyseeds in a saucepan. Add the remaining filling ingredients. Heat gently, stirring, until thick. Set aside and cool.

— 3 —

Roll out the dough to a 45 × 25 cm (18 × 10 inch) rectangle. Spread the filling over. Roll up the dough loosely from one narrow end like a Swiss roll. Place on the baking sheet. Cover with a clean cloth and leave to rise in a warm place until doubled in size.

— 4 —

Brush with the reserved egg and sprinkle with poppyseeds. Bake at 230°C (450°F) mark 8 for 10 minutes. Reduce the heat to 200°C (400°F) mark 6 and bake for 20 minutes.

GOODNESS GUIDE
MINERALS The teabread is rich in many essential minerals
VITAMINS Plenty of B vitamins are present in the poppyseed teabread

SULTANA RUM GINGERBREAD

MAKES 12 SLICES 275 calories each
PREPARATION 12–15 minutes
BAKING About 1 hour

350 g (12 oz) plain wholemeal flour
10 ml (2 tsp) ground ginger
10 ml (2 tsp) baking powder
225 g (8 oz) sultanas, rinsed
7.5 ml (1½ tsp) finely grated fresh root ginger
2 eggs, size 2
60 ml (4 tbsp) semi-skimmed milk
175 g (6 oz) molasses
100 g (4 oz) polyunsaturated margarine
45 ml (3 tbsp) rum

— 1 —

Grease a 900 g (2 lb) loaf tin. Sift the flour, ginger and baking powder into a large mixing bowl and add the bran in the sieve. Stir in half the sultanas.

— 2 —

Purée the remaining sultanas in a blender or food processor with the root ginger, eggs and milk.

— 3 —

Gently heat the molasses and margarine in a saucepan until the margarine has melted. Add the sultana mixture and the molasses mixture to the flour, with the rum. Stir well, adding a little more milk if needed to make a soft dropping consistency.

— 4 —

Pour into the tin. Bake at 170°C (325°F) mark 3 for about 1 hour, until the cake is springy in the centre. Leave in the tin until almost cold. Turn out and cut into slices.

MICROWAVE Follow steps 1 and 2. Put molasses and margarine into a bowl. Cook, uncovered, 100% (High) 1 minute. Stir well and complete step 3. Pour mixture into prepared tin. Cook uncovered, 100% (High) 11–12 minutes, turning tin 4 or 5 times until gingerbread is just dry all over surface. Leave in the tin for about 10 minutes. Turn on to a rack and leave to cool.

GOODNESS GUIDE
FIBRE The wholemeal flour and sultanas make this a high-fibre gingerbread
MINERALS This gingerbread is high in minerals, including iron, calcium and potassium

FLORENTINES

Florentines spread as they bake so space well apart. They are irregular in shape when cooked.

MAKES 28 100 calories each
PREPARATION 20 minutes
BAKING 12 minutes

100 g (4 oz) polyunsaturated margarine
100 g (4 oz) dark muscovado sugar
50 g (2 oz) sultanas, rinsed
50 g (2 oz) ready-to-eat dried apricots, rinsed and roughly chopped
50 g (2 oz) candied peel, rinsed and chopped
75 g (3 oz) whole hazelnuts
50 g (2 oz) flaked almonds
1 egg, size 2
20 ml (4 tsp) plain wholemeal flour
150 g (5 oz) unsweetened plain carob bar, broken into pieces

— 1 —

Line 2 large baking sheets with baking parchment and set aside. Heat 75 g (3 oz) of the margarine with the sugar in a saucepan.

SULTANA RUM GINGERBREAD

WHOLEMEAL PITTA BREAD

FLORENTINES

POPPYSEED TEABREAD

——2——

When beginning to bubble, remove from heat and stir in sultanas, apricots, peel, nuts, egg and flour.

——3——

Spoon the mixture in 28 small heaps on the baking sheets, allowing plenty of space to spread.

——4——

Bake at 180°C (350°F) mark 4 for 12 minutes. Leave to cool on the paper for a few minutes, then remove paper and cool on rack.

——5——

Gently heat the carob and remaining margarine together in a heatproof bowl over a pan of hot water. When just melted, spread over the smooth surface of each florentine with a palette knife. Leave to set.

GOODNESS GUIDE

FIBRE Florentines are exceptionally high in fibre, which is supplied by the dried fruit, nuts and flour. Fibre is necessary to help prevent diseases of the digestive system such as diverticulosis

VITAMINS B-complex vitamins are present, as well as vitamin A

WHOLEMEAL PITTA BREAD

Slit the warmed pitta bread open to make a pocket and fill with salad, cheese or meat. Or cut into fingers and dip in hummus.

MAKES 8 205 calories each
PREPARATION 15 minutes
BAKING 10 minutes
RISING 45 minutes

450 g (1 lb) plain wholemeal flour
5 ml (1 tsp) easy blend dried yeast
1.25 ml ($\frac{1}{4}$ tsp) sea salt (optional)
30 ml (2 tbsp) olive oil

——1——

Warm and lightly grease 1 or 2 baking sheets and set aside. Mix the wholemeal flour, yeast, sea salt and olive oil together, then add about 300 ml ($\frac{1}{2}$ pint) tepid water to make a soft but kneadable dough. Turn on to a well-floured work surface and knead for 8 minutes. Divide the dough into 8 pieces.

——2——

Using your palm, roll each piece of dough into a ball, then with a rolling pin into an oval about 0.5 cm ($\frac{1}{4}$ inch) thick.

——3——

Place on the baking sheets. Cover with a clean cloth and leave to rise in a warm place for about 45 minutes, until roughly doubled in size.

——4——

Bake at 230°C (450°F) mark 8 for 10 minutes. Remove from the oven. To keep in the steam and create a soft bread, wrap well in a clean cloth or foil and set aside for at least 10 minutes. Before serving, place under a moderate grill to puff up.

GOODNESS GUIDE

FIBRE One pitta bread provides 5.4 g of fibre, one-fifth of the recommended daily amount

MINERALS Minerals in this dish include potassium, calcium, iron and zinc

VITAMINS Thiamine (vitamin B_1) and vitamin E are present in the wholemeal flour

CARROT BISCUITS

MAKES ABOUT 20 115 calories each
PREPARATION 15 minutes
BAKING 10–12 minutes

75 g (3 oz) polyunsaturated margarine
75 g (3 oz) light muscovado sugar
60 ml (4 tbsp) clear honey
1 egg, beaten
100 g (4 oz) carrots, scrubbed and grated
175 g (6 oz) self-raising wholemeal flour
5 ml (1 tsp) baking powder
100 g (4 oz) porridge oats
25 g (1 oz) sesame seeds
50 g (2 oz) raisins, rinsed

——— 1 ———

Lightly grease 1 or 2 baking sheets and set aside. Place the margarine, sugar and honey in a small saucepan and heat gently until the margarine has melted and the sugar dissolved. Cool slightly.

——— 2 ———

Mix together the egg and carrots. Place remaining ingredients in a bowl and stir until mixed. Add the carrot and honey mixtures; stir well.

——— 3 ———

With moistened hands, shape heaped dessertspoons of the mixture into flat rounds. Place, a little apart, on the prepared baking sheets.

——— 4 ———

Bake at 200°C (400°F) mark 6 for 10–12 minutes, until lightly browned. Remove and cool on a wire rack. The biscuits will be crisp on the outside and soft in the centre. Store in an airtight container.

MICROWAVE Put margarine, sugar and honey into a bowl. Cook, uncovered, 100% (High) 1 minute. Stir well. Follow steps 2 and 3. Arrange biscuits around greased plates, 9–10 on each. Stand on upturned plate. Cook, uncovered, 60% (Medium) 6 minutes, turning plates 3 times, until dry all over the surface. Cool on a wire rack.

GOODNESS GUIDE
FIBRE The carrots, flour, oats, seeds and raisins make these biscuits high in fibre
VITAMINS Vitamin A is contributed by the carrots, egg and margarine and is needed for healthy skin and low-light vision
MINERALS The eggs, flour, oats, seeds and raisins supply iron, calcium and potassium

IRISH SODA BREAD

Soda bread is both healthy and easy to make—low-fat buttermilk is used here and soda replaces yeast as a raising agent.

MAKES 10 SLICES (SMALL LOAVES) OR 20 SLICES (LARGE LOAF) 120 calories each
PREPARATION 10 minutes
BAKING 35–70 minutes

450 g (1 lb) self-raising wholemeal flour, plus extra for sprinkling
225 g (8 oz) plain flour
salt, to taste
2.5 ml (½ tsp) bicarbonate of soda
600 ml (1 pint) buttermilk
a little semi-skimmed milk, if needed

——— 1 ———

Lightly flour a baking sheet and set aside. Sift the flours, salt and bicarbonate of soda into a bowl and add any bran left in the sieve.

——— 2 ———

Pour in the buttermilk and mix quickly with a large fork to form a soft dough. If the mixture is too dry add a little semi-skimmed milk. Knead very briefly on a lightly floured surface. Shape into one large or two small cob loaves.

——— 3 ———

Place on the prepared baking sheet and sprinkle with a little extra flour. Cut a deep cross in the top of each.

——— 4 ———

Bake at 200°C (400°F) mark 6 for about 35 minutes (small loaves) or 60–70 minutes (large loaf), until the base sounds hollow when tapped. Cool on a wire rack and serve warm.

MICROWAVE Follow steps 1 and 2 but do not flour a baking sheet. Place loaf on non-stick paper on a rack and cook, uncovered, 100% (High) 15 minutes, turning rack 3 times. If making 2 small loaves, cook each separately, 6–7 minutes.

GOODNESS GUIDE
PROTEIN The low-fat buttermilk and the flour contribute protein
CARBOHYDRATE Bread provides a range of nutrients, including complex carbohydrates for sustained energy and valuable fibre
VITAMINS The flour and buttermilk supply B-complex vitamins, which are used to provide energy from carbohydrates and fat, as well as from any excess protein not used by the body elsewhere

DATE AND WALNUT TOPPED SHORTBREAD

CARROT BISCUITS

CHEESE AND HERB SCONE WHIRLS

MAKES 10 SCONES 125 calories each
PREPARATION 15 minutes
BAKING 12–15 minutes

225 g (8 oz) self-raising wholemeal flour
salt, to taste
50 g (2 oz) polyunsaturated margarine,
chilled and cut into small pieces
100 g (4 oz) low-fat soft cheese
75 ml (5 tbsp) semi-skimmed milk
5 ml (1 tsp) Dijon mustard
semi-skimmed milk, for brushing
30 ml (2 tbsp) chopped fresh parsley
10 ml (2 tsp) chopped fresh herbs, such as
tarragon, mint, marjoram and rosemary, or
5 ml (1 tsp) dried mixed herbs
15 ml (1 tbsp) grated Parmesan cheese

———1———

Lightly grease a baking sheet and set aside. Mix the flour and salt in a bowl. Add the margarine and rub in until the mixture resembles fine breadcrumbs.

———2———

Mix together the cheese, milk and mustard, then add to the dry ingredients and mix lightly to form a soft dough.

———3———

Knead briefly on a lightly floured surface, then roll out to a 12 × 25 cm (5 × 10 inch) oblong. Brush with milk and sprinkle with the herbs.

———4———

Roll up from one long edge and cut into ten slices about 2.5 cm (1 inch) thick. Place on the backing sheet. Brush the tops with milk and sprinkle with Parmesan cheese. Bake at 220°C (425°F) mark 7 for 12–15 minutes, until risen and golden brown. Serve warm.

MICROWAVE Follow steps 1, 2, 3 and the beginning of step 4, but arrange on non-stick paper around the edge of a large plate. Cook, uncovered, 100% (High) 5 minutes, turning plate 3 times. Brown tops under the grill if liked.

GOODNESS GUIDE

MINERALS Cheese provides calcium, which is needed to maintain strong bones and the clotting ability of blood
FIBRE Wholemeal flour is a valuable source of fibre
FAT The use of low-fat cheese means that the overall fat content of these scones is fairly low

CHEESE AND HERB SCONE WHIRLS

IRISH SODA BREAD

DATE AND WALNUT TOPPED SHORTBREAD

For an alternative flavour, use ground mixed spice instead of cinnamon.

MAKES 18 BARS 175 calories each
PREPARATION 25 minutes
BAKING 30 minutes

150 g (6 oz) plain wholemeal flour
100 g (4 oz) plain flour
5 ml (1 tsp) ground cinnamon
150 g (6 oz) polyunsaturated margarine
30 ml (2 tbsp) clear honey
175 g (6 oz) stoned dates, rinsed and chopped
75 g (3 oz) walnuts, chopped
100 ml (4 fl oz) unsweetened orange juice
1 egg, beaten

———1———

Lightly grease a shallow 28 × 18 cm (11 × 7 inch) oblong tin and set aside. Place 100 g (4 oz) wholemeal flour with the plain flour and cinnamon in a bowl. Add the margarine and rub in until the mixture resembles fine breadcrumbs.

———2———

Drizzle the honey into the bowl and mix to form a soft dough. Knead on a lightly floured surface, then press into the prepared tin. Prick the shortbread and bake at 180°C (350°F) mark 4 for 15 minutes.

———3———

Meanwhile, make the topping. Mix together the remaining wholemeal flour, chopped dates and walnuts. Stir in the orange juice and egg until well mixed.

———4———

Spread the topping evenly over the shortbread and bake for a further 15 minutes, until the topping is set but still soft. Leave to cool in the tin, then cut into 18 bars and store in an airtight container.

GOODNESS GUIDE

MINERALS Iron and calcium are contributed by the flour and the nuts
VITAMINS B-complex vitamins, which play a part in so many of the body processes, are contributed by the flour, nuts, dates and egg
FIBRE The walnuts, dates and wholemeal flour provide fibre

HONEY LOAF

MAKES 12 SLICES 153 calories each
PREPARATION 15 minutes
BAKING 40 minutes
RISING 45 minutes

225 g (8 oz) plain wholemeal flour
225 g (8 oz) strong plain flour
15 g ($\frac{1}{2}$ oz) polyunsaturated margarine
10 ml (2 tsp) easy-mix dried yeast
1 egg, size 2
30 ml (2 tbsp) clear honey
150 ml ($\frac{1}{4}$ pint) semi-skimmed milk
5 ml (1 tsp) honey, to glaze
2.5 ml ($\frac{1}{2}$ tsp) poppy seeds, to decorate

——— 1 ———

Lightly grease a 1 kg (2 lb) loaf tin and set aside. Place the flours in a mixing bowl and rub in the margarine, then stir in the dried yeast. Beat the egg in a measuring jug and add the honey, then make up to 150 ml ($\frac{1}{4}$ pint) with water. Heat the milk in a saucepan, but do not boil. Pour on to the egg and honey mixture, stirring.

——— 2 ———

Add the liquid to the dry ingredients and mix to a soft dough. Knead thoroughly on a lightly floured surface for about 10 minutes, until smooth.

——— 3 ———

Divide the dough into four and roll each piece into a ball. Place side by side in the loaf tin and press down gently. Cover and leave to rise in a warm place for 45 minutes.

——— 4 ———

Uncover and bake at 220°C (425°F) mark 7 for 10 minutes, until risen and browned. Reduce the temperature to 190°C (375°F) mark 5 and continue baking for about 30 minutes, until hollow-sounding when tapped underneath. Heat the honey for the glaze, brush over the top of the loaf and sprinkle with poppy seeds. Cool on a wire rack. When the loaf is completely cold, cut into slices.

GOODNESSS GUIDE

PROTEIN This is an enriched loaf high in protein provided by the flour, egg and semi-skimmed milk
FIBRE The use of half wholemeal and half refined flour provides more fibre than using all refined, and enables you to become accustomed to the taste and texture of wholemeal flour

APPLE AND OAT LAYER

This dish is a tasty snack to have with coffee or tea, and also makes a good dessert after Sunday lunch or an evening meal.

MAKES 10–12 SLICES
205–170 calories each
PREPARATION 10 minutes
BAKING 30–40 minutes

100 g (4 oz) polyunsaturated margarine
60 g (2$\frac{1}{2}$ oz) light muscovado sugar
30 ml (2 tbsp) clear honey
225 g (8 oz) rolled oats
1 large cooking apple, about 250 g (9 oz), peeled, cored and thinly sliced
5 ml (1 tsp) ground cinnamon

——— 1 ———

Lightly grease an 18 cm (7 inch) square shallow baking tin and set aside. Put the margarine, 50 g (2 oz) sugar and the honey in a saucepan. Heat gently, stirring, until melted. Add the rolled oats and stir until coated in the melted mixture.

——— 2 ———

Spoon half the oat mixture into the tin and spread evenly over the base. Arrange the apples over the top in overlapping rows. Mix together the remaining sugar and cinnamon and sprinkle over the apples. Sprinkle the remaining oat mixture over the apples and gently press down.

——— 3 ———

Bake at 190°C (375°F) mark 5 for 30–40 minutes, until golden brown and crisp. Cut into slices while still hot, then leave in the tin to cool.

MICROWAVE In step 1, use a microwave oven bowl and cook, uncovered, 100% (High) 1 minute. Add remaining ingredients. Use a microwave oven dish and follow step 2, then cook, uncovered, 100% (High) 15 minutes, turning dish 3 times. Cut into slices, loosen underneath, lift out slices while warm so that the bottom of the oat layer does not become soggy.

GOODNESS GUIDE

FIBRE Oats and apple both provide excellent fibre, which aids better control of the absorption of the sugar present in this dessert
VITAMINS Cooking apples have a higher vitamin C content than eating apples. Oats have B vitamins, which help the body utilise the energy from carbohydrates

CAROB-MINT BISCUITS

With just a hint of mint, these biscuits have a crunchy texture and a rich chocolate-like flavour.

MAKES ABOUT 24 80 calories each
PREPARATION 15 minutes
BAKING 15 minutes

200 g (7 oz) plain wholemeal flour
45 ml (3 tbsp) carob powder
100 g (4 oz) polyunsaturated margarine, chilled
100 g (4 oz) light muscovado sugar
1 egg, size 6, beaten
1.25 ml ($\frac{1}{4}$ tsp) peppermint essence

——— 1 ———

Lightly grease 2 baking sheets and set aside. Sift the flour and carob into a bowl and add the bran from the sieve. Rub in the margarine until the mixture resembles fine breadcrumbs, then stir in the sugar. Add the egg and peppermint essence and mix to form a dough. Form into a ball and then knead the dough gently on a lightly floured surface.

——— 2 ———

Roll out to about 0.5 cm ($\frac{1}{4}$ inch) thick. Cut into about 24 rounds, re-

HONEY LOAF

238

rolling and using the trimmings. Place on the baking sheets and prick with a fork.

3

Bake at 180°C (350°F) mark 4 for about 15 minutes. Leave the biscuits to cool for a few minutes on the baking sheets, then transfer them to a wire rack. When the biscuits are crisp and cold store them in an airtight container.

MICROWAVE Follow steps 1 and 2 using microwave oven trays. In step 3 cook up to 8 biscuits at a time 60% (Medium) 5–7 minutes, turning trays once, until the surface is dry all over. Complete step 3. Cool the biscuits on wire racks.

GOODNESS GUIDE

FIBRE The wholemeal flour and the carob powder provide two types of fibre. The bran fibre absorbs water to ease food along the intestine, and the carob fibre enables better control of the glucose sugar uptake
MINERALS The flour and carob powder contribute iron, potassium, calcium and zinc

SHERRY FRUITCAKE

MAKES 12 SLICES 260 calories each
PREPARATION 30 minutes
BAKING $2\frac{1}{4}$–$2\frac{1}{2}$ hours
SOAKING At least 12 hours

finely grated rind and juice of
1 small orange
30 ml (2 tbsp) medium-dry sherry
5 ml (1 tsp) ground mixed spice
350 g (12 oz) mixed dried fruit, rinsed and chopped
50 g (2 oz) glacé cherries, (naturally coloured) well rinsed and chopped
50 g (2 oz) chopped mixed peel, rinsed
100 g (4 oz) polyunsaturated margarine
100 g (4 oz) light muscovado sugar
2 eggs, size 2
200 g (7 oz) plain wholemeal flour
15 g ($\frac{1}{2}$ oz) blanched almonds

1

Grease and line a 15 cm (6 inch) round deep cake tin and set aside. Place the orange rind and juice in a mixing bowl with the sherry and spice and mix together. Add the dried fruit, cherries and mixed peel and stir well. Cover and soak at least 12 hours, stirring occasionally.

2

Beat the margarine and sugar together in a mixing bowl until pale and creamy, then beat in the eggs one at a time, adding 15 ml (1 tbsp) of the flour with each egg.

3

Fold in the remaining flour with the soaked dried fruits to give a 'dropping' consistency. Spoon the mixture into the cake tin and level the surface. Arrange the almonds on top of the cake, pressing in gently.

4

Bake at 150°C (300°F) mark 2 for $2\frac{1}{4}$–$2\frac{1}{2}$ hours, until golden brown and firm to the touch in the centre and a skewer inserted in the centre comes out clean. Cover with a sheet of aluminium foil if the cakes start to overbrown. Cool in the tin before turning out on to a wire rack. When cold, store in an airtight container.

GOODNESS GUIDE

FIBRE The dried fruit, nuts and wholemeal flour all supply fibre
VITAMINS Dried fruit, eggs and wholemeal flour provide good quantities of B-complex vitamins
MINERALS To fully utilise the iron present in the cake, serve it with a vitamin C-rich drink, such as orange juice

APPLE AND OAT LAYER

SHERRY FRUITCAKE

CAROB-MINT BISCUITS

BOSTON BROWN BREAD

In the New England region of the United States, this bread was traditionally steamed in a coffee tin and eaten warm as an accompaniment to Boston Baked Beans on Sundays.

MAKES 10 SLICES 115 calories each
PREPARATION 15 minutes
STEAMING 2½ hours

75 g (3 oz) self-raising wholemeal flour
75 g (3 oz) rye flour
75 g (3 oz) cornmeal
2.5 ml (½ tsp) bicarbonate of soda
2.5 ml (½ tsp) salt
50 g (2 oz) raisins, rinsed (optional)
90 ml (6 tbsp) molasses
225 ml (8 fl oz) buttermilk

———1———
Lightly grease and line the base of a 1.1 litre (2 pint) pudding basin. Set aside. Put the flours and cornmeal into a bowl, add the bicarbonate of soda and salt and stir well to mix.

———2———
Add the raisins, molasses and buttermilk and beat well until evenly mixed. Transfer the mixture to the pudding basin. Cover with lightly greased and pleated aluminium foil and tie securely with string.

———3———
Stand the basin in a large saucepan and pour in enough hot water to come halfway up the sides. Bring to the boil, then cover the pan and steam for 2½ hours, topping up with more boiling water as necessary.

———4———
Leave the bread to stand in the basin for about 5 minutes, then turn out on to a board or plate and peel off the lining paper. Serve warm or cold, cut into thick wedges. Store, tightly wrapped, in an airtight container.

GOODNESS GUIDE
FIBRE The wholemeal and rye flours as well as the cornmeal and raisins provided plenty of fibre
MINERALS Iron, calcium and potassium are supplied by the flours, cornmeal, raisins and molasses. The buttermilk provides extra calcium
PROTEIN The buttermilk and flours provide protein

HAZELNUT AND DATE SLICES

These crunchy high-fibre oat slices with their rich date filling make an excellent sweet addition to a lunch box. Figs can be used instead of dates, and you can substitute orange rind and juice for the lemon.

MAKES 32 95 calories each
PREPARATION 15 minutes
BAKING 40 minutes

175 g (6 oz) plain wholemeal flour
175 g (6 oz) porridge oats
100 g (4 oz) polyunsaturated margarine
60 ml (4 tbsp) clear honey

DATE FILLING
225 g (8 oz) stoned dates, roughly chopped
finely grated rind and juice of 1 lemon
5 ml (1 tsp) ground cinnamon
50 g (2 oz) shelled hazelnuts, skinned and finely chopped

———1———
Lightly grease and line the base of a 20 cm (8 inch) square tin and set aside. To make the filling, put the dates in a heavy-based saucepan with the lemon rind and juice and 120 ml (8 tbsp) cold water. Cook, stirring constantly, for 5–7 minutes, until soft and all the liquid is absorbed. Remove from the heat.

———2———
Mix the flour and oats in a bowl, then rub in the margarine until the mixture resembles breadcrumbs. Add the honey and 30 ml (2 tbsp) cold water and mix well.

———3———
Press half of the oat mixture on to the base of the tin. Mix the cinnamon and hazelnuts into the date filling, then spread over the oat mixture. Press the remaining oat mixture evenly on top.

———4———
Bake at 190°C (375°F) mark 5 for 40 minutes, until golden brown. Remove from the oven and mark into 32 slices. Remove from tin when cold.

MICROWAVE Put dates, lemon rind, juice and water into a bowl. Part cover and cook 100% (High), stirring once, until soft and liquid almost absorbed. Complete steps 2 and 3. Cook, uncovered, 100% (High) 14–15 minutes, turning dish four times, until just dry all over the surface. Mark into slices. Cool.

WATER BISCUITS WITH CARAWAY

Home-made water biscuits are fresh, light and crisp. To complement the flavour of the caraway seeds serve with Edam or Gouda Cheese.

MAKES ABOUT 22 55 calories each
PREPARATION 20 minutes
BAKING 15–20 minutes

115 g (4½ oz) self-raising wholemeal flour
115 g (4½ oz) self-raising flour
1.25 ml (¼ tsp) salt
10–15 ml (2–3 tsp) caraway seeds
50 g (2 oz) polyunsaturated margarine

———1———
Put the flours in a bowl, add the salt and caraway seeds and stir well to mix. Rub in the margarine, then mix in 120 ml (8 tbsp) cold water to make a firm dough.

———2———
Roll out the dough as thinly as possible on a lightly floured work surface. Using a 7 cm (3 inch) biscuit cutter, cut out about 22 rounds.

———3———
Transfer to baking sheets and prick all over with a fork. Bake at 180°C (350°F) mark 4 for 15–20 minutes, until golden. Transfer to a wire rack. Leave to cool and become crisp. Store in an airtight tin.

GOODNESS GUIDE

WATER BISCUITS WITH CARAWAY
MINERALS The flour and caraway seeds are sources of potassium, iron, calcium and zinc. Potassium and calcium are two minerals involved in nerve conduction. Zinc aids the action of the enzymes responsible for mental and physical development
FIBRE The flour and caraway seeds provide fibre

HAZELNUT AND DATE SLICES
FIBRE The flour, oats, dates and hazelnuts make these slices high in fibre. Oat fibre enables better control of glucose absorption from the intestines. The fibre in the flour, dates and hazelnuts ensures good intestinal movement and thus presents constipation and related disorders

MUESLI CAKE

MAKES 10 SLICES   320 calories each
PREPARATION   20 minutes
BAKING   1 hour

175 g (6 oz) unsweetened muesli
150 ml (¼ pint) semi-skimmed milk
175 g (6 oz) plain wholemeal flour
100 g (4 oz) raw cane demerara sugar
10 ml (2 tsp) baking powder
175 g (6 oz) polyunsaturated margarine
3 eggs, size 2, beaten

———1———
Grease and line the base of an 18 cm (7 inch) round cake tin. Set aside. Put the muesli in a bowl, pour over the milk and mix well. Set aside.

———2———
Meanwhile, mix together the flour and sugar in a large bowl. Sift in the baking powder. Using a wooden spoon, beat in the margarine until well mixed, then add the eggs a little at a time and beat well.

———3———
Stir in the soaked muesli. Spoon the mixture into the prepared tin and smooth the surface.

———4———
Bake at 180°C (350°F) mark 4 for 1 hour, until well risen, golden brown and firm to the touch, or until a skewer inserted in the centre of the cake comes out clean. Turn out and cool on a wire rack. Cut into slices.

GOODNESS GUIDE

PROTEIN The combination of oats, nuts and dried fruit in the muesli together with the eggs, milk and wholemeal flour makes this a high-protein cake

VITAMINS Water-soluble B vitamins are present in the muesli, eggs, milk and flour. Fat-soluble vitamins A, D and E are supplied by the eggs and margarine

MUESLI CAKE

HAZELNUT AND DATE SLICES

WATER BISCUITS WITH CARAWAY

BOSTON BROWN BREAD

ENGLISH MADELEINES

These madeleines are a treat as a lunch box filler or simply eaten for afternoon tea.

MAKES 10 200 calories each
PREPARATION 10 minutes
BAKING 20 minutes
COOLING 20 minutes

100 g (4 oz) polyunsaturated margarine
100 g (4 oz) light muscovado sugar
2 eggs, beaten
50 g (2 oz) self-raising wholemeal flour
50 g (2 oz) self-raising flour
30 ml (2 tbsp) reduced-sugar strawberry or raspberry jam, sieved
50 g (2 oz) desiccated coconut
5 natural glacé cherries, halved and rinsed

——————1——————

Lightly grease 10 dariole moulds and set aside. Beat the margarine and sugar together until light and fluffy. Add the eggs, a little at a time, beating well after each addition. Sift the flours together, adding the bran left in the sieve, then fold into the egg mixture.

——————2——————

Spoon the mixture into the moulds, filling them three-quarters full. Bake at 180°C (350°F) mark 4 for about 20 minutes, until well risen and firm to the touch. Turn out on to a wire rack and cool for 20 minutes.

——————3——————

When the cakes are almost cold, trim the bases so they stand upright. Melt the jam over a gentle heat. Spread the coconut on a large plate. Insert a skewer into the base of each cake, then hold these when coating the cakes. Brush with the melted jam, then roll in the coconut to coat. Remove skewers. Decorate the top of each cake with half a glacé cherry.

MICROWAVE Lightly grease 10 small containers and set aside. Complete step 1. Spoon the mixture into containers until three-quarters full. Cook, uncovered, 100% (High) 5–6 minutes, rotating containers twice, until just set on the surfaces. Set aside for 5 minutes, then turn out to cool on a rack for 20 minutes. Warm sieved jam 100% (High) 20–30 seconds. Complete recipe.

RYE CRISPBREADS

MAKES 16 75 calories each
PREPARATION 15 minutes
BAKING 10–15 minutes

225 g (8 oz) rye flour
5 ml (1 tsp) mustard powder
2.5 ml ($\frac{1}{2}$ tsp) caraway seeds
2.5 ml ($\frac{1}{2}$ tsp) paprika
salt and pepper, to taste
50 g (2 oz) polyunsaturated margarine
105 ml (7 tbsp) semi-skimmed milk

——————1——————

Lightly grease 2 large baking sheets and set aside. Put the flour, mustard, caraway seeds, paprika and seasoning in a bowl. Rub in the margarine until the mixture resembles fine breadcrumbs. Add the milk and mix to a firm dough.

——————2——————

Roll out the dough on a lightly floured surface to a 30 × 40 cm (12 × 16 inch) rectangle. Cut into 7 × 10 cm (3 × 4 inch) rectangles and place on the baking sheets. Prick each rectangle several times with a fork to prevent rising during baking.

——————3——————

Bake at 200°C (400°F) mark 6 for 10–15 minutes or until golden brown. Cool slightly on the baking sheets, then transfer to wire racks to cool. Store in an airtight container.

GOODNESS GUIDE

RYE CRISPBREADS

PROTEIN The flour, seeds and milk provide a good source of complete protein
FIBRE The flour and seeds supply fibre
MINERALS Calcium, potassium and iron are supplied by the flour, seeds and spices. The milk supplies extra calcium

ENGLISH MADELEINES

FIBRE Wholemeal flour makes these madeleines a high-fibre version of an old favourite. The coconut also supplies fibre
SUGAR Using reduced-sugar or no-added-sugar jam greatly reduces the sugar in these cakes. Present dietary guidelines advise a reduction in our overall sugar intake

ORANGE BISCUITS

MAKES 20 85 calories each
PREPARATION 8–10 minutes
BAKING 10–15 minutes

100 g (4 oz) polyunsaturated margarine
75 g (3 oz) light muscovado sugar
grated rind of 2 oranges
1 egg yolk, beaten
150 g (5 oz) self-raising wholemeal flour
20 g ($\frac{3}{4}$ oz) rolled oats

——————1——————

Lightly grease 2 baking sheets and set aside. Cream the margarine, sugar and half the orange rind together, then beat in the egg yolk. Add flour and mix to a stiff dough.

——————2——————

Divide the dough into 20 walnut-sized balls. Mix the remaining orange rind with the oats and roll the balls in this to coat all over. Put on the baking sheets and bake at 190°C (375°F) mark 5 for 10–15 minutes, until golden brown.

——————3——————

Cool for a few minutes on the baking sheets, then transfer to wire racks to cool completely. Store in an airtight container.

GOODNESS GUIDE

ORANGE BISCUITS

VITAMINS The egg yolk, oats and flour provide a range of B-complex vitamins and vitamin E. The egg yolk and margarine are also sources of vitamins A and D. Vitamin D in the body controls absorption of calcium from food
MINERALS Iron, calcium, zinc and potassium are supplied by the egg yolk, flour and oats. The orange juice also provides potassium
FIBRE The oats and flour provide an important range of fibre

PUMPKIN MUFFINS

FIBRE The flour, pumpkin, raisins and walnuts provide plenty of fibre
MINERALS The flour, eggs, walnuts and raisins supply calcium, iron and potassium. The eggs, flour and walnuts also provide zinc, a mineral which aids the action of the enzymes responsible for mental and physical development

PUMPKIN MUFFINS

MAKES 12 145 calories each
PREPARATION 15 minutes
BAKING 20 minutes

450 g (1 lb) fresh pumpkin, seeded, peeled
and cut into 2.5 cm (1 inch) cubes
30 ml (2 tbsp) corn oil
60 ml (4 tbsp) clear honey
2 eggs
225 g (8 oz) plain wholemeal flour
5 ml (1 tsp) baking powder
5 ml (1 tsp) ground cinnamon
50 g (2 oz) raisins, rinsed
50 g (2 oz) walnut halves, coarsely chopped
polyunsaturated margarine or curd cheese,
to serve

——— 1 ———
Lightly grease 12 patty tins and set
aside. Cook the pumpkin in 1 cm
(½ inch) boiling water in a covered
saucepan for 10 minutes, until soft.
Drain and set aside to cool slightly.

——— 2 ———
Meanwhile, put the oil, honey and
eggs into a large bowl and beat
together well.

——— 3 ———
Sift the flour, baking powder and
cinnamon into a separate bowl,
adding the bran left in the sieve.
Mash the pumpkin and beat into
the egg mixture. Fold in the dry ingredients, the raisins and walnuts.

——— 4 ———
Divide the mixture equally between
the patty tins. Bake at 190°C (375°F)
mark 5 for 20 minutes, until risen.
Turn out on to a wire rack. Serve the
muffins warm or cold, spread with a
little polyunsaturated margarine or
curd cheese.

PUMPKIN MUFFINS

ENGLISH MADELEINES

RYE CRISPBREADS

ORANGE BISCUITS

243

OAT AND APRICOT SLICES

MAKES 8 SLICES 205 calories each
PREPARATION 15 minutes
BAKING 30–35 minutes

100 g (4 oz) ready-to-eat dried apricots,
rinsed and chopped
50 ml (2 fl oz) lemon juice

BASE
50 g (2 oz) polyunsaturated margarine
15 ml (1 tbsp) light muscovado sugar
50 g (2 oz) medium oatmeal
50 g (2 oz) plain wholemeal flour
50 g (2 oz) plain flour

ROLLED OAT TOPPING
15 ml (1 tbsp) light muscovado sugar
50 g (2 oz) rolled oats
25 g (1 oz) plain wholemeal flour
25 g (1 oz) polyunsaturated margarine

———1———
Lightly grease an 18 cm (7 inch) sandwich tin and set aside. Put the apricots, 175 ml (6 fl oz) water and lemon juice in a saucepan. Cover and simmer for about 15 minutes, stirring occasionally, until the apricots have softened and the liquid is well reduced. Set aside to cool.

———2———
To make the base, put all the ingredients in a blender or food processor and mix to form a smooth dough. Knead on a lightly floured surface and press into the tin. Cover with the cooked apricot mixture.

———3———
For the topping, mix together the sugar, oats and flour, then rub in the margarine to make a crumble. Sprinkle over the apricots and press down lightly. Bake at 190°C (375°F) mark 5 for 30–35 minutes, until golden. Slice and serve hot or cold.

MICROWAVE Put apricots, 100 ml (4 fl oz) water, lemon juice into a bowl. Part cover, cook 100% (High) 3½–4 minutes, until liquid is reduced, stirring once. Cool. Press prepared base into an 18 cm (7 inch) dish. Complete step 2 and follow step 3, but cook, uncovered, 60% (Medium) 17–18 minutes; turning dish 4 times, until topping is firm.

GOODNESS GUIDE
MINERALS The apricots, oats and flour are sources of iron, calcium and potassium

FIG ROLLS

MAKES 12 ROLLS 120 calories each
PREPARATION About 30 minutes
BAKING 25–30 minutes

175 g (6 oz) dried figs, rinsed and
coarsely chopped
75 g (3 oz) plain wholemeal flour
75 g (3 oz) plain flour
25 g (1 oz) light muscovado sugar
65 g (2½ oz) polyunsaturated margarine
1.25 ml (¼ tsp) salt

———1———
Lightly grease a baking sheet. Set aside. Put the figs in a saucepan with 300 ml (½ pint) water. Simmer for about 20 minutes, stirring occasionally, until the figs are tender and the liquid is well reduced. Set aside to cool, then purée in a blender or food processor. Set aside.

———2———
Put the remaining ingredients in a blender or food processor with 30 ml (2 tbsp) water and mix to a dough. Knead the dough on a lightly floured surface, then roll out to an oblong about 40 × 12 cm (16 × 5 inches).

———3———
Spread the fig purée down the centre of the dough rectangle and carefully fold in the sides so that they overlap over the filling. Trim the ends of the roll and cut into 3 cm (1¼ inch) wide slices. Turn the rolls over and place on the prepared baking sheet.

———4———
Mark the top of each roll with a wet fork and bake at 190°C (375°F) mark 5 for 25–30 minutes, until lightly browned. Cool on a rack.

MICROWAVE Put figs, 150 ml (¼ pint) water into a bowl. Part cover, cook 100% (High) 5 minutes, stirring once, until liquid is well reduced. Cool, then purée. Prepare fig rolls, arrange on a baking tray. Cook, uncovered, 100% (High) 9–11 minutes, turning 3 times until just dry all over the surface. Cool on a wire rack.

GOODNESS GUIDE
FIBRE Plenty of fibre is supplied by the figs and flour. Fibre is needed for healthy intestinal movement. People on high-fibre diets should drink plenty of fluids, as the fibre absorbs a great deal of liquid

PULL-APART WHOLEMEAL ROLLS

MAKES 4 195 calories each
PREPARATION 20 minutes
BAKING 20–25 minutes
RISING 1 hour

75 ml (3 fl oz) semi-skimmed milk
10 g (¼ oz) fresh yeast, or 5 ml (1 tsp) dried
yeast and 5 ml (1 tsp) light muscovado
sugar
225 g (8 oz) plain wholemeal flour
1.25 ml (¼ tsp) salt
semi-skimmed milk, to glaze
5 ml (1 tsp) sesame seeds

———1———
Lightly grease an 18 cm (7 inch) sandwich tin and set aside. Heat the milk and 50 ml (2 fl oz) water until tepid. Remove from the heat and crumble in the fresh yeast, stirring until dissolved. If using dried yeast, sprinkle it on to the tepid water mixed with the sugar and leave in a warm place for 15 minutes, until frothy.

———2———
Put the flour and salt into a warm bowl. Add the yeast mixture and mix to form a dough.

———3———
On a lightly floured surface, knead the dough for 5 minutes, then place in a lightly greased bowl and cover with a damp cloth. Leave in a warm place to rise for about 45 minutes or until doubled in size.

———4———
Knock back the dough and knead lightly. Divide into 4 equal pieces and shape each piece into a round. Place in the prepared tin and leave to prove for 15 minutes.

———5———
Brush with the milk and sprinkle with the sesame seeds. Bake at 200°C (400°F) mark 6 for 20–25 minutes until a rich brown. Pull apart and serve warm or cold.

GOODNESS GUIDE
MINERALS Iron, calcium, potassium and zinc are supplied by the ingredients. Potassium is necessary for proper fluid balance in the cells
VITAMINS The wholemeal flour and sesame seeds supply B-complex vitamins and vitamin E. The milk also provides B vitamins

HEALTHY BAKING

BITTER ORANGE TEABREAD

This teabread with the refreshing flavour of orange is a delightful summer treat. It can be stored for several days in an airtight container.

MAKES 10 SLICES 185 calories each
PREPARATION 10 minutes
BAKING 1 hour

coarsely grated rind of 2 oranges
100 ml (4 fl oz) orange juice
100 g (4 oz) chopped mixed peel, rinsed
100 g (4 oz) polyunsaturated margarine
75 g (3 oz) light muscovado sugar
1 egg
75 g (3 oz) self-raising flour
75 g (3 oz) plain wholemeal flour

———— 1 ————

Grease and line a 450 g (1 lb) loaf tin and set aside. Mix together the orange rind and juice and peel. Cream the margarine with the sugar until light and fluffy. Beat in the egg with 30 ml (2 tbsp) flour.

———— 2 ————

Add half the remaining flours with half the orange mixture and fold in carefully with a metal spoon. Add the remaining flours and orange mixture and mix well.

———— 3 ————

Spoon the mixture into the prepared tin and bake at 180°C (350°F) mark 4 for about 1 hour, until golden brown and beginning to leave the sides of the tin. Cool in the tin for 3–4 minutes, then turn out on to a wire rack to cool completely. Serve cut into slices.

MICROWAVE Put prepared mixture into a lined 450 g (1 lb) loaf dish. Cook, uncovered, 100% (High) 6 minutes, turning dish 4 times, until just dry all over the surface. Cool, then turn out.

GOODNESS GUIDE
VITAMINS The flour provides B-complex vitamins, which are essential for energy production in the body. The margarine is a source of fat-soluble vitamins A, D and E

OAT AND APRICOT SLICES

PULL-APART WHOLEMEAL ROLLS

FIG ROLLS

BITTER ORANGE TEABREAD

BAGELS

Serve these Jewish speciality rolls as soon as they come out of the oven, when they are soft and fresh.

MAKES 8 165 calories each
PREPARATION 40 minutes
RISING $1\frac{1}{2}$–2 hours
BAKING 20 minutes

50 ml (2 fl oz) semi-skimmed milk
150 g (5 oz) plain wholemeal flour
150 g (5 oz) strong plain flour
10 ml (2 tsp) easy blend yeast
1.25 ml ($\frac{1}{4}$ tsp) salt
1 egg, separated
30 ml (2 tbsp) corn oil
25 ml ($1\frac{1}{2}$ tbsp) poppy seeds

—1—

Lightly grease a baking sheet and set aside. Warm the milk with 50 ml (2 fl oz) of water until tepid.

—2—

Mix the flours, yeast and salt together in a warmed bowl. Make a well in the centre and add the warmed liquid, egg white and 30 ml (2 tbsp) oil. Mix well, adding a few more drops of water if dough seems dry.

—3—

Knead the dough on a lightly floured surface for 10 minutes, until smooth. Return to the bowl, cover and leave to rise in a warm place for 1–$1\frac{1}{2}$ hours, until doubled in size.

—4—

Turn out on to a lightly floured work surface. Divide the dough into 8 equal pieces, then roll each piece into a thick strip about 12 cm (5 inches) long. Press the ends of each strip together and insert the tip of your forefinger in the centre to make ring shapes. Place the bagels on a floured baking sheet and leave to prove in a warm place for 20–25 minutes, until risen.

—5—

Bring a large saucepan of water to the boil. Drop 2 or 3 of the risen bagels into the water. Leave for a few seconds until they rise to the surface, then immediately remove with a slotted spoon. Repeat with the remaining bagels.

—6—

Place the bagels on the greased baking sheet, spacing them apart. Brush gently with the egg yolk, then sprinkle with the poppy seeds.

—7—

Bake at 200°C (400°F) mark 6 for about 20 minutes, until the bagels are golden brown. Remove from the oven and serve as soon as possible.

STOUT CAKE

MAKES 12 SLICES 260 calories each
PREPARATION 5 minutes
BAKING 1 hour
SOAKING Overnight

100 g (4 oz) seedless raisins, rinsed
100 g (4 oz) sultanas, rinsed
75 g (3 oz) stoned prunes, rinsed and chopped
300 ml ($\frac{1}{2}$ pint) stout
225 g (8 oz) self-raising wholemeal flour
50 g (2 oz) walnuts, chopped
25 g (1 oz) chopped mixed peel, rinsed
2.5 ml ($\frac{1}{2}$ tsp) baking powder
10 ml (2 tsp) ground mixed spice
100 g (4 oz) polyunsaturated margarine
50 g (2 oz) dark muscovado sugar
2 eggs, beaten
8 walnut halves, to decorate

—1—

Grease and base line a deep 20 cm (8 inch) round cake tin. Put the raisins, sultanas, prunes and 200 ml ($\frac{1}{3}$ pint) of the stout in a large bowl and leave to soak overnight.

—2—

Add the remaining ingredients and about 50 ml (2 fl oz) more stout to make a soft dropping consistency. Beat thoroughly together.

—3—

Spoon into the prepared cake tin, level the surface and arrange the walnut halves on top. Bake at 170°C (325°F) mark 3 for about 1 hour or until a fine skewer inserted into the centre comes out clean. If the cake browns too quickly, cover it with several layers of greaseproof paper.

—4—

Cool in the tin for 15 minutes, then turn out on to a wire rack. Prick the bottom of the cake with a fine skewer and spoon over about 30 ml (2 tbsp) of the remaining stout. Leave to cool completely, then store in an airtight container.

GOODNESS GUIDE

FIBRE This is a very high-fibre cake
MINERALS The dried fruit, flour, nuts, dark muscovado sugar and eggs all contribute iron, calcium and potassium
VITAMINS B vitamins are contributed by the flour, nuts, eggs and stout

FRUIT BARS

These wholesome bars packed full of fruit contain no added sugar.

MAKES 8 225 calories each
PREPARATION 20 minutes
BAKING 40–50 minutes

450 g (1 lb) eating apples, peeled, cored and finely chopped
50 g (2 oz) stoned dates, rinsed and coarsely chopped
50 g (2 oz) ready-to-eat dried apricots, rinsed and chopped
100 g (4 oz) mixed nuts, chopped
50 g (2 oz) sultanas, rinsed
75 g (3 oz) rolled oats
75 g (3 oz) self-raising wholemeal flour
25 g (1 oz) unsweetened desiccated coconut
25 g (1 oz) sesame seeds
25 g (1 oz) pumpkin seeds
90 ml (6 tbsp) unsweetened apple juice
45 ml (3 tbsp) sunflower oil

—1—

Lightly grease an 18 cm (7 inch) square tin. Put the apples in a heavy based saucepan with 15 ml (1 tbsp) water. Cover tightly and cook for about 10 minutes, until the apples are very soft.

—2—

Uncover and cook apples, stirring, for a further 2 minutes or until the excess moisture has evaporated.

—3—

Add the remaining ingredients and beat well together. Pack into the prepared tin and level the surface. Bake at 170°C (325°F) mark 3, on a low shelf in the oven, for 40–50 minutes. Move the tin to the top of the oven for the last 10 minutes of cooking time. When cooked the mixture will be slightly brown around the edges and feel firm to the touch.

—4—

Mark into 8 bars while still warm. Leave to cool in the tin. When cold, turn out and cut into bars.

GOODNESS GUIDE

FIBRE These bars are very high in fibre, needed for the prevention of constipation and related disorders, the control of blood cholesterol levels and the absorption of glucose sugar by the blood
MINERALS Iron, calcium, zinc and potassium are all minerals provided by these bars

LEMON AND GINGER SHORTBREAD

MAKES 16   95 calories each
PREPARATION   10 minutes
BAKING   35–45 minutes

175 g (6 oz) plain wholemeal flour
100 g (4 oz) polyunsaturated margarine
5 ml (1 tsp) ground ginger
50 g (2 oz) light muscovado sugar
finely grated rind of 1 lemon

—————1—————
Put the flour into a bowl and rub in the margarine until the mixture resembles fine breadcrumbs.
—————2—————
Stir in the ginger, sugar and lemon rind. Knead to form a smooth dough. Turn out on to a lightly floured surface and divide in half.
—————3—————
Roll out each half to an 18 cm (7 inch) round and place on a baking sheet. Mark each round into 8 portions and prick all over with a fork. Crimp the edges to decorate.
—————4—————
Bake at 150°C (300°F) mark 2 for 35–45 minutes, until light golden brown. Leave to cool on the baking sheet. Cut into portions.

GOODNESS GUIDE

LEMON AND GINGER SHORTBREAD
FIBRE Using wholemeal flour makes these shortbreads high in fibre
VITAMINS The wholemeal flour supplies some B-complex vitamins and vitamin E. The margarine is a source of vitamins A, D and E as well as vitamin F—essential fatty acids needed for healthy cell membranes

BAGELS
FIBRE The addition of wholemeal flour adds important dietary fibre to these bagels
MINERALS The milk, egg and flours contribute calcium, potassium and zinc. The egg and flours also contain iron
VITAMINS Flour, eggs and milk are good sources of B vitamins

STOUT CAKE

BAGELS

FRUIT BARS

LEMON AND GINGER SHORTBREAD

ALMOND CHEESE TARTS

These make a tasty snack when served with tea or coffee. Sprinkle a little nutmeg over the top before baking for extra flavour.

MAKES 12 170 calories each
PREPARATION 20 minutes
BAKING 15–20 minutes
CHILLING 30 minutes

150 g (5 oz) low-fat soft cheese
100 g (4 oz) ground almonds
50 g (2 oz) light muscovado sugar
1 egg plus 1 egg yolk
grated rind of 1 lemon
thinly pared strips of lemon rind

PASTRY
75 g (3 oz) plain wholemeal flour
75 g (3 oz) plain flour
pinch of salt
10 ml (2 tsp) light muscovado sugar
65 g (2½ oz) polyunsaturated margarine

——— 1 ———

Lightly grease 12 patty tins and set aside. To make the pastry, put the flours, salt and sugar into a bowl and rub in the margarine until the mixture resembles fine breadcrumbs. Add enough water to bind and mix to a smooth dough.

——— 2 ———

Roll out thinly on a lightly floured surface. With a 7.5 cm (3 inch) round cutter, cut out 12 rounds and place one in each tin. Cover and chill for at least 30 minutes.

——— 3 ———

To make the filling, beat together the cheese, almonds, sugar, eggs and grated lemon rind until smooth. Fill each pastry cake to the top and bake at 190°C (375°F) mark 5 for 15–20 minutes, until the mixture has risen and is very light golden brown. Tie the pared strips of lemon rind into twists and decorate each tart. Cool on a rack and serve warm or cold.

GOODNESS GUIDE
FIBRE The wholemeal flour and the ground almonds are good sources of fibre
PROTEIN The low-fat soft cheese provides complete protein, which is increased by the eggs, almonds and flours
VITAMINS Eggs, nuts, cheese and flour are all rich in B vitamins which help release the energy from food

ALMOND CHEESE TARTS

CHORLEY CAKES

MAKES 10 210 calories each
PREPARATION 20 minutes
BAKING 20 minutes

100 g (4 oz) self-raising wholemeal flour
100 g (4 oz) self-raising flour
150 g (5 oz) polyunsaturated margarine
25 g (1 oz) light muscovado sugar plus 10 ml (2 tsp) light muscovado sugar
finely grated rind of 1 small orange
finely grated rind of 1 lemon
5 ml (1 tsp) mixed spice
100 g (4 oz) currants, rinsed
1 egg white, lightly beaten

———1———
Lightly grease two baking sheets and set aside. Put the flours into a bowl and rub in 100 g (4 oz) of the margarine until the mixture resembles fine breadcrumbs. Add enough cold water to make a stiff dough.

———2———
Cream the remaining margarine with the 25 g (1 oz) sugar. Beat in the grated citrus rinds and spice, then add the currants.

———3———
Divide the dough into 10 portions and roll each into a round about 10 cm (4 inches) across. Place a heaped teaspoon of the currant and spice filling in the centre of each round. Bring the edges together over the filling and seal them by pinching firmly together. Turn the pastry rounds over and roll out to a round about 7 cm (3 inches) across.

———4———
Place on the baking sheets and score the top of each cake with a knife. Brush with egg white and sprinkle with the extra sugar. Bake at 200°C (400°F) mark 6 for 20 minutes. Cool on a wire rack.

GOODNESS GUIDE
FIBRE The wholemeal flour and currants provide fibre
VITAMINS B vitamins are supplied by the flour and currants. Vitamins A, D and E are present in the margarine. The orange and lemon rind and juice provide a little vitamin C. Vitamin C is necessary for the maintenance of healthy connective tissue

CHORLEY CAKES

SAFFRON BREAD

MAKES 16 SLICES 170 calories each
PREPARATION 30 minutes
BAKING 40–50 minutes
RISING About 1¾ hours

300 ml (½ pint) semi-skimmed milk
2.5 ml (½ tsp) saffron threads
15 g (½ oz) fresh yeast or 7.5 ml (1½ tsp) dried
yeast and 2.5 ml (½ tsp) clear honey
225 g (8 oz) plain wholemeal flour
225 g (8 oz) plain flour
2.5 ml (½ tsp) ground mace
100 g (4 oz) polyunsaturated margarine
30 ml (2 tbsp) clear honey
100 g (4 oz) ready-to-eat mixed dried
fruit, rinsed
honey, to glaze

1

Lightly oil a 20 cm (8 inch) round cake tin and set aside. Heat the milk. Place the saffron in a bowl, pour the hot milk over and leave to infuse for 30 minutes.

2

Strain the milk and reheat until tepid. Crumble in the fresh yeast and stir until dissolved. If using dried yeast, sprinkle it into the tepid milk mixed with 2.5 ml (½ tsp) honey and leave in a warm place for 10 minutes, until frothy.

3

Mix the flours and mace in a large bowl. Add the margarine and rub in until the mixture resembles breadcrumbs. Make a well in the centre of the flour mixture and add the yeast liquid and honey. Mix well to form a soft dough.

4

Turn out on a lightly floured surface and knead for 10 minutes. Return to the bowl, cover with a clean cloth and leave to rise in a warm place for about 1 hour, until doubled in size.

5

Knead the dough again briefly, then gradually work in the dried fruit until evenly distributed. Shape the dough into a ball and place in the tin. Cover, and leave to rise for about 45 minutes, until well risen.

6

Bake at 200°C (400°F) mark 6 for 40–50 minutes, until firm to the touch. Turn out and brush the top with a little honey while still warm. Leave to cool.

GOODNESS GUIDE

PROTEIN Protein is supplied by the milk and flour
FIBRE The wholemeal flour and dried fruits are fibre-rich
VITAMINS B-complex vitamins, which will be used by the body to obtain energy from the bread, are provided by the flour, yeast, milk and dried fruit

SAFFRON BREAD

POTATO SCONES

MAKES 8 110 calories each
PREPARATION 15 minutes
BAKING 25–30 minutes

450 g (1 lb) potatoes, scrubbed
25 g (1 oz) polyunsaturated margarine
salt and pepper, to taste
100 g (4 oz) self-raising wholemeal flour
polyunsaturated margarine and no-added-sugar preserves, to serve

1
Lightly grease a baking sheet and set aside. Cook the potatoes in a small amount of boiling water for about 20 minutes, until soft. Drain well and leave until cool enough to handle, then peel.

2
Mash the potatoes well with the margarine, then add seasoning. Beat in the flour to make a soft dough. Roll or pat out to an 18 cm (7 inch) circle on a lightly floured surface. Place on the baking sheet and mark into 8 wedges.

3
Bake at 220°C (425°F) mark 7 for 25–30 minutes, until risen and a crisp golden brown.

GOODNESS GUIDE
FIBRE The potatoes and wholemeal flour contribute some fibre
VITAMINS Although potatoes contribute vitamin C, mashing destroys a large proportion of it, so even if you eat large amounts of mashed potatoes, you should still eat other sources of vitamin C in fruit and vegetables
FAT The fat content in these scones is relatively low

POTATO SCONES

INDEX